They Went to War:

A Biographical Register of the Green Mountain State in the Civil War

Compiled and edited by Erik S. Hinckley and Tom Ledoux

Order this book online at www.trafford.com
or email orders@trafford.com

Most Trafford titles are also available at major online book retailers.

Contact Tom Ledoux, webmaster@vermontcivilwar.org

Printed in Victoria, BC, Canada.

ISBN: 978-1-4269-3436-0

Our mission is to efficiently provide the world's finest, most comprehensive book publishing service, enabling every author to experience success. To find out how to publish your book, your way, and have it available worldwide, visit us online at www.trafford.com

Trafford rev. 06/23/2010

www.trafford.com

North America & international
toll-free: 1 888 232 4444 (USA & Canada)
phone: 250 383 6864 • fax: 812 355 4082

In memory of those who paid the ultimate sacrifice.

In their honor,

All proceeds from the sale of this book will be donated to the Vermont Old Cemetery Association (VOCA).

For more information about this organization please visit their website at http://www.voca58.org/

TABLE OF CONTENTS

Forward

When doing research on the Civil War, it is tough carrying around a copy of the 1892 Revised Roster, Benedict's Vermont in the Civil War, biographical works by Ullery, Dodge, Stone and others, town, county and state histories, not to mention general military histories, the official records, etc., for ready reference. Tom Ledoux had been toying with the idea of a Vermont version of Mark Boatner's Civil War Dictionary, and after several false starts, he enlisted Erik Hinckley, a contributor to the "Vermont in the Civil War" web project, who was hankering to get involved and contribute more than he already had. When it came down to scoping the project, due to the volume of material available, we decided to limit our study to biographical material only.

Who are we?

Erik S. Hinckley was born in Burlington and grew up there and in Florida. Five of his ancestors volunteered in various Vermont units during the Civil War. He attended Palm Beach Community College where he earned an A.S. in Land Surveying, in 1990, as well as an A.A. in General Education. He later attended Florida Atlantic University where he earned a B.A. in History (Summa Cum Laude) in 2007. While at FAU he won the Martin and Sylvia Shaw History Essay award for a paper entitled "Hungary, the Paris Peace Conference and Trianon: Peace without Foresight."

Tom Ledoux is an eighth-generation Vermonter, born and raised in Franklin County. He attended St. Michael's College in Winooski Park for three semesters before joining the U.S. Navy in 1970, serving several tours around the world, including Vietnam, the Philippines, Guam, Turkey, England and Japan. In 1985, he settled in suburban Maryland, completed a tour in Japan from 1989 to 1991, returned to Maryland and retired from the Navy in 1996. After 13 years as a Defense Department analyst, he is retiring in January 2010, hoping to devote more time to Civil War research. Tom earned a B.A. in Humanities from the University of Maryland, University College in 1996, and was awarded an M.A. in Military Studies (Civil War) from American Military University, Manassas, Virginia, in 2001.
He is the creator and webmaster of 'Vermont in the Civil War,' a major Civil War website dedicated to documenting the contributions of the Green Mountain Boys during "The Late Unpleasantness," according to a longtime friend, and unrepentant Confederate Rebel, who turns out to be a distant cousin of one of Vermont's Medal of Honor recipients. The project has won a number of web-based awards and accolades, and the Vermont Civil War Council's "Full Duty Award," for making significant contributions to preserving Vermont's Civil War history. In 2002, he published Quite Ready to the Sent Somewhere, The Civil War Letters of Aldace Freeman Walker.

Erik's Civil War ancestors include his 2nd great-granduncles; Edward Hinckley, 1st Vermont Cavalry, Jasper H. Fuller, 17th Vermont, Aaron Hinckley, 14th Vermont, James Hinckley, 2nd Vermont, and Dean Wilder Reed, 1st Vermont Cavalry. For good measure, he also has two cousins, Henry Hinckley, 5th and 7th Vermont and William W. Hinckley, 14th Vermont. Tom, on the other hand, has yet to identify any direct Civil War ancestors, and only a few distant cousins.

Credits

First and foremost, we want to acknowledge the folks at Google Books, for the incredible job they have been doing in posting digital versions of more than 2,200 public domain books that have information specifically on Vermont in the Civil War, including histories, biographies, encyclopedias, library catalogues, etc., plus tens of thousands of other books that gave us details and clues which aided in our research. Of the more than 500 sources we used, the overwhelming majority are digital versions of works we found on Google Books.

In general, and for their substantive and continued contributions to the Vermont in the Civil War project, some of which is included herein, we want to thank Tom Boudreau, Deanna French, John Gibson, Bob Hackett, Ed Italo, John Kimball, Alan Lathrop, Jen Snoots, Scott Sommer, Kathy Valloch and Linda Welch, plus hundreds of others, mostly descendants, too numerous to mention. Where applicable the last names of these individuals are noted as sources.

Thanks to Towner Blackstock, Curator of Archives, The Fraternity of Phi Gamma Delta, for death date and burial information on Oscar Hopestill Leland, and Lyman John Brooks, of Webster NH, for information on his great-grandfather, Nathaniel Grout Brooks. Thanks also to Tim Cooper, Commander & Historian of John D. Long Post #58, American Legion, Buckfield, ME, for material on Daniel L. C. Colburn.

Finally, thanks to Darla Hunley for designing the image on the front cover.

Abbreviations

[Also used but not listed are months (3 letters), directions, states (New style, e.g. VT, CA, etc.); Roman numerals are used for corps, Arabic numerals for brigades and divisions]

1LT – First Lieutenant
1SGT – First Sergeant
2SGT – Second Sergeant
2LT – Second Lieutenant
3SGT – Third Sergeant
4SGT – Fourth Sergeant
5SGT – Fifth Sergeant
6SGT – Sixth Sergeant
AAM - American Assoc of Medicine
AACS – Acting Assistant Commissary of Subsistence
AAG – Assistant Adjutant General
A.B. - Bachelor of Arts
ABA – American Bar Association
AC – Amherst College
Acad. - Academy/ies
ACG – Assistant Commissary General
ACGS – Acting Commissary General of Subsistence
ACS – Assistant Commissary of Subsistence
ADC - Aide-De-Camp
Add'l - Additional
ADJ - Adjutant
aft - after
AIG – Adjutant and Inspector General
ALS - Albany (NY) Law School
A.M. - Master of Arts (degree)
AMA - American Medical Assoc
AMP – Assistant Medical Purveyor
AMS - Albany (NY) Medical School
AOC - Army of the Cumberland (USA)
AOJ - Army of the James (USA)
AOP – Army of the Potomac (USA)
AOT – Army of the Tennessee (USA)
AQM – Assistant Quartermaster
APHA - American Public Health Assoc
Appt - Appointment
Apptd – Appointed
Arty – Artillery
Assoc – Associate/ion
Asst – Assistant
ATS - Andover Theological Seminary
Atty – Attorney
AuTS – Auburn Theological Seminary
AWOL - away without official leave
bef – before
BGD – Brigade
B.G. – Brigadier General
BMC – Berkshire Medical College
BRA – Black River Academy
BRFAL – Bureau of Refugees, Freedmen and Abandoned Lands
B.S. - Bachelor of Science
Btln - Battalion
Btry – Battery
BTS – Bangor (ME) Theological Seminary
Bvt – Brevet (honorary rank)
Cav – Cavalry
CDR – Commander (Navy)
Ch. - Chief
C.H. – Court House
Chair. - Chairman
CoS - Chief of Staff
CAPT – Captain (USN)
Chap. - Chaplain
CMC - Castleton Medical College
Cmdd - Commanded
cmdg – Commanding
CMDR - Commander (USN)
Cmdry - Commandery
CMO - Chief Medical Officer
CMP – Chief Medical Purveyor
Cmsy - Commissary
Co. - company
COL – Colonel
Coll. - College
COMO – Commodore (USN)
Conf. - Conference
ConCon - Constitutional Convention
Confed. - Confederate
CoS – Chief of Staff
CPL - Corporal
CPS - College of Physicians and Surgeons
CPT – Captain (USA)
CS – Commissary of Subsistence
CSA - Confederate States Army
CSN - Confederate States Navy
Cty – County
DAR – Daughters of the American Revolution
D.C. - District of Columbia
DC – Dartmouth College
DCMS - Dartmouth College Medical School
D.D. - Doctor of Divinity

Dept – Department
Dir(s) – Director(s)
dis – discharge/discharged
dis/dsb – discharged for disability
dis/wds – discharged for wounds
Dist. - District
Div - Division
DNC – Democratic National Convention
DPF – Delta Psi Fraternity
Dpy – Deputy
EGBS - East Gulf Blockading Squadron
Engr(s) - Engineer(s)
Enl - enlisted
ENS - Ensign
Flt Paymr - Fleet Paymaster
GAR – Grand Army of the Republic
GCM – General Court Martial
GEN – General (rank)
Gen – general
GMC – Green Mountain Club
Gov. – Governor
govt - government
GPO – Government Printing Office
HARTY – Heavy Artillery
HLS – Harvard Law School
HMS – Harvard Medical School
Hon. – Honorable/Honorary
hosp. - hospital
HQMC – Headquarters Marine Corps
H.S. – High School
ICC – Interstate Commerce Commission
I.G. - Inspector General
INF – Infantry
Inst. – Institute
Instr. - Instructor
IOOF – International Order of Odd Fellow
IRS – Internal Revenue Service
JAG - Judge Advocate General
j.p. – justice of the peace
kia – Killed in Action
KOP – Knights of Pythias
KSHS - Kansas State Historical Society
KUA – Kimball Union Academy
LARTY – Light Artillery
LCDR – Lieutenant Commander (USN)
LDS – Landsman (USN)
Legis. - Legislature
LL.B. – Bachelor of Law
LT – Lieutenant (USN)
LTCol – Lieutenant Colonel
LTG – Lieutenant General
LLD - Doctor of Laws (degree)
LOC – Library of Congress
M.A. – Master of Arts
MAJ – Major
MC – Middlebury College
M.D. - Doctor of Medicine (degree)
M.E. - Methodist-Episcopal
Mech. - Mechanical
M.G. – Major General
m/i – mustered in
Mid - Middle
Mil. – Military
Mil. Sci. – Military Science
mwia – Mortally Wounded in Action
M.M. – Master of Mathematics (degree)
mngr - Manager
m/o – mustered out
MOH – Medal of Honor
MOLLUS – Military Order of the Loyal Legion of the United States
MS – Medical Society
Mtd - Mounted
MUSC - Musician
NABS - North Atlantic Blockading Squadron
NARA – National Archives and Records Administration
nfi – No further information
NG - National Guard
n.g. – non-graduate
NGS – National Genealogical Society
NU – Norwich University
NYC – New York City
NYMC – New York University Medical College
NYPL – New York Public Library
NYU – New York University
OES - Order of the Eastern Star
ORD SGT - Orderly Sergeant
Paymr – Paymaster
p.g. – post-graduate
P.M. – Provost Marshall
pow – prisoner of war
pr - promoted
pres. – President
Princ. – principal
Prof - professor
Prov - Provisional
PVT - Private
QM – Quartermaster
QMG – Quartermaster General
QM SGT - Quartermaster
RAdm - Rear Admiral
reen – reenlisted

regt. – regiment
regtl – regimental
resgd - resigned
Rep. – Representative
ret. - retired
Rev. - Reverend
RNC – Republican National Convention
RPI - Rensselear Polytechnical Institute
RQM – Regimental Quartermaster
R.R. - Railroad
RSVO - Reunion Society of Vermont Officers
SABS - South Atlantic Blockading Squadron
SAR – Sons of the American Revolution
SCW - Society of Colonial Wars
SDLR – Saddler
Sec'y - Secretary
Sem. - Seminary
Sen. – Senator
SGM – Sergeant Major
SGT - Sergeant
Soc. - Society
SOV – Sons of Vermont
SOWD – Special Order Ward Department
SPCA – Society for the Prevention of Cruelty to Animals
Stew. - Steward
Strkpr - Storekeeper
Super. – Superintendent
SURG – Surgeon
SUVCW – Sons of Union Veterans of the Civil War
Svcs – services
Tac. - Tactics
TCF – Theta Chi Fraternity
Terr. – Territory/Territorial
Topo – Topographical
Tr - transferred
Univ. – University
UC – Union College
UM – University of Mississippi
UMI – University of Michigan
UNC – University of North Carolina
US - United States
USA - US Army
USAMHI – US Army Military History Institute
USCC – US Christian Commission
USCI – US Colored Infantry
USHR – US House of Representatives
USMA – US Military Academy
USMC – US Marine Corps
USMTS - US Military Telegraph Service
USN - US Navy
USSC – US Sanitary Commission
USSS – US Sharpshooters
USV - US Volunteers
UTS – Union Theological Seminary (NYC)
UVA – University of Virginia
UVM – University of Vermont
UW – University of Washington
UWI –University of Wisconsin
VBA – Vermont Bar Association
VHS – Vermont Historical Society
Vols - Volunteers
v.p. - Vice President
VRC – Veteran Reserve Corps
VT NG - Vermont National Guard
VTMS – Vermont Medical Society
WGBS - West Gulf Blockading Squadron
wdd - wounded
wds – wounds
WMC - Woodstock Medical College
WRC – Women's Relief Corps
XO – Executive Officer (USN)
YMCA – Young Men's Christian Association

They Went to War

Introduction

Just prior to the outbreak of the War Between the States, no northern state was less prepared for war than Vermont. Except in the feeble existence of four skeleton regiments, her militia was unorganized, the men subject to military service not being even enrolled. Some of the uniformed companies were without guns, others drilled with ancient flint-locks; and the State possessed but five hundred serviceable percussion muskets, and no tents nor camp equipage.

When the war broke out President Lincoln made a call for volunteers. Vermont filled its quotas and sent the state's fathers and sons into battle. They Went to War documents over 650 of those Vermonters who made that journey. Many of these men and boys had never even left the confines of their hometowns. Some of these men never returned home and are buried in locations that are now lost to time and memory. Others returned to their native state and their prior lives, while others left Vermont to make new lives for themselves and their families.

Who were these volunteers from Vermont? They were career soldiers, militia men, college students, farm boys, town fathers, immigrants and women. What capacities did these Vermonters serve in the war? Some were soldiers, sailors, musicians, chaplains, doctors, nurses and even a few that served in the confederate ranks. Many were wounded and yet returned to active duty to fight another day. Others served their terms in one unit and then reenlisted in other units. Some Vermonters also served in other state units as well. Over sixty of these men also were awarded the Medal of Honor for heroics on the battlefield.

The service of the Vermonters was commendable and has been widely documented in a number of other works. A bigger question remains, what happened to the numerous Vermonters that survived the war after it was over? Those that didn't remain in their native state moved to places like, France, Italy, Chile, Washington, DC, Florida, Iowa, Texas, Nebraska and other states. These same people held a variety of jobs after the war including; judge, prospector, farmer, journalist, senator and missionary. Many of those that died outside the state were returned "home" for burial, you can't take Vermont out of its native sons and daughters.

Each of the Vermonters documented here served their state and country during the war, but their contributions did not stop there. Vermont contributed greatly to the war effort it sent seventeen infantry units, four artillery units and one cavalry unit into the fray. The tiny state was represented at nearly every major engagement of the war. They Went to War is brief look into the lives of some of the Vermonters who served with grace and honor during the Civil War.

This undertaking took on many different forms in the early stages. We eventually were able to narrow our focus (a bit) and came up with a biographical dictionary of Vermonters who served during the war. Obviously we couldn't include every soldier, so there were some limitations. We have also included women and others who served the war effort in other capacities. The main criterion for inclusion within this opus is a connection to Vermont. Also included are those that held public office after the war or were otherwise engaged in other types of governmental work. While these Vermonters all contributed before, during or after the war, there are those that became entangled in plots, schemes and other types of disreputable activities. It is this combination of people and events that helped to shape our country and more specifically Vermont itself.

More specifically, we have included:

- Medal of Honor recipients
- Vermonters who attained the rank of Colonel and above in the army, or Captain and above in the navy
- Vermonters who had service in two or more wars (most of them turned out to be men with service in the Mexican-American War and later the Civil War, but a few had Civil War and then Spanish-American War Service).
- Vermonters who made major contributions in private or public life after the war, including postwar governors, U.S. Representatives or Senators, cabinet officials, philanthropists, etc.
- Vermonters who made the army (or navy) a career after the war was over

- Vermonters who served in units then called Colored Troops, black and white
- Vermonters who published diaries or unit histories after the war.
- Vermont women who made significant contributions
- Confederate Vermonters who made significant contributions on their side
- Membership in postwar organizations in Vermont (GAR, MOLLUS, Reunion Society, SUVCW, WRC, etc.)
- Soldiers for whom GAR posts were named (indicating the esteem they were accorded by their fellow soldiers)

Each biographical entry includes, ideally, the name, date and place of birth, parents' names, early lives including occupation and education, details of war service, life after the war, fraternal, political and religious affiliations, date of marriage and name of spouse, date of death and burial location and lastly, sources. In addition, where available, we have included the archives where diaries, correspondence and other papers for the individual are stored. Where applicable, books written by the individuals or biographies about them are included as well.

Sources are included parenthetically after each entry, coded and listed alphabetically by code in Sources Cited. Where a source has an asterisk (*) appended, that indicates the source for a photograph or likeness of the individual, which are included in sections after each alphabetical grouping.

Medal of Honor Recipients

Bates, Norman Francis (1839-1915)

Born: 6 Nov 1839, Derby Center VT, son of Portus and Ellen Judith Jannette (Harris) Baxter
Early Life: moved to Grinnell IA, Grinnell College, dropped out to enlist
War Service: PVT Co. E 4th IA CAV 16 Sep 1861, CPL 1 Oct 1862, 6SGT 5 Dec 1864, 5SGT 11 Jun 1865, m/o 8 Aug 1865 Atlanta GA
MOH Issued: 17 Jul 1865, for action at Columbus, GA, 16 Apr 1865
Citation: Capture of flag and bearer
Later Life: Poweshiek Cty Super. of schools, 1870, farmer Malcom IA 1880, hotel clerk Luverne MN 1900, railroad billing clerk Los Angeles CA 1910
Married: 31 Mar 1864, Almira Hatch Cummings
Died: 16 Oct 1915, Glendale CA; interment in Forest Lawn Memorial Park
Notes: SGT N. F. Bates Camp, No. 64, Department of IA, SUVCW named for him
(1880, 1900, 1910, LDI, LFP, MOHR, WFS)

Beattie, Alexander Mitchell (1828-1907)

Born: 29 Jul 1828, Ryegate VT, son of James and Margaret J. Beattie
Early Life: St. Johnsbury Acad. 1846
War Service: 2LT Co. I 3rd VT INF 11 Jun 1861, 1LT 7 Nov 1861, CPT Co. F 13 Oct 1862, m/o 27 Jul 1864
MOH Issued: 25 Apr 1894, for action at Cold Harbor VA, 5 Jul 1864
Citation: Removed, under a hot fire, a wounded member of his command to a place of safety
Later Life: State Rep. 1869, moved to Lancaster NH by 1870, farmer and lumberman Lancaster NH 1870-1900
Affiliations: RSVO, SOC. AOP, MOLLUS (#09663)
Married: 30 Dec 1869, Celestia Congdon
Died: 7 Mar 1907, Lancaster NH; interment in Summer Street Cemetery
(1870, 1880, 1900, C&S, FAG, FSO, JHR69, MOHR, SJA)

Benedict, George Grenville (1826-1907)

Born: 10 Dec 1826, Burlington VT, son of George Wyllys and Eliza (Dewey) Benedict
Early Life: A.B. UVM 1847, A.M. UVM 1850; teacher, railroad developer, journalist, postmaster
War Service: PVT Co. C 12th VT INF, 2LT Jan 1863, ADC B.G. Stannard, m/o 14 Jul 1863
MOH Issued: 27 Jul 1892 for action at Gettysburg, PA, 3 Jul 1863
Citation: Passed through a murderous fire of grape and canister in delivering orders and re-formed the crowded lines
Later Life: Asst I.G. State Militia, ADC Gov. Paul Dillingham, editor-in-chief, Burlington Free Press, State Sen. 1869-70
Affiliations: Republican VT Press Assoc, GAR, MOLLUS (#08267), VHS, SCW, SAR, RSVO
Married: (1) 1853, Mary Kellogg; (2) 1864, Katherine A. Pease
Died: 8 Apr 1907, Camden, NC; interment in Greenmount Cemetery, Burlington VT
Notes: Vermont's Civil War historian; cousin of George Dewey
Papers: UVM
(C&S, GFH*, JGW, LHC, MOHR, WHO3)

Blair, Robert M. (1836-1899)

Born: 1836, Peacham VT
War Service: Landsman USN 5 Nov 1862 Portland ME, *Huron*, m/o 31 Dec 1863, Boatswain's Mate 16 Jun 1864, *Pontoosuc, Pinta*, m/o 27 Aug 1865
MOH Issued: 22 Jul 1865, for action during capture of Fort Fisher and Wilmington, from 24 Dec 1864 to 22 Jan 1865

Citation: Served on board the USS *Pontoosuc* during the capture of Fort Fisher and Wilmington, 24 Dec 1864 to 22 Jan 1865. Carrying out his duties faithfully throughout this period, Blair was recommended for gallantry and skill and for his cool courage while under the fire of the enemy throughout these actions
Later Life: farmer Clear Creek KS 1880
Died: 2 Apr 1899, Enid OK; interment in Enid Cemetery
(1880, MOHR, RR)

Butterfield, Franklin George (1842-1916)

Born: 11 Mar 1842, Rockingham VT, son of David and Elmira (Randall) Butterfield
Early Life: Saxtons River Acad., MC 1860-62, left to enlist
War Service: 2LT Co. A 6th VT INF 4 Oct 1861, 1LT Co. C 21 Aug 1862, CPT Co. I 21 Apr 1864, LTCOL 21 Oct 1864, wdd Charlestown 21 Aug 1864, resgd 28 Oct 1864 as CPT Co. I
MOH Issued: 4 May 1891, for action at Salem Heights VA, 4 May 1863
Citation: Took command of the skirmish line and covered the movement of his regiment out of a precarious position
Later Life: mercantile pursuits 1865-77; atty 1880, US Census supervisor VT 1880-82, Bureau of Pensions 1882-92, manufacturer 1892-1913, Board of Visitors NU 1898-1900
Affiliations: GAR, MOLLUS (#02982), Mason, RSVO, SAR, SOC. AOP
Married: 1 Jun 1866, Maria Smith Frost
Died: 6 Jan 1916, Saxtons River VT; interment in Saxtons River Cemetery
(B&K, C&S, CLL*, JGU, MIDCat, MOHR, SAH, WAE)

Churchill, Samuel Joseph (1842-1932)

Born: 1 Nov 1842, Hubbardton VT, son of Samuel Sumner and Mary (Richardson) Churchill
Early Life: Sudbury Acad., moved to De Kalb, IL early 1861
War Service: QM SGT 6 Aug 1861 Btry G 2nd IL LARTY, m/o 4 Sep 1865
MOH Issued: 20 Jan 1897, for action at Nashville, TN, 15 Dec 1864
Citation: When the fire of the enemy's batteries compelled the men of his detachment for a short time to seek shelter, he stood manfully at his post and for some minutes worked his gun alone
Later Life: returned briefly to VT, moved to Lee's Summit, MO 1866, travelling salesman for Scutt barbed wire of Joliet, IL, moved to Las Cruces, NM, super. and v.p. Oregon Mountain Mining and Smelting Co., grocer, ret. to Lawrence KS
Affiliations: Congregational, GAR (AAG, AIG, KS Cmndry), IOOF
Married: (1) 4 May 1864, Adelia Augusta Holmes; (2) 4 Aug 1879, Louana Grant
Died: 3 Jun 1932, Lawrence, KS; interment in Oak Hill Cemetery
Publications: Genealogy and Biography of the Connecticut Branch of the Churchill Family in America (1901)
(B&K*, FAG, MOHR, SJC)

Clarke, Dayton Perry (1840-1915)

Born: 15 Dec 1840, Dekalb NY, son of Leonard Elliott and Calista M. (Warner) Clarke (both native Vermonters)
Early Life: moved to Hermon NY c1850, public schools, teacher; moved to Northfield VT, c1858, Northfield Acad., teacher in Roxbury, studying law
War Service: SGT Co. F 2nd VT INF 7 May 1861, 1LT, Co. D 29 Jan 1862, CPT Co. F 3 Nov 1863, m/o 29 Jun 1864
MOH Issued: 30 Jul 1892, for action at Spotsylvania C.H., 12 May 1864
Citation: Distinguished conduct in a desperate hand-to-hand fight while commanding the regiment
Later Life: resided Montpelier until his death, merchant, Lane Manufacturing Co., carriage, sign and house painter, first constable and collector, j.p. 1898
Married: 11 Sep 1865, Mary Bigelow Kent
Died: 10 Nov 1915, Montpelier VT; interment in Green Mount Cemetery
Notes: father served in 142nd NY INF

(BBObit, DAR2, FAG, HC4, JVS98, MOHR, TBP1)

Clark, John Wesley (1830-1898)

Born: 25 Oct 1830, Moretown VT, son of Oliver Grant and Lucia (Brown) Clark
Early Life: Newbury Sem.; mining and mercantile pursuits out west; sheriff, Mariposa Cty CA
War Service: QM 6th VT INF 28 Sep 1861, wdd, near Warrenton 28 Jul 1863, AQM (CPT) AQM USV 7 Apr 1864, m/o 6 Dec 1864
MOH Issued: 17 Aug 1891, for action near Warrenton VA, 28 Jul 1863
Citation: Defended the division train against a vastly superior force of the enemy; he was severely wounded, but remained in the saddle for 20 hours afterward until he had brought his train through in safety
Later Life: resided Montpelier until his death
Affiliations: RSVO, MOLLUS (#10074)
Married: 1854, Betsey Ann Dewey
Died: 4 Aug 1898, Montpelier VT; interment in Green Mount Cemetery
(C&S, FAG, FSO, GFH, MOHR, RR)

Coffey, Robert John (1842-1901)

Born: 15 Dec 1842, St. Johns, NB, Canada
Early Life: moved to Montpelier, local schools 1853-55 and Morristown 1855-59
War Service: PVT Co. F 1st VT INF 2 May 1861, m/o 15 Aug 1861, SGT Co. I 4th VT INF 5 Sep 1861, wdd, 18 Oct 1863, m/o 30 Sep 1864
MOH Issued: 13 May 1892, for action at Banks Ford VA 4 May 1863
Citation: single-handedly captured 2 officers and 5 privates of the 8th La. Reg't (CSA)
Later Life: hotel proprietor, Super. VT Soldiers' Home, MAJ and BGD P.M. on staff of GEN Julius J. Estey, VT NG (Total 15 years in NG)
Affiliations: Republican, GAR, Mason, RSVO
Married: 1867, Demis Hattie Burnham
Died: 9 Jul 1901, Montpelier VT; interment in Green Mount Cemetery
(FSO, JGU*, MOHR, SAH)

Coughlin, John (1837-1912)

Born: Jun 1837, Williamstown VT
Early Life: grocer, Manchester NH
War Service: LTCOL 10th NH INF 17 Jul 1862, m/I 5 Sep 1862, wdd 7 May 1864 Port Walthall VA, wdd 30 Jul 1864 Mine Explosion Petersburg VA; Bvt COL and B.G. (9 Apr 1865, m/o 21 Jun 1865, Richmond VA
MOH Issued: 31 Aug 1893, for action at Swifts Creek VA, on 9 May 1864
Citation: During a sudden night attack upon Burnham's Brigade, resulting in much confusion, this officer, without waiting for orders, led his regiment forward and interposed a line of battle between the advancing enemy and Hunt's Battery, repulsing the attack and saving the guns
Later Life: Colesville MD 1900, Washington DC 1910
Died: 27 May 1912, Washington D.C; interment in Arlington National Cemetery (Section 2, Lot 936, WS)
(1900, 1910, ADA, FAG, FBH, MOHR, RR)

Davis, George Evans (1839-1926)

Born: 26 Dec 1839, Dunstable MA, son of Mial and Lucy Davis
War Service: PVT Co. H 1st VT INF 2 May 1861, m/o 15 Aug 1861, 2LT Co. D 10th VT INF 5 Aug 1862, 1LT 26 Jan 1863, wdd Winchester 19 Sep 1864, wdd Cedar Creek 19 Oct 1864, CPT 2 Nov 1864, m/o 22 Jun 1865

MOH Issued: 27 May 1892, for action at Monocacy, MD, 9 Jul 1864
Citation: While in command of a small force, held the approaches to the 2 bridges against repeated assaults of superior numbers, thereby materially delaying Early's advance on Washington
Later Life: treasurer VT Shade Roller Co., Burlington, bookkeeper Burlington 1870, resided Essex 1880
Affiliations: MOLLUS (#09159), Baptist, YMCA (1st pres. Burlington, officer 13 years)
Married: Emma (nfi)
Died: 28 Jun 1926, Burlington VT; interment in Lakeview Cemetery
(1870, 1880, B&K*, C&S, EMH, FSO, MOHR)

Dolloff, Charles William (1844-1884)

Born: 10 May 1844, Parishville NY
Early Life: moved to VT 1846
War Service: PVT Co. K 11th VT INF 25 Nov 1863, CPL 23 Dec 1864, SGT 2 Jun 1865, Co. A 24 Jun 1865, m/o 25 Aug 1865
MOH Issued: 24 Apr 1865, for action at Petersburg VA, on 2 Apr 1865
Citation: Capture of flag (42nd MS INF)
Later Life: moved to WI 1871, bridge foreman for the Minneapolis, Sault Ste. Marie & Atlantic R.R, killed in railroad accident
Affiliations: Mason
Married: Mary Warner
Died: 2 Aug 1884, near Canton WI; interment in Forest Cemetery, Stevens Point WI
(AGC, FAG, MOHR, PTW, RR, Portage Cty Gazette)

Downs, Henry W. (1844-1911)

Born: 29 Aug 1844, Jamaica VT, son of Calvin and Elizabeth Knights (Hudson) Downs
War Service: PVT Co. I 8th VT INF 18 Feb 1862, reen 5 Jan 1864, SGT 13 Dec 1863, 1SGT 21 Mar 1865, 2LT 18 Apr 1865, m/o 28 Jun 1865
MOH Issued: 13 Dec 1893, for action at Winchester VA, 19 Sep 1864
Citation: With one comrade, voluntarily crossed an open field, exposed to a raking fire, and returned with a supply of ammunition, successfully repeating the attempt a short time thereafter
Later Life: Watertown MA, silk manufacturer, 1880, Manhattan NY, manufacturer, 1900, Newfane VT, 1910, ret.
Affiliations: GAR (MA Council of Administration 1896)
Married: 22 Apr 1868, Louisa B. Rawson
Died: 2 Jul 1911, Dayton OH; interment in Dayton National Cemetery (Section Q, Row 7, Grave 24)
(1880, 1900, 1910, FAG, FSO, GARM2, GNC, JGU*, MOHR)

Drury, James John (1835-1919)

Born: 15 Aug 1835, Cty Clare, Ireland, son of Michael and Mary (Sullivan) Drury
Early Life: emigrated to Chester VT 1845, stonemason, farm laborer Chester 1860
War Service: PVT Co. C 4th VT INF 26 Aug 1861, CPL 27 Oct 1863, SGT 18 Jun 1864, 2LT, 4 Jun 1865, m/o 26 Jul 1865 as SGT
MOH Issued: 18 Jan 1893, for action at Weldon Railroad, 23 Jul 1864
Citation: Saved the colors of his regiment when it was surrounded by a much larger force of the enemy and after the greater part of the regiment had been killed or captured
Later Life: stonemason, farmer, Chester VT, moved to Albia IA 1869
Affiliations: Republican, Mason, GAR, Bluff Creek (IA) Veterans Assoc
Married: 28 Dec 1868, Jane Daugherty
Died: 25 Dec 1919, Lovilia IA; interment in St. Peter Cemetery
(1860, B&K*, FAG, MOHR)

Eddy, Samuel Edwin (1822-1909)

Born: 2 Jun 1822, Whitingham VT, son of Henry and Catherine (Bemis) Eddy
Early Life: moved to Chesterfield MA, blacksmith
War Service: PVT 23 Jul 1862 Co. D 37th MA INF, m/o 9 Jun 1865
MOH Issued: 10 Sep 1897 for action at Sailor's Creek VA, 6 Apr 1865
Citation: Saved the life of the adjutant of his regiment by voluntarily going beyond the line and there killing one of the enemy then in the act of firing upon the wounded officer. Was assailed by several of the enemy, run through the body with a bayonet, and pinned to the ground, but while so situated he shot and killed his assailant
Later Life: blacksmith and farmer Chesterfield MA 1870-1900
Affiliations: GAR
Married: 3 Jul 1849, Sarah D. Todd
Died: 7 Mar 1909, Chesterfield MA; interment in West Chesterfield Cemetery
(1870, 1880, 1900, FSO, MOHR, RR)

Evans, Ira Hobart (1844-1922)

Born: 11 Apr 1844, Piermont NH, son of Ira and Emeline H. Evans
Early Life: student, Barre VT
War Service: PVT Co. B 10th VT INF 1 Sep 1862, dis 22 Dec 1863 for pr as 1LT, 9th USCI, CPT Co. B 31 Jan 1865 116th USCI, Bvt MAJ USV 13 Mar 1865, m/o 7 Feb 1866
MOH Issued: 24 Mar 1892 for action at Hatcher's Run, 2 Apr 1865
Citation: Voluntarily passed between the lines, under a heavy fire from the enemy, and obtained important information
Later Life: Freedmen's Bureau, IRS, businessman, politician; Texas State Rep., railroad executive
Affiliations: Republican
Died: 19 Apr 1922, San Diego CA; interment in Hobart Corners Cemetery, Berlin VT
Notes: selected as one of the officers of the honor guard to march in President Lincoln's funeral cortège
Papers: University of Tulsa
(FSO, FWJ, MOHR, RR)

Ferris, Eugene W. (1842-1907)

Born: 26 Nov 1842, Springfield VT, son of Robert and Fanny Ferris
Early Life: bookkeeper, moved to Lowell MA by 1850
War Service: 1SGT Co. D 30th MA INF 1 Jan 1862, 2LT Co. E 19 Aug 1862, 1LT 26 Nov 1863, ADJ 15 Feb 1865, CPT 21 Apr 1865, m/o 5 Jul 1866, Charleston SC
MOH Issued: 16 Oct 1897, for action at Berryville, 1 Apr 1865
Citation: Accompanied only by an orderly, outside the lines of the Army, he gallantly resisted an attack of 5 of Mosby's cavalry, mortally wounded the leader of the party, seized his horse and pistols, wounded 3 more, and, though wounded himself, escaped
Later Life: hotel keeper, Delaware, IN 1900; never married
Affiliations: MOLLUS (#10287)
Died: 26 Feb 1907, Rockville IN; interment in Rockville Cemetery (Section B, Lot 32)
(1850, 1900, C&S, JHA, MOHR, RR)

Gould, Charles Gilbert (1845-1916)

Born: 5 May 1845, Windham VT
War Service: PVT Co. G 11th VT INF 1 Sep 1862, CPL 27 Dec 1863, SGM 12 Feb 1864, 2LT Co. E 30 Jun 1864, CPT Co. H 5th VT INF 10 Nov 1864, Bvt MAJ 2 Apr 1865, wdd, Petersburg, 2 Apr 1865, m/o 19 Jun 1865
MOH Issued: 30 Jul 1890, for action at Petersburg VA, on 2 Apr 1865

Citation: Among the first to mount the enemy's works in the assault, he received a serious bayonet wound in the face, was struck several times with clubbed muskets, but bravely stood his ground, and with his sword killed the man who bayoneted him
Later Life: Pension clerk, Washington; US Patent Office
Affiliations: Republican, MOLLUS (#08814)
Died: 5 Dec 1916, Windham VT; interment in Windham Central Cemetery
Correspondence: UVM (B&K, C&S, FAG, JGU, MOHR, RR)

Grant, Lewis Addison (1829-1918)

Born: 17 Jan 1829, Winhall VT
Early Life: teacher, Washington NJ 1850, atty
War Service: MAJ 15 Aug 1861 5th VT INF, LTCOL 25 Sep 1861, COL 16 Sep 1862, wdd 14 Dec 1862, B.G. USV 27 Apr 1864, Bvt M.G. USV 19 Aug 1864, m/o 24 Aug 1865
MOH Issued: 11 May 1893, for action at Salem Heights VA, on 3 May 1864
Citation: Personal gallantry and intrepidity displayed in the management of his brigade and in leading it in the assault in which he was wounded
Later Life: atty, Moline, later Des Moines IL (20 years); Assistant Secretary of War 1890-93 (Harrison administration), real estate dealer, resided Minneapolis 1889-1918
Affiliations: RSVO
Marriage: (1) 11 Mar 1857, S. Agusta Hartwell; (2) 9 Sep 1863, Mary Helen Pierce
Died: 20 Mar 1918, Minneapolis MN; interment in Lakewood Cemetery (Section 8, Lot 416, Grave 2)
(1850, 1880, B&K*, EJW, GGB, MOHR, NYTObit, SAH, WHC)

Hack, Lester Goodell (1841-1928)

Born: 18 Jan 1841, Cadwell NY, son of Joseph and Mary (Fay) Hack
War Service: PVT Co. F 5th VT INF 27 Aug 1861, reen 15 Dec 1863, CPL, SGT 1 Mar 1865, wdd, Wilderness, 5 May 1864, m/o 29 Jun 1865
MOH Issued: 10 May 1865, for action at Petersburg VA, 2 Apr 1865
Citation: Capture of flag of 23rd Tenn. INF (CSA) with several of the enemy
Later Life: farmer/farm laborer 1870-1920, Ticonderoga NY
Married: 1874, Emma Jane Burt
Died: 24 Apr 1928, Copenhagen NY; interment in Mt. Hope Cemetery, Ticonderoga NY
(1870, 1880, 1890, 1900, 1910, 1920, B&K*, FAG, MOHR)

Harrington, Ephraim Wood (1833-1914)

Born: 16 Jan 1833, Waterford ME, son of David and Lucinda Harrington
Early Life: Brunswick ME 1860, moved to Kirby VT, laborer
War Service: 2SGT Co. G 2nd VT INF 20 Jun 1861, wdd 3 May 1864, 2LT Co. B 20 Jun 1864, 1LT Co. G 8 Aug 1864, CPT 24 Dec 1864, Bvt MAJ 2 Apr 1865, m/o 15 Jul 1865
MOH Issued: 13 Dec 1893, for action at Fredericksburg VA, on 3 May 1863
Citation: Carried the colors to the top of the heights and almost to the muzzle of the enemy's guns
Later Life: farmer Hodgdon ME 1870, carpenter St. Johnsbury 1880, cabinet maker Attleboro MA 1900, farmer Brunswick 1910
Married: (1) abt 1865, Sarah Dudley Wheeler; (2) Lucretia (nfi)
Died: 10 Dec 1914, Attleboro MA; interment in Grove Cemetery, East St. Johnsbury VT
(1850, 1860, 1870, 1880, 1900, 1910, B&K, FAG, MOHR, SAH)

Hawkins, Gardner C. (1846-1913)

Born: 11 Feb 1846, Pomfret VT, son of Lewis and Hannah Hawkins
War Service: PVT Co. F 3rd VT INF 28 Jan 1864, 2LT Co. I 18 Oct 1864, 1LT Co. E 15 Feb 1865, wdd, Petersburg, 2 Apr 1865, dis/wds 2 Jun 1865
MOH Issued: 30 Sep 1893 for action at Petersburg VA, 2 Apr 1865
Citation: When the lines were wavering from the well-directed fire of the enemy, this officer, acting adjutant of the regt, sprang forward, and with encouraging words cheered the soldiers on and, although dangerously wounded, refused to leave the field until the enemy's works were taken
Later Life: mech. engr Winthrop MA 1910
Died: 15 Dec 1913, Winthrop MA; interment in Lindenwood Cemetery, Stoneham MA
(1850, 1900, 1910, B&K*, CCC, MOHR)

Henry, William Wirt (1831-1915)

Born: 21 Nov 1831, Waterbury VT, son of James M. and Matilda (Gale) Henry
Early Life: Waterbury schools, People's Acad., Morrisville; in California 1852-57, constable; businessman, drug merchant Waterbury 1860
War Service: 1LT Co. D 2nd VT INF, 20 May 1861, resgd 15 Jan 1861; MAJ 10th VT INF, 26 Aug 1862, LTCOL 17 Oct 1862, COL 26 Apr 1864, wdd, Cold Harbor, 3 Jun 1864, wdd, Monocacy, 9 Jul 1864, wdd, Cedar Creek, 19 Oct 1864; resgd 17 Dec 1864; Bvt B.G. USV 7 Mar 1865
MOH Issued: 21 Dec 1892 for action at Cedar Creek VA, on 19 Oct 1864
Citation: Though suffering from severe wounds, rejoined his regiment and led it in a brilliant charge, recapturing the guns of an abandoned battery
Later Life: State Sen. 1874-75; US Marshall 1879-86; Burlington mayor 1887-88; Immigrant inspector 1892-
Married: Mary J. (nfi)
Affiliations: Mason, GAR, MOLLUS (#05875), SOC. AOP, KOP, RSVO
Died: 31 Aug 1915, Burlington VT; interment in Lakeview Cemetery (Maple Block, Lot 1)
Publications: Patrick Henry: Life, Correspondence, and Speeches (1891), The First Legislative Assembly in America (1894)
(1860, C&S,EMH*, GFH, JGU, LHC, MOHR, RR)

Holton, Edward A. (1835-1906)

Born: 28 Aug 1835, Westminster VT, son of Erastus Alexander and Hannah Brainerd (Chase) Holton
War Service: PVT Co. H 1st VT INF 2 May 1861, m/o 15 Aug 1861, 1SGT, Co. I, 6th VT INF 28 Aug 1861, 2LT 18 Jan 1862, 1LT 5 Jun 1863, CPT Co. F 15 May 1864, wdd Wilderness 5 May 1864, dis/wds 17 Aug 1864
MOH Issued: 9 Jul 1892, for action at Lee's Mill VA, 16 Apr 1862
Citation: Rescued the colors of his regiment under heavy fire, the color bearer having been shot down while the troops were in retreat
Later Life: miner Lee MA 1870, moved to Burlington, carpenter 1880-88, deputy collector and inspector 1888-90, ret. to Bernardston MA
Affiliations: RSVO
Married: 15 Sep 1863, Catherine Matilda Chase
Died: 29 Jan 1906, Bernardston MA; interment in Old Cemetery, Westminster VT
Correspondence: Fredericksburg and Spotsylvania National Military Park Archive; UVM
(1870, 1880, 1890, 1900, B&K, FAG, HC1, MOHR, SAH)

Hooker, George White (1838-1902)

Born: 6 Feb 1838, Salem NY, son of Samuel Smith and Esther (White) Hooker
Early Life: moved to Londonderry VT, public schools, West River Acad., clerk, traveling salesman
War Service: PVT Co. F 4th VT INF 6 Sep 1861, SGM 18 Dec 1861, 2LT, Co. E 21 Apr 1862, 1LT, 1 Aug 1862, CPT and AAG USV, 31 Jul 1861, Bvt MAJ and LTCOL USV, 4 Nov 1865), m/o 4 Jan 1866

MOH Issued: 17 Sep 1891, for action at South Mountain, MD, 14 Sep 1862
Citation: Rode alone, in advance of his regiment, into the enemy's lines, and before his own men came up received the surrender of the MAJ of a Confederate regiment, together with the colors and 116 men
Later Life: banker and broker; COL and CoS to Gov. Redfield Proctor (q.v.); State Rep., Sergeant-at-Arms, US Rep.
Affiliations: Dept Cmdr, GAR, RSVO, MOLLUS (#10666)
Died: 6 Aug 1902, Brattleboro VT; interment in Prospect Hill Cemetery
(C&S, JGU, MOHR, MRC*, RR, WAE)

Howard, Oliver Otis (1830-1909)

Born: 8 Nov 1830, Leeds ME, son of Rowland B. and Eliza (Otis) Howard
Early Life: Monmouth and Yarmouth Academies, Bowdoin College 1850, USMA 1854 (4/46); 2LT 1 Jul 1855; 1LT 1 Jul 1857, instr. USMA
War Service: COL 3rd ME INF; B.G. USV 3 Sep 1861; wdd, right arm amputated, 1 Jun 1862; cmdg BGD at 2nd Bull Run; cmdg Div Antietam; M.G. USV Apr 1863; cmdg XI Corps; Gettysburg, Cemetery Hill; Chattanooga TN; Mission Ridge; Knoxville TN; Sherman's March to Atlanta; cmdg Army of Tenn.; B.G. USA Dec 1864; Bvt M.G. USA 13 Mar 1865
MOH Issued: 29 Mar 1893 for action at Fair Oaks, on 1 Jun 1862
Citation: Led the 61st NY INF in a charge in which he was twice severely wounded in the right arm, necessitating amputation
Later Life: cmdg BRFAL 1865-71; founded Howard University 1867; pres., Howard Univ. 1869-73; cmdg Dept of the Columbia 1874-81; M.G. 1886; cmdg Division of the East 1886-94; ret. 1894
Affiliations: MOLLUS (#03808)
Died: 9 Oct 1909, Burlington VT; interment in Lakeview Cemetery (Pine Grove 1 Section, Lot 40)
Notes: Ludlow GAR Post #33 named after him
Papers: Lincoln Memorial University
Publications: General Taylor. (1892), Autobiography of Oliver Otis Howard. (1908)
(C&S, FAG, GFH, GWC, HGW, LPB, MOHR, SAH*, TCE)

Howard, Squire Edward (1840-1912)

Born: 15 May 1840, Jamaica VT, son of Nathaniel Stoddard and Calista Church (Bills) Howard
Early Life: teacher of penmanship, Jamaica 1860
War Service: 1SGT, Co. H 8th VT INF 19 Nov 1861, 2LT, Co. H 13 Jan 1863, 1LT, 27 Oct 1863, CPT Co. C 26 Jul 1864, wdd, Cedar Creek, 19 Oct 1864, dis 9 Dec 1864
MOH Issued: 29 Jan 1894 for action at Bayou Teche LA, on 14 Jan 1863
Citation: Voluntarily carried an important message through the heavy fire of the enemy to bring aid and save the gunboat *Calhoun*
Later Life: hardware merchant, Brattleboro VT 1870, resided Newton MA 1890-1900
Married: Helen (nfi)
Affiliations: RSVO, Mason
Died: 26 Nov 1912, West Newton MA; interment in Newton Cemetery
(1860, 1870, 1880, 1890, 1900, B&K*, FAG, MOHR, RR)

Ingalls, Lewis J. (1837-1913)

Born: 11 Oct 1837, Boston MA
War Service: PVT Co. K 8th VT INF 2 Nov 1861, wdd 4 Sep 1862, reen 5 Jan 1864, wdd Winchester 19 Sep 1864, m/o 28 Jun 1865
MOH Issued: 20 Oct 1899 for action at Boutte Station, LA, 4 Sep 1862

Citation: A railroad train guarded by about 60 men on flat cars having been sidetracked by a misplaced switch into an ambuscade of guerrillas who were rapidly shooting down the unprotected guards, this soldier, under a severe fire in which he was wounded, ran to another switch and, opening it, enabled the train and the surviving guards to escape
Died: 31 Dec 1913, Irasburg VT; interment in Irasburg Cemetery
(MOHR, RR)

Jewett, Erastus W. (1839-1906)

Born: 1 Apr 1839, St. Albans VT, son of Eleazer and Adorethy (Abells) Jewett
War Service: 2LT Co. A 9th VT INF 14 Jun 1862, 1LT 24 May 1863, pow 3 Sep 1862, prld 28 Sep 1862, resgd 21 Nov 1864
MOH Issued: 8 Sep 1891, for action at Newport Barracks, NC, 2 Feb 1864
Citation: By long and persistent resistance and burning the bridges kept a superior force of the enemy at a distance and thus covered the retreat of the garrison
Later Life: moved to Swanton, lime and hay business, several town offices, inc. village pres. Swanton
Affiliations: Republican, RSVO, GAR (Post 73), Mason, SAR, MOLLUS (#05876)
Married: 28 Oct 1863, Fanny L. Brigham
Died: 20 Feb 1906, Swanton VT; interment in Church Street Cemetery
(B&K*, C&S, FAG, FSO, LHC, LCA1, MOHR, SAH)

Johndro, Franklin (1835-1901)

Born: 1835, Highgate Falls VT
Early Life: moved to Queensbury NY
War Service: PVT Co. A 118th NY INF 9 Aug 1862, m/o 13 Jun 1865
MOH Issued: 6 Apr 1865, for action at Chaffin's Farm, 30 Sep 1864
Citation: Capture of 40 prisoners
Later Life: Medal of Honor Legion 1891 (Surg. GEN)
Died: 5 Apr 1901, North Bay City MI; interment in Glens Falls Cemetery, Glens Falls NY
(B&K*, FAG, FP, MOHR, NYAG, SAH)

Johnston, Willie (1850-?)

Born: Jul 1850, Morristown NY
War Service: Musician Co. D 3rd VT INF 1 May 1862, tr to VRC 5 Feb 1864, reen 15 Feb 1864, m/o 31 Aug 1865
MOH Issued: 16 Sep 1863, for an unknown action and date
Citation: Date and place of act not on record in War Department
Died: date unknown; interment unknown
Notes: Youngest MOH recipient on record
(MOHR)

Livingston, Josiah O. (1837-1917)

Born: 3 Feb 1837, Walden VT
Early Life: student, atty
War Service: 1LT Co. I 9th VT INF 30 Jun 1862; ADJ 4 Jun 1863; CPT Co. G 19 Oct 1864; wdd Newport Barracks 2 Feb 1864; m/o 13 Jun 1865
MOH Issued: 8 Sep 1891 for action at Newport Barracks, NC, on 2 Feb 1864
Citation: When, after desperate resistance, the small garrison had been driven back to the river by a vastly superior force, this officer, while a small force held back the enemy, personally fired the railroad bridge, and, although wounded himself, assisted a wounded officer over the burning structure
Later Life: atty, Montpelier, city assessor, grand juror

Affiliations: Democrat, GAR, MOLLUS (#09180), RSVO, Soc. of the Medal of Honor
Died: 23 Jul 1917, Calais VT; interment in Robinson Cemetery
(B&K*, C&S, GFH, MOHR, RR)

Lonergan, John (1839-1902)

Born: 7 Apr 1839, Ireland
War Service: CPT Co. A 13th VT INF, m/o 21 Jul 1863, SGT Co. M Frontier CAV 10 Jan 1865, m/o 27 Jun 1865, Brattleboro
MOH Issued: 28 Oct 1893 for action at Gettysburg, PA, 2 Jul 1863
Citation: Gallantry in the recapture of 4 guns and the capture of 2 additional guns from the enemy; also the capture of a number of prisoners
Affiliations: RSVO
Died: 6 Aug 1902, Montreal, PQ; interment in St. Joseph Cemetery, Burlington VT (Section F, Lot 85)
(B&K, FAG, MOHR, RR)

Lyon, Frederick A. (1843-1911)

Born: 25 Jul 1843, Williamsburg MA
Early Life: moved to Burlington VT
War Service: SGT Co. A 1st VT CAV 9 Feb 1863, CPL 1 Jul 1864, SGT 1 Nov 1864, tr to Co. B 21 Jun 1865, m/o 9 Aug 1865
MOH Issued: 26 Nov 1864, for action at Cedar Creek VA, 19 Oct 1864
Citation: With one companion, captured the flag of a Confederate regiment, 3 officers, and an ambulance with its mules and driver (Not to mention CSA M.G. Ramseur)
Died: 23 Sep 1911, Jackson, MI; interment in Mt. Evergreen Cemetery
(B&K, MOHR, SAH)

Mattocks, Charles Porter (1840-1910)

Born: 11 Oct 1840, Danville VT, son of Henry and Martha Osgood (Porter) Mattocks
Early Life: Andover Acad. 1858; Bowdoin College 1862
War Service: 1LT 17th ME INF 2 Aug 1862; CPT 4 Dec 1862; MAJ 22 Dec 1863; captured at the Wilderness, 5 May 1864, escaped, recaptured, exchanged; Bvt COL 9 Apr 1865; Bvt B.G. 13 Mar 1865; COL 15 May 1865; m/o 4 Jun 1865
MOH Issued: 29 Mar 1899 for action at Sailor's Creek VA, on 6 Apr 1865
Citation: Displayed extraordinary gallantry in leading a charge of his regiment which resulted in the capture of a large number of prisoners and a stand of colors
Later Life: HLS 1867; atty; State's Atty 1869-72; State Rep. 1880-84; judge of probate 1900; Spanish-American War: B.G. 9 Jun 1898, 3rd Corps, Chickamauga, GA; dis 31 Oct 1898
Married: 1875, Ella Robinson
Died: 16 May 1910, Portland ME; interment in Evergreen Cemetery (Section R, Lot 845)
Publications: In Six Prisons (1898), Unspoiled Heart: The Journal of Charles Mattocks of the 17th Maine (posthumously, 1994)
(E&E, FAG, FSO, MOHR, RJ)

Nichols, Henry Clay (1832-1904)

Born: 30 Mar 1832, Brandon VT
Early Life: farming
War Service: PVT Co. H 1st VT INF 9 May 1861, m/o 15 Aug 1861, SGT Co. F 8th VT INF 18 Feb 1862, reduced, dis 8 Oct 1863 SOWD, to accept Captaincy in 73rd USCI, additional service in 96th USCI
MOH Issued: 3 Aug 1897 for action at Fort Blakely, AL, on 9 Apr 1865

Citation: Voluntarily made a reconnaissance in advance of the line held by his regiment and, under a heavy fire, obtained information of great value
Later Life: farmer
Died: 10 Feb 1904, Coventry VT; interment in Coventry Cemetery
(B&K, FAG, MOHR, RR)

Noyes, Wallace William (1846-1910)

Born: 23 Apr 1846, Montpelier VT, son of William and Miranda (Guernsey) Noyes
War Service: PVT Co. F 2nd VT INF 21 Jul 1863, wdd Petersburg 2 Apr 1865, m/o 21 Oct 1865
MOH Issued: 22 Mar 1892, for action at Spotsylvania C.H., on 12 May 1864
Citation: Standing upon the top of the breastworks, deliberately took aim and fired no less than 15 shots into the enemy's lines, but a few yards away
Later Life: resided Montpelier, carpenter, fireman Capitol Engine No. 5 1865-67, killed when he fell from a building
Married: (1) Emma Vincent; (2) abt 1900, Addie Vincent
Died: 1 Jul 1910; interment in Cutler Cemetery, East Montpelier
Notes: Inaccurately listed as William Wallace Noyes in 1892 Revised Roster
(1880, 1890, 1910, B&K, DBK, MOHR, SAH)

Peck, Cassius (1842-1913)

Born: 3 Mar 1842, Brookfield VT, son of Reuben and Hannah G. (Edson) Peck
Early Life: Newbury Sem., West Randolph Acad
War Service: PVT Co. F 1st USSS 11 Sep 1861, CPL 1 Dec 1862, SGT 1 May 1863, m/o 12 Sep 1864
MOH Issued: 12 Oct 1892, for action near Blackburn's Ford VA, on 19 Sep 1862
Citation: Took command of such soldiers as he could get and attacked and captured a Confederate battery of 4 guns. Also, while on a reconnaissance, overtook and captured a Confederate soldier
Later Life: farmer 1864-97; State Rep. 1882-83, 1886-87; State Sen. 1896-97; super. experimental farm, State Agricultural College (1897-1913)
Affiliations: Republican, Congregational, Mason, GAR, RSVO
Died: 12 Jul 1913, Brookfield VT; interment in Brookfield New Cemetery
(FSO, GFH, MOHR, PCD)

Peck, Theodore Safford (1843-1918)

Born: 22 Mar 1843, Burlington VT, son of Theodore Augustus and Delia (Safford) Peck
Early Life: student
War Service: PVT Co. K 1st VT CAV 27 Jun 1862, QM SGT 9th VT INF 9 Jul 1862, 2LT Co. C 8 Jan 1863, 1LT Co. H 10 Jun 1864, wdd Chapin's Farm 29 Sep 1864, AQM (CPT) USV 11 Mar 1865, declined, m/o 23 Jun 1865
MOH Issued: 8 Sep 1891, for action at Newport Barracks, NC, on 2 Feb 1864
Citation: By long and persistent resistance and burning the bridges, kept a superior force of the enemy at bay and covered the retreat of the garrison
Later Life: insurance executive; military officer; State AIG 1881-1900
Affiliations: Republican, GAR, MOLLUS (#01397), RSVO, SAR, Mason
Died: 15 Mar 1918, Burlington VT; interment in Lakeview Cemetery (Pine area, Lot 6)
Papers: UVM
(B&K*, C&S, FAG, FSO, GFH, JGU, MOHR, SAH, VHS20, WHO3)

Phelps, Charles Edward (1833-1908)

Born: 1 May 1833, Guilford VT, son of John and Almira (Hart) Phelps

Early Life: moved to NJ in 1837, MD in 1841; Princeton College 1852; HLS; atty 1855-62; Baltimore MD City Council 1860
War Service: LTCOL 7th MD INF, 20 Aug 1862; pr COL 13 Apr 1864; wdd/pow Laurel Hill VA 8 May 1864; released and dis/wds
MOH Issued: 30 Mar 1898, for action at Laurel Hill VA, on 8 May 1864
Citation: Rode to the head of the assaulting column, then much broken by severe losses and faltering under the close fire of artillery, placed himself conspicuously in front of the troops, and gallantly rallied and led them to within a few feet of the enemy's works, where he was severely wounded and captured
Later Life: US Rep. 1865-69; atty; commissioner of public schools; judge 1892-1908; law faculty, University of MD 1884-1907
Married: 29 Dec 1868, Mary Eleanor Woodward
Died: 27 Dec 1908, Baltimore MD; interment in Woodlawn Cemetery
Publications: Juridical Equity: Abridged for the use of Students (1894), Falstaff and Equity: An Interpretation (1902)
(CB, FAG, FSO, JGU)

Pingree, Samuel Everett (1832-1922)

Born: 2 Aug 1832, Salisbury NH, son of Stephen and Judith (True) Pingree
Early Life: DC 1857; atty
War Service: 1LT Co. F 3rd VT INF 24 May 1861, CPT 13 Aug 1861, wdd, Lee's Mill, 16 Apr 1862, MAJ 27 Sep 1862, LTCOL, 15 Jan 1863, m/o 27 Jul 1864
MOH Issued: 17 Aug 1891 for action at Lee's Mill VA, on 16 Apr 1862
Citation: Gallantly led his company across a wide, deep creek, drove the enemy from the rifle pits, which were within 2 yards of the farther bank, and remained at the head of his men until a second time severely wounded
Later Life: State's Atty 1868-69; RNC delegate 1868; LT Gov. 1882-83; VT Gov. 1883-84; Chaired State R.R. Commission 1886-94; Honorary LLD NU 1898; Town Clerk, Hartford, 60 years
Affiliations: RSVO
Married: 15 Sep 1869, Lydia M. Steele
Died: 1 Jun 1922, Hartford VT; interment in Hartford Cemetery, White River Jct VT
Speeches: An oration before the Re-union Society of Vermont Officers, in the representative's hall, Montpelier, Vt., November 7th, 1872
(B&K*, BBObit, FAG, GFH, JGU, MOHR)

Rich, Carlos H. (1841-1918)

Born: 11 Feb 1841, Canada
War Service: PVT Co. F 1st VT INF 2 May 1861, m/o 15 Aug 1861, CPL Co. K, 4th VT INF 21 Sep 1861, reen 15 Dec 1863, SGT 21 Sep 1864, Co. E 25 Feb 1865, wdd, Wilderness, 5 May 1864, m/o 13 Jul 1865
MOH Issued: 4 Jan 1895 for action at the Wilderness VA, 5 May 1864
Citation: Saved the life of an officer
Later Life: farmer, Roxbury VT 1880, Bennington Soldiers Home 1900
Married: 21 Dec 1865, Ellen Wolfendale
Died: 29 Mar 1918, Bennington VT; interment in Roxbury Cemetery, Roxbury VT (Lot 217)
(1880, 1900, B&K, FAG, MOHR, VM)

Ripley, William Young Warren (1832-1905)

Born: 31 Dec 1832, Middlebury VT, son of William Young and Jane (Warren) Ripley
Early Life: ???????????????????;
War Service: CPT Co. K 1st VT INF, 28 Nov 1859, m/o 15 Aug 1861; LTCOL, 1st USSS, 1 Jan 1862, wdd, Malvern Hill, 1 Jul 1862, dis 6 Aug 1862 to become COL, 10th VT INF, declined on account of wds
MOH Issued: 11 Mar 1893 for action at Malvern Hill VA, 1 Jul 1862

Citation: At a critical moment brought up two regiments, which he led against the enemy himself, being severely wounded
Later Life: M.G. VT Militia 1864-65, Ripley Brothers marble business, pres. Rutland Cty National Bank 1875-
Affiliations: MOLLUS (#07092), RSVO
Married: Cornelia Ann Thomas
Died: 16 Dec 1905, Rutland VT; interment in Evergreen Cemetery, Rutland. (Block 27, Lot 22.)
Publications: Vermont Riflemen in the War for the Union, 1861-1865. A history of Company F, First United States Sharp Shooters (1883)
(C&S, E&E, FAG, Jones*, MOHR, SR)

Robbins, Augustus J. (1839-1909)

Born: 17 Nov 1839, Grafton VT, son of Nathaniel and Jane M. (Chaffee) Robbins
War Service: CPL Co. A 2nd VT INF 20 Jun 1861; Cmsy SGT 16 Jan 1862, 2LT 20 Dec 1862, wdd, Spotsylvania, 12 May 1864; m/o 29 Jun 1864
MOH Issued: 24 Mar 1892 for action at Spotsylvania VA, 12 May 1864
Citation: While voluntarily serving as a staff officer successfully withdrew a regiment across and around a severely exposed position to the rest of the command; was severely wounded
Later Life: grocer, Northfield 1870, hotel keeper Northfield 1880, laborer, Lakewood NJ 1900
Affiliations: Mason, RSVO
Married: (1) 9 Sep 1863, Helen M. Burnham; (2) 1884, Lucy (Nfi)
Died: 16 Sep 1909; interment in Woodlawn Cemetery, Lakewood NJ
(1870, 1880, 1900, FAG, FSO, MOHR)

Sargent, Jackson George (1841-1921)

Born: 29 Dec 1841, Stowe VT, son of Jeremiah and Sophronia (Robinson) Sargent
War Service: PVT Co. D 5th VT INF 16 Sep 1861, reen 15 Dec 1863, SGT 17 Oct 1864, wdd, Spotsylvania, 12 May 1864, 1LT, Co. K, 10 May 1865, m/o 29 Jun 1865
MOH Issued: 28 Oct 1891 for action at Petersburg VA, on 2 Apr 1865
Citation: First to scale the enemy's works and plant the colors thereon
Later Life: farmer, Stowe-Hyde Park, 1870-1910
Married: Carrie M. (Nfi)
Died: 2 Oct 1921, Stowe VT; interment in Riverbank Cemetery (Section 42 East-B, Lot 55)
(1870, 1880, 1910, FSO, MOHR, RR)

Scott, Alexander Jr. (1844-1923)

Born: 19 Aug 1844, Montreal PQ, Canada, son of Alexander Scott
Early Life: moved to Burlington 1850; public schools
War Service: PVT Co. D 10th VT INF 1 Sep 1862, CPL 1 Jan 1864, wdd, Cedar Creek, 19 Oct 1964, m/o 22 Jun 1865
MOH Issued: 28 Sep 1897, for action at Monocacy, MD, on 9 Jul 1864
Citation: Under a very heavy fire of the enemy saved the national flag of his regiment from capture.
Later Life: clerk, Burlington; lumber business, MI 1866-70; draughtsman, US Patent Office 1870-82+
Died: 27 May 1923; interment in Arlington National Cemetery (Section 17, Grave 204772)
Notes: father served in Co. I 5th VT INF, and died 17 Oct 1862, interment in Annapolis National Cemetery
(EMH*, MOHR, RR)

Scott, Julian A. (1846-1901)

Born: 15 Feb 1846, Johnson VT, son of Charles and Lucy (Kellum) Scott
War Service: Musician Co. E 3rd VT INF 16 Jul 1862, m/o 28 Apr 1863

MOH Issued: Feb 1865, for action at Lees Mill, on 16 Apr 1862
Citation: Crossed the creek under a terrific fire of musketry several times to assist in bringing off the wounded
Later Life: painter
Died: 4 Jul 1901; interment in Hillside Cemetery, Scotch Plains NJ
Paintings: "Rear-Guard at White Oak Swamp," "Battle of Cedar Creek" (at Vermont Statehouse), "Battle of Golding's Farm: The Recall," "On Board the Hartford"
(MOHR, RJT)

Seaver, Thomas Orville (1833-1912)

Born: 23 Dec 1833, Cavendish VT, son of James Seaver
Early Life: Green Mountain Acad., Woodstock; Tufts University, 1855-56, NU 1856-58, A.B. UC 1859; atty
War Service: CPT Co. F 3rd VT INF 24 May 1861; MAJ 13 Aug 1861, LTCol 27 Sep 1862, COL 15 Jan 1863, m/o 27 Jul 1864
MOH Issued: 8 Apr 1892 for action at Spotsylvania C.H., on 10 May 1864
Citation: At the head of three regiments and under a most galling fire attacked and occupied the enemy's works
Later Life: atty, probate judge
Affiliations: RSVO
Died: 11 Jul 1912, Woodstock VT; interment in River Street Cemetery
(MOHR, WAE, Welch*)

Sherman, Marshal (1823-1896)

Born: 1823, Burlington VT
Early Life: moved to MN in 1849; painter
War Service: PVT Co. C 1st MN INF 29 Apr 1861, 1st Btln MN INF 24 Mar 1864; dis/wds 24 Jul 1865
MOH Issued: 1 Dec 1864 for action at Gettysburg, PA, 3 Jul 1863
Citation: Capture of flag of 28th VA INF (CSA)
Later Life: painter, insurance agent
Died: 19 Apr 1896, St. Paul MN; interment in Oakland Cemetery
(FAG, FMCW, MOHR)

Sperry, William Joseph (1840-1914)

Born: 28 Dec 1840, Cavendish VT, son of John J. and Roxana Sperry
War Service: PVT Co. E 1st VT INF 2 May 1861, m/o 15 Aug 61, SGT Co. E 6th VT INF 26 Sep 1861, 2LT 21 Aug 1862, 1LT 3 Mar 1863, CPT Co. C 8 Aug 1864, MAJ 7 Jan 1865, Bvt LTCOL 2 Apr 1865, LTCOL 4 Jun 1865, m/o 26 Jun 1865 as MAJ
MOH Issued: 12 Aug 1892 for action at Petersburg VA, 2 Apr 1865
Citation: With the assistance of a few men, captured 2 pieces of artillery and turned them upon the enemy
Later Life: Painter, Titusville PA 1870, Cavendish 1880 VT Sen. doorkeeper 1890
Affiliations: RSVO
Married: (1) Ella J. (nfi); (2) Lucy M. (nfi)
Died: 3 Mar 1914, Cavendish VT; interment in Mount Union Cemetery
(1850, 1870, 1880, 1900, B&K*, GGB, JHR90, MOHR, NARA, OFW)

Steele, John Whedon (1835-1905)

Born: 21 Dec 1835, Middlebury VT, son of Robert and Sarah (Carson) Steele
Early Life: moved to OH, admitted to bar 1861
War Service: 1LT 41st OH INF 16 Sep 1861, CPT 3 Feb 1862, MAJ ADC USV 27 Oct 1864, Bvt LTCOL USV 13 Mar 1865, m/o 20 Jan 1866
MOH Issued: 28 Sep 1897, for action at Spring Hill, TN, 29 Nov 1864

Citation: During a night attack of the enemy upon the wagon and ammunition train of this officer's corps, he gathered up a force of stragglers and others, assumed command of it, though himself a staff officer, and attacked and dispersed the enemy's forces, thus saving the train
Later Life: probate judge 1867-71, atty, moved to Oberlin 1877, atty
Married: Ella Frances Clarke
Died: 1905, Oberlin OH; interment in Westwood Cemetery
(FAG, FBH, MOHR, NARA, family)

Sweeney, James (1845-1931)

Born: 24 Sep 1845, England
War Service: Pvt Co A 1st VT CAV 30 Dec 1863, wdd 10 Jun 1864, m/o 14 Jun 1865
MOH Issued: 26 Oct 1864, for action at Cedar Creek 19 Oct 1864
Citation: With one companion captured the State flag of a North Carolina regiment, together with 3 officers and an ambulance with its mules and driver
Died: 26 Jun 1931, Los Angeles CA; interment in National Cemetery, Los Angeles, CA
Notes: received his medal in Washington, from Secretary of War Stanton
(MOHR)

Thomas, Stephen (1809-1903)

Born: 6 Dec 1809, Bethel VT, son of John and Rebecca (Batchelder) Thomas
Early Life: apprenticed to woolen manufacturer 1827. **e**ntrepreneur in Thetford, Strafford and West Fairlee, State Rep. 1838-39, 1845-46, 1860-61; State Sen. 1848-49; ConCon delegate 1843, 1850; Registrar of Probate 1842-46; Judge of Probate 1847-49; delegate, DNC 1852, 1856, 1860
War Service: COL 8th VT INF 12 Nov 1861, wdd Port Hudson 27 May 1863, m/o 21 Jan 1865, B.G. USV, 1 Feb 1865, m/o 24 Aug 1865
MOH Issued: 25 Jul 1892, for action at Cedar Creek 19 Oct 1864
Citation: Distinguished conduct in a desperate hand-to-hand encounter, in which the advance of the enemy was checked
Later Life: resided West Fairlee until 1870**,** LT Gov. 1867-68; moved to Montpelier 1870, pension agent 1870-77; farmer; pres. U.S. Clothespin Co., North Haverhill Granite Co, trustee NU
Affiliations: Democrat until 1861, joined Republican Party**,** RSVO, MOLLUS (#09174)
Married: Ann Peabody
Died: 18 Dec 1903, Montpelier VT; interment in Green Mount Cemetery
(C&S, FAG, FSO, FTM*, JGU, MOHR, TWH, WAE)

Thompson, Charles Augustus (1843-1900)

Born: 16 Feb 1843, Perrysburg OH, son of Augustus and Ann Thompson
Early Life: resided Perrysburg 1860, moved to Kalamazoo MI
War Service: CPL Co. D 17th MI INF, SGT 15 Nov 1862, 1SGT 3 Feb 1865, 2LT 25 Apr 1865, m/o 3 Jun 1865
MOH Issued: 27 Jul 1896, for action at Spotsylvania, 12 May 1864
Citation: After the regiment was surrounded and all resistance seemed useless, fought single-handed for the colors and refused to give them up until he had appealed to his superior officers
Later Life: Rutland VT 1870, quarry foreman Rutland 1880, monumental dealer
Married: 1868, Helen E. Tuttle
Died: 24 Aug 1900, Rutland VT; interment in Evergreen Cemetery
(1850, 1860, 1870, 1880, 1890, 1900, FAG, MOHR, NARA)

Tilton, William (1834-1910)

Born: 27 Oct 1834, St. Albans VT, son of Benjamin and Electa Tilton
Early Life: farmer Danville VT 1850, moved to Hanover NH
War Service: PVT Co. C 7th NH INF 6 Nov 1861, CPL 26 Nov 1861, SGT 28 Dec 1863
MOH Issued: 20 Feb 1884, for action during the Richmond Campaign, 1864
Citation: Gallant conduct in the field
Later Life: farmer Hanover NH 1870, carpenter Enfield NH 1880-1900
Married: Susan (nfi)
Died: 8 Mar 1910, Enfield NH; interment in Oak Grove Cemetery
(1850, 1870, 1880, 1900, FAG, MOHR)

Tompkins, Charles Henry (1830-1915)

Born: 12 Sep 1830, Ft Monroe VA, son of Daniel D. Tompkins
Early Life: cadet USMA 1 Jul 1847, resgd 23 Jun 1849, 1st US Dragoons 21 Jan 1856, dis 10 Jan 1861
War Service: 2LT 2nd US CAV 23 Mar 1861, 1LT 30 Apr 1861, Fairfax C.H. VA Jun 1861, transferred 5th US CAV 3 Aug 1861, RQM Aug-Nov 1861, CPT AQM 13 Nov 1861, COL 1st VT CAV 24 Apr 1862, Bvt MAJ 26 Jun 1862, Malvern Hill VA Jul 1862, resgd 9 Sep 1862, AQM, Dept of Washington 1864, AQM, I Corps 1865, Bvt LTC, Bvt COL, Bvt B.G. 13 Mar 1865
MOH Issued: 13 Nov 1893 for action at Fairfax C.H.
Citation: twice charged through the enemy's lines and taking a carbine from an enlisted man shot the enemy's captain
Later Life: Member, Lincoln Conspirators Commission May-Jul 1865, QM (LTCol) 1 Jul 1865, COL 13 Jun 1866, Deputy QM GEN, 29 Jul 1866, AQM GEN 24 Jan 1881, ret. 12 Sep 1894, B.G. on ret. list 23 Apr 1904
Died: 18 Jan 1915, Washington, DC; interment in Oak Hill Cemetery, Washington, DC
(E&E, GGB, GWC, MOHR, TWH)

Tracy, Amasa Sawyer (1829-1908)

Born: 16 Mar 1829, Dover ME, son of David and Sarah Sawyer (Fowler) Tracy
War Service: 1LT Co. K 2nd VT INF 28 May 1861, CPT Co. H 24 Jan 1862, MAJ 2 Apr 1864, LTCOL 17 Jun 1864; COL 7 Jun 1865; wdd Marye's Heights 3 May 1863, wdd Cedar Creek 19 Oct 1864 m/o 15 Jul 1865 as LTCol; Bvt COL 2 Apr 1865
MOH Issued: 24 Jul 1892 for action at Cedar Creek, on 19 Oct 1864
Citation: Took command of and led the brigade in the assault on the enemy's works
Later Life: Postmaster, Middlebury 1870-81
Affiliations: RSVO, MOLLUS (#10072)
Married: (1) Feb 1849, Helen Sarah Dow; (2) Mar 1858, Sarah M. Crane
Died: 26 Feb 1908, Orleans VT; interment in West Cemetery, Middlebury VT
Correspondence: 1851-89, USAMHI
Manuscripts: Reminiscence of Cedar Creek, 19 Oct 1864 (USAMHI)
Notes: "Colonel Tracy's military record is one that does him honor in every sense, and his services are appreciated by his fellow citizens at their true worth" (HPS)
(1870, C&S, FAG, HPS, MOHR, WHP1)

Veazey, Wheelock Graves (1835-1898)

Born: 5 Dec 1835, Brentwood NH, son of Jonathan and Ann (Stevens) Veazey
Early Life: Phillips Exeter Acad., DC 1858; ALS 1860; admitted to the bar 1860, atty, Springfield VT
War Service: CPT Co. A 3rd VT INF, 21 May 1861; MAJ 10 Aug 1861; LTCOL 13 Aug 1861; COL 16th VT INF 27 Sep 1862, m/o 10 Aug 1863
MOH Issued: 8 Sep 1891 for action at Gettysburg, PA, on 3 Jul 1863
Citation: Rapidly assembled his regiment and charged the enemy's flank; changed front under heavy fire, and charged and destroyed a Confederate brigade, all this with new troops in their first battle

Later Life: VT Supreme Court recorder 1864-73, State Rep. 1872-73, Register in Bankruptcy 1874-78, revised State laws 1878-80, State Supreme Court Judge 1879-88, ICC 1889-94, DC Trustee 1879-91, NU trustee, LLD DC 1887
Affiliations: RSVO (President), GAR (National Cmdr), MOLLUS (#07406)
Married: 22 Jun 1861, Julia A. Beard
Died: 22 Mar 1898, Washington, D.C; interment in Arlington National Cemetery
Speeches: Memorial day address Wheelock G. Veazey as a soldier and comrade (1898)
(B&K, C&S, JGU, Jones*, PCD, RJ, MOHR, SAH, WAE)

Webster, Henry S. (1845-1910)

Born: 7 Jan 1845, Stockholm NY, son of Alva P. and Adaline (Holmes) Webster
Early Life: farm laborer
War Service: LDS, USN, at Brooklyn NY
Citation: On board USS *Susquehanna* during the assault on Fort Fisher, 15 Jan 1865, when enemy fire halted the attempt by his landing party to enter the fort and more than two thirds of the men fell back along the open beach, Webster voluntarily remained with one of his wounded officers, under fire, until aid could be obtained to bring him to the rear
Later Life: farmer, Stockholm NY
Married: abt 1875, Julia E. Phelps
Died: 2 Jul 1910, Brattleboro VT; interment in Cedar Grove Cemetery, Fairhaven VT
(NARA, ORN)

Wells, William (1837-1892)

Born: 14 Dec 1837, Waterbury VT, son of William Wellington and Eliza (Carpenter) Wells
Early Life: clerk, Waterbury 1860
War Service: 1LT, Co. C 1st VT CAV, 14 Oct 1861; CPT Co. C 18 Nov 1861; MAJ 30 Oct 1862; pow, Herndon Station, 17 Mar 1863; prld 5 May 1863; wdd, Hagerstown, 6 Jul 1863; wdd, Culpeper C.H., 13 Sep 1863; COL 24 Jun 1864; Bvt B.G. 22 Feb 1865; Bvt M.G. 13 Mar 1865, B.G. USV 19 May 1865; m/o 15 Jan 1866
MOH Issued: 8 Sep 1891 for action at Gettysburg, PA, on 3 Jul 1863
Citation: Led the second battalion of his regiment in a daring charge
Later Life: wholesale druggist; State Rep. 1865-66; State A&IG 1866-72; State Sen. 1886-87; pres Burlington Trust Co., Burlington Gas-Light Co., Burlington Board of Trade; dir. Burlington Cold Storage Co., Rutland R.R. Co., Champlain Transportation Co.
Affiliations: RSVO, MOLLUS (#03897), GAR, SAR
Died: 29 Apr 1892, New York City; interment in Lakeview Cemetery, Burlington VT
Notes: St. Johnsbury GAR Post # 1 and Williamstown GAR Post #113 were named after him
Correspondence: UVM
(1860, C&S, FAG, GFH*, GGB, LHC, MOHR, SAH)

Wheeler, Daniel Davis (1841-1916)

Born: 12 Jul 1841, Cavendish VT, son of Daniel H. and Susan Wheeler
Early Life: student, clerk
War Service: 2LT 4th VT INF 21 Sep1861, 1LT 21 APR 1862, AAG (CPT) USV 30 Jun 1864, Bvt MAJ USV 29 Sep 1864, AAG (MAJ) USV 27 Dec 1864, AAG (LTCOL) USV 26 May 1865 to 11 Jun 1866, Bvt COL USV 1 Dec 1865, m/o 19 Oct 1866
MOH Issued: 28 Mar 1892 for action at Salem Heights VA, 3 May 1863
Citation: Distinguished bravery in action where he was wounded and had a horse shot from under him
Later Life: 2LT 1st US ARTY 11 May 1866, 1LT 12 Feb 1867, Bvt CPT 2 Mar 1867, AQM (CPT) 2 Jul 1879, QM (MAJ) 6 Sep 1893, Deputy QM GEN (LTCOL) 11 Nov 1898, ARTY School, 1873; Chief QM (LTCOL) USV 9 May 1898 to 10 Nov 1898, QM (COL) USV 3 Sep 1898 to 2 Mar 1899
Died: 27 Jul 1916, Fredericksburg VA; interment in City Cemetery

(DBEK, MOHR, SAW, TWH, WHP)

Williston, Edward Bancroft (1836-1920)

Born: 15 Jul 1836, Norwich VT, son of Ebenezer Bancroft and Elmira (Partridge) Williston
Early Life: NU 1856; engr PA, 1855-56, rancher 1856-61
War Service: 2LT 2nd US ARTY, 1LT 27 Sep 1861; Bvt CPT 3 May 1863, Bvt MAJ 3 Jul 1863, Bvt LTCOL 19 Sep 1864, Bvt COL 13 Mar 1864; CPT 8 MAR 1865
MOH Issued: 6 Apr 1892, for action at Trevillian Station VA, 2 Jun 1864
Citation: Distinguished gallantry in action
Later Life: California 1865-67, instr. US ARTY. School, Fort Monroe VA 1867-69, Alaska 1869-70, San Francisco 1870-72, Raleigh, NC 1872-74, suppression of illicit distilling, NC 1877, Washington DC 1877, Texas 1877-81, Indian Terr. 1881-82, KS 1882-85, MAJ 3rd US ARTY 22 Mar 1885; Washington, 1885-89; KS 1889-92; MO 1892-94; FL 1894-96, LTCOL 12 FEB 1895; San Francisco 1896-98, COL 6th US ARTY. 8 Mar 1898; Spanish-American War, B.G. USV 4 Mar 1898; m/o USV 12 Jun 1899; ret. USA 15 Jul 1900, B.G. on ret. list 23 APR 1904
Died: 24 Apr 1920, San Diego CA; interment in Arlington National Cemetery
(MOHR, WAE*)

Woodbury, Eri Davidson (1837-1928)

Born: 30 May 1837, Francestown NH, son of Henry and Hannah (Davidson) Woodbury
Early Life: AC 1859, DC 1863
War Service: PVT Co. E 1st VT CAV 14 Dec 1863, SGT 1 Jul 1864, 2LT 19 Nov 1864, 1LT Co. B 9 Feb 1865; wdd Appomattox Station 8 Apr 1865, Bvt CPT 13 Mar 1865, m/o 21 Jun 1865
MOH Issued: 26 Oct 1864, for action at Cedar Creek, 19 Oct 1864
Citation: During the regiment's charge when the enemy was in retreat SGT Woodbury encountered 4 Confederate infantrymen retreating. He drew his saber and ordered them to surrender, overcoming by his determined actions their willingness to further resist. They surrendered to him together with their rifles and 12th North Carolina (CSA) regimental flag
Later Life: headmaster Episcopal Acad. Cheshire CT 1865-1900
Married: 8 Jul 1873, Anna Austine Jarvis
Died: 14 Apr 1928, Cheshire CT; interment in St. Peter Cemetery
Correspondence: Dartmouth College
(1880, 1900, ACBR, B&K, GTC, MOHR, SAH*, WLM)

Benedict, George G.

Butterfield, G. F.

Churchill, S. J.

Coffey, Robert J.

Davis, George E.

Downs, H. W.

Drury, J. J.

Grant, Lewis A.

Hack, Lester

Hawkins, Gardner C.

Henry, William W.

Hooker, George W.

Howard, Oliver O.

Howard, Squire E.

Jewett, Erastus W.

Johndro, Franklin

Livingston, Josiah O.

Peck, Theodore S.

Pingree, Samuel E.

Ripley, William Y. W.

Scott, Alexander

Seaver, Thomas O.

Sperry, William J.

Thomas, Steven

Veazey, Wheelock G.

Wells, William

Williston, W. B.

Woodbury, Eri D.

Civilians, Soldiers and Sailors

AAAAA

Abbott, Lemuel Abijah (1842-1911)

Born: 24 Aug 1842, Barre VT, son of Richard Flagg and Mary (Norris) Abbott
Early Life: B.S. NU 1864
War Service: 1SGT Co. B 10th VT INF 1 Sep 1862, 2LT Co. D 26 Jan 1863, 1LT Co. E 17 Jun 1864, wdd Winchester 19 Sep 1864, CPT Co. G 19 Dec 1864, m/o 22 Jun 1865
Later Life: 1LT and ADJ 97th USCI 6 Nov 1865, m/o 10 Sep 1867, 2LT 6th US CAV 2 Jul 1867, 1LT 10 Sep 1869; RQM 1869-73, CPT 3 Jun 1880, Bvt MAJ 17 Jul 1881, ret. 3 Jan 1885, COL USA 1899 by special act of Congress, historian, genealogist
Affiliations: MOLLUS (#14398), RSVO
Died: 3 Feb 1911, Aberdeen WA; interment in Wilson Cemetery, Barre VT
Publications: <u>Descendants of George Abbott, of Rowley MA</u> (1906), <u>Personal Recollections and Civil War Diary, 1864</u> (1908)
(C&S, EMH, HFW12, WAE*)

Abell, Charles Emmet (1836-1913)

Born: 2 May 1836, Orwell VT, son of Mason S. and Mary H. (Dickinson) Abell
Early Life: Troy Conf. Acad., A.B. MC 1861, A.M. MC 1864
War Service: SGT Co. H 5th VT INF 4 Sep 1861, dis/dsb 20 Jan 1862, CPT Co. D 14th VT INF 29 Aug 1862, m/o 30 Jul 1863
Later Life: farmer, Orwell, State Rep. 1876, State Sen. 1892
Affiliations: Republican, Congregational, Mason, RSVO
Married: 12 Mar 1867, Mary Jane Root
Died: 20 May 1913, Orwell VT; interment in Mountain View Cemetery
(EJW, PCD)

Adams, Cephas Gardner (1829-1901)

Born: 13 Mar 1829, Morgan VT, son of Levi Preston and Ruth (Carlton) Adams
Early Life: M.D. UVM 1855, first physician in East Charleston 1855, physician Brighton 1860
War Service: Fredericksburg and Washington (May 1864), among a contingent of Vermont doctors who volunteered their services to care for Vermonters who were wounded in the battles of the Wilderness and Spotsylvania C.H.
Later Life: physician Charleston, Island Pond, State Rep. 1880, moved to Portland ME, died as a result of injuries received in carriage accident 1899
Affiliations: SAR
Married: 24 Nov 1856, Sara Bates Cobb
Died: 12 Apr 1901, Portland ME; interment unknown
(1860, 1870, 1880, BMJ3, FSO, HC2, JHR80, LHC, UVMCat3)

Adams, Charles Abraham (1837-1902)

Born: 3 Nov 1837, Ludlow VT, son of Abraham and Esther Penther (Chandler) Adams
War Service: 2LT Co H 1st VT CAV 19 Oct 1861, 1LT 30 Oct 1862, CPT 1 Apr 1863, wdd Gettysburg 3 Jul 1863, wdd/pow Brandy Station 11 Oct 1863, MAJ 18 Nov 1864; escaped Libby Prison 16 Feb 1865, Bvt LTCOL and COL 13 Mar 1865, m/o 21 Jun 1865
Later Life: farmer, dairyman and creamery owner, Livingston Cty MO 1870-1900
Affiliations: RSVO
Married: 26 Nov 1860, Eliza Ann Peabody

Died: 11 Mar 1902, Chillicothe MO; interment in Jones Cemetery
Notes: military papers in University of Missouri/State Historical Soc. of MO "Western Historical Manuscript Collection – Columbia"
(FSO, LMW3)

Alford, Albert Gallatin (1847-1925)

Born: 14 Oct 1847, St. Albans VT, son of Ammi and Clarissa G. (White) Alford
Early Life: moved to Waterville, local schools
War Service: Artificer, US Engr Corps 21 Feb 1865
Later Life: enl 1874, Chicago, 1st IL NG, mngr, arms Dept E. Remington & sons, Chicago 1874-83; moved to Baltimore MD, gen. mngr Remington, Baltimore, CPT Ordnance officer and inspector of rifle practice, 1st MD NG 1886-93, started A. G. Alford Sporting Goods Co.
Affiliations: Republican, GAR
Married: 1886, Clara Augusta Robinson
Died: 2 Jan 1925, Baltimore MD; interment unknown
(1920, JGU*, T289)

Allen, Benjamin (1807-1873)

Born: 26 Aug 1807, Woodstock VT, son of Cyrus A. and Sally (Fletcher) Allen
Early Life: WI State Sen. 1853-54, Postmaster Pepin Cty WI, District Atty Pepin Cty 1858-59
War Service: COL 16th WI INF 21 Jan 1862, wdd Shiloh 6 Apr 1862, resgd 17 Jul 1863
Later Life: atty
Married: 2 Mar 1834, Calista Sabrina Dike
Died: 5 Jul 1873, Pepin WI; interment in Oakwood Cemetery
(DWV, FAG, FSO, HCC, HNW, RMB)

Allen, Charles Linnaeus (1820-1890)

Born: 21 Jun 1820, Brattleboro VT, son of Jonathan Adams and Betsey (Cheney) Allen
Early Life: Addison Cty Grammar School, A.B. MC 1842, M.D. CMC 1846, physician, Middlebury, prof. Chemistry CMC 55, pres VT MS 1858, prof. Practice of Medicine UVM 1858, pres CMC 1861
War Service: State Board for examining candidates for regtl surgeons 1861; prof. civil and Military Hygiene UVM 1862, SURG (MAJ) USV 23 Jun 1862, Med. Purveyor Dept. of the South, 1864, resgd 5 Aug 1864, pres. State Board for examination of candidates for regtl SURG 1865
Later Life: pres. US Board of Pension Surgeons 1880; Sec'y State Board of Health 1886
Affiliations: AAM, AMA, APHA, RSVO
Married: (1) 14 Jun 1854, Harriet (Warren) Garfield; (2) 30 May 1865, Gertrude Margaret Lyon
Died: 2 Jul 1890, Rutland VT; interment in Glade Mills PA
(FBH, MIDCat, SLA)

Allen, Cyrus Hamilton (1833-1908)

Born: 5 Sep 1833, North Thetford VT
Early Life: Montpelier Acad., M.D. UVM 1857, physician Union Village VT
War Service: Asst SURG 8th VT INF 1 Dec 1862, SURG 5th VT INF 1 Oct 1864, m/o 29 Jun 1865
Later Life: moved to Lima NY 1865-67, moved to Centreville CA 1867, physician Washington CA 1870, Centerville 1880
Affiliations: CA MS, Alameda Co. MS, Mason
Married: 8 Mar 1859, Myra Ann Johnston
Died: 7 Sep 1908; interment in Centerville Pioneer Cemetery, Freemont CA

(1870, 1880, FAG, NAS, VM, WBA)

Allen, Heman Woods (1844-1915)

Born: 3 Apr 1844, Westford VT, son of John and Clarissa (Rice) Allen
Early Life: Eastman Business College, Poughkeepsie NY 1864
War Service: PVT Co A 13th VT INF 10 Oct 1862, m/o 21 Jul 1863
Later Life: 1LT VT Militia 1864-68, partner Lyman and Allen Dry Goods, Burlington VT 1868-90, proprietor H. W. Allen & Co., Burlington 1890-1910, dir. merchants National Bank Burlington 1894-96, COL VT NG 1894-96, State Sen. 1896-98, RNC delegate 1904, v.p. merchants National Bank, farmers and Mechanics Loan and Trust, Burlington
Affiliations: Republican, SAR
Married: (1) 1869, Jennie D. Dodds; (2) 1881, Juliette W. Keeler
Died: 6 Jun 1915; interment in Lakeview Cemetery, Burlington VT
(PCD, VHS16)

Allen, John Hamilton (1838-1914)

Born: 18 Jul 1838, Hinesburg VT, son of John and Roxanna (Carpenter) Allen
Early Life: People's Acad., Morrisville, Potsdam (NY) Acad., harness maker, Hinesburg
War Service: 1LT, Co G, 14th VT INF, 8 Sep 1862, m/o 30 Jul 1863
Later Life: Harness Maker, Hinesburg, CPT Co H VT NG 1872-73, State Rep. 1880, 1900-04, asst judge, Chittenden Cty, j.p. Hinesburg
Affiliations: Republican
Married: 1857, Elizabeth Burns
Died: 3 Nov 1914; interment in Village cemetery, Hinesburg VT
(AGO, PCD, WSR)

Allen, Samuel Johnson (1819-1886)

Born: 8 Jan 1819, Newport NH, son of David and Hannah (Wilcox) Allen
Early Life: CMC 1842; principal, Hartford H.S. 1855-56
War Service: SURG 4th VT INF 15 Aug 1861, BGD SURG 1862, wdd Opequon Creek 13 Sep 1864, m/o 30 Sep 1864, SURG USV 1864, 2 DIV VI Corps1864, Med. Inspector VI Corps 1864-65
Later Life: physician VT SURG GEN, Hon. degree DC 1870
Affiliations: RSVO
Married: 14 Jun 1844, Mary Jane Lyman
Died: 8 Aug 1886, Hartford VT; interment in Hartford Point Cemetery
(GGB, Italo*, VTMS)

Alvord, Benjamin (1813-1884)

Born: 18 Aug 1813, Rutland VT, son of William and Lucy (Claghorn) Alvord
Early Life: USMA 1833 (22/43), 4th US INF, LA 1833-36, 2LT 21 Jul 1835, 1LT 23 Sep 1836, Seminole War 1836-37, math instr. USMA 1837-39, OK Terr. 1839-41, Seminole War 1841-42, LA 1844-45, Mexican-American War 1846-47, CPT 9 Sep 1846, Western Frontier 1847-53, Pacific Northwest 1853-62, MAJ 22 Jun 1854, M.M. UVM 1854
War Service: cmdg Dept of OR 1862-65, B.G. USV 15 Apr 1862, Bvt LTCOL and COL USA, 13 Mar 1865, Bvt B.G. USA, 9 Apr 1865
Later Life: Paymr NYC 1865-67, Ch. Paymr, Dist. of Omaha 1867-69, Ch. Paymr, Platte River region 1869-72, Paymr GEN, USA, Washington 1872-80, ret. 8 Jun 1880; mathematician
Married: 17 Sep 1846, Emily Louisa Mussey
Died: 16 Oct 1884, Washington D.C.; interment in Arlington National Cemetery (Sect. 4 Grave 2215-WS)

Papers: University of Washington
Publications: The Tangencies of Circles and of Spheres. (1856)
Notes: published many highly regarded books/articles on mathematics and agriculture, pre- and postwar
(BSObit, CCPL, E&E, FBH, FSO, GWC, HGW, LOC*)

Andrews, Sumner A. (1844-1905)

Born: 28 Dec 1844, Johnson VT, son of J. Atwood and Angeline (Davinson) Andrews
Early Life: pubic and grammar schools; farmer
War Service: PVT Co. E 13th VT INF 8 Sep 1862, m/o 21 Jul 1863, PVT Co. F Frontier CAV (26th NY CAV) 4 Jan 1865 - 27 Jun 1865
Later Life: store clerk 6 years, Super. State Primary School, Monson MA 1875-83, merchandiser 1883-89, State Rep. 1884, asst judge, Lamoille Cty Court, Super. VT Reform School
Affiliations: Republican, Baptist
Married: 28 Sep 1868, Mary A. Story
Died: 16 Jun1905; interment in Lamoille View cemetery, Johnson VT
(AGO, AMH, HC2, JGU*, OLC)

Andross, Dudley Kimball (1823-1910)

Born: 12 Sep 1823, Bradford VT, son of Broadstreet Spafford and Mary (Kimball) Andross
Early Life: lumberman, railroad builder, gold miner in CA, miller, militia officer
War Service: CPT Co D 1st VT INF 1 May 1861; m/o 15 Aug 1861, LTCOL 9th VT INF 26 May 1862; COL 20 Mar 1863, resgd 22 May 1863
Later Life: Town Selectman 1867-69, COL 7th VT Mil., farmer
Affiliations: RSVO
Married: 17 Mar 1878, Marcella Wassen nee Harris
Died: 28 Nov 1910; interment in Village Cemetery, Bradford VT
(HC3, JGU*, SK)

Arms, Austin Davis (1817-1896)

Born: 26 Dec 1817, Montpelier VT, son of Austin and Sally (Davis) Arms
Early Life: NU 1835-37 (n.g.), farmer, East Montpelier, Town Clerk 1856-61
War Service: civilian AQM under GEN P. P. Pitkin, served in Fairfax C.H. Culpeper C.H., Richmond, City Point and Washington
Later Life: farmer East Montpelier 1880
Affiliations: Mason
Married: 14 Jan 1841, Fanny Dodge
Died: 19 Sep 1896, East Montpelier VT; interment in Cutler Cemetery
(1880, WAE*)

Arthur, Chester Alan (1829-1886)

Born: 5 Oct 1829, Fairfax VT, son of Rev. William and Melvina (Stone) Arthur
Early Life: UC 1848, Principal, Pownal Acad. 1851, atty NYC, JAG 2nd BGD NY Militia, Engr-in-chief, Gov. staff
War Service: I.G., QM Gen, State of NY
Later Life: atty, customs collector 1871-78, US Vice President 1881, US President 1881-85
Affiliations: Republican
Married: Oct 1859, Ellen Lewis Herndon
Died: 18 Nov 1886 NYC; interment in Rural Cemetery, Albany NY

Papers: LOC, UVA
(CB, JGU*)

Atwood, Augustus Adelbert (1828-1867)

Born: 1828, Barnard VT, son of Alfred and Matilda Atwood
Early Life: NYMC 1856, physician Sharon VT 1860
War Service: Asst SURG 2nd VT INF, 22 Sep 1862, resgd 25 Jun 1863
Later Life: physician, Sharon VT
Married: 28 Aug 1853, Melissa A. Thorn
Died: 18 Jun 1867; interment in Pine Hill Cemetery, Sharon VT
(1860, RR, VTMS)

Atwood, Henry C. (1837-1876)

Born: 21 Jan 1837, Chester VT, son of Nathan and Hannah Atwood
Early Life: CMC 1858, physician, Salisbury 1860
War Service: Asst SURG, 5th VT INF, 6 May 1863, resgd 25 Jun 1863
Later Life: physician, Castleton VT 1866-70
Married: before 1860, Martha (nfi)
Died: 9 Aug 1876; interment in Hillside Cemetery, Castleton VT
(1860, 1870, AGO, JMC)

Aubery, James Madison (1843-1926)

Born: 1 Jan 1843, Burlington VT, son of Albert and Almira (Blish) Aubrey
Early Life: Burlington Acad., employed by H.L. Moore and George L. Warner, Burlington, moved to Milwaukee WI 1863
War Service: PVT Co G 36th WI INF 29 Feb 1864, SGM 1 Sep 1864, QM SGT 1 Nov 1864, 2LT Co G 15 Jun 1865, m/o 12 Jul 1865
Later Life: teacher, cashier, People's and Merchants' Dispatch, Milwaukee, 1869-77, mngr, Merchants' Dispatch Transportation Co., Chicago, IL 1877-93, mngr, Packing House 1893+, Chicago 1900, Los Angeles CA 1903-20, hotel mngr 1903-08
Affiliations: Republican, Unitarian, Mason, GAR (CA/NV Rep. 1920 Encampment), IOOF, SOV (Chicago, Los Angeles)
Married: 14 Jun 1866, Frances Cook
Died: 13 Dec 1926, Huntington Park CA; interment unknown
Publications: <u>The Thirty-Sixth Wisconsin Volunteer Infantry</u> (1900)
(1900, 1910, 1920, GAR54, JMA, PCD)

Austine, William (1815-1904)

Born: Jan 1815, Stonington CT (birth name William Alfred Brown), son of Denison and Sarah (Main) Brown
Early Life: USMA 1838 (25/45), 2LT 2nd US Dragoons, 1LT 3rd US ARTY, Seminole Indian Wars 1838-42, Mexican-American War, CPT 3rd US ARTY 13 Aug 1847, Bvt MAJ 1847, ret. 1862
War Service: Super. of mustering and volunteer recruiting service VT 1862-66
Later Life: Bvt LTCOL Sep 1865 for long and faithful service; LTCOL 23 May 1904
Died: 4 Sep 1904, Brattleboro VT; interment unknown
Correspondence: UNC
(FSO, GGB, GWC, MRC*)

Avery, Matthew Henry (1836-1881)

Born: 27 Mar 1836, Middletown Springs VT, son of John Ayers and Emeline (Baldwin) Avery
Early Life: bookseller
War Service: MAJ 10th NY CAV 25 Nov 1861, COL 28 Dec 1864, 1st Prov. NY CAV 17 Jun 1865, Bvt B.G. USV 13 Mar 1865, m/o 19 Jul 1865
Later Life: oil pipeline operator
Died: 1 Sep 1881, Geneva NY; interment in Oakwood Cemetery, Syracuse NY
(E&E, FAG, FBH, FSO, Greenhagen*)

Abbott, Lemuel A.

Alford, Albert G.

Allen, Samuel J.

Alvord, Benjamin

Andrews, Sumner A.

Andross, Dudley K.

Arms, Austin D.

Arthur, Chester A.

Austine, William

Avery, Matthew H.

BBBBB

Babbitt, Elbridge Harris (1844-1920)

Born: 23 Jan 1844, Bethel VT, son of Simon Augustus and Emily (McKinstry) Babbitt
Early Life: Randolph Acad., NU 1861, but left to enlist
War Service: SGT 17th US INF 7 Jun 1862 from Portland ME, wdd Gettysburg 2 Jul 1863, Mar 1864, joined brother Robert as 2LT 1st NC Union Vols 2LT Mar 1864, acting Asst AIG, Dept of NC until close of war
Later Life: businessman, Jamestown NY 1867-80
Married: 1867, Minnie Rees
Died: 24 Jan 1920; interment in Arlington National Cemetery
(FAG, WAE)

Babbitt, Robert Augustus (1842-1864)

Born: 21 Jan 1842, Bethel VT, son of Simon Augustus and Emily (McKinstry) Babbitt
Early Life: AMS 1860
War Service: PVT Co. D 8th CT INF 25 Sep 1861, Hosp. steward 1862, Super. Hammond Gen Hosp., Beaufort NC, SURG 1st NC Union Vols 1 Jan 1863, Post SURG, Beaufort NC 1864; died of yellow fever
Died: 17 Oct 1864, Beaufort NC; interment in South View Cemetery, Randolph VT
(AGO, AMH, RR)

Babcock, Orville Elias (1835-1884)

Born: 25 Dec 1835, Franklin VT, son of Elias and Clara (Olmstead) Babcock
Early Life: USMA 1861 (3/45)
War Service: Bvt 2LT, 2LT US ENGRS 6 May 1861, 1LT 17 Nov 1861, Bvt CPT 4 May 1862, CPT 1 Jun 1863, Bvt MAJ 29 Nov 1863; AIG (LTCOL), 1 Jan 1863-64, Bvt LTCOL 6 May 1864, ADC (LTCOL) to LTG Grant 1864-66, Bvt COL USV 24 Jul 1865, Bvt COL, Bvt B.G. 13 Mar 1865
Later Life: ADC (COL) GEN Grant 1866-69, MAJ ENGRS 21 Mar 1867, COL Super. Public Buildings Washington 1873-77, Secretary to Pres Grant, lighthouse inspector 1882-84
Married: 8 Nov 1866, Ann Eliza Campbell
Died: 2 Jun 1884, Mosquito Inlet FL; interment in Arlington National Cemetery (Section 2 Lot 3828)
(E&E, FBH, FSO, GWC, HC3, LOC*, RR)

Babcock, Volney Chauncey (1833-1912)

Born: 14 May 1833, Bridgewater VT, son of Chauncey and Sally (Barrows) Babcock
Early Life: farmer
War Service: PVT Co. E 13th VT INF 10 Oct 1862, dis/dsb 27 Nov 1862
Later Life: wheelwright Stowe VT 1870, merchant Bridgewater 1880, wheelwright and cabinet maker, 1880-96, postmaster, State Rep. 1900, Stowe 1910
Affiliations: Republican
Married: 1855, Harriet E. Barrows
Died: 4 May 1912; interment in West Branch Cemetery, Stowe VT
(1870, 1880, 1890, 1900, 1910, AGO, PCD)

Bailey, Myron W. (1835-1898)

Born: 9 Feb 1835, Waterville VT, son of Richard and Sally (Barrows) Bailey
Early Life: local schools, Bakersfield Acad., People's Acad., ALS 1859, atty
War Service: PVT Co. H 3rd VT INF 16 Jul 1861, wdd while on picket duty, dis 5 Feb 1862
Later Life: judge of probate 1867-94, R.R. commissioner 1872-78
Affiliations: Mason, RSVO
Married: 20 Nov 1862, Mary Lemira Sears
Died: 1898; interment Greenwood Cemetery, St. Albans VT
(FSO, JGU*)

Baker, Edward (1847-aft 1930)

Born: 13 May 1847, Manchester NH, son of Jabez and Louisa (Gove) Baker
Early Life: Royalton Acad.
War Service: PVT Co G 17th VT INF 12 Apr 1864, wdd 4 times during Wilderness Campaign, m/o 14 Jul 1865
Later Life: Cab Shop, Montpelier VT, wheelwright, Berlin VT 1880, bookkeeper, Montpelier 1900, CPT military storekeeper, later AAG VT Militia, cmdg VT Arsenal, Montpelier, Montpelier 1920-30
Affiliations: GAR (VT Commander)
Married: (1) 15 Sep 1873, Alma F. Evans; (2) 15 Sep 1890, Alice C. Gould
Died: aft 1930; interment unknown
(1880, 1900, 1920, 1930, PCD, WRC1)

Baker, Joel Clarke (1838-1904)

Born: 16 Apr 1838, Danby VT, son of Edia and Seleucia A. (Davenport) Baker
Early Life: Poultney Acad., atty, Rutland Cty
War Service: SGT Co. B 9th VT INF 27 May 1862, 1SGT 28 May 1863, 2LT Co. K 22 Dec 1862, 1LT 1 Dec 1864, resgd 16 Apr 1865
Later Life: atty, Wallingford 1866-68, moved to Rutland 1868, real estate, dir. Clement National Bank, Howe Scale Co., P. E. Chase Manufacturing Corp., editor Rutland Herald 1869-73, State Sen. 1886, Cty Auditor, City Atty
Affiliations: Republican, Episcopal, Mason, YMCA, MOLLUS (#09165)
Married: 8 Oct 1866, Ada O. Howe
Died: 6 Jun 1904, Rutland; interment in Evergreen Cemetery
(AGO, C&S, JGU*)

Baldwin, Melvin Riley (1838-1901)

Born: 12 Apr 1838, Chester VT, son of E. T. and Sophia Baldwin
Early Life: moved to WI 1847, Lawrence Univ. 1855, Civil Engr, Chicago & North Western R.R. 1855-61
War Service: PVT Co. E 2nd WI INF 21 Apr 1861, SGT MAJ 13 Oct 1861, 2LT 21 Apr 1862, 1LT 2 Jan 1863, CPT 3 Mar 1863, pow at Gettysburg, 18 months at Libby, Macon, Charleston and Columbia, escaped twice, recaptured, m/o 16 Dec 1864
Later Life: railroad work, KS, moved to MN 1875, Duluth 1885, US Rep. 1893-95, chair. Chippewa Indian commission 1894-97, miner in Alaska 1897
Affiliations: Democrat
Died: 15 Apr 1901, Seattle, WA; interment in Forest Hill Cemetery, Duluth, MN
(CB, FAG, JGU)

Ballard, Henry (1839-1906)

Born: 20 Apr 1839, Tinmouth VT, son of Jeffrey B. and Amelia (Thompson) Ballard
Early Life: Castleton Sem. 1857, A.B. UVM 1861, ALS 1863, atty Burlington, Tinmouth
War Service: 2LT Co. I 5th VT INF 12 Sep 1861, resgd 30 Jul 1862 due to ill health

Later Life: atty Burlington, State Sen. 1878-79, State Rep. 1888-89, City Atty, RNC delegate 1884, 1888
Affiliations: Republican, Episcopal, YMCA, GAR (Stannard), RSVO, MOLLUS (#09164)
Married: 15 Dec 1863, Annie J. Scott
Died: 23 Sep 1906, Burlington VT; interment in Lakeview Cemetery
Notes: in his first court case, successfully defended a recently discharged soldier named Burns against premeditated murder charges
(AGO, C&S, GFH, JGU*)

Ballou, Newton Herrick (1816-1895)

Born: 3 Jul 1816, Sheldon VT, son of Milton and Laura (Herrick) Ballou
Early Life: Jefferson Med. College, Philadelphia PA 1839, physician St. Albans 1839-59, Burlington 1859-61
War Service: SURG 2nd VT INF 11 Jun 1861, resgd 18 Dec 1862
Later Life: physician Mechanicville NY 1862-81, village trustee 1870, village pres 1879, trustee St. Luke's Episcopal Church, Lansingburgh 1887
Married: (1) 6 Nov 1839, Harriet Brayton Hall; (2) 10 Nov 1846, Abigail Green Farnham
Died: 9 Sep 1895, Mechanicville NY; interment in Hudson View Cemetery
(BIA, GBA, PL)

Barber, Merritt L. (1838-1906)

Born: 31 Jul 1838, Pownal VT, son of Benjamin S. and Caroline (Wright) Barber
Early Life: Williams College 1857, State and Union Law College, Cleveland OH, atty, assist clerk VT House 1860-61
War Service: 1LT Co. B 10th VT INF 7 Aug 1862, CPT 17 Jun 1864, CPT and Asst A.G. USV 31 Dec 1864, Bvt MAJ 19 Oct 1864, m/o 19 Sep 1865
Later Life: 2LT and 1LT 16th US INF 23 Feb 1866, 34th US INF 21 Sep 1866, ADJ and RQM 1868-69, Bvt CPT and MAJ 2 Mar 1862, 16th US INF 14 Apr 1869, ADJ 1869-72, CPT 4 Mar 1879, AAG (MAJ) 29 Jun 1882, LTCOL 2 Aug 1890, COL 15 Nov 1892, LLD Williams College 1900, B.G. USV 26 Apr 1901, ret. USA 30 Jun 1901
Affiliations: MOLLUS (#02614), GAR, SAR
Died: 19 Apr 1906, Watervliet NY; interment in Arlington National Cemetery (section 1, site 113
(C&S, EMH, FBH, GGB, JGU*, LAA, RR)

Barney, Elisha L. (1832-1864)

Born: 13 Apr 1832, Swanton VT, son of George and Eunice D. (Goodrich) Barney
Early Life: Jewett & Barney merchants
War Service: CPT Co. K 6th VT INF 15 Oct 1861, MAJ 15 Oct 1862, LTCOL 18 Dec 1862, COL 18 Mar 1863, wdd Crampton's Gap 14 Sep 1862, mwia Wilderness 5 May 1864, died of wds 10 May 1864
Married: (1) 1856, Sarah A. Burton; (2) 14 Oct 1862, Martha M. Blake
Died: 10 May 1864, Fredericksburg VA; interment in Church Street Cemetery, Swanton VT
Notes: Wheelock GAR Post #58 named after him
(AMH, FSO, Jones*)

Barstow, John Lester (1832-1913)

Born: 21 Feb 1832, Shelburne VT, son of Heman and Loraine (Lyon) Barstow
Early Life: teacher, clerk, businessman out west
War Service: ADJ 8th VT INF 19 Feb 1862, CPT Co. K 21 Mar 1863, MAJ 28 Dec 1863, m/o 22 Jun 1864
Later Life: State Rep. 1864-67; US Pension Agent 1870-77; LT Gov. 1880-81 Gov. 1882-84; LLD, NU 1909, Burlington Savings Bank trustee, UVM trustee
Affiliations: Republican, Episcopal, RSVO, Mason, GAR, MOLLUS (#09173)

Married: 28 Oct 1858, Laura Meach
Died: 28 Jun 1913, Shelburne VT; interment in Village Cemetery
Notes: cmdd State Militia BGD in aftermath of St. Albans Raid
(BBObit, C&S, JGU, PCD)

Barto, Alphonso (1834-1899)

Born: 27 May 1834, Hinesburg VT, son of William R. and Mary (Gage) Barto
Early Life: moved to IL early, farmer
War Service: PVT Co. K 52nd IL INF 14 Sep 1861, 2LT and CPT 16 Oct 1861, m/o 25 Oct 1865
Later Life: furniture manufacturer 1864-70, atty, moved to MN, j.p. Kane Cty IL, treasurer Kane Cty 1867-69, State Rep. 1871-72, Lt Gov 1873-75, register of U.S. Land Office, organizer, dir. and v.p. St. Cloud Merchants National Bank
Affiliations: Republican, Mason, GAR, MOLLUS (#08926), Soc. AOT
Married: (1) 13 Oct 1854, Harriet E. Hitchcock; (2) 17 Oct 1867, Charlotte A. Allen
Died: 4 Nov 1899, St. Cloud MN; interment in Sauk Center Cemetery
Publications: Letters, 1861-1864 (1875)
(C&S, JGU*, SAT)

Batchelder, James Edwin (1847-1888)

Born: 12 Nov 1847, Highgate VT, son of Rev. C. R. and Frances Batchelder
Early Life: Episcopal Institution, Burlington, NU 1862-63 (n.g.)
War Service: PVT Co. E 5th VT INF 5 May 1864, wdd, 12 May 1864, dis 22 Sep 1864 to attend to USMA
Later Life: USMA 1868, 2LT Jun 1868, 2LT 2nd US CAV 15 Jun 1868, LT 4 May 1870, Fort D. A. Russell, WA, resgd 4 Dec 1871, prof. French, descriptive geometry, drawing, asst prof. Mil. Sci, Dec 1871 until 25 Jun 1873, asst engr, railway construction MT, killed in an explosion
Married: 1871, Frances E. Cady
Died: 3 Mar 1888, MT; interment unknown
(GWC, WAE)

Bates, Norman Francis – See Part I, Medal of Honor

Baxter, Henry Clay (1844-1890)

Born: 16 Dec 1844, Derby VT, son of Portus (q.v.) and Ellen Judith Jannette (Harris) Baxter
Early Life: St. Johnsbury Acad., Green Mountain Inst, NU 1862-63, left to enlist
War Service: 2LT Co. D 11th VT INF 12 Dec 1863, 1LT 16 Oct 1864, wdd 19 Oct 1864, Bvt CPT 19 Oct 1864, Bvt MAJ 2 Apr 1865, m/o 24 Jun 1865
Later Life: proprietor, American House, Boston 1865-89, mngr Bellevue House, Seattle 1889-90)
Affiliations: RSVO
Married: (1) 21 Sep 1866, Laura Lillian White; (2) 2 Apr 1873, Mary Emma Carter
Died: 15 Sep 1890, Seattle, WA; interment in Strafford VT
Notes: GEN LA Grant wrote September 22 1885: "He was quite a young man to perform the duties of a staff officer but he did it well and merited the commendations on every occasion he was a noble boy and a gallant officer"
(FSO, GGB, RR, TJL, WAE)

Baxter, Horace Henry (1818-1884)

Born: 18 Jan 1818, Saxtons River VT, son of Horace and Elvira (Webb) Baxter
Early Life: railroad executive
War Service: Peace Conf. delegate 1861, AIG

Later Life: railroad executive, mining, banking
Married: Mary E. Roberts
Died: 17 Feb 1884, New York NY; interment in Evergreen Cemetery, Rutland VT
Notes: Gaysville GAR Post #111 named after him
(BBObit, BML, FSO, LHC)

Baxter, Jedediah Hyde (1837-1890)

Born: 11 Mar 1837, Stafford VT, son of Portus (q.v.) and Ellen Judith Jannette (Harris) Baxter
Early Life: UVM 1859, 1860; resident physician, Bellevue and Blackwell's Island Hosp. NYC
War Service: SURG 12th MA INF 26 Jun 1861; AOP 1861-62; Campbell Gen Hosp. 1862; CMO Paymr GEN Bureau 1862-65; Bvt COL USV 13 Mar 1865
Later Life: LTCOL, AMP 20 Jul 1867; CMP 12 Mar 1872, COL and CMP 23 Jun 1874; LL.B., Columbia University, 1875; SURG Gen. 16 Aug 1890
Affiliations: MOLLUS (#02402)
Died: 4 Dec 1890, Washington, D.C; interment in Arlington National Cemetery
Publications: Statistics, Medical and Anthropological, of the Provost-Marshal General's Bureau, of over a Million Men Examined (1875)
Notes: medical attendant to Presidents Garfield and Harrison, son of Congressman Portus Baxter (q.v.)
(C&S, DPF, E&E, FBH, NYTObit, RR, WCW, WAE*)

Baxter, Luther Loren (1832-1915)

Born: 8 Jun 1832, Cornwall VT, son of Chauncey and Philena (Peet) Baxter
Early Life: NU 1851; atty 1852-53; moved to Chicago 1853, Geneva WI 1855, Chaska MN 1857; judge of probate 1858; prosecuting atty 1859
War Service: CPT Co. A 4th MN INF 10 Apr 1861; MAJ 18 Apr 1862; resgd Oct 1862; MAJ 1st MN HARTY 21 Nov 1864; LTCOL 25 Feb 1865; COL 1865; State Sen. 1864, granted leave of absence; returned to unit Mar 1865; Ch. ARTY, Chattanooga until m/o 27 Sep 1865
Later Life: State Sen. 1865-68; State Rep. 1869, 1871-82; judge 1885-1910
Affiliations: Democrat, Mason, MOLLUS (#05855), GAR
Died: 1915, Chaska MN; interment in Mt. Pleasant Cemetery
Notes: Baxter, MN named after him
Papers: University of Washington
(C&S, JGU, WAE*)

Baxter, Portus (1806-1868)

Born: 4 Dec 1806, Brownington VT, son of William and Lydia (Ashley) Baxter
Early Life: NU 1824, UVM 1852, farmer and merchant, Whig Presidential elector 1852, Republican Presidential elector 1856
War Service: US Rep. 1861-67
Affiliations: Whig, Republican
Died: 4 Mar 1868, Washington, D.C; interment in Strafford Cemetery, Strafford VT
Notes: Known as "Soldier's Friend" for his support of troops, especially for work in hospitals at Fredericksburg during battle of the Wilderness; two sons served in Civil War, Jedediah and Henry C.; Burlington Marine Hosp. renamed in his honor
(CB, HGW, JGU, LOC*, PCD, TJL, WAE)

Bayne, Thomas (1823-aft 1900)

Born: 26 Jan 1823, Dunblane, Perth, Scotland, son of William and Margaret (Miller) Bayne
Early Life: immigrated to US 1843, farmer, Lincoln VT 1850, Congregational minister, Irasburgh VT 1860, A.M. MC 1863
War Service: Chap. 8th VT INF 23 Feb 1865, m/o 28 Jun 1865
Later Life: minister, New Haven NY 1870, minister, Gibbon, NE 1880, farmer, Richland SD 1900
Affiliations: Congregational, later Presbyterian
Married: 1847, Jane N. (nfi)
Died: aft 1900; interment unknown
Notes: delivered a sermon entitled "Scatter Thou the People that Delight in War" at funeral of CPT Henry Clay Flint, 1st VT CAV in Irasburgh 12 Apr 1863
(1850, 1860, 1870, 1880, 1890, 1900, FSO, GNC, MDG, MIDCAT)

Beaman, Fernando Cortez (1814-1882)

Born: 28 Jun 1814, Chester VT, son of Joshua N. and Hanna (Olcott) Beaman
Early Life: moved to Franklin Cty NY 1819, Malone Acad., teacher, moved to Rochester NY 1836, moved to Manchester MI 1838, admitted to the bar, moved to Adrian MI 1843, prosecuting atty, City Atty, RNC delegate 1856, mayor of Adrian 1856,
War Service: US Rep. 1861-71
Later Life: atty, Adrian, judge of probate 1871-72, 1876, declined appt. to US Sen. Due to ill health
Married: Mary Goodrich (nfi)
Died: 27 Sep 1882, Adrian MI; interment in Oakwood Cemetery
(CB, FSO, HGW)

Beaman, George William (1837-1917)

Born: 7 May 1837, Rutland VT, son of George Hudson and Eleanor Kettelle (Gookin) Beaman
Early Life: student, Rutland H.S., Troy Conf. Acad
War Service: PVT 3rd Regt, MO US Reserve Corps 1861; correspondent, Missouri Democrat 1861-62, Acting Asst Paymr USN, 5 Mar 1862, gunboat *Seneca* 1862-64, screw steamer *Union* 1864, Mound City, IL 1864-65, Mississippi Flotilla 1865
Later Life: steamer *Algonquin* 1865-66, Paymr 28 Mar 1866, practice ship *Marion* 1866-68, storeship *Cyane* 1869, steam sloop Ossipee 1869-72, Norfolk Navy Yard 1872-76, frigate Franklin 1876-77, steamer *Monongahela* 1877-79, Philadelphia Naval Asylum 1879-83, steamer *Shenandoah* 1885-86, Gen. Strkpr, Boston Navy Yard 1887-89, cruiser *Baltimore* 1889-90, Gen. Strkpr, Mare Island Navy Yard 1890-92, Pay Inspector 12 Sep 1891, Paymr Flagship *New York* 1893-96, Flt Paymr, 1894-96, Paymr, Boston Navy Yard 1896-99; Pay Dir. 9 Apr 1899, ret. 7 May 1899 with rank of RAdm
Affiliations: MOLLUS (#08875)
Died: 3 May 1917, Cambridge MA; interment in Evergreen Cemetery, Rutland.
(C&S, TJL2)

Beattie, Alexander Mitchell – See Part I, Medal of Honor

Beckwith, Amos Smith (1825-1894)

Born: 4 Oct 1825, Sutton VT, son of John and Matilda (Shaw) Beckwith
Early Life: USMA 1850 (21/44), Bvt 2LT 1st US ARTY 1 Jul 1850, Seminole War 1850-53, 2LT, 22 Feb 1851, garrison duty 1853-61, 1LT, 21 Aug 1854
War Service: CS (CPT) 10 May 1861, CS (MAJ) 29 Sep 1861 USMA staff, COL Asst ADC, 1 Jan 1862, Atlanta campaign May-Sep 1864, Bvt LTCOL 1 Sep 1864, Bvt B.G. USV, Bvt M.G, 13 Mar 1865, m/o 31 May 1866 Asst ADC
Later Life: CS Dept of the Gulf, LTCOL USA 28 Jun 1874, purchasing and depot commissary of subsistence, St. Louis MO 1886, ret. 4 Oct 1889
Died: 25 Oct 1894, St. Louis MO; interment in Jefferson Barracks National Cemetery
(ATA, FSO, GWC, NYTObit, RJ, RLO, WHP, WPG4)

Bedell, Henry Edson (1836-1911)

Born: 26 Jul 1836, Troy VT, son of James G. and Amanda (Smith) Bedell
Early Life: local schools, Westfield, farmer
War Service: CPL Co. D 11th VT INF 4 Aug 1862, SGT 11 Aug 1863, 2LT 28 Dec 1863, wdd Edward's Ferry 13 Sep 1864, dis/wds 20 Feb 1865
Later Life: US Customs House officer, Richford, Berkshire and Newport, auctioneer
Married: 3 Mar 1856, Emeline Burba
Affiliations: Republican, Methodist, GAR
Died: 15 Mar 1911, Newport VT; interment in East Main Street Cemetery
Notes: see also Betty Van Metre (q.v.)
Biography: Chittenden, L. E. The Unknown Heroine. New York: Richmond, Croscup & Co., 1893
(HC2, JGU*)

Bell, Charles James (1845-1909)

Born: 10 Mar 1845, Walden VT, son of James Dean and Caroline (Warner) Bell
Early Life: common schools, Peacham Acad
War Service: PVT Co. B 15th VT INF 22 Oct 1862, m/o 5 Aug 1863; PVT Co. C 1st VT CAV 17 Aug 1864, CPL 19 Nov 1864, wdd Appomattox Station 8 Apr 1865, m/o 21 Jun 1865
Later Life: farmer, town officer, State Rep. 1882-83; State Sen. 1894-95; State Board of Railroad Commissioners 1894-96, State Board of Agriculture 1896-1904, VT Gov. 1904-06, LLD NU 1906
Affiliations: Republican, Congregationalist, State and National Grange
Married: 4 Oct 1870, Mary Louise Perry
Died: 25 Sep 1909, New York City; interment in North Walden Cemetery VT
(FSO, PCD, RR, VHS10, WAE*)

Benedict, George Grenville – See Part I – Medal of Honor

Benton, Jacob (1814-1892)

Born: 19 Aug 1814, Waterford VT, son of Samuel Slade and Esther (Prouty) Benton
Early Life: Lyndon Acad., Randolph Acad; Burr and Burton Sem., Manchester NH 1839, teacher, atty, State Rep. 1854-56, RNC delegate 1860
War Service: B.G., cmdg NH Vols
Later Life: US Rep. 1867-71; atty Lancaster 1880
Married: Louisa D. (nfi)
Died: 29 Sep 1892, Lancaster NH; interment in Summer Street Cemetery
(1880, CB, FAG, FSO)

Benton, Reuben Clark (1830-1895)

Born: 13 May 1830, Waterford VT, son of Reuben C. and Almira (Fletcher) Benton
Early Life: St. Johnsbury Acad., A.B. UVM 1854, teacher, atty
War Service: CPT Co. D 5th VT INF, 28 Aug 1861, wdd, Savage's Station, LTCOL 11th VT INF 26 Aug 1862, resgd 21 Jun 1864
Later Life: atty Hyde Park 1864-67, St. Albans 1867-75, Minneapolis, MN 1875-95
Affiliations: Republican, RSVO, MOLLUS (#05863)
Married: 18 Mar 1856, Sara M. Leland
Died: 8 Jan 1895, Minneapolis MN; interment unknown
Publications: The Distinction between Legislative and Judicial Functions (1885), The Vermont Settlers and the New York Land Speculators (1894)

(C&S, JGU*, MDG, WU)

Bissell, Simon Backus (1808-1883)

Born: 28 Oct 1808, Fairlee VT, son of Simon Backus and Martha (Morey) Bissell
Early Life: Acting Midshipman, US Navy, 1 Mar 1825, Midshipman 4 Jun 1831, sloop *Delaware*, Mediterranean 1833-36, Passed Midshipman and LT 9 Feb 1837, cmdg sloop *Albany*, Home Squadron, during Mexican-American War, siege of Vera Cruz, cmdg steamer *Petrita*, 1846-47, Commander 10 Apr 1860
War Service: sloop *Cyane*, Pacific Squadron, 1861-62, Mare Island Naval Yard 1863-64
Later Life: COMO 10 Oct 1866, cmdg sloop-of-war *Monongahela*, North Atlantic 1866-67, special service 1869, Examining Board, Washington 1870, ret. 1 Mar 1870, relieved of duty Sep 1871, Board of Examiners 1872-73
Married: 13 May 1841, Sarah Mariah Loughborough (bro. served in VA CAV CSA)
Died: 18 Feb 1883, Paris, France; interment unknown
(AMH, E&E, EWC, GGB)

Bixby, Armentus Boyden (1834-1909)

Born: 26 Jun 1834, Mt. Holly VT, son of William and Hannah (Stoddard) Bixby
Early Life: Black River Acad., KUA, CMC 1858, physician, Londonderry 1860
War Service: Asst SURG, 4th VT INF, 6 Oct 1862, m/o 30 Sep 1864
Later Life: physician, Londonderry 1864-72, ret. to Poultney 1882
Married: (1) 17 Mar 1857, Annie French; (2) 9 Oct 1862, Elnora E. Howard
Died: 3 May 1909, Poultney VT; interment in Hillsdale Cemetery
Notes: 1905 Passport application from Moore Cty, N.C.: 5'7", blue eyes, gray hair, fair complexion, thin face, prominent forehead, medium nose and mouth, dimpled chin, thin face
(1870, 1880, AGO, JGU*, PA)

Bixby, Orville (1834-1864)

Born: 7 Aug 1834, Chelsea VT, son of Nathan and Lydia (Lathrop) Bixby
Early Life: Hackett & Bixby furniture business
War Service: 2LT Co. E 2nd VT INF 21 May 1861, 1LT 11 Jan 1862, CPT 4 Aug 1862, mwia at the Wilderness
Married: 1858, Frances Wills
Died: 5 May 1864, Wilderness; interment unknown
Notes: South Royalton GAR Posts #35 and #93 named after him
Correspondence: UVM
(GGK, HC3)

Blackmar, Armand Edward (1826-1888)

Born: 30 May 1826, Bennington VT, son of Reuben Harmon and Amanda (Cushman) Blackmar
Early Life: moved to Cleveland OH, Western Reserve College 1845, prof. of music, Centenary College, Jackson LA 1852-55, music publishing house, New Orleans 1856-65, violinist, pianist, chess expert
War Service: Confederate music publisher
Later Life: published 232 compositions
Married: 1861, Margaret B. Meara
Died: 28 Oct 1888, New Orleans LA; interment unknown
Publications: Dixie War Song 1861, The Beauregard Manassas Quick-step 1861, The Southern Marseillaise 1861, Maryland, My Maryland 1861, The Bonnie Blue Flag 1861, God and our Rights 1861, Washington Artillery Polka March 1863, The Camp Jester or, Amusement for the Mess1864, Let us have pease, ha, ha (1883), Harmony Simplified and Made Clear (1888)

Notes: arrested by Butler, songs banned in New Orleans
(APM, LOC)

Blackmer, John Collins (1840-1907)

Born: 25 Aug 1840, Manchester Depot VT, son of Hiram J. and Fannie (Collins) Blackmer
Early Life: common schools, Burr and Burton Sem., store clerk Sunderland, moved to Indiana
War Service: PVT/SGT 16th IN INF, wdd, Richmond, KY, 1LT 11th IN INF, 1LT 135th IN, m/o Sep 1864
Later Life: returned to VT 1865, Sunderland 1865-69, Manchester 1869 until death, general merchandiser
Affiliations: Republican, GAR, MOLLUS (#13404), Mason, Eastern Star
Married: 7 May 1874, Jennie E. Pratt
Died: 27 Oct 1907; interment unknown
Notes: Manchester Depot Sons of Veterans Camp No. 60 named for him.
(GFH*, MOLLUS)

Blair, Robert M. – See Part I – Medal of Honor

Blaisdell, Edson George (1846-1923)

Born: 13 Dec 1846, Richford VT, son of Josiah and Cleora (Munsill) Blaisdell
Early Life: public schools, Fairfax H.S., Commercial College, Burlington 1864
War Service: clerk, QM Dept., City Point VA
Later Life: moved to TX, returned to VT by 1870, M.D. UVM 1871, physician, Bridport 1880-1910
Affiliations: Republican, Congregational, Addison Cty MS, Mason
Married: 17 Jun 1874, Mary E. Eldredge
Died: 16 Oct 1923; interment unknown
(1870, 1880, 1910, CPT FSO, JGU)

Blake, Harrison Gray Otis (1818-1876)

Born: 17 Mar 1818, Newfane VT, son of Harrison Gray and Lucy (Goodell) Blake
Early Life: moved to OH, atty, State Rep. 1846-47, State Sen. 1848-49, merchant 1850, founder, Phoenix Bank, Medina OH 1857, US Rep. 1859-63
War Service: COL 166th OH INF 2 May 1864 - 9 Sep 1864
Later Life: declined appointment as Gov. of ID Ter., Loyalist Convention 1866, atty 1870, banker
Married: 1 Jan 1840, Betsey A. Bell
Died: 16 Apr 1876, Medina OH; interment in Spring Grove Cemetery, Medina OH
Notes: drafted legislation in Congress which created money-order system of US Postal service
(CB, EHN, FEB, HGW, WD)

Blake, Isaac (1804-1883)

Born: 10 Jun 1804, Derby VT, son of Samuel and Sarah (Atkins) Blake
Early Life: M.E. clergyman, circuit in Canada and VT, farmer Derby 1850, saw-mill operator
War Service: Musician Co. B 8th VT INF 26 Nov 1861, Chap. 3rd LA Native Guards (75th USCI), dis/dsb 12 Jul 1863 New Orleans
Later Life: M.E. clergyman
Married: (1) 24 Dec 1826, Azubah Caswell Aldrich; (2) 8 Apr 1873, Lucy S. Rowell
Died: 29 Sep 1883, Lowell VT; interment in Mead Hill Cemetery, Holland VT
Notes: Morgan Center GAR Post #104 was named after him
(1850, FSO, GGK, HHB)

Blanchard, Enoch (1830-1889)

Born: 4 Jul 1830, Peacham VT, son of Jacob and Thomasine Jefferson (Cameron) Blanchard
Early Life: B.S. DC 1852, M.D. DC 1857, physician M'Indoes Falls VT, moved to Lyndon VT
War Service: Asst SURG 7th VT INF, 25 Jan 1862, SURG 15 Sep 1862, m/o 20 Sep 1865
Later Life: physician, Lacon IL 1870, Minonk IL 1880, Super. of schools
Married: 16 Feb 1862, Susan Bugbee
Died: 11 Mar 1889; interment in City Cemetery, Mclean Cty IL
Notes: court-martialed 1862 for misappropriation of food and striking an enlisted man, found innocent of all charges
(1870, 1880, CWB, GTC, TPL, WCH)

Blinn, Charles Henry (1843-1926)

Born: 27 Jan 1843, Burlington VT, son of Chauncy and Edatha (Harrington) Blinn
Early Life: public schools, UVM, left to enlist
War Service: PVT Co. A 1st VT CAV 21 Sep 1861, pow 24 May 1862, prld 13 Sep 1862, m/o 18 Nov 1864
Later Life: clerk, Central Pacific R.R., later chief clerk, Welden House, St. Albans 1864-68, moved to CA 1868, Wells-Fargo Express, editorial writer, Alta California, 1875, chief permit clerk, San Francisco Customs House 1878-1902
Affiliations: Methodist, GAR, SAR, Veteran Guard, Native SOV
Married: 15 Dec 1870, Nellie Holbrook
Died: 11 May 1926, San Francisco CA; interment in San Francisco National Cemetery
(JGU, LHI)

Bliss, Charles Miller (1827-1905)

Born: 1 Jan 1827, Hartford, CT, son of Charles and Lucia (Coe) Bliss
Early Life: Hartford H.S., Yale 1852, traveled abroad, moved to Woodford VT 1854, farmer, lumberman
War Service: SGT Co. A 2nd VT INF 20 Jun 1861, 2LT Co. B 21 Sep 1861, m/o 4 Oct 1862, USSC
Later Life: newspaperman, editor/proprietor Bennington Free Press, businessman, Rutland 1872-75
Married: 15 Feb 1870, Sarah Adell Godfrey
Died: 21 Dec 1905; interment unknown
(BYU, DKECat, VHS06)

Blodgett, Gardner Spring (1819-1909)

Born: 10 Nov 1819, Rochester VT, son of Luther P. and Mary (Jefferson) Blodgett
Early Life: Jericho Acad., clerk, country store, dry-goods salesman NYC until 1852, returned to VT, mail agent, Burlington & Boston R.R., invented galvanized iron portable oven
War Service: AQM (CPT), USV, 3 Aug 1861, Chief Depot QM, Annapolis, MD, May 1862, supervised building of parole camp, duty as Chief QM, VIII Corps, laid out national cemetery, AQM (CPT), USA 2 Jul 1864, Bvt MAJ 13 Mar 1865, ordered to Washington, in charge of all rail and river transportation, resgd Oct 1865
Later Life: G.G. Blodgett & Co. (sheet and galvanized iron, dealer in furnaces, plumbers' material, stoves & ranges)
Affiliations: Congregational, MOLLUS (#05026), GAR, SAR
Married: 5 May 1849, Sarah H. Ellis
Died: 16 Apr 1909, Burlington VT; interment unknown
(C&S, CLL*, FBH, GFH, HC1, LHC, NYTObit)

Blunt, Asa Peabody (1826-1889)

Born: 19 Oct 1826, Danville VT
Early Life: cotton mill overseer; draughtsman

War Service: ADJ 3rd VT INF 6 Jun 1861, LTCOL 6th VT INF 25 Sep 1861, COL 12th VT INF 19 Sep 1862, m/o 14 Jul 1863, Bvt B.G. 13 Mar 1865
Later Life: Depot QM Norfolk 1865; Chief QM Richmond VA 1866. Chief QM Dept of the Potomac 1866; AQM (CPT) USA 28 Mar 1867, Bvt MAJ, Bvt LTCOL USA 28 Mar 1867, Richmond VA 1867; Washington, 1868; Charleston SC 1869; Commandant, US Disciplinary Barracks, Ft. Leavenworth 1877-88
Married: before 1850, Mary (nfi)
Died: 4 Oct 1889, Manchester NH; interment in Pine Grove Cemetery
(1850, AGC, E&E, FAG, FBH, Gibson*, RR)

Bond, George Herbert (1846-1928)

Born: 31 Jan 1846, Dummerston VT, son of Luke T. and Elsie (Stoddard) Bond
Early Life: local schools
War Service: PVT Co. I 16th VT INF 20 Sep 1862, m/o 10 Aug 1863
Later Life: PVT 4SGT, 1SGT Co. I 1st VT Militia 1864-67, CPT 18 Jul 1881, MAJ 11 Dec 1886, LTCOL 6 Jan 1893, Bvt COL 28 Nov 1894, COL 10 Jan 1895, Bvt B.G. 16 Dec 1897, ret. 18 Dec 1897, in civil life, Stanley Rule and Level Co., Brattleboro, 1867-68; New Home Sewing Machine Co., Orange, Lowell and Boston MA 1868-70, Estey Organ Co., Brattleboro, 1872-86; retail coal business in Brattleboro 1886-99; messenger in US Sen. 1900-13, US govt clerk, Washington, 1920
Affiliations: Republican, Mason, IOOF, GAR
Married: 1870, Addie Richardson Carpenter
Died: 3 May 1928; interment in Prospect Hill Cemetery, Brattleboro VT
(1920, AGO, JGU*, PCD)

Boutin, Charles W. (1839-1912)

Born: 8 Nov 1839, Chester VT, son of Joachim and Martha (Warner) Boutin
Early Life: moved to Windham, local schools, farmer until 1858, carpenter until 1865
War Service: CPL Co. E 1st VT INF 2 May 1861, m/o 15 Aug 1861, 1LT Co. K 4th VT INF 14 Sep 1861, CPT Co. D 14 Dec 1862, pow Weldon Railroad 23 Jun 1864, prld 1 Mar 1865, MAJ 4 Jun 1865, m/o 13 Jul 1865 as CPT
Later Life: dry goods, Chicago, nursery business, Webster City IA, 1865-67, moved to Hampton IA, architect and builder, 16 years in IA NG (CPT through COL, 6th IA NG)
Married: (1) 25 Aug 1861, Marinda A. French; (2) Mar 1869, Julina A. French (sister); (3) Nov 1888, Emma S. Kennedy
Affiliations: Republican, Mason, GAR, MOLLUS (#04111)
Died: 4 Jan 1912, Des Moines IA; interment unknown
(C&S, ERH, JGU*)

Boynton, Edward Carlisle (1824-1893)

Born: 1 Feb 1824, Bennington VT, son of Thomas and Sophia (Cabot) Boynton
Early Life: Union Acad., Meriden NH, USMA 1846 (12/59); Bvt 2LT 2nd US ARTY 1 Jul 1846; 2LT 1st ARTY 16 Feb 1847; 1LT 20 Aug 1847; Bvt CPT 20 Aug 1847, instr. USMA 1848-55; Florida 1855-56; resgd 16 Feb 1856; professor of chemistry U. of MS; dismissed 1861 for "evincing a want of attachment to the government of the confederate states"
War Service: CPT 11th US INF 23 Sep 1861 at USMA, Bvt MAJ 13 Mar 1865
Later Life: unassigned 1869; 3rd US ARTY 15 Dec 1870; resgd 1 Dec 1872
Married: bef 1854, Mary J. Hubbard
Died: 3 May 1893, Newburg NY; interment unknown
Publications: History of West Point and its Military Importance during the Revolution, and the Origin and Progress of the Military Academy (1863); Guide to West Point and the United States Military Acad. (1863); Register of Cadets Admitted to the Military Academy from its Origin to June 30, 1870 (1870); Several Orders of George Washington, Commander-in-Chief, etc., Issued at Newburg (1883); contributed to Webster's Army and Navy Dictionary (1886)
Photographs: UM (collection of glass plate negatives of photos taken by Mr. Boynton between 1856-61)

(FBH, FSO, GWC, JGW, WPG1)

Boynton, Joseph Jackson (1833-1897)

Born: 9 Jun 1833, Stowe VT, son of David and Melinda Boynton
War Service: CPT Co. E 13th VT INF 8 Sep 1862, MAJ 5 May 1863, m/o 23 Jul 1863
Later Life: M.D. UVM 1878, phys, Stowe VT until 1882, moved to South Framington, MA
Affiliations: RSVO
Married: 1852, Vodica Maria Fuller
Died: 17 Jun 1897, South Framingham MA; interment unknown
(DAR3, FSO, HC2, ROS, RSVO2)

Bradford, James Henry (1836-1913)

Born: 24 Aug 1836, Grafton VT, son of Rev. Moses Bradstreet Bradford
Early Life: district school, Charleston SC, dry goods clerk 3 years, Williston Sem., Yale Coll. 1863
War Service: Chap. 12th CT INF 4 Feb 1862, m/o 2 Dec 1864
Later Life: home missionary, Hudson WI, 2 years, Westboro MA State Reform School 3 years, CT Industrial School 4 years MA Primary School 3 years, Howard Mission NY, Washington 12 years federal service in census, pension and Indian bureau
Affiliations: GAR, MOLLUS (#06659)
Married: 19 Aug 1865, Ellen J. Knight
Died: 22 Dec 1913; interment in Arlington National Cemetery
Publications: The Chaplains in the Volunteer Army. (1892), Crises of the Civil War (1897), A Tribute to Tom, or, the Servant Question Among the Volunteers (1895)
(AGO, C&S, CAB*, JGU)

Bradford, Philander Drury (1811-1892)

Born: 11 Apr 1811, Randolph VT, son of John and Lucy (Brooks) Bradford
Early Life: WMC 1834, A.M. UVM 1850, A.M. NU 1882, physician, Braintree, Randolph, Bethel, Northfield, State Rep. 1853-54, State Sen. 1862-63, Commissioner of Insane 1854-55, prof. of Physiology and Pathology CMC 1857-62
War Service: SURG, 5th VT INF 3 Dec 1862; resgd 1 Mar 1863
Later Life: prof. of Natural Sciences NU 1866-70, Physiology 1866-74, 1883-89, Anatomy 1883-89, Histology 1870-74, Natural history 1874-83, Physiology 1874-80, Natural Sciences 1866-70, SURG 1878-89, librarian 1870-75
Married: (1) 1835, Susan H. Edson; (2) May 1867, Olive Moore
Affiliations: Free Soiler, Republican, Episcopal, Mason, IOOF, Sons of Temperance
Died: 16 Jul 1892, Northfield VT; interment in Elmwood Cemetery
(AGO, WAE*)

Brainerd, Anna Eliza (1819-1905)

Born: 7 Oct 1819, St. Albans VT, daughter of Lawrence and Fidelia Burnett (Gadcomb) Brainerd
War Service: honorary LTCOL for gallant conduct during the raid at St. Albans (1864)
Later Life: Author, writing under the name, Mrs. J. Gregory Smith, Pres. Board of Mngrs, Warner Home for Little Wanderers, Pres. VT Woman's exhibit, Centennial Exposition, Philadelphia (1876)
Affiliations: Congregationalist, VT Soc. Colonial Dames, DAR
Married: 27 Dec 1843, John Gregory Smith (q.v.)
Died: 6 Jan 1905, St. Albans VT; interment in Greenwood Cemetery
Publications: From Dawn to Sunrise: A Review Historical and Philosophical of the Religious Ideas of Mankind (1876), Seola (1878), Selma (1880), The Iceberg's Storm (a poem, 1881), Atla (1886), Poems (1889), Notes of Travel (1896)
Notes: brother Aldis O. served in the 5th VT INF; her husband named Brainerd MN after her in 1871.

(JGU, LAB, MDG)

Brainerd, Charles Deming (1842-1906)

Born: 11 Sep 1842, Danville VT, son of Hiram and Mehitable (Brown) Brainerd
Early Life: public schools, Phillips Acad., farmer
War Service: 1SGT, Co. B 15th VT INF, 2LT Co. G 1 Apr 1863, m/o 5 Aug 1863, 2LT Co. G 17th VT INF 12 Apr 1864, 1LT, Co. F 1 Nov 1864, Bvt CPT 2 Apr 1865, CPT 18 Apr 1865, m/o 14 Jul 1865
Later Life: Assoc Cty Judge, State Sen. 1882, town agent, j.p. 60 years
Affiliations: Republican, Methodist Episcopal, RSVO
Married: 3 Nov 1868, Elizabeth A. Carter
Died: 25 Apr 1906, Danville; interment in Danville Green Cemetery VT
Publications: Danville in the War of the Rebellion (1879)
(AFS*, AGO, FSO, MDG, TPG)

Branch, Charles Franklin (1845-1910)

Born: 9 Dec 1845, Orwell VT, son of Orson and Rodilla (Felton) Branch
Early Life: local schools
War Service: CPL, Co. C 9th VT INF 23 Jun 1862, SGT 27 Jan 1864, 1SGT 1 Feb1864, 2LT Co. H 21 Dec 1864, 1LT Co. C 20 May 1865, CPT Co. A 3 Jul 1865, m/o 1 Dec 1865
Later Life: farmer 1865-75, M.D. UVM 1879, physician, Med. Examiner, nine life insurance companies, SURG, southern div., CPRR, SURG 1st Reg't VT NG, VT SURG GEN 1886-88, prof. of sanitary science and hygiene, UVM 1892
Affiliations: Congregational, GAR, MOLLUS (#09662), Orleans Cty MS, VTMS, AMA
Married: (1) Mar 1868, Emma Cook; (2) Ida H. Burbank; (3) Oct 1891, Martha J. Stewart
Died: 1910; interment unknown
(C&S, FSO, JGU*, UVMCat2, UVMMED)

Brastow, Lewis Orsmond (1834-1912)

Born: 23 Mar 1834, Brewer ME, son of Dr. Deodat and Eliza (Blake) Brastow
Early Life: Bowdoin College 1857, BTS 1860, Pastor, South Congregational Church, St. Johnsbury VT 1861-62
War Service: Chap. 12th VT INF 19 Sep 1862, m/o 14 Jul 1863
Later Life: Pastor, South Congregational Church, St Johnsbury VT 1862-73, Pastor, First Congregational Church, Burlington VT 1873-84, D.D., Bowdoin College 1880, Professor, Yale Theological Sem. 1887-1905, Professor Emeritus, Yale 1907
Affiliations: Congregational, RSVO
Married: 15 May 1872, Martha Brewster Ladd
Died: 10 Aug 1912, Woodmont CT; interment unknown
Publications: Representative Modern Preachers (1904), The Modem Pulpit: a Study of Homiletic Sources and Characteristics (1912)
(AGC, FCB, JOW, RJ)

Brookins, Harvey S. (1835-1907)

Born: 25 Jan 1835, Shoreham VT, son of Philip C. and Lucina (Forbes) Brookins
Early Life: local schools, Bakersfield Acad., moved to MN 1856, surveyor, sheriff, farmer Silver Creek 1860
War Service: 2LT 8th MN INF Aug 1862, CPT 1 May 1865, scout, MN 1864, wdd, Murfreesboro, TN, m/o 17 May 1865
Later Life: clerk, Treasury Dept, resgd 1866; farmer, State Rep. 1876-78, town constable 1872-80, farmer Shoreham 1880-1900
Affiliations: Republican
Married: 3 Sep 1866, Emma L. Wright

Died: 1 Sep 1907; interment in East Cemetery, Shoreham VT
(1850, 1880, 1900, AGO, JGU*)

Brooks, Nathaniel Grout (1838-1918)

Born: 14 Oct 1838, Acworth NH, son of Dr. Lyman and Mary (Graham) Brooks
Early Life: KUA, AMS 1861, Albany City Hosp. 1861
War Service: Asst SURG, 16th VT INF, 23 Oct 1862, m/o 10 Aug 1863, also Acting Asst SURG, U.S.A., Brattleboro Hosp.
Later Life: physician, Acworth 1865-74, Charlestown 1874-1904, town clerk, super. of schools, Board of Health, State Rep. 1896-97, State Sen. 1900-01
Affiliations: Republican, Episcopal, NH MS, CT Valley MS, Mason
Married: 5 Dec 1876, Emma Preston
Died: 10 Mar 1918; interment unknown
(ESS, Family*, HHM, RR, WHO3)

Brooks, William Thomas Harbaugh (1821-1870)

Born: 28 Jan 1821, Lisbon OH (father was born Montpelier VT)
Early Life: USMA 1841 (46/52), Seminole War 1841-42, KS 1843-45, Louisiana 1845, TX 1845-46, Mexican-American War 1846-48, Twigg's division 1848-51, NM and AZ 1851-58, sick leave 1858-60, TX 1860 NY 1861
War Service: mustering duty WI Aug-Sep 1861, B.G. USV Sep 1861, Defenses of Washington 1861-62, cmdg 2 BGD 2 Div IV Corps, AOP, Peninsular Campaign 1862, wdd, Seven Days, 29 Jun 1862, cmdg 2 BGD 2 Div IV Corps, AOP, Maryland Campaign 1862, wdd Antietam, cmdg 1 Div/VI Corps, AOP 1862-63, cmdg Dept of the Monongahela 1863-64, M.G. USV Jun 1863, cmdg 1 Div XVIII Corps, AOJ 1864, cmdg X Corps 1864, resgd 14 Jul 1864
Later Life: farmer, Huntsville AL
Died: 19 Jul 1870, Huntsville, AL; interment in Maple Hill Cemetery
(CCPL, GGB, GWC, RR, WR)

Brown, Andrew Chandler (1828-1911)

Born: 10 Jul 1828, Sutton VT, son of Rev. Elisha and Phoebe (Fletcher) Brown
Early Life: Newbury Sem. 1847, teacher, Waitsfield VT 1849-51, publisher, Northern Inquirer, Bradford VT 1852-54, business mngr, Watchman and Journal, Montpelier VT 1854-57, Editor, Watchman and Journal 1857-62
War Service: LTCOL 13th VT INF 24 Sep 1862, resgd, 5 May 1863
Later Life: Commissioner, Board of Enrollment, 1st Congressional District of Vermont, Rutland, Official Reporter, House of Representatives, State Rep. 1865-80, Insurance business, Montpelier, Lessee, American Bell Telephone Co. 1880-1907
Affiliations: MOLLUS (#13865)
Married: 1 May 1851, Lucia Almira Green
Died: 29 Oct 1911, Montpelier VT; interment unknown
(C&S, PCD, WRC1)

Brown, Stephen Flavius (1841-1903)

Born: 4 Apr 1841, Swanton VT, son of Samuel Gibson and Anna Maria (Crawford) Brown
Early Life: local schools, Swanton Falls Acad.
War Service: 1LT, Co. K, 13th VT INF, 11 Sep 1862, at Gettysburg armed solely with a hatchet, captured sword and pistol of rebel officer, m/o 21 Jul 1863, CPT Co. A 17th VT INF 11 Nov 1863, wdd Wilderness 6 May 1864 (left arm amputated), dis/wds 22 Aug 1864
Later Life: ALS 1868; admitted to the bar, moved to Chicago, lost everything in Great Chicago Fire of 1871, rebuilt practice, returned to Swanton when his parents became enfeebled, and remained
Affiliations: Mason, MOLLUS (#09178), SAR, GAR, IL SOV

Died: 8 Sep 1903, Swanton VT; interment in Church Street Cemetery
Notes: lost a bet with his father as to who would serve in 1st VT INF, after father's return, Stephen enlisted; 13th VT INF monument at Gettysburg is topped with statue of him, including the camp hatchet he was armed with; Brown donated captured sword to VHS in 1902
(C&S, FAG, LCA1, LHC, ROS, VHS02)

Browne, Francis Fisher (1843-1913)

Born: 1 Dec 1843, South Halifax VT, son of William Goldsmith Browne
Early Life: student, printer, moved to Chicopee, MA
War Service: PVT Co. D 46th MA INF 27 Aug 1862, m/o 29 Jul 1863
Later Life: studied law, Rochester NY, UMI 1866-67; edited the Lakeside Monthly (Chicago) 1869-74, The Alliance 1878-79, and The Dial 1880-1913, a semimonthly literary review
Died: 1913 CA; interment unknown
Publications: Every-Day Life of Abraham Lincoln (1886, 1913), Volunteer Grain (1896)
(JCR, JGW, MAG)

Browne, William Frank (abt 1839-1867)

Born: abt 1839, Northfield VT
Early Life: farm laborer
War Service: PVT Co. C 15th VT INF 22 Aug 1862, m/o 5 Aug 1863; camp photographer, 5th MI CAV; contract photograph for Alexander Gardner 1864-65
Died: 12 Sep 1867, Northfield VT; interment unknown
Notes: took earliest portraits of George Custer after pr to B.G.
Publications: View of Confederate Water Batteries on James River
(LOC, RR)

Brush, Daniel Harmon (1813-1890)

Born: 25 Apr 1813, Vergennes VT, son of Elkanah and Lucretia (Harmon) Brush
Early Life: moved to IL 1819, clerk, dry goods store, judge of probate 1836, clerk of circuit court, clerk of Cty Court, Recorder of Deeds, founded Carbondale IL 1852, banker Carbondale 1860
War Service: CPT 18th IL INF 28 May 1861; MAJ 27 Jul 1862; LTCOL 27 Sep 1862; COL 25 May 1863; Bvt B.G. USV 13 Mar 1865, resgd 8 Sep 1863
Later Life: atty Carbondale 1870-80, mine operator, newspaper publisher; died in a tree-cutting accident
Married: (1) 2 Nov 1841, Julia M. Etherton; (2) 9 Dec 1868, Elizabeth Parnham Bliss
Died: 10 Feb 1890, Carbondale IL; interment in Woodlawn Cemetery
Publications: Growing Up in Southern Illinois 1820-1861 (1944)
(1860, 1870, 1880, CAB*, DHB2, E&E, FBH, FSO)

Brush, Edwin Ruthven (1836-1908)

Born: 15 Apr 1836, Cambridge VT, son of Salmon and Sara (Lovegroove) Brush
Early Life: M.D. UVM 1858, farmer Cambridge 1860
War Service: drafted as PVT Co. H 2nd VT INF 17 Jul 1863, Asst SURG 15 Oct 1863, m/o 15 Jul 1865
Later Life: physician Cambridge 1870-1900, j.p.
Married: 25 Jul 1860, Amy R. Fletcher
Died: 27 Feb 1908, Cambridge VT; interment in Mount View Cemetery
(1860, 1870, 1900, AGO, FSO, JVS02, UVMMED)

Bullard, Gates Bezaleel (1829-1901)

Born: 1 Feb 1829, Plainfield NH, son of Jonathan and Rebecca (Gates) Bullard
Early Life: M.D. DC 1855, physician, Canaan, St. Johnsbury
War Service: Asst SURG, 15th VT INF, 2 Oct 1862, SURG 4 May 1862, field Hosp. 2 DIV I AC, Gettysburg, m/o 5 Aug 1863
Later Life: State Rep. 1863-64, State Sen. 1867-68, VT SURG-Gen. 1869-70, physician St. Johnsbury 1870-80
Affiliations: VT MS, RSVO, MOLLUS (#09192)
Married: 1879, Lefie Fenton Wheeler
Died: 4 Sep 1901, St. Johnsbury VT; interment unknown
(1860, 1870, 1880, C&S, DCN, GFS)

Burdick, Arthur Franklin (1828-1921)

Born: 26 Oct 1828, Underhill VT, son of Timothy and Sylvia (Lewis) Burdick
Early Life: Green Mt. Acad., Med. Sch. UVM 1858, MD from CPS NYU 1869, moved to CA 1849, physician, Underhill 1859-62
War Service: Asst SURG, 5th VT INF, 23 Sep 1862, resgd 26 May 1863
Later Life: physician Jericho VT 1870-1900, Med. Examiner NY Life Insurance
Affiliations: Republican, Congregational, VTMS
Married: 29 Oct 1867, Mary C. Church
Died: 21 Feb 1921, Underhill VT; interment in Underhill Flats Cemetery
(1870, 1900, UVMMED, WHO3)

Burleson, George Washington (1845-1920)

Born: 23 Mar 1845, Berkshire VT, son of Caleb Nicholas and Amanda Hannah (Bowdish) Burleson
Early Life: Franklin Acad.
War Service: PVT Co. C 1st VT INF 9 May 1861, m/o 15 Aug 1861, SGT Co. K 6th VT INF 15 Oct 1861, QM SGT 1 Dec 1862, 1LT Co. F 29 Oct 1864, Co. C 16 Oct 1864, wdd Petersburg 2 Apr 1865, CPT 22 Apr 1865, m/o 26 Jun 1865
Later Life: St. Mary's College, law studies, Highgate VT, admitted to bar 1876, atty Fairfield VT 1880, State's Atty 1884-86, atty Ballard & Burleson 1885-90, Deputy US Customs Collector, St. Albans VT 1886-1903, Special US Customs Deputy 1903-20
Affiliations: MOLLUS (#10076)
Married: 1865, Irene E. Spaulding
Died: 19 Jul 1920, Fairfield VT; interment in Egypt Cemetery
(1880, 1920, C&S, FSO, GFH, LCA1, PCD)

Burnap, Wilder Luke (1839-1905)

Born: 3 Sep 1839, Canojoharie NY, son of Luke and Abigail (Robbins) Burnap
Early Life: moved to Groton VT, Leland Sem., DC 1859, left to enlist
War Service: Co. B 1st Regt RI CAV, Jun-Oct 1862
Later Life: DC 1863, moved to Burlington, admitted to the bar 1866, attorney, Solicitor in Bankruptcy, State's Atty 1871-75, State Sen. 1882, prof. Med. Jurisprudence, UVM 1895-1905
Affiliations: DC Alumni Assoc
Married: May 1870, Fannie Castle
Died: 15 Jul 1905; interment unknown
(1890, ADA, VHS06)

Burton, Henry Stanton (1818-1869)

Born: Sep 1818, Norwich VT, son of Oliver G. and Almira (Partridge) Burton
Early Life: NU, USMA 1839 (9/31), 2LT, 3rd Artillery, 1 Jul 1839, 1LT, 3rd Artillery, 1 Nov 1839, Seminole War 1839-42, garrison duty 1842-43, instr. INF Tactics & ARTY USMA 16 Jun 1843-5 Aug 1846, LTCOL NY Vols, Mexican-American War 1847-48, CPT 3rd US ARTY 22 Sep 1847, frontier duty, California 1848-59, leave of absence 1860-61
War Service: Ft. Monroe VA 1861, MAJ 3rd US ARTY 14 May 1861, Alcatraz Island CA 1861-62, cmdg Ft. Delaware, DE 1862-63, LTCOL, 4th US ARTY 25 Jun 1863, COL 5th US ARTY 11 Aug 1863, Dist. of Monongahela 1863-64, Inspector of Arty AOP, May-Jun 1864, cmdg ARTY XVIII Corps Jun-Jul 1864, cmdg 5th US ARTY, Dept of the East Sep-Dec 1864, board for retiring disabled officers 1864-65, Bvt B.G. 13 Mar 1865
Later Life: cmdg 5th ARTY May-Nov 1865, cmdg Ft. Monroe VA, 1865-67, Court Martial Committee 1868-69
Married: (1) 1840, Elizabeth Furgurson Smith; (2) 1849, Maria Amparo de Ruiz
Died: 4 Apr 1869, Ft. Adams, Newport, RI; interment in West Point Cemetery, NY
(E&E, GWC, MAR, WAE*)

Butterfield, Franklin George – See Part I – Medal of Honor

Butterfield, Frederick David (1838-1918)

Born: 14 May 1838, Rockingham VT, son of David and Elmira Ward (Randall) Butterfield
Early Life: local schools, Saxtons River Acad., hardware store clerk
War Service: 2LT, Co. B 8th VT INF, 19 Dec 1861, 1LT 15 Jun 1863, CPT 7 Nov 1863, signal corps, m/o 8 Jun 1864
Later Life: businessman 1864-66, deputy customs collector 1866-72, manufacturer, later partnered with brother Franklin George Butterfield (q.v.), tap and die manufacturer Derby VT 1900, pres. Olive Growers Assoc. Los Angeles CA 1910
Affiliations: Mason, GAR, MOLLUS (#04470), RSVO, SAR
Married: 8 Oct 1868, Ellen Jeannette Morrill
Died: 12 Jul 1918, Los Angeles CA; interment in Derby Line VT
(1900, 1910, AGO, C&S, CLL*, JGU, LHC)

Butts, Lemuel Porter (1844-1932)

Born: 23 Jan 1844, Stowe VT, son of Prosper and Mary (Luce) Butts
Early Life: Stowe H.S.
War Service: PVT Co. E, 13th VT INF 10 Oct 1862, m/o 21 Jul 1863, PVT Co. D 5th VT INF 19 Aug 1864, m/o 19 Jun 1865
Later Life: farmer Johnson VT 1870, proprietor Valley House Hotel, North Hyde Park VT, State Rep. 1896, Postmaster, Hyde Park 1897-1912
Married: 1866, Luranna A. Munn
Died: 9 Nov 1932, Stowe VT; interment in Riverbank Cemetery
(1870, 1890, AGO, HC2, PCD)

Buxton, Albert (1835-1864)

Born: 26 Dec 1835, Londonderry VT, son of Nathan and Elizabeth S. (Griswold) Buxton
Early Life: farmer
War Service: 2LT Co. H 2nd USSS 24 Dec 1861, CPT 1 Dec 1862, wdd Gettysburg 3 Jul 1863, kia Wilderness 6 May 1864
Married: 24 Aug 1863, Hattie A. Rice
Died: 6 May 1864, Wilderness VA; interment in Village Cemetery, Londonderry VT
(FSO, LSH)

Buxton, Charles (1834-1864)

Born: 1 Mar 1834, Londonderry VT, son of Nathan and Elizabeth S. (Griswold) Buxton
Early Life: saddler, harness maker, Bellows Falls

War Service: CPT Co. G 11th VT INF 12 Aug 1862, kia Winchester 19 Sep 1864, MAJ (posthumously) 2 Sep 1864
Married: Sophia W. Frost
Died: 19 Sep 1864, Winchester VA; interment in Immanuel Cemetery, Rockingham VT
Diary: VHS
(FSO, LSH, RR, TJL)

Babcock, Orville E.

Bailey, Myron W.

Baker, Joel C.

Ballard, Henry

Barber, Merritt L.

Barney Elisha L.

Barstow, John L.

Barto, Alphonso

Baxter, Jedediah H.

Baxter, Luther L.

Baxter, Portus

Bedell, Henry E.

Bell, Charles J.

Benton, Reuben C.

Bixby, Armentus B.

Blackmer, John C.

Blodgett, Gardner S.

Blunt, Asa P.

Bond, George H.

Boutin, Charles W.

Bradford, James H.

Bradford, Philander D.

Branch, Charles F.

Brookins, Harvey S.

Brooks, Nathan

Brown, Andrew C.

Brush, Daniel H.

Burnap, Wilder L.

Burton, Henry S.

Butterfield, Frederick. D.

CCCCC

Cahoon, Charles Shaw (1829-1881)

Born: 30 Sep 1829, Lyndon VT, son of William and Nancy (Shaw) Cahoon
Early Life: physician Lyndon 1860
War Service: Fredericksburg and Washington (May 1864), among a contingent of VT doctors who volunteered services to care for Vermonters wdd in the battles of the Wilderness and Spotsylvania C.H.
Later Life: physician Lyndon 1870-80
Affiliations: VT MS
Married: 4 Dec 1857, Charlotte Chase
Died: 8 Apr 1881; interment unknown
(1860, 1870, 1880, AMT1860, BMJ2, FSO)

Caldwell, John Curtis (1833-1912)

Born: 17 Apr 1833, Lowell VT, son of George Morrison and Betsey (Curtis) Caldwell
Early Life: AC 1855, princ., Washington Acad., East Machias ME 1856-61
War Service: COL 11th ME INF 1861, B.G. USV, 13 May 1862, cmdg 1 BGD 1 Div II Corps, AOP, Peninsula Campaign 1862, wdd Fredericksburg Dec 1862, relieved of duty from AOP Mar 1864, Bvt M.G. USV, 19 Aug 1865
Later Life: ME AG 1867-69, US Consul Valparaiso Chile, 1869-74, US Minister to Uruguay 1874-82, atty, Topeka KS 1882-85, Chair. KS Board of Pardons 1885-93, 1895-97, US Consul to Costa Rica 1897-1909
Married: 15 May 1857, Martha Helen Foster
Died: 31 Aug 1912, Calais, ME; interment in St. Stephen Rural Cemetery, New Brunswick, Canada
Notes: Possibly the only Civil War General buried in Canada; served in honor guard in procession of Lincoln's body from Washington to Springfield
(ACBR, FAG, HGW, JGW, LOC*, RJ, WLM)

Camp, Lyman Lovell (1838-1926)

Born: 10 Jun 1838, Elmore VT, son of Abel and Charlotte (Taplin) Camp
Early Life: public schools, Barre Acad., farmer
War Service: PVT Co. E 3rd VT INF 1 Jun 1861, co. cook, m/o 27 Jul 1864
Later Life: farmer
Affiliations: Republican, Methodist, GAR (Post #4, Morrisville)
Married: 19 Mar 1868, Hattie E. White
Died: 14 Apr 1926, Morrisville VT; interment in Riverside Cemetery
(JGU, Morrisville Messenger)

Canfield, Thomas Hawley (1822-1897)

Born: 29 Mar 1822, Arlington VT, son of Samuel and Mary A. (Hawley) Canfield
Early Life: local schools, Burr Sem., Manchester, farm laborer, Troy Episcopal Inst., UC 1839, returned to farming, moved to Williston 1844, merchant, moved to Burlington 1847, wholesale stores, boat lines to NYC and Montreal, set up telegraph line between Troy NY and Montreal Feb 1848, constructed Bellows Falls to Burlington R.R. 1849, also Rutland & Washington, Ogdensburg and others in NY and PA lines, involved with many other railroads across the northern U.S., involved with Sec. of War Jefferson Davis in developing transcontinental lines
War Service: asst mngr, railroads about Washington, cooperated with Hon. Solomon Foote to raise 1st VT CAV

Later Life: super. steamers on Lake Champlain, transcontinental railroads, most importantly Northern Pacific R.R., ret. to Lake Park, MN
Affiliations: Republican, M.E. Church
Married: (1) 1844, Elizabeth A. Chittenden; (2) 2 Nov 1858, Caroline A. Hopkins
Died: 20 Jan 1897; interment unknown
Papers: UVM
(FSO, JGU*)

Cargill, John D. (abt 1825-1883)

Born: abt 1825, Canada
Early Life: ordained Universalist clergyman 1851, Lenox NY 1850s, Woodstock VT 1860
War Service: CPL Co K 5th VT INF 16 Sep 1861, SGT Jun 1863, wdd Fredericksburg 5 Jun 1863, Chap. 29 Sep 1864, m/o 29 Jun 1865
Later Life: pastor, Camilla GA 1880
Married: Margaret (Nfi)
Died: 25 Sep 1883, Brewton AL; interment unknown
(1850, 1860, CLS, GGB, HWR)

Carpenter, Benjamin Walter (1836-1906)

Born: 31 Oct 1836, Randolph VT, son of Dr. Walter and Olivia Chase (Blodgett) Benjamin
Early Life: M.D. UVM 1857, demonstrator of anatomy UVM 1858-60
War Service: Asst SURG 2nd VT INF 11 Jun 1861, SURG 9th VT INF 21 Jun 1862; resgd 4 Nov 1864
Later Life: VT SURG Gen. 1867-70, physician, druggist
Affiliations: RSVO
Died: 20 Mar 1906, Burlington VT; interment in Greenmount Cemetery
(1850-1890, GGB, Gibson*, UVMCat3, WSR)

Carr, Anthony (1837-1918)

Born: 15 Apr 1837, Farnham, PQ, Canada, son of Peter and Nancy (Maloy) Carr
Early Life: farm laborer Ferrisburg VT 1860
War Service: PVT Co. I 1st VT INF 9 May 1861, m/o 15 Aug 1861, SGT Co. C 9th VT INF 9 Jul 1862, m/o 13 Jun 1865
Later Life: A.B. MC 1869, civil engr, Chicago, Michigan Lake Shore RR, St. Joe to Pentwater MI 1870-72, Tuscarawas Valley RR, Elyria OH Mar to Sep 1872, Pittsburg, Wheeling & Kentucky RR, Wheeling, WV 1872-73, Birmingham PA 1874-75, Pittsburg & Castle Shannon RR 1879, Thos. Scott & Jay Gould RR in Texas, M.K. & T., Fort Worth & Denver City, Texas Pacific East Line and Red RR, 1881-83, real estate business Wise Cty TX 1884-1900, Cinnabar Mining Co. Brewster Cty TX, inmate, VT Vets Home, unmarried
Died: 2 Jul 1918, Bennington VT; interment in Vermont Veterans Home Cemetery
(1860, AGO, MIDCat)

Carter, Henry Gray (1836-1896)

Born: 11 Oct 1836, Weston VT, son of Dr. Seneca and Mary (Gray) Carter
Early Life: moved to TX 1852
War Service: LT, 4th TX CAV (Tom Green's Brigade) CSA 1861, CPT 1862, wdd Pleasant Hill 9 Apr 1864
Later Life: banker, rancher, businessman
Married: 1864, Mary Cleopatra Williams
Affiliations: Confed.
Died: 2 Jun 1896, Marlin, TX; interment unknown

Notes: visited relatives in Vermont frequently after the war
(ACD, THC)

Chamberlin, Preston S. (1832-1916)

Born: 28 Nov 1832, Newbury VT, son of Abner and Mary (Haseltine) Chamberlin
Early Life: local schools, Newbury Sem., farmer, moved to Bradford
War Service: SGT Co. D 1st VT INF 2 May 1861, m/o 15 Aug 1861, CPT Co. H 12th VT INF 22 Sep 1862, m/o 14 Jul 1863
Later Life: farmer (sugar and fruit trees, cattle, sheep and horses), town offices, State Rep. 1890, trustee of Bradford Acad. 15 years
Affiliations: GAR, RSVO
Married: 17 Jan 1856, Hannah S. Corliss
Died: 27 Apr 1916; interment in Village Cemetery, Bradford VT
(HC3, JGU)

Chandler, Albert Brown (1840-1923)

Born: 20 Aug 1840, West Randolph, son of William Brown and Electa (Owen) Chandler
Early Life: bookseller, telegrapher, mngr, Western Union, Bellaire OH 1858, mngr, Pittsburgh OH 1859-63
War Service: cipher operator, USMTS, War Dept Washington, also disbursing clerk for Gen. T. T. Eckert, Dept of the Potomac
Later Life: chief clerk, Eastern Div., in charge of Trans-Atlantic cable traffic 1866, Super. 6th Dist. Eastern Div. 1869-75, asst gen. mngr, Atlantic and Pacific Telegraph Co. 1875-79, pres. of same 1879-82, treasurer, Western Union 1881, pres. Fuller Electrical Co. 1881-84, counsel, later receiver, Postal Telegraph and Cable Co., 1884-86, gen mngr United Lines Telegraph Co. 1887, pres. and gen mngr New York Quotation Co. 1890
Married: (1) 11 Oct 1864, Marilla Eunice Stedman; (2) 14 Dec 1910, Mildred Vivian
Died: 3 Feb 1923; interment in South View Cemetery, Randolph VT
(FAG, JGU, NYTObit, PCD*)

Chandler, Charles Marcellus (1827-1889)

Born: 1 Jul 1827, Tunbridge VT, son of Charles B. and Nancy Chandler
Early Life: HMS 1854; physician
War Service: Asst SURG, 6th VT INF 10 Oct 1861, SURG 29 Oct 1861; SURG in charge, II BGD II DIV VI Corps Hosp., Peninsula Campaign, SURG in charge, VI Corps Hosp., Hagerstown, MD fall/winter 1862, resgd 7 Oct 1863; Acting Asst SURG USV 1864-65, hosp. steamer *State of Maine*, Sloan US Gen. Hosp.
Later Life: physician, Montpelier; pension examiner
Affiliations: VT MS, AMA, RSVO
Married: 15 May 1860, Abby Hazen
Died: 19 Mar 1889, Montpelier VT; interment in Green Mount Cemetery
(AFS, FHB, GC, TFH, VTMS)

Chandler, George Cornelius (1831-1901)

Born: 16 Aug 1831, Tunbridge VT, son of Charles B. and Nancy Chandler
Early Life: merchant, Waterbury VT, lived 2-3 years in Lawrence, KS
War Service: Sutler, 2nd VT INF
Later Life: farmer, real estate broker
Married: (1) Apr 1843, Margaret R. Sears; (2) Alathea M. Smith
Died: 28 Sep 1901; interment unknown
(GC, VHS02)

Chapin, Cornelius Augustus (1838-1863)

Born: 1838, Williston VT, son of Horatio and Beulah (Bliss) Chapin
Early Life: MD UVM 1857
War Service: Asst SURG 6th VT INF, 8 Jul 1863, d. typhoid fever
Affiliations: Sigma Phi Fraternity
Died: 14 Sep 1863, New York NY; interment in East Cemetery, Williston VT
(FSO, GGB, JDM, SP)

Chase, Charles Monroe (1829-1902)

Born: 6 Nov 1829, Lyndon VT, son of Epaphras Bull and Louisa (Baldwin) Chase
Early Life: Lyndon Acad., St. Johnsbury Acad. and Meriden (NH) Acad., DC 1853, studied law, farmer's College, Cincinnati, atty, Sycamore, IL, 1857-63, music dir. and composer
War Service: BGD Band 13th IL INF 1861
Later Life: police magistrate, Sycamore, IL, newspaper editor KS, publisher Vermont Union, Lyndon, j.p., Lyndon, DNC delegate 1876, dir. Lyndon Nat. Bank & Savings Bank & Trust Co.
Affiliations: Democrat
Married: 15 Jun 1865, Mary E. Wells
Died: 1 Nov 1902; interment in Lyndon Center cemetery, Lyndon VT
Correspondence: KSHS
Publications: Editor's Run in New Mexico and Colorado (1882)
(DCN, JGU*)

Chesmore, Alwyn Harding (1837-1891)

Born: 17 Oct 1837, Warren VT, son of Alvah W. and Harriet (Thorn) Chesmore
Early Life: M.D. UVM 1860
War Service: Asst SURG 5th VT INF 25 Sep 1862, SURG 1 Mar 1863, m/o 15 Sep 1864
Later Life: State Sen. 1874, State Rep. 1886, pres. VT State Board of Health 1886-91
Affiliations: RSVO, VTMS
Died: 27 Jan 1891, Huntington VT; interment in Riverview Cemetery
(AGO, FSO, Italo*, RR, UVMMED)

Child, Willard Augustus (1828-1878)

Born: 16 Sep 1828, Pittsford VT, son of Willard and Catherine (Kent) Child
Early Life: sailor, CMC 1858, physician, Mooers NY
War Service: Asst SURG 1st VT INF 26 Apr 1861, m/o 15 Aug 1861, Asst SURG, 4th VT INF 15 Aug 1861, SURG 10th VT INF 6 Aug 1862, BGD SURG, m/o 22 Jun 1865
Later Life: physician, Mooers NY
Married: 28 Mar 1863, Emma Knapp
Died: Feb 1878, Pittsford VT; interment in Pittsford VT
(EC, EMH*, GGB)

Chittenden, Lucius Eugene (1824-1920)

Born: 24 May 1824, Williston VT, son of Giles and Betsey (Hollenbeck) Chittenden
Early Life: atty, politician, anti-slavery and Free Soil movement; Republican; State Sen. 1856-60
War Service: Peace Conf. delegate 1861; Registrar of Treasury 1861-64
Later Life: atty, author

Died: 22 Jul 1920, Burlington VT; interment in Lakeview Cemetery
Publications: A Report of the Debates and Proceedings in the Secret Sessions of the Conference Convention, for Proposing Amendments to the Constitution of the United States (1864), The Capture of Ticonderoga (1872), Recollections of President Lincoln and his Administration (1891), An Unknown Heroine, An Historical Episode of the War Between The States (1893), Personal Reminiscences 1840-1890 (1893), Abraham Lincoln's Speeches (1908), Lincoln and the Sleeping Sentinel, The True Story (1909)
(FAG, GGB, JGU, LOC*)

Churchill, Samuel Joseph – See Part I – Medal of Honor

Churchill, Sylvester (1783-1862)

Born: 2 Aug 1783 Woodstock VT, son of Joseph and Sarah (Cobb) Churchill
Early Life: editor and publisher of The Vermont Republican 1808, 1LT, 3rd US ARTY 12 Mar 1812, CPT 15 Aug 1813, AIG (MAJ) 29 Aug 1813, Bvt MAJ 15 Aug 1823, transferred to 1st US ARTY, MAJ, 3rd US ARTY, 6 Apr 1835, I.G. (COL), 25 Jun 1841, Bvt B.G. 23 Feb 1847
War Service: ret. 25 Sep 1861
Married: 30 Aug 1812, Lucy Hunter
Died: 7 Dec 1862 Washington, interment in Oak Hill Cemetery
Notes: Churchill Cty NV and Fort Churchill in Silver Springs NV named after him 1861
(CKG, FHC, FSO, RR)

Clark, Charles Edgar (1843-1922)

Born: 10 Aug 1843, Bradford VT, son of James Dayton and Mary (Sexton) Clark
Early Life: Midshipman, USNA, 29 Sep 1860
War Service: Midshipman's cruise, *John Adams* 1862, Midshipman's cruise, corvette *Macedonian* 1863, Ensign 1 Nov 1863, steam sloop *Ossipee* 1863-65
Later Life: steamer *Vanderbilt* 1865-68, LCDR, wrecked *Suwanee* 1868, West Indies Station 1868-70, instr. USNA 1870-73, ironclad *Dictator* 1875-77, shore duty 1878-81, CDR 15 Nov 1881, battleship *New Hampshire* 1882, screw steamer *Ranger*, conducting survey of west coast of Mexico and Central America 1883-86, shore duty 1886-94, screw sloop *Mohican* 1894-96, CPT 21 Jun 1896, battleship *Oregon*, bombardment of Santiago, Cuba 1898, Gov. Naval Home, Philadelphia 1901-04, RAdm 16 Jun 1902, pres. of Naval Examining and Retiring Board 1904-1905, ret. 10 Aug 1905
Affiliations: MOLLUS (#09210)
Died: 1 Oct 1922, San Diego CA; interment in Arlington National Cemetery
Correspondence: NYPL
Publications: My 50 Years in the Navy (1917)
(C&S, GFH*, SK, TJL2)

Clark, Francis Gary (1838-1920)

Born: 17 Apr 1838, Roxbury VT, son of Theophilus Flagg and Mary Ann (Taylor) Clark
Early Life: moved to Bridgewater 1843, common schools, South Woodstock Acad., Barre Acad. MC 1860, left to enlist
War Service: PVT Co. G 16th VT INF 28 Aug 1862, 2LT Co. F 26th NY CAV (Frontier Cavalry) 4 Jan 1865
Later Life: A.B. MC 1864, law student, Woodstock 1864-66, admitted to the bar 1866, atty, Belle Plain IA 1867-76, Cedar Rapids 1876, State Rep. 1872-73, member and pres. School Board, Alderman and Referee in Bankruptcy
Married: (1) 5 Sep 1865, Harriet Newell Newton; (2) 1 Sep 1896, Mary V. Loy
Died: 3 Feb 1920, Cedar Rapids IA; interment unknown
(MIDCat, TBP1)

Clark, John Wesley – See Part I - Medal of Honor

Clarke, Albert (1840-1911)

Born: 13 Oct 1840, Granville VT, son of Jedediah and Mary (Woodbury) Clarke (Twin of Almon Clarke, q.v.)
Early Life: public schools, West Randolph Acad., Barre Acad., atty, Montpelier, Rochester
War Service: 1SGT Co. I 13th VT INF 25 Aug 1862, 1LT Co. G 22 Jan 1861, m/o 21 Jul 1863
Later Life: atty Rochester, St. Albans, editor, St. Albans Messenger, publisher 1870-80, Washington, 1 yr, moved to Boston 1881, journalist, pres. Vermont & Canada R.R., editor Rutland Herald, State Sen. 1874, MA RNC delegate 1892, COL, Staff of Gov. Paul Dillingham.
Affiliations: GAR, MOLLUS (#05950), RSVO, Vermont Veteran Assoc
Married: 21 Jan 1864, Josephine Briggs
Died: 16 Jul 1911; interment unknown
(C&S, FSO, JGU*)

Clarke, Almon (1840-1904)

Born: 13 Oct 1840, Granville VT, son of Jedediah and Mary (Woodbury) Clarke (Twin of Albert Clarke (q.v.)
Early Life: CMC, MD UMI 1862
War Service: Asst SURG, 10th VT INF, 11 Aug 1862, SURG 1st VT CAV 6 Mar 1865, m/o 9 Aug 1865
Later Life: physician, Thetford VT, Sheboygan WI, Cty Insane Asylum 1866-79, Commissioner of Pensions 1877, SURG, WI Soldiers' Home 1895-1904
Married: 1868, Emma J. Adams
Affiliations: WI MS, AMA, MOLLUS (#08086)
Died: May 1904, Wauwatosa WI; interment unknown
(C&S, EMH, SCW)

Clarke, Dayton Perry - See Part I – Medal of Honor

Cleveland, James P., Jr. (1828-1908)

Born: 21 Sep 1828, Bethel VT, son of James P. and Anna P. (Huntington) Cleveland
Early Life: moved to Braintree in 1845, farmer
War Service: 1LT Co. F 12th VT INF, 11 Sep 1862, resgd 27 Feb 1863
Later Life: farmer, moved to West Randolph in 1880, insurance agent
Affiliations: Republican, IOOF, Mason, GAR, RSVO
Married: 3 Aug 1850, Martha Flint
Died: 29 Apr 1908; interment in Randolph VT
(AGO, JGU*)

Closson, Henry Whitney (1832-1917)

Born: 16 Jun 1832, Whitingham VT, son of Henry and Emily (Whitney) Closson
Early Life: USMA 1854 (8/46), 2LT 1st ARTY 1 Jul 1854, frontier duty CA 1854-55, frontier duty TX 1856, 1LT 1st ARTY 31 Oct 1856, Seminole War 1857, garrison duty 1858-59, frontier duty TX 1860-61
War Service: CPT 1st US ARTY 14 May 1861, Ft. Pickens FL May 1861-May 1862, Chief of ARTY Dist. of Pensacola, 16 May-24 Dec 1862, Btry Cmdr, Baton Rouge, 27 Dec 1862-13 Mar 1863, Chief of ARTY XVIIII Corps, 13 Mar-Aug 1863, Bvt MAJ (Port Hudson) 8 Jul 1863, Chief of ARTY XVIIII Corps, 4 Oct 1863-31 Jul 1864, Chief of ARTY Mobile expedition Aug 1864, Bvt LTCOL 23 Aug 1864, Chief of ARTY CAV Corps, Mid Mil Div, 1 Nov-31 Dec 1864, Btry Cmdr, Winchester VA Apr-Jul 1865
Later Life: garrison duty 1865-66, MAJ 5th US ARTY 1 Nov 1876, LTCOL 14 Sep 1883, COL 4th US ARTY 25 Apr 1888, ret. 16 Jun 1896, B.G. (ret. list) 23 Apr 1904
Married: 5 Oct 1857, Olivia Adelaide Burke
Died: 16 Jul 1917, Washington D.C; interment in Arlington National Cemetery

(GWC, JAB, WHP)

Coburn, Joseph Leander (1809-1890)

Born: 1809 VT, son of Joseph Coburn
Early Life: USMA 1834 (26/36), Bvt 2LT 3rd US INF, 1 Jul 1834, Florida 1834-36, sick leave 1836-38, 1LT 7 Jul 1838, A.G. office, Washington 1838-43, Jefferson Barracks, MO 1843-44, Ft. Jessup, LA 1844-45, CPT 1845, military occupation of Texas until resignation 18 May 1846, agent for US Subsistence Dept, Texas 1846-51, farmer, Matagorda Island TX 1851-57
War Service: civilian employee Subsistence and QM Departments, Chicago 1861-65, ACS (CPT) USV 1864, Bvt MAJ 11 Nov 1865 (service), m/o 22 Nov 1865
Later Life: govt employee working on Chicago harbor improvements 1867-68. Chicago, 1870
Died: 9 Sep 1890, Chicago IL; interment unknown
(1870, FSO, GWC, WPG2)

Coffey, Robert John – See Part I – Medal of Honor

Colburn, Amanda M. (1833-1893)

Born: 12 Nov 1833, West Dover VT, daughter of Ira and Celana (Cicso) Colburn
War Service: Nurse, hosp. matron, 3rd VT INF, 5 Jul 1861, dropped from rolls Dec 1861, but stayed in the field; Women's Nursing Bureau May 1864 dis Jun 1865
Later Life: govt pension by Special Act of Congress 3 Mar 1891
Married: (1) c1853, Albert Farnham; (2) 16 Dec 1865 Marshall P. Felch
Died: 31 Dec 1893; interment in Greenwood Pioneer Cemetery, Canon City, CO
(FAG, JAL, MAH*)

Colburn, Daniel L. C. (1834-1877)

Born: 1834, Fairfield VT, son of Daniel and Anna (Wells) Colburn
Early Life: MD UVM 1862
War Service: Asst SURG, 5th VT INF, 18 Aug 1863, m/o 29 Jun 1865
Later Life: unknown
Married: 2 Mar 1865, Ruth Cordelia Royce (his 1st cousin)
Died: 6 Jun 1877, Baraboo WI; interment in Walnut Hill Cemetery
(FAG, UVMMED)

Collamer, Jacob (1791-1865)

Born: 8 Jan 1791, Troy NY, son of Samuel and Elizabeth (Van Orman) Collamer
Early Life: moved to Burlington 1795, UVM 1810, War of 1812, admitted to the bar 1813, atty 1813-33, State Rep. 1821-22, 1827-28, State's Atty 1822-24, superior court judge 1833-42, 1850-54, US Rep. 1843-49
War Service: US Sen. 1855-65
Affiliations: Republican
Married: 15 Jul 1817, Mary N. Stone
Died: 9 Nov 1865; Woodstock VT; interment in Riverside Cemetery
(CB, FSO, HGW; LOC*)

Colvocoresses, George Musalas (1816-1872)

Born: 22 Oct 1816, Chios, Greece, son of Constantine and Franka (Grimaldi) Colvocoresses

Early Life: Midshipman USN 1832; *United States*, Mediterranean Squadron 1836-37; Passed Midshipman 1838; *Porpoise, Peacock, Vincennes*, Oregon, Wilkes Exploration Expedition 1838-42; LT 7 Dec 1843; *Shark*, Pacific Squadron, Mexican-American War 1846; Mediterranean Squadron 1847-49; African coast 1851-52; shore duty, New York 1853-55; XO, *Levant*, East India Squadron 1855; Portsmouth Navy Yard 1858-61
War Service: storeship Supply 1861-63; sloop Saratoga 1863-65;
Later Life: St. Mary's, Pacific Squadron 1865-66; CAPT 11 Jan 1867, ret.; businessman
Died: 3 Jun 1872, Bridgeport, CT (murdered); interment in East Burying Ground, Litchfield CT
Publications: Four Years in a Government Exploring Expedition (1853)
(TJL2, WAE*)

Colvocoresses, George Partridge (1847-1932)

Born: 3 Apr 1847, Norwich VT, son of CAPT George M. and Eliza Freelon (Halsey) Colvocoresses
War Service: two years as captain's clerk on *Supply* and *Saratoga*, his father's ships, Midshipman, 28 Sep 1864
Later Life: USNA 4 Jun 1869, flagship, South Atlantic Station, *Lancaster*, then *Portsmouth* 1869-71, Ensign 12 Jul 1870, Master 18 Jun 1872, *Hartford* and *Lackawanna*, Asiatic Station 1872-75, LT, 1 Jul 1875, Hydrographic Office, Washington, *Gettysburg*, *Enterprise*, European Station 1876-79, Hydrographic Office 1879-82, *Hartford* 1882-84, *Saratoga* 1884-86, instr. USNA 1886-90, XO, *Enterprise* 1890-91, *Concord*, South Atlantic Station 1891-93, instr. USNA 1893-97, LCDR 4 Jun 1897, XO, *Concord*, Manila Bay, honorary M.A. NU 1898, CDR 30 Jun 1900, assisted in publication of Official Navy Records from Civil war 1899-01, commanding *Lancaster* 1901-03, shore duty in New York 1903-04, Commandant, Naval Station Key West 1904-05, CAPT Jan 1905, Commandant, USNA, 1905-07, ret. Jun 1907 as RAdm. after 45 years of service
Died: 10 Sep 1932, Litchfield, CT; interment in New East Cemetery
(TJL2, WAE*)

Conline, John (1844-1916)

Born: 9 Feb 1844, Rutland VT, son of Thomas and Mary (Cunningham) Conline
War Service: PVT Co. E 1st VT INF 9 May 1861, m/o 15 Aug 1861, PVT Co. E 4th VT INF 12 Apr 1862, m/o 5 Sep 1863 to accept appointment to USMA (from GA)
Later Life: USMA in 1863, dis 1868, reinstated 1868, graduated 1870 (54/59), 2LT 9th US CAV (Buffalo Soldiers), 1LT 1875, Bvt CPT 1880, CPT 1887, served in TX, LA, NM, DC, NE, ret. 25 Feb 1891, in charge of the "Pingree Potato Farms" in Detroit 1896, Detroit Police Commissioner 1896-1900, moved to Washington 1910, traveled to Europe 1913-14
Affiliations: Mason, MOLLUS (#4926)
Married: (1) 1872, Emma Jane Leland (divorced 1879); (2) 1 Sep 1887, Fannie Strickland
Died: 16 Oct 1916, Washington DC; interment in Arlington National Cemetery VA (Section 2 #1183)
Publications: Recollections of the Battle of Antietam and the Maryland Campaign (1897), Report of Agricultural Committee, Detroit, Michigan, of the Cultivation of Idle Land by the Poor and Unemployed (1896), The Campaign of 1880 Against Victorio (1903)
(C&S, CLK, CLL*, GWC1, FBH, FSO, WHP)

Conn, Granville Priest (1832-1916)

Born: 25 Jan 1832, Hillsboro NH, son of William and Sally (Priest) Conn
Early Life: WMC 1855, M.D. DC 1856; physician, East Randolph 1856-61
War Service: Asst SURG 12th VT INF 19 Sep 1862, m/o 14 Jul 1863
Later Life: physician, Concord NH 1864-81, pres. NH Board of Health, US Board of Pension Examiners, SURG, Boston & Maine R.R., prof. of Hygiene, DC, member NH Railroad Commission
Affiliations: Mason, GAR, AMA, VTMS, NH MS, NH Hist. Soc., APHA, SCW
Married: 25 May 1859, Helen M. Sprague
Died: 24 Mar 1916; interment in Wayne, PA

Publications: Observations Upon the Importance and means of Ventilation (1882), Railway Hygiene 1890, Prevention and Cure of Disease (1891), Notes on Sanitary Conditions of Mexico (1894), Report of the Committee on Car Sanitation (1896), History of the New Hampshire Surgeon in the War of the Rebellion (1906)
(WAE*)

Connor, Seldon (1839-1917)

Born: 25 Jan 1839, Fairfield ME
Early Life: Tufts College 1859; moved to VT; atty
War Service: PVT 1st VT INF 2 May 1861; m/o 15 Aug 1861; LTCOL 7th ME INF 22 Aug 1861; COL 19th ME INF 11 Jan 1864; B.G. USV 11 Jun 1864; m/o 7 Apr 1866
Later Life: IRS collector; ME ADJ, militia; Gov. ME 1876-79; US pension agent; banker
Affiliations: MOLLUS (#02390)
Died: 9 Jul 1917, Augusta ME; interment in Forest Grove Cemetery
Correspondence: 1861 and 18 Oct 1864, USAMHI
(C&S, CLL*, E&E, FBH, MOLLUS, RR)

Converse, George Albert (1844-1909)

Born: 13 May 1844, Norwich VT, son of Shubael and Luvia (Morrill) Converse
Early Life: Norwich public schools 1852-58, NU 1861
War Service: USNA 1865; steam sloop *Canandaigua*, European Station 1865-68; ENS 1 Dec 1866; *Frolic* 1868; Master 12 Mar 1868, LT 26 Mar 1869; Torpedo Service, *Colorado, Lackawanna, Hartford,* Asiatic Station 1869-71; Torpedo Service 1874-77; LCDR 12 Jul 1878; *Marion*, European Station 1878-79; sick leave 1879-81; *Lancaster*, European Station 1883-85; Torpedo Station 1885-89; CDR Mar 1889; screw sloop *Enterprise* 1890-91; Bureau of Ordnance 1891-92; Torpedo Station, 1893-97; cruiser *Montgomery*, North Atlantic Squadron 1897-99; witness at court of inquiry on loss of *USS Maine* in Cuba 1898; CAPT 3 Mar 1899; bureau of navigation 1899-1901; New Orleans Naval Station 1901-03; RADM 21 Oct 1903; Bureau of Equipment and Recruiting 1903-04; Bureau of Ordnance 1904; Bureau of Navigation 1904-06; ret. 13 May 1906; pres. Board on Construction 1907-08
Died: 29 Mar 1909, Washington D.C; interment in Arlington National Cemetery (Section East, Site 937)
Notes: Considered one of the ablest officers in the Navy, and well known as an expert on ordnance, especially torpedoes, RADM Converse was one of the first officers involved in the introduction of electricity aboard men-of-war, and pioneered in experimentation with and the introduction of smokeless powder in the Navy
(TJL2, WAE*)

Cook, John Bray (1836-1919)

Born: 3 Jul 1836, Greensboro VT, son of Charles, Jr., and Caroline (Huntington) Cook
Early Life: public schools, St. Johnsbury and Barre Acad., farmer, moved to IA 1861
War Service: PVT Co. A 14th IA INF Oct 1861, fought Indians in Dakota Terr.
Later Life: moved to Greensboro VT, held several town offices, j.p., pres. Library Assoc 1883
Affiliations: Republican, Congregational, Caledonia Grange
Married: 14 Nov 1865, Katharine Kallamyer
Died: 2 Sep 1919; interment in Greensboro VT
(AGO, JGU, PDW)

Copeland, John Wesley (1840-1919)

Born: 17 Jun 1840, Moretown VT, son of Rev. Edmund and Mary Ann (Gladding) Copeland
Early Life: public schools, Barre Acad., Montpelier Acad., Newbury Sem.
War Service: CPL Co. F 12th VT INF 22 Aug 1862, m/o 14 Jul 1863

Later Life: M.D. UVM 1866, general practitioner Lyndonville, dir. Lyndonville National Bank 1889-1901, dir. Lyndonville Savings Bank, trustee Cobleigh Public Library, town health officer 25 years, village trustee
Affiliations: Independent, Congregational, GAR, Mason
Married: (1) 10 Nov 1868, Martha Augusta Sanborn; (2) 29 Mar 1904, Regina A. McLean
Died: 8 Apr 1919, Lyndon VT; interment in Lyndon Center Cemetery
(AFS, AGO)

Corbin, Job (1834-1915)

Born: 23 Nov 1834, South Hero VT, son of David and Rebecca A. (Atkins) Corbin
Early Life: Burlington H.S., M.D. UVM 1859, King Co. Hosp. 1859-61
War Service: Asst SURG USN 9 May 1861, Passed Asst SURG 26 Oct 1861, SURG USN 9 Mar 1864, resgd 9 May 1867
Later Life: physician, Brooklyn NY
Affiliations: Kings Cty MS, MOLLUS (#06958)
Married: 16 May 1867, Maria Louisa Weaver
Died: 14 Jun 1915, Brooklyn NY; interment unknown
Publications: articles relative to Diphtheria, NY Medical Journal (1888)
(C&S, TJL2, UVMMED)

Coughlin, John – See Part I – Medal of Honor

Cowdin, Robert J. (1805-1874)

Born: 18 Sep 1805 Jamaica VT, son of Angier and Abbie Cowdin
Early Life: Lumber business, MA State Militia
War Service: COL 1st MA INF 25 May 1861, cmdg BGD Oct 1861-Feb 1862, B.G. 1 Oct 1862, appointment not confirmed by Congress and expired 4 Mar 1863, relieved 30 Mar 1863
Later Life: Served on Common Council and Board of Alderman, Boston, MA
Married: 5 Oct 1832, Sara Dana Bugbee
Died: 9 Jul 1874, Boston MA; interment in Mt. Auburn Cemetery, Cambridge MA (Asphodel Path, Lot 2921)
(OAR, WAE*, WRC1)

Cram, Dewitt Clinton (1825-1903)

Born: Nov 1825, Andover VT, son of Caleb and Sarah (Hadley) Cram
Early Life: Chester Acad., DC 1850, teacher, school principal, atty
War Service: Indian Campaign, Missouri River 1863-65, CPT 6th IA CAV, 31 Jan 1863, MAJ 23 Oct 1864, Bvt LTCol, Bvt COL 13 Mar 1865, m/o 17 Oct 1865
Later Life: atty, Dubuque city School Board 1875-81, US District Atty, Asst US District Atty, Northern Dist. of IA 1882-1903
Married: 15 Sep 1858, Emily Edwards or 22 Oct 1851, Sarah A. Hutchins
Died: 18 Apr 1903, Dubuque, IA; interment in Linwood Cemetery
Notes: Known as the "Blind Lawyer" in IA, as he lost his eyesight a number of years after the war, but continued to practice law
(1900, DCI, EH, MDE)

Crandall, John Bradley (1839-aft 1904)

Born: 21 Feb 1839, Duxbury VT, son of Daniel Burnett and Lydia (Bailey) Crandall
Early Life: Barre Acad., UVM 1863
War Service: Hosp. Stew. 6th VT INF 15 Oct 1861, Asst SURG 13th VT INF 7 Oct 1863, m/o 21 Jul 1863, later Baxter Gen Hosp. 1864 and Sloan Gen Hosp. 1865-66

Later Life: P.G. study at CPS NYU, Asst SURG, USA, Dept of MO 1866-68, Pension Examining Board, health officer, Med. Examiner several Insurance Companies, Sec'y Rock River Valley MS
Affiliations: IL MS, Sterling Club, GAR, MOLLUS (#12716), RSVO
Married: 1869, Eliza J. Fluelling
Died: after 17 Aug 1904; interment in Sterling Cemetery, Whiteside Cty IL
(C&S, FSO, UVMMED, WWD)

Crandall, Richard Bailey (1837-1864)

Born: 14 Aug 1837, Duxbury VT, son of Daniel Burnett and Lydia (Bailey) Crandall
Early Life: Barre Acad. 1854-59, DC 1859-61, left to enlist
War Service: ADJ 6th VT INF 10 Oct 1861, CPT Co. K 1 Nov 1862, MAJ 18 Mar 1863, kia Cold Harbor
Died: 7 Jun 1864, Cold Harbor VA; interment in Berlin Corners Cemetery, Berlin VT
Notes: Barre GAR Post #56 named after him
Diary: VHS (1864)
(DC63, FSO, GGK)

Crooker, Lucien Bonaparte (1840-1926)

Born: 12 Nov 1840, Pomfret VT, son of Orasmus and Salana Crooker
Early Life: teacher
War Service: PVT 12th IL INF, 26 Aug 1861, 1SGT Co I 55th IL INF, 1LT, 5 Mar 1862, wdd, Shiloh Apr 1862, CPT Co. I 1 Jul 1862, Co F 29 Dec 1862, wdd, Vicksburg, 19 May 1863, resgd due to wds, 3 Aug 1863
Later Life: atty, police magistrate, mayor, Mendota, IL, State Rep. 1876-80, Federal Revenue Collector, Aurora District, IL 1881-87
Married: 1866, Annette E. Wirick
Died: 14 Oct 1926, Mendota IL; interment in Restland Cemetery
(55IL, JMP, UJH)

Cross, Lewis Bartlett (1839-1915)

Born: 9 Aug 1839, Montpelier VT, son of Charles Harrison and Caroline Webster (Houston) Cross
Early Life: Fort Edward and Newbury Seminaries; baker's apprentice
War Service: enrolled but not mustered due to illness, later sutler of 3rd VT INF, served one year
Later Life: C. H. Cross & son 1863-98, sold business in 1908; RNC delegate 1880, Presidential elector 1896-7, trustee & v.p Montpelier Savings Bank and Trust Co.
Affiliations: Republican, Appolo Club, Country Club of Montpelier, Mason, SAR
Married: 25 Dec 1862, Lucia A. Chaplin
Died: 18 Jul 1915, Montpelier VT; interment in Green Mountain Cemetery
(PCD, VHS16, WRC1)

Cummings, Ephraim Chamberlain (1825-1897)

Born: 2 Sep 1825, Albany ME, son of Francis P. and Lois (Chamberlain) Cummings
Early Life: Student, North Yarmouth Acad., ME 1841, Bowdoin College 1853, Professor, Bowdoin 1855, BTS 1857, Pastor, North Church, St. Johnsbury VT, 10 May 1860
War Service: Chap. 15th VT INF 26 Sep 1862 - 5 Aug 1863
Later Life: missionary Asia 1863-64, Europe 1869-71, prof. of Mental and Moral Philosophy Bowdoin Coll. 1873, minister Portland ME 1880, trustee Portland Public Library
Married: 18 Oct 1866, Annie Louise Pomeroy
Died: 14 Dec 1897; interment unknown

Publications: <u>A Man in Christ.</u> (1865), <u>Birth and Baptism: Discourses of First Principles.</u> (1873), <u>Nature in Scripture: A Study of Bible Verification in the Range of Common Experience.</u> (1887)
(1880, AGC, FSO, CCM, TBC)

Cummings, William G. (1839-1911)

Born: 3 Mar 1839, Barnet VT, son of Joseph Cummings
Early Life: Peacham Acad., DC 1859-61, left to enlist
War Service: 2LT, Co D 1st VT CAV, 15 Oct 1861, 1LT, 30 Oct 1862, pow Annandale VA, 25 Dec 1862, Libby Prison 28 Dec 1862, prld 5 May 1863, CPT 1 Jun 1863, wdd Stony Creek 28 Jun 1864, MAJ 22 Oct 1864, Bvt COL 13 Mar 1865, LTCol 23 May 1865, COL (Never mustered) 25 Jun 1865, m/o 9 Aug 1865
Later Life: US Customs official, Island Pond VT 1867-70, moved to IA 1871, coal & ice business IA 1871-93
Affiliations: RSVO
Married: Cora Pinney
Died: 11 May 1911, Kansas City MO; interment unknown
(CCI, FPW)

Currier, John Winnick (1835-1909)

Born: 5 Apr 1835, North Troy VT, son of John Winnick and Mary (Elkins) Currier
Early Life: "little red schoolhouse," cotton mills, Palmer MA, jeweler, Holyoke MA, wholesale jewelry store, Boston, 1854, Springfield City Guards 1854
War Service: civilian employee Springfield Arsenal, SGT Co. F 10th MA INF 31 May 1861, ADJ 1st VA Vols 26 Nov 1862, Add'l Paymr USV 14 Jan 1863 (declined), accepted position as trade agent AOP, for furnishing military clothing and equipments, City Point VA, Paymr Gen. AOP Jun 1864, served until end of war
Later Life: moved to North Troy 1871, farmer, wintered in Boston or on his Southern plantation, town offices, State Rep. 1878, 1882, U.S. Deputy Marshal 1893-97, livestock breeder and dealer, lumber and flouring mills, interests in R.R. construction
Affiliations: Democrat, Episcopal, GAR, RSVO, Orleans Cty Vets Assoc, Mason
Married: 9 Nov 1866, Eveline Chamberlain
Died: 1909; interment unknown
(ASR, HC2, JGU)

Currier, Samuel Hammond (1835-1895)

Born: 6 Jun 1835, Norwich VT, son of Samuel Quimby and Mahala (Blaisdell) Currier
Early Life: Thetford Acad., NU 1852, DC, M.D. UVM 1857, physician Shelburne 1857-61
War Service: Asst SURG 8th VT INF
Later Life: physician Norwich VT, State Rep. 1880-81
Affiliations: Republican, Mason, GAR
Married: (1) 16 May 1858, Abbie Kimball Hersey; (2) 21 Sep 1871, Emily H. Hersey
Died: 25 May 1895, Norwich VT; interment unknown
(UVMMED, WAE)

Curtis, Edward Malcolm (1840-1874)

Born: 16 Feb 1840, Warren VT, son of H. and Elizabeth Curtis
Early Life: B.S. UVM 1862
War Service: PVT Co. H 1st VT INF 2 May 1862 - 15 Aug 1861; Hosp. Stew. 4th VT INF 21 Sep 1861, Asst SURG 6th VT INF 29 Jan 1863, SURG 24 Oct 1864, m/o 13 Jul 1865
Later Life: moved to NY, moved to CO for health 1870, moved to Sacramento CA 1871, traveled to Australia

Died: 12 May 1874; interment in Lakeview Cemetery, Burlington VT
(CMS, FSO, UVMMED)

Cushman, Henry Theodore (1844-1922)

Born: 16 May 1844, Bennington VT, son of John and Sophronia (Hurd) Cushman
Early Life: Bennington Acad
War Service: QM SGT 4th VT INF 1 Mar 1862, QM (1LT) 29 Jan 1863, m/o 30 Sep 1864
Later Life: H. T. Cushman Manufacturing 1865-1910, pr. Village of North Bennington 1895-1911, State Sen. 1910, VT Soldiers Home trustee Bennington
Affiliations: MOLLUS (#09186), GAR, VHS
Married: 4 Oct 1867, Eliza Davis Hall
Died: 11 May 1922, Bennington VT; interment in Village Cemetery
Notes: probably the youngest Quartermaster in the Union army
(1910, AGO, C&S, GFH, JGU, PCD)

Cutting, Oliver B. (1837-1924)

Born: 12 Sep 1837, Concord VT, son of Franklin and Prudence (Isham) Cutting
Early Life: teacher, farm laborer, Concord 1860
War Service: PVT Co. A 11th VT INF 20 Aug 1864, wdd Cedar Creek 19 Oct 1864, m/o 22 May 1865
Later Life: druggist, Concord 1870-1920, postmaster Concord 1877-85, book dealer, State Rep. 1900, Asst judge, Essex Cty VT 1904-10
Affiliations: Republican, Mason, GAR
Married: (1) 1865, Lavina Powers; (2) 1872, Lois B. Robinson
Died: 16 Jan 1924, Concord VT, interment in Village Cemetery
(1860, 1870, 1880, 1890, 1900, 1910, 1920, AGO, FSO, PCD)

Caldwell, John C.

Canfield, Thomas H.

Carpenter, Benjamin W.

Chandler, Albert B.

Chase, Charles M.

Chesmore, Alwyn H.

Chittenden, Lucius E.

Clark, Charles E.

Clarke, Almon

Cleveland, James P.

Colburn, Amanda

Colburn, Daniel

Collamer, Jacob

Colvocoresses, George M.

Colvocoresses, George P.

Conline, John

Connor, Seldon

Conn, Granville P.

Converse, George A.

Cowdin, Robert J.

Currier, John W.

Cushman, Henry T.

DDDDD

Damon, George Bowen (1835-1885)

Born: 31 Mar 1835, Hatley, PQ, Canada, son of Dr. George and Lucy J. (Burt) Damon
Early Life: law studies in Montpelier VT, Poughkeepsie NY and Wells River VT, admitted to the Caledonia Cty Bar, 8 Dec 1858, admitted to the IL Bar 3 Oct 1859, atty, Chicago IL 1859-60, atty, Bradford VT 1860-61
War Service: CPT Co G 10th VT INF 12 Aug 1862, JAG, div. staff for Gens Carr, James B. Ricketts, and Seymour, Bvt MAJ 19 Oct 1864, MAJ 19 Dec 1864, LTCOL 2 Jan 1865, Bvt COL 2 Apr 1865, COL 15 Jun 1865, m/o 28 Jun 1865
Later Life: admitted to Ohio Bar, 6 Jan 1866, atty, Cincinnati OH, 1866, agent for Cincinnati, Boston and NYC publishing companies 1866-85
Married: Feb 1859, Susan Underwood
Died: 20 Apr 1885, Des Moines, IA; interment unknown
(EMH*, HC3)

Dana, Samuel Jackson (1833-1926)

Born: 18 May 1833, Warren VT, son of Samuel and Calista (Pastor) Dana
Early Life: carpenter, Fayston VT 1860, insurance agent
War Service: PVT Co B 13th VT INF 10 Oct 1862, wdd Gettysburg 3 Jul 1863, m/o 21 Jul 1863
Later Life: farmer Fayston 1870, State Rep. 1872, carpenter Fayston 1880, S. J. & H. W. Dana Co., Shingle Manufacturers, Fayston 1900, Asst judge Washington Cty 1902-04, farmer Fayston 1910, town offices 30 years (Town clerk, j.p., treasurer)
Affiliations: Republican
Married: (1) 5 Oct 1853, Adeline White Benton; (2) 10 Jan 1888, Miranda W. Davis (3) 27 Feb 1894, Mary Jane Fisher (4) 23 Jul 1910, Mrs. Hattie E. Richardson
Died: 15 Mar 1926, Fayston VT; interment in Irasville Cemetery
Notes: one of six Dana brothers who served in the war
(1860, 1870, 1880, 1890, 1900, 1910, 1920, EED, AGO, PCD)

Darling, Joseph Kimball (1833-1910)

Born: 8 Mar 1833, Corinth VT, son of Jesse and Rebecca (Whitaker) Darling
Early Life: local schools, farmer, Corinth Acad., moved to CA, mining and surveying 1853-61, returned to Corinth VT, farmer
War Service: PVT Co. H 12th VT INF 4 Oct 1862, m/o 14 Jul 1863
Later Life: mercantile pursuits, postmaster East Corinth 1864-71, admitted to the bar 1874, removed to Chelsea 1884, State's Atty 1882, dpy clerk Cty Courts, State Rep. 1890-94, super. and teacher Sabbath school 20 years
Affiliations: Republican, Congregationalist, GAR,
Married: (1) 6 Oct 1859, Mary Alice Knight; (2) Emma Webster (3) Mary A. Dow
Died: 25 Oct 1910, Corinth VT; interment in Old East Corinth Cemetery
(AFS, AGO, JGU*)

Dartt, Justus N. (1836-1915)

Born: 17 Feb 1836, Weathersfield VT, son of Erastus and Rebecca (Jackson) Dartt
Early Life: Wesleyan Sem., Newbury Sem., teacher, Springfield VT 1854, farm Laborer, Weathersfield 1860
War Service: 2LT Co D 9th VT INF 25 Jun 1862, pow Winchester 3 Sep 1862, prld 15 Sep 1862, resgd 13 Nov 1862
Later Life: merchant, Springfield 1870, State Rep. 1874-76, 1878-82, 1902-06, 1910-12, State Sen. 1882, teacher and school super. 1880-88, trustee, Vermont State Agricultural College 1879-85, super. of schools, Conway and Gardner MA 1889-91 VT Super. of Education 1888-96, farmer Springfield 1900-10, trustee Bennington Soldiers' Home 1906-12

Affiliations: Republican, Congregational, GAR, Mason
Married: 13 Oct 1859, Abbie Patton Knight
Died: 1 Aug 1915, Springfield VT; interment in Summer Hill Cemetery
Publications: History of the Town of Springfield, Vermont (1895) with C. Horace Hubbard
(1860, 1870, 1880, 1890, 1900, 1910, AGO, CHH*, PCD, TLB, TPG, UVMCat)

Davis, George Evans – See Part I – Medal of Honor

Davis, George Franklin (1815-1901)

Born: 20 Dec 1815, Springfield VT, son of John Davis
Early Life: Cavendish Acad; hotel keeper/banker 1838-53), State Sen. 1849-60, QM Gen. 1857-64
War Service: VT Q.M. Gen. (relieved by Perley Pitkin Nov 1864)
Later Life: farmer Cavendish 1870-1900
Married: Bertia (nfi)
Died: 27 Feb 1901, Cavendish VT; interment in Cavendish Cemetery
Notes: Instrumental in purchase and construction of military hospitals in Brattleboro, Burlington and Montpelier. Oversaw deployment of all Vermont's troops to the war.
(1870, 1880, 1900, AGO, FSO, Gibson*, RR)

Davis, Henry Greene (1819-1898)

Born: 5 Jun 1819, Goshen VT, son of Joseph Cortland and Dorothy (Maynard) Davis
Early Life: farmer Concord IN 1850, Jefferson IN 1860, lumberman
War Service: 1LT 29th IN INF 27 Aug 1861; CPT 1 Mar 1862; LTCOL 101st USCI 2 Sept 1864; Bvt COL and B.G. USV 13 Mar 1865, m/o 21 Jan 1866
Later Life: Munro MI 1890
Married: Cynthia (nfi)
Died: 26 Aug 1898, Forest Glen MD; interment in Pine Hill Cemetery, Cheboygan, MI
(1850, 1860, 1890, E&E, FBH)

Davis, Thomas Treadwell (1810-1872)

Born: 22 Aug 1810, Middlebury VT, son of Henry and Hanna (Phoenix) Davis
Early Life: moved to NY 1817, Clinton (NY) Acad., Hamilton College 1831, admitted to the bar 1833, atty, Syracuse NY
War Service: US Rep. 1863-67, favored conscription, higher taxes, railroad legislation
Later Life: atty, Syracuse NY
Married: 1837, Sarah Matilda Henry
Died: 2 May 1872, Washington D.C.; interment in Oakwood Cemetery
(CB, FSO, HGW)

Day, Hannibal (1804-1891)

Born: 17 Feb 1804, Montpelier VT, son of Dr. Sylvester Day
Early Life: pow with his father during War of 1812, USMA 1823 (23/35), 2LT, 2nd US INF 1 Jul 1823, garrison duty 1823-31, 1LT, 2nd US INF 4 Apr 1832, Black Hawk Expedition 1832, garrison duty 1832-36, recruiting service 1836-38, Seminole War 1838-39, CPT 2nd US INF 7 Jul 1838, sick leave 1839-41, Seminole War 1841-42, garrison duty 1842-46, Mexican-American War 1846-47, recruiting service 1847-48, frontier duty CA 1848-53, MAJ 2nd US INF 23 Feb 1852, frontier duty 1854-61, LTCOL, 2nd US INF 25 Feb 1861
War Service: 2nd US INF Washington Aug-Dec 1861, recruiting service Dec 1861-Jun 1863, cmdg 1 BGD 2 Div V Corps, AOP, Pennsylvania Campaign, ret. 1 Aug 1863, Bvt B.G. 13 Mar 1865

Later Life: Military Commissions and Courts Martial, 1864-69
Married: 1831, Anna Maria Houghton
Died: 25 Mar 1891, Morristown, NJ; interment in Evergreen Cemetery, Leominster, MA
Notes: son of Dr. Sylvester Day, Asst SURG, USA
(FAG, GWC, WPG2)

Dayton, Durell Williams (1826-1909)

Born: 17 Oct 1826, Poughkeepsie NY
Early Life: Troy Conf. M.E. Church 1851, pastor in Williston and Middlebury
War Service: Chap. 2nd VT INF 18 Aug 1862 - 6 Jan 1863, apptd. again 10 Mar 1863 and 9 Oct 1863, but not accepted
Later Life: pastor in Burlington VT, Gloversville, Albany, and Saratoga NY, Amsterdam NH, Fairhaven VT, Fort Plain NY, Fairhaven VT and Shelburne VT
Married: (1) 17 Sep 1845, Clarinda Benton, 22 Oct 1856; (2) Jane Ann Doud
Died: 22 Jun 1909, Rensselaer NY; interment in Evergreen Cemetery, Rutland VT
(1900, AGO, DWD, MTC)

Derby, Buel John (1839-1924)

Born: 8 Mar 1839, Huntington VT, son of John and Sarah (Buel) Derby
Early Life: post office clerk, Burlington 1859, Rutland 1860-62
War Service: CMSY SGT 12th VT INF 4 Oct 1862, QM SGT 15 May 1863, m/o 14 Jul 1863, QM, 17th VT INF 12 Apr 1864-14 Jul 1865
Later Life: furniture business, Bristol VT 1865-67, Asst postmaster Burlington 1867-75, postmaster 1875-87, 1899-1912, school commissioner 1887-89, 1898-99, RNC delegate 1888, Dir. Denison (TX) Land Co. 1889-1903, Dir. Burlington Grocery Co. 1894-1912
Affiliations: Republican, Mason, MOLLUS (#13769), GAR
Married: 1 Jan 1866, Arvilla C. Wheeler
Died: 25 Jun 1924, Burlington VT; interment in Lakeview Cemetery
(AGO, AWE, C&S, GFH, GFH, PCD)

Dewey, George (1837-1917)

Born: 26 Dec 1837, Montpelier VT, son of Dr. Julius Yeamans and Mary (Perrin) Dewey
Early Life: local schools, NU, USNA 1858, steamer *Wabash*, Mediterranean Squadron 1858-59, steamer *Powhatan*, West Indies Squadron, 1860
War Service: XO, side-wheel steamer *Mississippi* 1861-63, prize commissioner, New Orleans, 1863, XO, steamers *Monongahela*, *Brooklyn* (temp. command), *Agawam, Minnesota, Colorado* through January 1865, LCDR 3 Mar 1865
Later Life: European Squadron, XO, *Kearsarge*, *Canandaigua*, XO, flagship *Colorado* 1865-67; Assist to Commandant of Midshipmen, in charge of practice ships and other vessels at the Naval Acad. 1867-70; screw sloop *Narragansett* 1870-71, storeship *Supply* 1871, Boston Navy Yard 1871, Torpedo Station, Newport, RI 1871-72; CDR 13 Apr 1872; *Narragansett* 1873-75, shore duty, Washington 1877-82; screw sloop *Juniata* 1882-83, *Dolphin* 1884-85, CAPT 27 September 1884; flagship *Pensacola* European Station, 1885-88; shore duty, Washington 1889-97; COMO 28 February 1896, Destroyed Spanish Fleet in Manila Bay, Philippines 1898, RADM 1898, ADM 1899, Admiral of the Navy 1899
Married: (1) 14 Oct 1867, Susie Goodwin; (2) 9 Nov 1899, Mildred McLean Hazen (widow of M.G. William B. Hazen)
Affiliations: MOLLUS (#02397)
Died: 16 Jan 1917, Washington, D.C; interment in Arlington National Cemetery; reinterred in Bethlehem Chapel, Protestant Episcopal Cathedral, Washington, D.C. in 1925.
Publications: Autobiography of George Dewey, Admiral of the Navy (1913)
(C&S, PCD*, TJL2)

Dewey, Joel Allen (1840-1873)

Born: 20 Sep 1840, Georgia VT, son of Horace Mosely and Harriet M. (Peck) Dewey
Early Life: Oberlin College 1858; withdrew to accept commission in the Union Army
War Service: 2LT 58th Ohio INF 10 Oct 1861, CPT Co. H 43rd Ohio INF 28 Dec 1861, New Madrid, Iuka, Corinth, on staff of Gen. Rosecrans, LTCOL 111th USCI, COL 14 Feb 1864, captured Athens, AL 1864, B.G. USV 20 Nov 1865, declined post-war appointment as CPT USA 13 Dec 1865, mustered out 31 Jan 1866
Later Life: ALS 1867, atty Dandridge TN 1867-69), atty Gen. 1869-73
Married: 14 Nov 1871, Victoria Josephine Branner
Died: 17 Jun 1873 Knoxville, TN; interment in Old Presbyterian Church Cemetery, Dandridge TN
(FAG, FBH, FSO, JGW, RJ, RR)

Dickinson, John Quincy (1836-1871)

Born: 26 Nov 1836, Benson VT, son of Isaac and Cornelia (Coleman) Dickinson
Early Life: A.B. MC 1860; reporter, correspondent for Rutland Herald
War Service: 2LT, Co. C 7th VT INF, 15 Jan 1862; 1LT, Co. C 9 Oct 1862; QM, 13 Sep 1864; CPT Co. F 22 Oct 1865; resgd 10 Oct 1865
Later Life: lumberman, Pensacola, Fl; asst secr. State Sen.; Cty Clerk; COL State Militia; atty
Died: 3 Apr 1871, Marianna FL; interment in Old Cemetery, Benson VT
Epitaph: John Quincy Dickinson; CPT Dickinson was assassinated by the Ku Klux Klan near his home on the night of Apr 3. He fell at the post of Duty in the integrity of a true patriot; CPT John Q., son of Isaac & grandson of CPT Joel, b. Benson Nov. 26, 1836, graduated Middlebury College 1860, Served in the War of the Rebellion from 1861-65
(AGO, MIDCat, MIDCat2)

Dickinson, Lucius Chandler (1822-1887)

Born: 7 Jul 1822, Weathersfield VT, son of John and Mary (Chandler) Dickinson
Early Life: M.E. minister admitted to VT Conf. 1850, served in Proctorsville and Ludlow
War Service: Chap. 9th VT INF 2 Jul 1862, m/o 13 Jun 1865
Later Life: presiding elder, Springfield VT, 1867-70, pastor, Waterbury Centre 1872
Died: 3 Dec 1887, St. Johnsbury VT; interment in Center Cemetery
(AGO, FSO, H&D, ME72)

Dillingham, Edwin (1839-1864)

Born: 13 May 1839, Waterbury VT, son of Paul and Julia C. (Carpenter) Dillingham
Early Life: local schools, Poughkeepsie Law School 1859, admitted to the bar 1860, atty 1860-62
War Service: CPT Co. B 10th VT INF 4 Aug 1862, MAJ 17 Jun 1864, pow Orange Grove 27 Nov 1863, prld 21 Mar 1864, kia Winchester
Died: 19 Sep 1864, Winchester VA; interment in Village Cemetery, Waterbury VT
Notes: Waterbury GAR Post #22 was named after him
Papers: Rice University
(EMH, HC4)

Dimick, Justin (1800-1871)

Born: 5 Aug 1800, Hartford, CT
Early Life: USMA 1819 (11/29), 2LT, LARTY 1 Jul 1819, garrison duty, New England 1819-22, 2LT, 1st US ARTY 1 Jun 1821, instr. USMA 14 Feb-28 Sep 1822, garrison duty 1822-36; 1LT 1st US ARTY 1 May 1824, Bvt CPT 1 May 1834; CPT 1st US ARTY 6 Apr 1835; Seminole War 1836; Bvt MAJ 8 May 1836; recruiting service 1837-38; Canadian border disturbance at

Rouse's Point NY 1838-39; garrison duty, New England 1839-45; occupation of Texas 1845-46; recruiting service 1846-47; Mexican-American War 1847-48; Bvt LTCOL 20 Aug 1847; wdd, Chapultepec, and Bvt COL 13 Sep 1847; Commander, Vera Cruz 1847-48; garrison duty 1848-49; Seminole War 1849-50; MAJ, 1st US ARTY, 1 Apr 1850; Vermont Civil Court, to defend actions at Rouse's Point NY 1851-53; garrison duty, Ft. Moultrie SC 1853-54, 1855-56; Vermont Civil Court 1854, Board on Armament of Fortifications, 10 Oct 1854-24 Mar 1855; Seminole War 1856-57; garrison duty 1857-59; LTCOL, 2nd US ARTY, 5 Oct 1857; commanding ARTY. School at Ft. Monroe VA, 1859-61
War Service: COL, 1st US ARTY, 26 Oct 1861; commanding prison depot, Ft. Warren MA, 1861-63, ret. 1 Aug 1863, Gov. Soldiers Home near Washington, 1864-68; Bvt B.G. 13 Mar 1865
Died: 13 Oct 1871, Philadelphia PA; interment in Proprietors Cemetery, Portsmouth NH
Notes: son Justin 1LT 2nd US ARTY during war, mwia at Chancellorsville
(FAG, GWC)

Dix, Samuel Nevins (1839-1899)

Born: 4 May 1839, Troy VT, son of Samuel and Maria B. (Church) Dix
Early Life: local schools, Albany Acad., farmer
War Service: PVT Co. I 15th VT INF 3 Sep 1862, m/o 16 Jun 1863
Later Life: farmer, businessman, financier, j.p., town grand juror, State Rep. 1880, 1882, Asst postmaster
Affiliations: Republican, GAR
Married: 28 Oct 1875, Annette L. Stiles
Died: 30 Jun 1899; interment in New Protestant Cemetery, Montgomery VT
(AGO, JGU)

Dixon, Lucius Jerome (1829-1902)

Born: 22 Nov 1829, Underhill VT
Early Life: M.D. UVM 1858, physician, Milton VT, 1858-60, Madison WI 1860-61
War Service: SURG 1st WI INF 24 Apr 1861, BGD SURG 28 Aug 1861, m/o 13 Oct 1864; 2 years more as Staff SURG USA
Later Life: physician, Milton VT, 1867-1902, State Rep. 1874-5
Married: 1856, Charlotte Wood
Died: 8 Aug 1902, Milton VT; interment unknown
(EBQ, UVMMED, WBA)

Dodge, George Sullivan (1838-1881)

Born: 3 Aug 1838, Irasburg VT, son of William P. and Nancy Dodge
Early Life: merchant
War Service: AQM (CPT) USV 12 May 1862, AQM, Bermuda Hundred Campaign May 1864, MAJ, QM, 2 Aug 1864, COL, QM, 17 Sep 1864, Chief QM, AOJ, 25 Sep 1864, Ft Fisher NC Dec 1864, Bvt B.G. 15 Jan 1865, m/o 7 Mar 1866
Later Life: US Consul to Bremen 1866-69, Olympia R.R. & Mining Co. 1873, railroad, mining and banking interests in California and the Pacific Northwest
Died: 24 Aug 1881, Oakland CA; interment in Newton Cemetery, Newton, NJ
(BFB, E&E, FSO, GWH)

Dolloff, Charles William – See Part I – Medal of Honor

Doolittle, Charles Camp (1832-1903)

Born: 16 Mar 1832 Burlington VT, son of Matthew Jesse and Elizabeth (Camp) Doolittle
Early Life: Clerk and Banker

War Service: 1LT, Co. E 4th MI INF, 20 Jun 1861, CPT Co. H 4th MI INF 20 Aug 1861, COL 18th MI INF 13 Aug 1862, wdd Gaines's Mill Jun 1862, Army of the Ohio, Kentucky 1862-63, Tennessee 1862-64, Commander at Decatur, AL where he repulsed GEN Hood Oct 1864, Commander 1st BGD 3rd Div XXIII Corps, Nashville Dec 1864, Commander, Nashville 1865, Commander, Northeast District of Louisiana, B.G. USV, 11 May 1865, Bvt M.G., 13 Jun 1865, m/o 30 Nov 1865
Later Life: cashier, merchants' national bank, Toledo
Affiliations: GAR, MOLLUS (#06516)
Died: 20 Feb 1903 Toledo OH; interment in Woodlawn Cemetery
(C&S, EJW, FAG, RJ, WFD)

Dorsey, Stephen Wallace (1842-1916)

Born: 28 Feb 1842, Benson VT, son of John W. and Marie Dorsey
Early Life: painter; moved early to OH
War Service: 1LT Btry E, 1st OH LARTY 23 Aug 1861, CPT 13 Apr 1864, m/o 14 Jun 1865, served on staffs of GENs James A. Garfield and U.S. Grant
Later Life: pres. Sandusky Tool Co., Arkansas Railway Co; US Sen. 1873-79; cattle rancher, miner; involved in Star Route Frauds 1876
Affiliations: Republican
Died: 20 Mar 1916, Los Angeles CA; interment in Fairmont Cemetery, Denver, CO;
Publications: Statistical and Other Facts Relating to Narrow Gauge Railways, 1871
Biography: Caperton, Thomas J., Rogue! Being an Account of the Life and High Times of Stephen W. Dorsey, United States Senator and New Mexico Cattle Baron (1978)
(CB, DAB, FSO, MG)

Doty, George W. (1838-1910)

Born: 16 Feb 1838, Montpelier VT, adopted by O. L. Metcalf of Morristown.
Early Life: local schools and People's Acad., moved to Mapleton KS, constable, Free Soil forces under COL Montgomery and Lane
War Service: PVT Co. F 2nd VT INF 7 May 1861, CPL 1 Oct 1861, wdd, Fredericksburg, 13 Dec 1862, tr to VRC 1 Sep 1863, m/o 29 Jun 1864
Later Life: station agent, express agent, telegraph operator, St. J. & L. C. R.R. 12 years, furniture dealer and undertaker 10 years, deputy sheriff, sheriff, prudential committee of People's Acad
Affiliations: Republican, Mason, GAR
Married: 30 Apr 1863, Flora A. Bundy
Died: 20 Aug 1910; interment in Pleasant View Cemetery, Morrisville VT
(AGO, JGU, WHJ*)

Draper, Alonzo Granville (1835-1865)

Born: 6 Sep 1835, Bennington VT, son of Alonzo and Hannah Vose (Cram) Draper
Early Life: moved to Boston 1843; newspaper editor
War Service: CPT 1 MA ARTY 5 Jul 1861; MAJ 28 Feb 1863; COL 36th USCI 1 Aug 1863; Bvt B.G. USA 28 Oct 1864
Later Life: killed by stray bullet after the war
Married: 24 Aug 1856, Sarah Elizabeth Andrews
Died: 3 Sep 1865, Brazos de Santiago, TX; interment in Pine Grove Cemetery, Lynn MA
(E&E, FBH, TWD)

Drury, James John – See Part I – Medal of Honor

Drury, Lucius H. (1824/25-1883)

Born: 20 Dec 1825 or 21 Dec 1824, Highgate VT, son of Abel Jr. and Caroline (Hollenbeck) Drury
Early Life: Madison WI, 1861 Berlin WI
War Service: CPT 3rd WI LARTY 26 Aug 1861, Chief of Arty, Gen. Van Cleve's Division, m/o 10 Oct 1864, MAJ 1st WI HARTY 9 Sep 1864, m/o 14 Jul 1865
Later Life: Customs House mngr 1880, Chicago IL
Affiliations: MOLLUS (#02325), IL Assoc SOV
Married: Florilla C.
Died: 11 Mar 1833, Chicago IL; interment unknown
Notes: WI GAR Post#167, Eagle River, Vilas Cty, named after him
(1850, 1880, C&S, FSO, JF, TJM, SOVI, T289)

Dudley, William Wade (1842-1909)

Born: 2 Aug 1842 Weathersfield Bow VT
Early Life: Phillips Acad., Danville VT; Russell Mil. Acad., New Haven, CT
War Service: CPT Co. B 19th IN INF 29 Jul 1861, MAJ 18 Sep 1862, wdd, Antietam, 17 Sep 1862, LTCOL 7 Oct 1862; wdd (right leg amputated) Gettysburg, USA Inspector, JAG, dis/wds 30 Jun 1864; US Pension office 1864-65; Bvt MAJ, LTCOL, COL and B.G. 13 Mar 1865; CPT VRC, 25 Mar 1865, m/o 30 Jun 1866
Later Life: atty, clerk of Circuit Court, Wayne Cty IN 1866-70, US Marshall 1879-81, US Commissioner of Pensions 1881-84, Treasurer RNC 1888
Died: 15 Dec 1909, Washington, D.C; interment in Arlington National Cemetery
Notes: Involved in 1888 Presidential election scandal in which he penned a letter about buying Republican votes in Indiana
(E&E, FAG, RJ, RMS)

Dunton, Charles Henry (1844-1921)

Born: 24 Jan 1844, Underhill VT, son of Elijah and Mary Ann (French) Dunton
Early Life: New Hampton Inst., Fairfax
War Service: PVT Co. F 13th VT INF 10 Sep 1862, dis/dsb 17 Mar 1863
Later Life: UVM 1870, Methodist Church, Johnson 1871-72, p.g. course Boston Univ. pastor at Manchester and East Dorset, teacher, natural science, Troy Conf. Acad., Poultney, later principal, D.D. Syracuse Univ. 1886
Affiliations: Republican
Married: 26 Jun 1872, Nettie W. Belding
Died: 6 Apr 1921, Poultney VT; interment in Poultney Cemetery
(AGO, JGU, PCD*)

Dunton, Walter Chipman (1830-1890)

Born: 29 Nov 1830, Bristol VT, son of Ezekiel and Mandana (Holley) Dunton
Early Life: Franklin Acad. Malone NY, MC 1857, admitted to the bar 1858, atty, Manhattan KS 1858-61, Terr. Rep. 1861, returned to Rutland VT 1862
War Service: CPT Co. H 14th VT INF 10 Sep 1862 - 30 Jul 1863
Later Life: jp Rutland Dist. 1865-77, VT Supreme Court judge 1877-79, State Sen. 1880-82, pres. VBA 1881. State ConCon 1870, prof. law IA State Univer. 1888-89, MC trustee 1870-90
Affiliations: RSVO, GAR
Married: 11 Sep 1862, Miriam Emma Barrett
Died: 23 Apr 1890, Rutland VT; interment in Evergreen Cemetery
Notes: Bristol GAR Post #110 was named after him
(AGO, MIDCAT, RJ, RSVO)

Dunton, Warren Robbins (1839-1902)

Born: 14 May 1839, Dorset VT, son of G. W. and Sara Dunton
War Service: 1SGT Co. F 5th VT INF 16 Sep 1861, 2LT 21 Jun 1862, 1LT 14 Dec 1862, wdd Fredericksburg 14 Dec 1862, m/o 31 Mar 1863, 1LT VRC 15 Oct 1863, CPT 5 Jan 1865, Bvt MAJ USV 13 May 1865, m/o 30 Jun 1866
Later Life: 2LT 2nd US INF 22 Jan 1867, 19th US INF 3 Aug 1870, 1LT 31 Dec 1872, ret. 28 Jun 1878
Affiliations: GAR, MOLLUS (#10069), OES
Married: abt 1865, Caroline E. (nfi)
Died: 28 Apr 1902, Dorset VT; interment in Maple Hill Cemetery
(1850, 1900, AGO, C&S, FBH, GGB)

Dustin, Daniel (1820-1892)

Born: 5 Oct 1820, Topsham VT, son of John Knight and Sally (Kendall) Dustin
Early Life: M.D. DC 1846, physician 1846-50, moved to CA 1850, State Rep. Nevada Cty CA, moved to Sycamore IL 1858, mercantile business
War Service: CPT 8th IL CAV 18 Sep 1861; MAJ 12 Jan 1862; COL 105th IL INF 2 Sep 1862; Bvt B.G. USV 16 Mar 1865, m/o 7 Jun 1865
Later Life: physician, Cty Clerk, Cty Treasurer, circuit clerk and recorder, Sycamore, IL (16 years), published Republican Sentinel 1857-58
Affiliations: MOLLUS (#08421)
Married: 20 Oct 1844, Isabel Taplin
Died: 29 Mar 1892, Sycamore IL; interment in Elmwood Cemetery
(FAG, FBH, FSO, FWS, HFK, LMG*, PK)

Dutton, Ira Barnes (1843-1931)

Born: 27 Apr 1843, Stowe VT, son of Ezra and Abigail (Barnes) Dutton
Early Life: removed to WI, Old Acad. and Milton Acad., Janesville WI, Janesville City Zouaves 1860
War Service: PVT Co. B 13th WI INF 9 Sep 1861, QM SGT 26 Oct 61, 2LT 10 Aug 1864, 1LT 15 Feb 1865, QM 24 Mar 1865, m/o 13 Dec 1865
Later Life: employed in cemetery operations, gathering Federal dead, 1865-67; US Government 1867-70; Clerk L&NRR 1870-75; Investigating agent, War Dept. US Commission 1876-84; became a Catholic 1883; Trappists, Gethsemani Abby Kentucky 1884-85; Redemptorists 1886; Helper at Leper Settlement, Molokai, Hawaii assoc w/Father Damien, 1886-89; succeeded Father Damien 1889
Affiliations: Congregationalist, later Catholic; WI Hist Soc., 3rd Order of St. Francis
Died: 26 Mar 1931, Honolulu, HI; interment in Saint Philomena Catholic Church Cemetery, Kalaupapa, HI
Notes: Founded Baldwin Home, a residence for leper men and boys, in Molokai, Hawaii.
(CE, FSO, JWS)

Dwinell, Melvin (1825-1887)

Born: 9 Jul 1825, East Calais VT, son of Israel and Phila G. Dwinell
Early Life: UVM 1849, teacher, Morrisville Acad. 1849-51, moved to Rome GA, teacher, newspaper publisher
War Service: 2LT Rome Light Guard, part of 8th GA INF, wdd, Gettysburg, elected to GA Legis., resgd commission; ADJ (CPT) 1864 GA state forces
Later Life: newspaper publisher
Affiliations: Confederate, Methodist
Died: 28 Dec 1887, Rome GA; interment in Fairview Cemetery, East Calais VT
Publications: Common Sense Views of Foreign Lands (1878)
(Argus and Patriot, AMH, MDG)

Dyer, Jay (1819-1906)

Born: 30 Nov 1819, Clarendon VT, son of Jonathan and Hannah (Dwinell) Dyer
Early Life: A.B. NU 1838, Asst Engr IL Central R.R. 1839-49, teacher IL and Ohio 1840-50, mining in CA 1850-60
War Service: CPT Co. I 32nd Ohio INF 31 Aug 1861, resgd 10 Apr 1862
Later Life: Delaware Cty (Ohio) surveyor 1863-66, Asst Engr Cleveland, Akron & Columbus R.R. 1870-72, farming, raising stock 1862-1906
Married: 4 Oct 1847, Hortensia Norton
Died: 24 Dec 1906, Galena OH; interment unknown
(WAE)

Damon, George B.

Darling, Joseph K.

Dartt, Justus N.

Dayton, Durell W.

Dewey, George

Doty, George W.

Dunton, Charles H.

Dustin, Daniel

EEEEE

Eaton, Henry Augustus (1838-1864)

Born: 8 Nov 1838, Granville VT, son of David and Sarah E. (Perry) Eaton
Early Life: Free Soiler in KS 1856, MC 1862
War Service: CPT Co. A 16th VT INF 26 Aug 1862, wdd Gettysburg 3 Jul 1863 (Treated at Peter Myers House), m/o 10 Aug 1863, CPT Co. D 17th VT INF 4 Mar 1864, MAJ 12 Aug 1864, kia Poplar Spring Church
Died: 30 Sep 1864, Poplar Spring Church VA; interment on the battlefield, cenotaph at North Hollow, Rochester VT
Notes: Rochester GAR Post #38 named after him
(AGO, GGK, TBP1)

Eddy, Samuel Edwin – See Part I – Medal of Honor

Edson, Ptolemy O'Meara (1833-1928)

Born: 27 Dec 1833, Chester VT, son of Ptolemy and Susan (Pratt) Edson
Early Life: B.S. UVM 1857, M.D. UVM 1860, physician, Chester VT
War Service: Asst SURG 1st VT CAV 5 Nov 1861, SURG 17th VT INF 1 Apr 1864; m/o 27 Feb 1865
Later Life: physician, Chester VT, physician, Roxbury MA 1866-1915
Married: 30 Oct 1865, Mary Augusta Young
Affiliations: Unitarian, GAR, MOLLUS (#03876), RSVO, MA MS
Died: 13 Feb 1928, Boston MA; interment in Elm Hill Avenue Cemetery
Publications: Address Delivered at the Second Annual Meeting of the First Vermont Cavalry Reunion Society, at Montpelier, November 4, 1874, UVM
(C&S, FHB, MDG, WHO3)

Emmons, George Foster (1811-1884)

Born: 23 Aug 1811, Clarendon VT, son of Horatio and Abigail (Foster) Emmons
Early Life: Midshipman USN 1 Apr 1828; New York Naval School; *Brandywine* 1830-33; Passed Midshipman 1834; *Consort* 1836-38; Wilkes Exploring Expedition 1838-42; LT 25 Feb 1841; *Boston*, Brazil Squadron 1843-46; *Ohio*, Pacific Squadron, Mexican-American War; Bureau of Construction and Repair, Washington 1850-53; *Savannah* 1853-56; CDR 28 Jan 1856; awaiting orders 1856-61
War Service: Lighthouse Board 1861; *Hatteras* 1861-62; gunboat *R. R. Cuyler* 1863; screw sloop *Monongahela* 1863-64; *Brooklyn* 1864; Fleet Captain, SABS 1863; screw sloop *Lackawanna* 1864-65
Later Life: steam sloop *Ossipee* 1866-8, CMDR 29 Sep 1868, Ordnance Board 1869, Commandant, Philadelphia Navy Yard 1870-71; Hydrographic Office, Washington 1872; RADM 25 Nov 1872; commandant, Philadelphia Navy Yard 1872-73; ret. 23 Aug 1873
Affiliations: MOLLUS (#00135)
Died: 23 Jul 1884, Princeton, NJ; interment in Green Mount Cemetery, Baltimore, MD
Publications: The Navy of the United States, from the Commencement, 1775 to 1853. (1853)
(C&S, DAB, RR, TJL2)

English, Charles Henry (1841-1917)

Born: 18 Dec 1841, Woodstock VT, son of Henry Walbridge and Eliza Ann (Steele) English
Early Life: Green Mountain Perkins Acad
War Service: PVT Co. B 12th VT INF 4 Oct 1862, m/o, 14 Jul 1863

Later Life: town selectman Woodstock 1872-78, farmer, Woodstock 1880, proprietor English's Saw, Grist & Cider Mill, Woodstock, State Rep. 1892, grocer Woodstock 1900, rural mail carrier 1903-12, j.p.
Married: (1) 24 May 1869, Lizzie M. Vaughan (his cousin); (2) 1882, Nellie E. Gilbert
Died: 5 Nov 1917; interment in Woodstock VT
(1870, 1880, 1900, AGO, BWD, FSO, HC5, HSD, PCD)

Evans, Goin Bailey (1842-1922)

Born: 4 Dec 1842, Moretown VT, son of Osgood and Mary (Bailey) Evans
Early Life: public schools, Newbury Sem., Bryant and Stratton Business Coll., farmer and drover
War Service: PVT Co. G 6th VT INF 22 Feb 1862, dis/dsb 24 Apr 1863
Later Life: businessman, State Rep. 1874, 1876, 1878, 1884, Deputy collector and Customs inspector 1885, postmaster Waterbury 1894-98, deputy sheriff, Washington Cty 1912, DNC delegate 1908
Affiliations: Democrat
Married: (1) 30 Oct 1864, Abbie M. Goodrich; (2) Margaret May Thompson
Died: 24 Aug 1922, Waterbury VT; interment in Village Cemetery
(AFS, AGO)

Evans, Ira Hobart – See Part I – Medal of Honor

Emmons, George F.

FFFFF

Fairbanks, Erastus (1792-1864)

Born: 28 Oct 1792, Brimfield MA, son of Joseph F. and Phoebe (Paddock) Fairbanks
Early Life: merchant, inventor, State Rep. 1836, VT Gov. 1852-54, railroad executive
War Service: VT Gov. 1860-61; organized and mustered in first six infantry regts, first sharpshooter co., 1st CAV
Later Life: philanthropist
Affiliations: Republican
Died: 20 Nov 1864, St. Johnsbury VT; interment in Mt. Pleasant Cemetery
Papers: UVM
(DAB, FSO, FGH, GWH, HC6, JGU*, RR)

Fairchild, Benjamin (1804-1887)

Born: 12 Aug 1804, Georgia VT, son of Joel and Mehitable (Eastman) Fairchild
Early Life: UVM 1830, physician, Milton VT 1830-60
War Service: Fredericksburg and Washington May 1864, among a contingent of Vermont doctors who volunteered their services to care for Vermonters who were wounded in the battles of the Wilderness and Spotsylvania C.H.
Later Life: Physician, Milton 1870-80, Delegate, Burlington Med. College
Affiliations: Chittenden Cty MS
Married: (1) 7 Oct 1830, Sarah A. Sischo; (2) 26 Aug 1847, Ann Mary Barton; (3) 17 Feb 1852, Charlotte A. Tillison
Died: 23 Aug 1887, Milton VT; interment unknown
(1860, 1870, 1880, HC1, UVMMED, VMS64)

Fairman, Erastus Philo (1828-1904)

Born: 15 Jul 1828, Albany VT, son of Erastus and Susan (McIntire) Fairman
Early Life: Derby, Craftsbury and St. Johnsbury Acad., M.D. CPS NYU 1854, Lamoille Cty Sheriff 1859-61
War Service: PVT Co. C 17th VT INF 29 Feb 1864, Asst SURG, 9th VT INF, 9 Apr 1864, m/o 13 Jun 1865
Later Life: physician in Wolcott 1870-80, State Rep. 1874-75, post-grad studies 1878-82, moved to Hardwick 1890-1900
Affiliations: Republican
Married: (1) 29 Sep 1852, Laura Elmina Hubbell; (2) 29 Sep 1861, Eliza Cornelia Bailey
Died: 6 Apr 1904; interment in Fairmont Cemetery, Wolcott VT
(1870, 1880, 1900, FSO, GFH, HC2, RR)

Farmer, Edward (1836-1918)

Born: 1 Mar 1836, Perkinsville VT, son of Edward and Lydia A. Farmer
Early Life: early education in the local public schools and from private tutors; 3rd Assistant ENGR 3 May 1859; Home Squadron 1859-60
War Service: 2nd Asst ENGR USN 16 Oct 1861; screw sloop *Mohican,* SABS, gunboat *Kanawha,* WGBS 1862-64; 1st Asst ENGR 20 May 1863; side-wheel steamer *Alabama, NABS* 1864-65
Later Life: screw sloop *Shenandoah,* East India Station 1866-68; Boston Navy Yard 1868-71; Chief ENGR, 4 Mar 1871; on *Ticonderoga,* South Atlantic Station 1871-74; Boston Navy Yard 1874-77; Asiatic Station 1877-81 on *Alert*, Asiatic Station 1877-81; Naval Acad. 1881-88; Chief ENGR (CMDR), 2 December 1887; *Chicago*, Squadron of Evolution 1888-91; Portsmouth Navy Yard 1891-93; Boston Navy Yard 1893-95; New York Navy Yard 1895-98; ret. list 1 Mar 1898; Inspector of Machinery, for Bureau of Steam Engineering, Washington, 1898-99; RADM on ret. list 29 Jun 1906
Affiliations: MOLUS (#08645)

Died: 20 Feb 1918, Concord MA; interment in Sleepy Hollow Cemetery
(TJL2)

Farnham, Roswell (1827-1903)

Born: 23 Jul 1827, Boston MA, son of Roswell Farnham and Nancy (Bixby) Farnham
Early Life: moved to VT 1840, Bradford Acad., UVM 1849, 1852; teacher, admitted to the bar 1857, State's Atty 1859-62
War Service: 2LT Co. D 1st VT INF 2 May 1861, P.M. Newport News, m/o 15 Aug 1861, CPT Bradford Guards 1862, MAJ 12th VT INF 19 Sep 1862, m/o 14 Jul 1863
Later Life: state militia; State Sen. 1868-69; atty Bradford VT 1870, RNC delegate 1876; VT Gov. 1880-82, resided Bradford 1900
Affiliations: RSVO, MOLLUS (#09160)
Married: 25 Dec 1849, Mary Elizabeth Johnson
Died: 5 Jan 1903, Bradford VT; interment in Village Cemetery
Correspondence: VHS
(1870, 1900, C&S, JGU*, JHB, LHC, PCD, SK)

Farnsworth, Orrin (1831-1863)

Born: 16 May 1831, Haverhill NH, son of Stephen and Anna (Martin) Farnsworth
War Service: PVT Co. G 3rd VT INF 16 Jul 1861, CPL, mwia Marye's Heights 3 May 1863
Died: 4 May 1863, Fredericksburg VA; interment in Lyndon Center Cemetery, Lyndon VT
Notes: Lyndonville GAR Post #106 was named after him (AGO, FSO, GGB, GGK)

Ferrin, Chester M. (1837-1932)

Born: 27 Sep 1837, Holland VT, son of Micah and Lucinda (Sonant) Ferrin
Early Life: Derby and Hinesburg Acad
War Service: PVT Co. B 8th VT INF 28 Nov 1861, Hosp. Steward, m/o 22 Jun 1864
Later Life: M.D. UVM 1865, physician St. Johnsbury 1870, Essex 1880, p.g. School NY 1893, attending physician, teacher in school for nurses, Fanny Allen Hosp., resided Burlington 1920
Affiliations: GAR, 8th VT Soc. (secretary 30+ years)
Married: 1866, Marian E. Benedict
Died: 28 Sep 1932, Essex Jct VT; interment in Village Cemetery
(1870, 1880, 1920, AGO, FGH, GNC, TWH, UVMMED)

Ferris, Eugene W. – See Part I – Medal of Honor

Fisk, Perrin Batchelder (1837-aft 1910)

Born: 30 Jul 1837, Waitsfield VT, son of Deacon Lyman and Mary (Spofford) Fisk
Early Life: cooper, farmer, Barre Acad., BTS 1863, Congregational minister
War Service: USCC AOP
Later Life: pastor of churches in MA VT, and MN, field agent, Carleton Coll., MN, home missions in IL and FL 5 years, returned to Peacham VT 1870, Chap. VT Sen. 1869-70, Congregational Church, Springfield 1874-77), Mt. Dora, FL 1887, Lake, MN 1880, St. Johnsbury VT 1895, Greensboro 1900, Plainfield 1910, poet
Married: 25 Aug 1863, Harriet L. Bigelow
Died: aft 1910; interment unknown
(1870, 1880, 1890, 1900, 1910, H&D, JGU, KC)

Flagg, George W. (1839-1919)

Born: 9 Apr 1839, Braintree VT, son of Austin and Mary E. (Harwood) Flagg
Early Life: local schools, Randolph Acad., farmer, day laborer
War Service: PVT Co. F 2nd VT INF 7 May 1861, CPL 1 Jul 1864, SGT 1 Sep 1864, 1SGT 7 Feb 1864, reenlisted 31 Jan 1864, wdd Petersburg 2 Apr 1865, m/o 15 Jul 1865 as 1SGT, champion collar and arm wrestler AOP
Later Life: farmer, collar and elbow wrestler (200 matches), many town offices, State Rep. 1886
Affiliations: Republican, GAR, Mason, RSVO
Married: 16 May 1865, Delia A. Howard
Died: 14 Sep 1919, Braintree VT; interment in Village Cemetery
(AGO, JGU*)

Flagg, Joel (1841-1928)

Born: 17 Sep 1841, Heath MA, son of Joel and Delight (Wait) Flagg
Early Life: Guilford public schools, farmer
War Service: CPL Co. B 16th VT INF 28 Aug 1862, reduced 14 Feb 1863, m/o 10 Aug 1863
Later Life: farmer, selectman, town lister, overseer of the poor, license commissioner, State Rep. 1906-08
Affiliations: Democrat, Universalist, Mason, Grange
Married: (1) 21 Feb 1872, Lizzie A. Barber; (2) 13 Oct 1925, Mrs. Alice Tracy nee Thomas
Died: 25 Aug 1928, Guilford VT; interment in Christchurch Cemetery
(AFS, AGO)

Fletcher, Henry Addison (1839-1897)

Born: 11 Dec 1839, Cavendish VT, son of Ryland and Mary Ann (May) Fletcher
Early Life: farmer
War Service: 2SGT Co. C 16th VT INF 23 Oct 1862, 1SGT Co. C 23 Oct 1862, SGT MAJ, 2LT, 2 Apr 1863, m/o 10 Aug 1863
Later Life: farmer; State Rep. 1867-82; State Sen. 1886, LT Gov. 1890-91, unmarried
Affiliations: Republican, GAR, RSVO
Died: 19 Apr 1897, Cavendish VT; interment in Cavendish Cemetery
(JGU, RR)

Floyd, Horace W. (1834-1870)

Born: 27 Nov 1834, Lebanon NH, son of Benjamin and Martha (Whitmore) Floyd
Early Life: Tailor, Springfield VT
War Service: 2LT 21 May 1861 Co A 3rd VT INF 1LT, Co F 13 Aug 1861, Co. A. 1 Dec 1861, CPT Co. C 22 Sep 1862, wdd 21 Jun 1864, MAJ, 4 Aug 1864, LTCOL, 18 Oct 1864, Bvt COL 19 Oct 1864, COL (not mustered) 4 Jun 1865, m/o 11 Jul 1865
Later Life: Tailor, Springfield
Affiliations: RSVO
Married: 3 Feb 1862, Caroline L. Parker
Died: 4 Oct 1870, Springfield VT; interment unknown
(CDC, H&D)

Foot, Solomon (1802-1866)

Born: 19 Nov 1802, Cornwall VT, son of Solomon and Betsey (Crossett) Foot
Early Life: MC 1826; teacher (1826-31), atty, State Rep. 1833, 1836-38, State ConCon 1836, State's Atty 1836-42, US Rep. 1843-47
War service: US Sen. 1851-66
Married: (1) 9 Jul 1839, Emily Fay; (2) 2 Apr 1844, Mary Ann (Hodges) Dana
Affiliations: Whig, Republican

Died: 28 Mar 1866, Washington D.C.; interment in Evergreen Cemetery, Rutland VT
Notes: Funeral services held in the Chamber of the US Sen.
(CB, HGW, LOC*, MIDCat)

Ford, Arba A. (1841-1864)

Born: 1841, Granville VT, son of Alvin and Lucia A. Ford
Early Life: farm laborer
War Service: PVT Co. K 4th VT INF 30 Dec 1863, kia Cold Harbor
Died: 8 Jun 1864, Cold Harbor VA; originally interred in VI Corps Hosp. plot; final interment in Cold Harbor National Cemetery
Notes: Granville GAR Post #76 was named after him
(1850, 1860, GGK, RR)

Foster, Ebenezer J. (1847-1930)

Born: 15 Jan 1847, Moretown VT, son of Leonard R. and Jane B. Foster
Early Life: public schools
War Service: Musician Co. B 10th VT INF 1 Sep 1862, m/o 22 Jun 1865
Later Life: Homeopathic College Philadelphia, MA Metaphysical College, adopted Nov 1888 by Rev. Mary B. G. Eddy, Emerson College of Oratory, Boston, pres. National Christian Science Association, La Cross WI 1900, Waterbury VT 1910-30
Affiliations: GAR, VT Veterans' Assoc. Boston
Died: 12 Nov 1930; interment in Moretown Common Cemetery, Moretown VT
(1900, 1910, 1930, AGO, EMH, JGU*)

Foster, Elihu S. (1829-1867)

Born: 1829
Early Life: physician, Corinth 1860, Topsham 1862
War Service: Asst SURG, 7th VT INF, 1 Oct 1862, resgd 20 Feb 1865
Died: 9 Jan 1867, Hyde Park VT; interment in Green Mount Cemetery, Montpelier VT
Notes: VHS has his sword
(1850, AMH, NAS)

Foster, George Perkins (1835-1879)

Born: 3 Oct 1835, Walden VT, son of Ephraim and Emily (Perkins) Foster
Early Life: teacher
War Service: CPT Co. G 4th VT INF 11 Sep 1861, MAJ 18 Jul 1862, LTCOL 5 Nov 1862, COL 3 Feb 1864, wdd, Wilderness VA 5 May 1864; Bvt B.G. 1 Aug 1864, m/o 13 Jul 1865
Later Life: US Marshall 1870-79
Affiliations: RSVO, GAR (1st Cdr VT Cmdry)
Died: 19 Mar 1879, Burlington VT; interment in Lakeview Cemetery
Notes: Wolcott GAR Post #55 was named after him
(FAG, FSO, GGB, RR)

Fremont, Sewell L. (1816-1886)

Born: 1816, VT
Early Life: USMA 1841 (17/52); Florida War 1841; Mexican-American War 1846; survey party, determined border between TX and MX; 3rd US ARTY; resgd 5 Apr 1854; chief engr Wilmington (NC) and Weldon R.R. 1854-61

War Service: COL 1st Corps NC ARTY. and Engrs, CSA 1861-65; cmdg Cape Fear region NC 31 Aug 1861; designed and constructed Fort Fisher
Later Life: super. and chief engr Wilmington and Weldon R.R. 1861-71
Died: 1 May 1886; interment unknown
Notes: Changed name from Sewall L. Fish sometime after USMA graduation
(CCPL, CEF, GWC, WHP)

French, Winsor Brown (1832-1910)

Born: 28 Jul 1832, Proctorsville VT
Early Life: moved to Wilton NY 1836, clerk Cavendish VT 1850, Tufts College 1859, studied law in Saratoga, admitted to the bar 1861, moved to Burlington 1862
War Service: ADJ (1LT) 77th NY INF 24 Sept 1861. MAJ 1 Jun 1862; LTCOL 18 Jul 1862. Bvt B.G. USV 13 Mar 1865, m/o 13 Dec 1864
Later Life: atty; District Atty 1868-79, moved to Jackson MI
Affiliations: Republican, GAR, MOLLUS (#04342), Theta Delta Chi, Saratoga Anthaneum
Died: 24 Mar 1910, Saratoga Springs NY; interment in Greenridge Cemetery
(1850, C&S, FAG, FBH, TDC*)

Frost, Carlton Pennington (1830-1896)

Born: 29 May 1830, Sullivan NH, son of Benjamin and Mary C. (Brant) Frost
Early Life: Thetford Acad., A.B. DC 1852, M.D. DC, NYMC 1856, physician St. Johnsbury 1857-62
War Service: SURG, 15th VT INF, 2 Oct 1862, resgd 3 May 1863, SURG, Board of Enrollment 1863-65
Later Life: physician, Brattleboro 1865-71, Asst prof. of Science and Practice of Medicine, DC 1868-69, prof. of same 1870-72, dean of faculty 1872-96
Affiliations: RSVO, VT MS, NH MS, CT River Valley MS, White Mountains MS
Married: 1857, Eliza Ann Dubois
Died: 24 May 1896; interment in Hanover NH
(BAAM, WBA)

Frost, Henry Martyn (1835-1866)

Born: 26 Mar 1835, Sullivan NH, son of Henry Martyn and Mary Catherine (Brant) Frost
Early Life: farmer, Thetford VT 1850, DC 1857, ATS 1858-59, Teacher, Thetford Acad., honorary A.M. MC 1860, Episcopal Deacon, Frankfort, KY, 20 Apr 1860, ordained Episcopal Priest, Middlebury VT, 26 Feb 1862
War Service: Chap. 7th VT INF 25 Jan 1862 - 9 Aug 1862
Later Life: rector, St. Stephen's Church, Middlebury VT 1860-64
Died: 20 Feb 1866, Thetford VT; interment unknown
Notes: two brothers also served in the war, Dr. Carlton Pennington Frost, SURG 15th VT INF and Edwin Brant Frost, CPT 10th VT INF
(1850, GTC, JLS, NSR)

Fairbanks, Erastus

Farnham, Roswell

Flagg, George W.

Foot, Solomon

Foster, George P.

French, Winsor B.

GGGGG

Gale, George F. (1827-1907)

Born: 19 May 1827, Petersham MA, son of Jesse and Hannah (Holland) Gale
Early Life: Petersham Acad., MC, moved to CA, returned, M.D. BMC 1855, physician, Amherst, Cummington and Deerfield MA, Janesville WI, moved to Brattleboro 1858
War Service: SURG, 8th VT INF, 10 Dec 1861- 24 Jun 1862
Later Life: physician, surgeon, gen. mngr. Higby Sewing Mach. Co., Brattleboro 1884, incorporator VT and Brattleboro Savings Banks, Prospect Hill Cemetery Assoc, advisory board Memorial Hosp., village bailiff
Affiliations: SPCA
Married: 1849, Vesta Richards Orcutt
Died: 14 Apr 1907, Brattleboro VT; interment in Prospect Hill Cemetery
Notes: Bridport GAR Post #107 was named after him
(MRC, GGK, HC7, HFW12)

Gates, Amasa O. (1842-1895)

Born: 25 Apr 1842, Morrisville VT, son of Daniel F. and Lavina (Jordan) Gates
Early Life: common schools, People's Acad., MC 1860 (n.g.)
War Service: 1SGT Co. C 17th VT INF 22 Jan 1864, reduced to 2SGT 24 Dec 1864, tr to VRC 22 Feb 1865, in charge of muster rolls at Sloan Hosp., Montpelier, m/o 28 May 1865
Later Life: druggist, St. Johnsbury 1865-68, moved to Morrisville, ret. 1893, town auditor of accounts 15 years, trustee People's Acad., school dir. Morristown, COL and CoS to Gov. Fuller
Affiliations: Republican, Mason, GAR
Married: 7 Jun 1869, Florence H. Cutting
Died: 6 Dec 1895, Morrisville VT; interment in Pleasant View Cemetery
(AGO, JGU)

Gilchrist, Charles Allen (1834-1906)

Born: 13 Feb 1834, Saxtons River VT, son of Charles Grandison and Minerva (Holton) Gilchrist
Early Life: railroad civil engineer, surveyor Tennessee IL 1860
War Service: CPT 10th MO INF 21 Aug 1861; COL 50th USCI 27 Jul 1863; Bvt B.G. USV 26 Mar 1862, m/o 9 Jun 1866
Later Life: civil engineer, Carthage IL 1870, Keokuk IL 1880, High Springs FL 1900
Married: 1 Oct 1857, Lucy Ellen Walker
Died: 22 Jan 1906 New York NY; interment in Scottsburg Cemetery, Scottsburg IL
Publications: An Illustrated Historical Atlas of Hancock County, Illinois (1874)
(1860, 1870, 1880, 1890, E&E, FBH, FSO)

Gilfillan, John Bachop (1835-1924)

Born: 11 Feb 1835, Barnet VT, son of Robert and Janet (Bachop) Gilfillan
Early Life: Caledonia Acad., Peacham Acad., teacher St. Anthony MN 1855, admitted the bar 1860
War Service: 1LT Co E 1st MN INF Apr-Jul 1861
Later Life: Cty Atty 1863-67, 1869-71, 1873-75, atty 1871-1900, State Sen. 1875-85, Board of Regents, Univ. of MN 1880-88, US Rep. 1885-87, pres. 1st Nat. Bank of Minneapolis 1894-1912
Married: (1) 1870, Rebecca Corse Oliphant; (2) Jun 1893, Lavinia Coppock
Died: 19 Aug 1924, Minneapolis MN; interment in Lakewood Cemetery

(CB, FAG, HFS, MHS, PCD, THS)

Gillette, Henry Oliver (1836-1877)

Born: 18 Dec 1836, Readsboro VT, son of Waters and Brittania (Whitney) Gillette
Early Life: farmer
War Service: 1LT, Co F 16th VT INF, 3 Sep 1862, Gettysburg Jul 1863, m/o 10 Aug 1863
Later Life: farmer, Whitingham VT, Selectman, Whitingham VT 1871-72, State Rep., Whitingham VT 1876-77, j.p. Whitingham VT 1876-77
Married: Sophronia M. Read
Died: 19 Dec 1877 VT; interment unknown
(1870, FSO, GFH, JHR77, LB, WRC1)

Gillett, Herman Hosford (1823-1907)

Born: 22 May 1823, Thetford VT, son of Henry and Hannah Gillett
Early Life: M.D. DC 1847, physician Corinth VT 1850-60
War Service: Asst SURG 8th VT INF, 10 Dec 1861, SURG 25 Jun 1862, m/o 28 Jun 1865
Later Life: physician, Thetford 1870-80, health officer, Fairlee 1893
Married: Rosetta (nfi)
Died: 7 May 1907, Dorchester MA; interment in Post Mills Cemetery, Thetford VT
(1850, 1860, 1870, 1880, DCN, WVR)

Gilmore, Joseph Albree (1811-1867)

Born: 10 Jun 1811, Weston VT, son of Asa and Lucy (Dodge) Gilmore
Early Life: grocer, Concord NH 1842, super. Concord and Claremont R.R. 1848, super. Manchester and Lawrence R.R. 1853-56, super. Concord R.R. 1856, State Rep. 1858-59
War Service: NH Gov. 1863-65
Later Life: ret. due to ill health
Died: 17 Apr 1867, Concord NH; interment unknown
Publications: The Conscription in New Hampshire (1863)
(HGW, TWH)

Gilmore, William H. (1839-1910)

Born: 17 Oct 1839, Fairlee VT
Early Life: farmer
War Service: PVT Co. D 8th VT INF 18 Feb 1862; QM SGT 1 Jul 1862; m/o 22 Jun 1864
Later Life: farmer; Fairlee Town Treasurer 39+ years, State Rep. 1878, State Sen. 1882; QM Gen., VT NG 1886; A&IG 1900-10
Affiliations: Republican, Episcopal, RSVO; GAR
Died: 18 Apr 1910, Fairlee VT; interment in Town Cemetery, Bradford VT
Notes: GAR Post in Williamstown named for him
(BBObit, FGF, RR, VHS10)

Glazier, Nelson Newton (1838-1922)

Born: 12 Dec 1838, Stratton VT, son of John Newton and Phebe Cass (Bourn) Glazier
Early Life: local schools, Leland Sem., AC 1856-61

War Service: PVT Co. G 11th VT INF 11 Aug 1862, CPL 23 Nov 1862, 2LT Co. A 2 Nov 1863, wdd, Spotsylvania, 18 May 1864, dis/wds 3 Sep 1864
Later Life: A.B. Brown Univ. 1866, A.M. 1869, Newton Theological Institution; State Rep. 1865, 1867, super. schools, Montpelier 1872-75, State Sen. 1872-78, pastor, Central Falls, RI 1869-70, Montpelier, 1872-78, South Abington MA 1880-84, Westboro MA 1884-86, Greenfield MA, 1887-1905, Sharon MA 1910, ret. to Beatrice NE
Affiliations: Republican, Baptist, GAR, MOLLUS (#14182), RSVO
Died: 1922, Ashland NE; interment in Willow Creek Cemetery, Prague NE
(1910, BrownCat, C&S, JGU, TJL)

Gleason, Joseph Thomas (1844-1923)

Born: 18 Jun 1844, Lunenburg VT, son of George and Sabrina (Thomas) Gleason
Early Life: local schools
War Service: tried to enl Dec 1861, Co. K 8th VT INF, rejected on account of extreme youth, PVT Co. E 15th VT INF 15 Sep 1862, m/o 5 Aug 1863
Later Life: farming, atty, assoc judge Caledonia Cty Court, moved to Lyndonville, town auditor, moderator, chair of Republican town committee
Affiliations: Republican, Congregational, Mason, GAR, OES
Married: 9 Sep 1884, Mary S. Aldrich
Died: 23 May 1923, Lyndonville; interment in Lyndon Center Cemetery
(AGO, JGU*)

Gleason, Newell (1827-1886)

Born: 11 Aug 1827, Wardsboro VT (born Newell Sargent)
Early Life: NU 1849; teacher, civil engr; asst engr Jeffersonville R.R, Columbus, Piqua & Indiana R.R.; chief engr Cincinnati, Peru & Chicago R.R.; 1857, in charge of construction of Dubuque Western R.R. and western div. of Pittsburg, Fort Wayne & Chicago R.R.
War Service: LTCOL 87th IN INF 28 Aug 1862; COL 22 Mar 1863; cmdg 2nd BGD 3rd DIV XIV Corps 24 Jun 1864 until end of war; Bvt B.G. 13 Mar 1865
Later Life: State Rep. 1865—66; chief engr Ionia & Lansing R.R. 1866; chief engr Indianapolis & Chicago R.R. 1867-68; chief engr, Grand River Valley R.R. 1869, later, chief engr Grand Rapids & Lake Shore R.R., Mansfield, Coldwater & Lake Michigan R.R., Chicago, Danville & Vincennes R.R.; ret. due to ill health 1875
Affiliations: IOOF, GAR, Soc. AOC
Died: 6 Jul 1886, Chicago IL; interment in Pine Lake Cemetery, LaPorte IN
(FAG, FBH, WAE*)

Godfrey, Frederick (1841-1923)

Born: 16 May 1841, Bennington VT, son of Bradford and Sarah (McGowan) Godfrey
Early Life: public schools, Manchester Sem., apprentice potter
War Service: 3SGT Co. A 4th VT INF 10 Aug 1861, reen. 9 Feb 1864, reduced 1 Sep 1863, m/o 13 Jul 1865
Later Life: stoneware maker 1865-83, knitting mill, Bennington, Deputy sheriff 1891-1906, sheriff 1908-13, town constable 15 years, tax collector 8 years
Affiliations: Republican, Mason, GAR
Married: (1) 1865, Eldora Bradford; (2) 10 Nov 1894, Margaret Beeman
Died: 26 Feb 1923, Bennington VT; interment in Village Cemetery
(AFS, AGO)

Goodwin, David Marks/Marcus (1833-1908)

Born: 12 Oct 1833, Tunbridge VT, son of Moses Goodwin
Early Life: M.D. DC, NYMC 1856, staff Blackwell Island Hosp., moved to Cabot VT 1857, member Cabot Cornet Band
War Service: Asst SURG, 3rd VT INF, 20 Jun 1861, SURG 29 Apr 1863, m/o 27 Jul 1864
Later Life: Cabot, 1864-66, Minneapolis MN 1866-80, Los Angeles 1900
Married: Harriet (nfi)
Died: 14 Sep 1908, Los Angeles CA; interment unknown
(1870, 1880, 1900, DCN, IA, WU)

Goodrich, John Ellsworth (1831-1915)

Born: 19 Jan 1831, Hinsdale MA, son of Elijah Hubbard and Mary Northrop (Washburn) Goodrich
Early Life: UVM 1853, school principal 1853-56, ATS 1860
War Service: Chap. 1st VT CAV 7 Apr 1864, m/o 9 Aug 1865
Later Life: School Super., Burlington VT 1868-70, Professor, UVM 1872-1906, Dean of Academics, UVM 1902-06, Professor Emeritus, UVM 1906-15
Affiliations: RSVO, MOLLUS (#09163)
Married: 8 Feb 1869, to Ellen Miranda Moody
Died: 24 Feb 1915, Burlington VT; interment unknown
Notes: contributor and compiler of many university publications
(AS, C&S, PCD, WRC1)

Goss, Story Norman (1831-1905)

Born: 7 Feb 1831, Waterford VT, son of Abel and Amanda (Hebard) Goss
Early Life: public schools of Waterford, St. Johnsbury and Chelsea Acad., DC 1856, NYMC 1857, physician Georgia VT 1858-62
War Service: Asst SURG 9th VT INF 26 Sep 1862, resgd 15 Oct 1863
Later Life: physician Georgia 1863-70, physician Chelsea 1870-1905, super. of schools in both towns
Affiliations: GAR
Married: 4 Jan 1858, Ann Eliza Vincent (sister of Walter Scott Vincent)
Died: 27 Apr 1905, Chelsea VT; interment in Highland Cemetery
Biography: Story Norman Goss, Doctor of Medicine of Chelsea, Vermont, 1831-1905, 1905
(DCN, HC3, HFW12, JGU*)

Gray, Edmund Baldwin (1825-aft 1895)

Born: 17 Jun 1825, Canton NY, son of Burr D. and Amy (Baldwin) Gray (Native Vermonters)
Early Life: UVM, text book business, instructor, school superintendent
War Service: CPT Co C 4th WI CAV 23 Apr 1861; resgd 10 Apr 1862, MAJ 28th WI INF 30 Aug 1862, LTCOL 29 May 1863, COL (Not mustered) 16 Mar 1864, m/o 23 Aug 1865
Later Life: Postmaster, Whitewater WI, 1865-68, school book business, Chicago IL 1868-75, Asst State Super. Schools IL 1875-78, State Pension Office 1895
Affiliations: GAR
Died: aft 1895; interment in Oak Woods Cemetery, Cook Cty IL
(CZ, JG, HCAS, MDR, FSO)

Gray, Jacob G. (1841-1913)

Born: 27 May 1841, Sheffield VT, son of Reuben and Annie (Miles) Gray
Early Life: farmer, Haverhill NH

War Service: PVT Co K, 4th VT INF, 12 Aug 1863, pr CPL, wdd, Wilderness, 5 May 1864, tr to VRC 10 Dec 1864, m/o, 24 Nov 1865
Later Life: Topeka, KS, farmer, Barton VT 1878-1901, Brownington VT 1901-03, moved to Sheffield 1903, Road Commissioner, Sheffield 1908-09, j.p. 1909-10
Married: 1868, Elvira W. Pearl
Died: 4 Jan 1913; interment in Dexter Cemetery, Sheffield VT
(AGO, PCD)

Greene, Theodore Phinney (1809-1887)

Born: 1 Nov 1809, Montreal PQ, Canada, son of Eli and Patience (Phinney) Green
Early Life: raised by uncle in Brattleboro; Acting Midshipman 1826; Mediterranean Squadron, *Warren*, *Java*, *Ontario*, *Brandywine* and *Constellation* 1826-31; Passed Midshipman 28 Apr 1832; sloop *Vincennes*, Pacific Squadron, 1833-36; New York Navy Yard 1836-37; razee *Independence*, Brazil Squadron 1837-40; LT 20 Dec 1837; receiving ship *Columbia*, Boston 1840-42; *Grampus*, Home Squadron, *St. Louis*, *Norfolk*, *Lexington*, Mediterranean Squadron 1842-44; *Congress*, Pacific Squadron, Mexican-American War 1845-49; *Cyane*, Home Squadron 1851-53; Boston Navy Yard 1853-57; CDR 14 Sep 1855; First Lighthouse District, Portland ME 1857-60
War Service: Mare Island Navy Yard 1861-63; CAPT 16 Jul 1862; *Shenandoah* 1863; *Santiago de Cuba*, West India Squadron 1863; screw frigate *San Jacinto*, EGBS 1863-64; steam sloop *Richmond*, WGBS 1865
Later Life: Ordnance Officer, Portsmouth Navy Yard 1865-66; *Powhatan*, Pacific Squadron 1866-68; COMO 24 Jul 1867; Board of Visitors, Naval Acad. 1867; Pensacola Navy Yard 1867-70; on leave 1870-71; ret. 1 Nov 1871
Died: 30 Aug 1887, Jaffrey NH; interment unknown
(TJL2)

Greenleaf, William Luther (1842-1902)

Born: 1 Sep 1842, Derby VT, son of William Fairbanks and Abigail (Ward) Greenleaf
Early Life: moved to Burlington 1846, Winooski 1847, district schools, Williston Acad., moved to IA 1857, compositor, North Iowa Gazette, returned to VT 1858
War Service: 2SGT Co. L 1st VT CAV 29 Sep 1862, wdd thrice, 2LT 28 Feb 1864, wdd 23 Jun 1864, 1LT 9 Feb 1865, dis/dsb 15 Jun 1865
Later Life: CPT Co. E 1st VT Militia 1869, MAJ, LTCOL, COL, B.G. 1 Dec 1866, cmdd VT NG until retirement on1 Dec 1892, retail druggist 1866-84, deputy collect of Internal Revenue 1882, Colchester town clerk, village clerk, trustee, treasurer, fire department chief at various times
Affiliations: GAR (AQM, Cmdr), Mason, MOLLUS (#01958)
Married: 25 Dec 1865, Adelaide Barrett
Died: 18 Dec 1902; interment in Greenmount Cemetery, Burlington VT
Publications: 1st Vermont Cavalry History in Peck's Revised Roster (1892), "From the Rapidan to Richmond." (1994)
(AGO, C&S, FSO, GFH, MOLLUS)

Grinnell, Josiah Bushnell (1821-1891)

Born: 22 Dec 1821, New Haven VT, son of Myron and Catherine (Hastings) Grinnell
Early Life: Oneida Inst. 1842, Auburn Theol. Sem. 1846, pastor, Congr. Churches in Union Village NY and Washington, founded Grinnell IA 1854, State Sen. 1856-60, sheltered John Brown 1859, RNC delegate 1860
War Service: US Rep. 1863-67, supported black troops, broad use of war powers
Later Life: atty, dir. Rock Island R.R., receiver, IA Central R.R., pres. State Horticultural Soc., pres. 1st National Bank Grinnell
Affiliations: Republican, Congregational, Abolitionist
Married: 5 Feb 1852, Julia Ann Chapin
Died: 31 Mar 1891, Grinnell IA; interment in Hazelwood Cemetery
Biography: Payne, Charles E. Josiah Bushnell Grinnell. Iowa City: State Historical Soc. of Iowa, 1938

Publications: Sketches of the West, Home of the Badgers (1845), Cattle Industries of the United States (1882), New Haven: A Rural Historical Town of Vermont (1887), Men and Events of Forty Years: Autobiographical Reminiscences of an Active Career from 1850-1890 (1891)
(HGW, JHB, TWH)

Grout, Josiah (1842-1925)

Born: 28 May 1842, Compton PQ, Canada, son of Josiah and Sophronia (Ayer) Grout
Early Life: student, teacher Kirby VT 1860
War Service: 2LT, Co. I, 1st VT CAV, 21 Oct 1861, 1LT 25 Apr 1862, CPT 1 Apr 1863, wdd, Broad Run, 1 Apr 1863, dis/dsb 1 Oct 1863; CPT Co. M, Frontier CAV (26th NY CAV), 10 Jan 1865, MAJ 22 Mar 1865, m/o 27 Jun 1865
Later Life: atty; Customs agent 1866-69; State Rep. 1872-74; in IL 1874-80; State Rep. 1884-88; State Sen. 1892; VT Gov. 1896-98, atty, Newport 1910
Affiliations: RSVO, MOLLUS (#09170)
Married: Oct 1867, Harriet Hinman
Died: 9 Jul 1925, Derby VT; interment in Derby Center Cemetery, Derby Line
Publications: Memoir of Gen'l William Wallace Grout and Autobiography of Josiah Grout (1919), A Lincoln Book: A Soldier's Tribute to his Chief (1925)
(1860, 1910, C&S, JGU, PCD*)

Grout, William Wallace (1836-1902)

Born: 24 May 1836, Compton, PQ, Canada, son of Josiah and Sophronia (Ayer) Grout
Early Life: common schools, local Acad., Poughkeepsie Law School 1857; admitted to the bar 1857, atty; nom. State's Atty, but declined to enlist
War Service: LTC, 15th VT INF, 26 Sep 1862, m/o 5 Aug 1863; B.G. cmdg prov forces, eastern VT, after St. Albans Raid 19 Oct 1864
Later Life: State's Atty 1865-67; State Rep. 1868-71, 1874-75; State Sen. 1876-77; US Rep. 1881-83, 1885-1901
Affiliations: RSVO, MOLLUS (#02695)
Died: 7 Oct 1902, Kirby VT; interment in Pine Grove Cemetery, East St. Johnsbury VT
Speeches: An oration before the Re-union Society of Vermont Officers, in the Representatives' Hall, Montpelier, Vermont, November 4, 1869
(C&S, CB, FAG, JGU*, LHC, VHS02)

Grow, Milo Walbridge (1825-1864)

Born: 28 Mar 1825, Craftsbury VT, son of Silas and Lamoille Grow
Early Life: DC 1852, studied law, teacher, Albany GA, atty Milford GA 1860
War Service: PVT Co. D 51st GA INF "Miller Guards" 15 Mar 1862, wdd, Gettysburg, 2 Jul 1863, pow 3 Jul 1863, imprisoned Fort Delaware, Point Lookout VA, died in prison
Married: 13 Dec 1860, Sarah Catherine Baughn
Affiliations: Confederate
Died: 23 Jan 1864, Point Lookout VA; interment in Mt. Pleasant Cemetery, St. Johnsbury VT
(1860, GTC, GG)

Gleason, Joseph T.

Gleason, Newell

Goss, Story N.

Greenleaf, William L.

Grout, Josiah

Grout, William W.

HHHHH

Hale, Charles Stuart (1835-1905)

Born: 30 Apr 1835, Brandon VT, son of Dr. Josiah and Marcia (Tracy) Hale
Early Life: Brandon Acad., Trinity College
War Service: Chap. 5th VT INF 24 May 1862, resgd, 25 May 1863, recommissioned 8 Aug 1863, m/o 15 Sep 1864
Later Life: Rector, St. James Church, Arlington VT 1865-68, Emmanuel Church, Bellows Falls VT, St. Mary's-on-the-hill, Buffalo NY, 1874-78, St. Paul's Church, Buffalo NY, Christ Church, New Bern, NC, Trinity Church, Claremont NH 1881-85, Claremont NH 1890
Married: (1) 6 Jul 1875, Louise Weed Stevens; (2) 1884, Clara Farwell Blodgett
Died: 1905, Claremont NH; interment in Bellows Falls VT
(1890, GRB, HWH, PEC)

Hall, Elmore John (1834-1897)

Born: 28 Feb 1834, Beamsville ON, Canada
Early Life: Morrisville Acad., teacher in Morrisville, Stowe and Burke, M.D. UVM 1858, p.g. study at Burlington and NY
War Service: Asst SURG 1st VT CAV 1863-64
Later Life: US Pension Examiner 21 years, Med. Examiner, Old Line Ins. Co.
Affiliations: VT MS, Lamoille Cty MS
Married: 15 Feb 1859, Ophelia Sophia Titus
Died: 1 May 1897, Morrisville VT; interment unknown
(GFH, UVMMED)

Hall, George B. (1844-1914)

Born: 24 Jun 1844, Richmond VT, son of Benjamin and Lovina Delight (Carroll) Hall
Early Life: Northfield H.S., VT Conf. Sem.
War Service: PVT Co. I, 9th VT INF 9 Jul 1862, Co. B 17th US INF 15 Jan 1863, m/o 15 Jun 1863, PVT 3rd VT LARTY 1 Jan 1864, CPL 21 Jan 1864, reduced 3 Dec 1864, m/o 15 Jun 1865
Later Life: farm laborer Roxbury VT 1870-80, j.p. 1878-88, town clerk 1903-12, insurance agent 1910
Married: 1877, Evelyn S. Pearson
Died: 13 Jun 1914, Roxbury VT; interment in Roxbury Cemetery
(1870, 1880, 1910, AGO, PCD)

Hall, Horace P. (1829-1883)

Born: 4 Sep 1829, St. Albans VT, son of Charles and Charlotte (Hubbard) Hall
Early Life: BMC 1853, physician St. Albans 1860
War Service: Asst SURG 9th VT INF 30 Jun 1862, resgd 13 Mar 1863
Later Life: physician St. Albans 1870-83
Affiliations: VT MS 1853-88
Married: 16 Oct 1854, Mary E. Walworth
Died: 12 Mar 1883, St. Albans VT; interment in Greenwood cemetery
(1860, 1870, 1880, CAW, Gibson*, NAS)

Hall, Josiah (1835-1912)

Born: 5 Feb 1835, Westminster VT, son of Edward and Orpha (Goodell) Hall
Early Life: NU 1858-59, cattle driver, MO, NU 1859-60, store clerk, MO
War Service: Recruiting Officer, 4th VT INF 1861, CPT Co F 1st VT CAV 17 Oct 1861, MAJ 4 Oct 1862, wdd/pow Brandy Station 12 Oct 1863, Libby Prison, prld 3 Aug 1864, LTCOL 19 Nov 1864, cmdg 1st VT CAV 1 Feb 1865, COL 23 May 1865, m/o 21 Jun 1865
Later Life: farmer, Greenfield MA 1866-75, surveying and construction work CA 1876-80, farmer Fresno CA 1880-1912, B.S. NU 1904
Died: 15 Mar 1912, Fresno CA; interment in Mountain View Cemetery
(FAG, WAE*, WSR)

Hanrahan, John David (1844-1927)

Born: 18 Jan 1844, Rathkeale Cty Limerick Ireland, son of James and Ellen (O'Connor) Hanrahan
Early Life: local schools, moved to NYC 1850, NYMC until 1861
War Service: Asst SURG USN, Potomac Flotilla 1861-63, pow 23 Aug 1863, prld after six weeks, attended lectures Georgetown Univ., exchanged and ordered to duty in NABS, m/o Jul 1865
Later Life: M.D. NYMC, physician NY 1869, moved to Rutland bef 1880, grand juror Rutland 1880, Cty Pension Board 1885-93, postmaster 1893-97, DNC delegate 1884, 1888, 1892
Affiliations: Democrat, Catholic, GAR (Surg. Gen. 1911), RSVO
Married: (1) 12 Feb 1870, Mary A. Riley; (2) 31 Oct 1883, Frances Keenan
Died: 1927; interment unknown
(AMM, GFH, JGU*)

Hannon, Thomas (1843-1928)

Born: 17 Nov 1843, Danville VT, son of James and Mary (Hayes) Hannon
Early Life: public schools, Guilford.
War Service: PVT Co K 9th VT INF 9 Jul 1862, CPL 11 Apr 1863, SGT 15 Dec 1864, m/o 13 Jun 1865
Later Life: foreman, Estey Organ Co., Brattleboro VT 1870-1901, Asst. QMG, VT NG 1892-1900, super., VT Soldiers Home, Bennington 1901-21
Affiliations: GAR (VT Cdr 1915)
Married: 1869, Ellen M. Weatherhead
Died: 3 Dec 1928, Bennington VT; interment in Brattleboro VT
(PCD)

Hanscom, Willis G. (1847-1938)

Born: 3 Mar 1847, Barnston PQ, son of Elias Bean and Rosella (Danforth) Hanscom
Early Life: moved to US 1851
War Service: PVT Co K, 11th VT INF, 17 Aug 1864, m/o, 24 Jun 1865
Later Life: farmer, Sheffield VT 1870-80, auctioneer, Sheffield 1875-1920, mngr, Greensboro & Glover Telephone Co., Sheffield 1898, Sheffield 1930
Married: 1866, Eliza A. Barber
Died: 27 Jul 1938, Lyndon VT; interment in Lyndon Center Cemetery
(1870, 1880, 1900, 1920, 1930, PCD)

Harmon, James Clark (1840-1906)

Born: 19 Jan 1840, Milton VT
Early Life: Grand Isle Acad
War Service: CPL Co. D 13th VT INF 6 Sep 1862, SGT 1 Mar 1863, wdd, Gettysburg 3 Jul 1863, m/o 21 Jul 1863

Later Life: M.D. UVM 1866, physician Westford VT 1870, Rantoul IL 1880-1900, Pension Board 12 years in IL
Affiliations: Champaign Cty MS, IL MS, Esculapian MS
Married: 1868, Edna E. Johnson
Died: 1 Aug 1906, Champaign IL; interment in Maplewood Cemetery
(1870, 1880, 1900, GNK, UVMMED)

Harrington, Joseph Lysander (1840-1893)

Born: 5 Aug 1840, Jamaica VT
Early Life: entered college from Londonderry VT, M.D. UVM 1862
War Service: PVT Co. I 4th VT INF 14 Sep 1864, tr to Co. F 25 Feb 1865, Asst SURG 11th VT INF 4 Mar 1865, m/o 25 Aug 1865
Later Life: State Rep. 1878, physician Halifax 1880, Owatonna MN 1890
Affiliations: CT River Valley MS, VT MS, Steel Cty MN MS
Married: 1867, Catherine McAllister
Died: 11 Jan 1893, Owtonna MN; interment unknown
(1880, 1890, CPT UVMMED, WBA1)

Harris, Broughton Davis (1822-1899)

Born: 16 Aug 1822, Chesterfield NH, son of Wilder and Harriet (Davis) Harris
Early Life: Chesterfield Acad., KUA, DC 1845, atty, editor, Vermont Phoenix, founded and published Eagle 1847-56, register of probate 1847, 1st secretary of Utah Terr. 1850, conflicted with Gov. Brigham Young, returned to VT 1852, State Sen. 1860-62
War Service: Peace Conf. delegate 1861
Later Life: railroad constructor, pres. Brattleboro Savings Bank
Married: 24 Mar 1851, Sarah Buell
Died: 19 Jan 1899, Brattleboro VT; interment unknown
(GSM, JGU)

Haskell, Franklin Aretas (1828-1864)

Born: 13 Jul 1828, Tunbridge VT, son of Aretas and Annie E. (Folsom)
Early Life: DC 1854, atty, militia officer
War Service: ADJ (1LT), 6th WI INF, ADC B.G. John Gibbon; COL 36th WI INF, cmdg 1st BGD 2nd DIV II Corps at Cold Harbor just before being killed leading a charge
Died: 3 Jun 1864, Cold Harbor VA; interment in Silver Lake Cemetery, Portage WI
Notes: his account of the battle of Gettysburg, posthumously published in 1898, was hailed by historian Bruce Catton as "one of the genuine classics of Civil War literature"
(ADG, FLB, FSO, RR)

Haskins, Kittredge (1836-1916)

Born: 8 Apr 1836, Dover VT, son of Asaph and Amelia (Ward) Haskins
Early Life: admitted to the bar, 14 Apr 1858, atty Wilmington VT 1858-61, moved to Williamsville VT 1861
War Service: 1LT Co. I 16th VT INF 20 Sep 1862, resgd 19 Mar 1863
Later Life: State's Atty, Windham Cty 1871-72, State Rep. 1872-73, 1896-99, State Sen. 1892-93, US Atty Vermont District 1880-87, US Rep. 1901-09, Judge, Municipal Court, Brattleboro VT 1910, Postmaster, Brattleboro 1912-15
Affiliations: MOLLUS (#13263)
Married: 1860, Esther Maria Childs
Died: 7 Aug 1916, Brattleboro VT; interment Prospect Hill Cemetery

(BDAC, C&S, JGU*, PCD)

Hatch, Isaac W. (1838-1934)

Born: 25 Aug 1838, Panton VT, son of Warren E. and Phebe C. Hatch
Early Life: Vergennes H.S., farmer, Panton 1860
War Service: PVT Co. K 2nd VT INF 30 Aug 1861, wdd Wilderness 5 May 1864, m/o 29 Aug 1864
Later Life: farmer, Addison VT 1866-71, hotel business NY 1871-75, farmer, Lewis NY 1880, lumber business and farmer Lincoln VT, road commissioner Lincoln 1900, hotel keeper Queen City Hotel Burlington 1900, Richmond VT 1910, real estate agent, Burlington 1920
Married: (1) 1864, Ann E. Matthews; (2) 7 Sep 1891, Mrs. Phebe H. Batchelder
Died: 1 Jan 1934; interment in Greenwood Cemetery, Bristol VT
(1860, 1880, 1900, 1910, 1920, AGO, FSO, GFH, PCD)

Hathaway, Forrest Henry (1844-1912)

Born: 7 Oct 1844, Boston MA, son of Arthur and Mary Hathaway (native Vermonters)
Early Life: Charlestown MA 1860, moved to Hartford VT
War Service: PVT Co. G 16th VT INF 23 Oct 1862, m/o 10 Aug 1863, CPT 107th USCI 30 Jun 1864, Bvt MAJ 25 Jul 1866, m/o 20 Feb 1867
Later Life: 2LT 41st US INF 7 Mar 1867, tr to 40th US INF 27 Nov 1867, tr to 5th US INF 17 Dec 1869, Ft. Harker KS 1870, 1LT 4 Sep 1878, CPT AQM 13 Feb 1882, MAJ QM 12 Sep 1894, LTCOL QM 3 Sep 1898-2 Mar 1889, LTCOL Dpy QM Gen. 12 Aug 1900, COL AQM Gen. 12 Apr 1903, B.G. 20 Jan 1904, ret. 21 Jan 1904, resided Portland OR 1910
Affiliations: SAR, SCW, MOLLUS (#05701)
Married: Abt 1869, Alice (nfi)
Dled: 29 Jul 1912, Portland OR; interment in Fort Vancouver Military Cemetery, Vancouver WA
(1870, 1910, FAG, FBG, FGW, WHO13)

Hathorn, Ransom E. (1843-1931)

Born: 3 Nov 1843, Londonderry VT, son of Eleazer and Lydia (Foster) Hathorn
Early Life: public schools, harness-maker
War Service: PVT Co. G 11th VT INF 11 Aug 1862, wdd Petersburg 2 Apr 1865, m/o 24 Jun 1865
Later Life: harness-maker 1865-1915, electric light commissioner, organized Ludlow boys' drum corps 1894, State Sen., Ludlow trustee, COL on Gov. Ormsbee's staff
Affiliations: Republican, RSVO, Mason, GAR (5 times post commander, twice Senior Vice-Commander, 1902 Dept Commander)
Married: (1) 1868, Jennie Ward; (2) 13 Jan 1875, Clara Wright
Died: 9 Jan 1931, Ludlow VT; interment in Ludlow Cemetery
(AFS, AGO)

Hawkins, Rush Christopher (1831-1920)

Born: 14 Sep 1831, Pomfret VT, son of Lorenzo Dow and Maria Louisa (Hutchinson) Hawkins
Early Life: 2nd US Dragoons, Mexican-American War, studied law NYC,
War Service: COL 9th NY INF (Hawkins' Zouaves) 3 May 1861; m/o 20 May 1863; Bvt B.G. 13 Mar 1865
Later Life: atty, book collector, NY State Rep. 1872, Art Commissioner, Paris, 1889
Married: 1860, Annmary Brown
Died: 25 Oct 1920, New York NY; interment in Annmary Brown Library, Brown University, Providence RI
Correspondence: University of Glasgow

Publications: A Biographical Sketch of the Rev. Aaron Hutchinson, A.M.: of Pomfret, Vermont (1888), An Account of the Assassination of Loyal Citizens of North Carolina (1897)
(RJ*, VHS20)

Haynes, Edwin Mortimer (1836-1910)

Born: 12 Apr 1836, Concord MA
Early Life: Shelburne Falls Acad. (MA), Univ. of Rochester (NY); clergyman, Wallingford VT Jun 1857
War Service: Chap. 10th VT INF 18 Aug 1862; resgd 2 Oct 1864
Later Life: clergyman, Palmer MA, Lewiston ME, Whitehall NY, Meadville PA. LLD DC 1885, pres. Reunion Soc. of VT Officers (1894), Baptist Clergyman, Rutland VT 1900
Died: 15 Dec 1910; interment in Evergreen Cemetery, Rutland VT
Affiliations: Baptist, MOLLUS (#10073), RSVO (pres. 1894)
Publications: A History of the Tenth Regiment, Vermont Volunteers (1894)
(1900, C&S, EMH*, MDB, RSVO2, WT)

Hazelton, Daniel Walker (1824-1901)

Born: 11 May 1824, Hebron NH, son of Daniel and Mary (Walker) Hazelton
Early Life: Hebron Acad., D.M., WMC 1848, physician, Boston MA, physician, Antrim NH 1850-53, physician, Cavendish VT 1854-79
War Service: Fredericksburg and Washington (May 1864), among a contingent of Vermont doctors who volunteered their services to care for Vermonters who were wounded in the battles of the Wilderness and Spotsylvania C.H.
Later Life: State Rep. 1876, physician, Springfield VT 1879-1901
Affiliations: Republican, Baptist, VT MS, CT Valley MS
Married: 5 Nov 1850, Laurette L. Hammond
Died: 31 Jan 1901, Bellows Falls VT; interment unknown
(1860, 1870, 1900, PAH)

Hazelton, John H. (1838-1878)

Born: 1838, Vermont
Early Life: Clerk, Rutland VT 1860
War Service: PVT Co. H 1st VT Cav 18 Sep 1861, QM SGT 19 Nov 1861, 1SGT, 1 Aug 1862, 2LT 30 Oct 1862, 1LT 1 Apr 1863, CPT Co M 6 Jul 1863, escort for M.G. Hancock, VA Campaign 14 May 1864, Bvt LTCOL, Bvt COL 13 Mar 1865, MAJ 23 May 1865, m/o 9 Aug 1865
Later Life: landlord, Barnes House, Rutland 1870
Affiliations: GAR (charter member, Roberts Post #14, Rutland), RSVO
Died: 21 Aug 1878, Rutland VT; interment in Evergreen Cemetery
(1860, 1870, AAH, JEP, JHG, RHObit, SR)

Hazen, William Babcock (1830-1887)

Born: 27 Sep 1830, West Hartford VT, son of Stillman and Ferone (Fenno) Hazen
Early Life: 1833 moved to Huron OH, USMA 1855 (28/34), Bvt 2 LT, 4th US INF 1855, Pacific Northwest 1855-57, Texas 1857-59, wdd by Comanche Indians, Texas 1859, Instr. INF Tactics, USMA 1861, 1 LT, 8th US INF, 1 Apr 1861, CPT 8th US INF, 14 May 1861
War Service: COL 41st OH INF 29 Oct 1861, B.G. USV 29 Nov 1862, cmdg 19 Brig 4 DIV, Shiloh 1862, Cmdg. 2 Brig 2 DIV XIV Corps, Stone's River 1862-63, Cmdg. 2 Brig 2 Div XXI Corps at Chickamauga 1863, Cmdg 2 Brig 3 Div IV Corps, Knoxville 1863, cmdg 2 Div XV Corps, M.G. USV, 13 Dec 1864, cmdg XV Corps, 19 May 1865

Later Life: COL 38th US INF, 28 Jul 1866; 6th US INF 1869, observed Franco-Prussian War, Paris 1869, frontier duty, Military Attaché, Vienna 1877, B.G. and Chief Signal officer USA, 15 Dec 1880
Married: 15 Feb 1871, Millie McLean (remarried George Dewey (q.v.))
Died: 16 Jan 1887 Washington, D.C; interment in Arlington National Cemetery (Section 1, Grave 15)
Papers: Smithsonian Institution
Publications: The School and the Army in Germany and France, With a Diary of Siege Life at Versailles (1872), A Narrative of Military Service (1885)
Notes: Brevetted on five separate occasions during the war. Close friend of future President James Garfield
(BEO, E&E, GWC, LOC*, WR)

Hebard, Salmon Blodgett (1835-1894)

Born: 15 Nov 1835, Randolph VT, son of William and Elizabeth S. (Brown) Hebard
Early Life: Randolph grammar school, Chelsea Acad., atty, deputy clerk Orange Cty Court
War Service: 1LT 1st VT LARTY 15 Jan 1862, CPT 13 Feb 1863, m/o 10 Aug 1864
Later Life: atty, town agent, Deputy clerk Orange Cty Court 1860-87, clerk 1887-94, State's Atty, State Sen. 1884; never married
Affiliations: RSVO
Died: 17 Nov 1894, Chelsea VT; interment in Highland Cemetery
(JGU, RSVO2, VBA)

Hemenway, Lewis Hunt (1841-1925)

Born: 30 Nov 1841, Bangkok, Siam, son of Asa and Lucia (Hunt) Hemenway
Early Life: Burr and Burton Sem., Manchester VT, MC 1859
War Service: PVT Co. K, 12th VT INF 19 Aug 1862 - 14 Jul 1863
Later Life: A.B. MC 1864, CPS NYU 1864-66, M.D. UVM 1866, physician, Manchester VT 1868-77, St. Paul, MN 1877-79, Manchester VT, 1879-1916
Affiliations: AMA, Bennington Cty and VT MS, Nat. Geo. Soc., Delta Kappa Epsilon Fraternity
Married: 21 Sep 1870, Maria Reed
Died: 30 Aug 1925, Honolulu, HI; interment unknown
(UVMMED, WHO3)

Hendee, George Whitman (1832-1906)

Born: 30 Nov, 1832, Stowe VT
Early Life: atty; Super. of Schools; State's Atty 1858-59
War Service: Deputy Provost Marshall; State Rep. 1861-63
Later Life: State Sen. 1866-69; LT Gov. 1869-70; VT Gov. 1870; US Rep. 1873-79; railroad constructor; banker 1879-85
Married: 23 Dec 1863, Viola L. Bundy
Died: 6 Dec 1906, Morristown VT; interment in Pleasant View Cemetery
(CB, FAG, FSO, JGU*)

Henry, Hugh (1838-1920)

Born: 21 Mar 1838, Chester VT, son of Hugh Horatio and Sarah (Henry) Henry
Early Life: public schools, Chester Acad., Deerfield (MA) Acad., admitted to the bar May 1862
War Service: QM SGT 16th VT INF 15 Sep 1862, 2LT Co. I, 12 May 1863, m/o 10 Aug 1863
Later Life: atty, judge of probate, Windsor district 1884-98, one of founders of Bennington Soldiers' Home 1884, later pres. board of trustees 1886, State Rep. 1870, 1872, 1874, 1876, 1884, State Sen. 1880, pension agent, Concord NH 1898-1906, atty Chester VT 1910

Affiliations: Republican, Unitarian, GAR (VT Dept Commander 1892), MOLLUS (#09167, Cmdr, 1910 VT Cmdry), Mason, IOOF
Married: 9 Jan 1872, Emma J. Ordway; (2) Alice A. Ordway
Died: 3 Feb 1920, Chester VT; interment in Brookside Cemetery
Notes: Hugh Henry Camp. Sons of Veterans, of Chester was named for him
(1910, AFS, AGO, C&S)

Herrick, Lucius Carroll (1840-1903)

Born: 2 Sep 1840, West Randolph VT, son of Lorenzo Dow and Zilpha Ann (Haskins) Herrick
Early Life: Randolph Acad., printer, studied medicine under Dr. D. L. Stewart, attended lectures at CMC and Michigan University Med. School
War Service: PVT Co. G 8th VT INF 21 Nov 1861, m/o 5 Dec 1863, Asst SURG, 1st CAV Corps d'Afrique (4th US COL INF) 13 Nov 1863, m/o 20 Mar 1866
Later Life: M.D. UVM 1864; student/physician Bellevue Hosp. NYMC, moved to OH 1869, Columbus OH 1882
Affiliations: OH State MS, Champaign Cty MS
Married: 1871, Louise Taylor
Died: 30 Apr 1903, Columbus OH; interment unknown
Publications: Herrick Genealogy (1885, 1890)
(HFW12, LMW4, WHO1, UVMMED)

Heyer, Charles Alfred (1849-1942)

Born: 11 Mar 1849, Rochester MA, son of Walter Isaac and Deborah (Bacon) Heyer
Early Life: unknown
War Service: PVT Co. C 8th VT INF 15 Feb 1865, m/o 28 Jun 1865;
Later Life: machinist, scale shop, St. Johnsbury 1870-1910
Affiliations: GAR (AAG to National Cdr George A. Gay, last Commander VT Cmdry)
Married: (1) Josephine E. Bonnette; (2) 18 Jun 1876, Matilda Louise Wheeler
Died: 12 Jul 1942, St. Johnsbury VT; interment in Mt. Pleasant Cemetery
Notes: one of the last 10 surviving Vermont veterans
(1870, 1890, 1930, AB, FSO, RR)

Higley, Edwin Hall (1843-1916)

Born: 15 Feb 1843, Castleton VT, son of Rev. Harvey O. and Sarah (Little) Higley
Early Life: Castleton Sem.
War Service: 1SGT Co. K 1st VT CAV 30 Sep 1861, 2LT 16 Jul 1862, wdd, Weldon Railroad 23 Jun 1864, pow, Nottoway C.H. 23 Jun 1864, at Columbia SC, prld 1 Mar 1865, Bvt 1LT, Bvt CPT Bvt MAJ, 13 Mar 1865, m/o 15 May 1865
Later Life: MC 1868, studied music and philology in Boston & Cambridge, also royal conservatory, Leipsic, Germany 1882-84, taught music, Boston, 18686-72, prof. German and Greek, MC 10 years, taught music, Worcester MA 1884-86, prof. Greek and German, Groton School, choir master and organist
Married: 2 Jun 1870, Jane Shepard Turner
Died: 5 May 1916, Groton MA; interment in Hillside Cemetery, Castleton VT
Publications: The Puritans and their Psalm Tunes (1885), Exercises in Greek Composition (1897)
(ANM, DUCat2, JGU, MDICat)

Hill, Charles Wesley (1812-1881)

Born: 7 Jul 1812, Starksboro VT, son of John and Laura (Bushnell) Hill
Early Life: moved to Ohio 1818; Oberlin College; atty

War Service: B.G. OH militia 15 Jun 1861; Hill's Army of Occupation, Dept of the Ohio 1861-; AG OH Militia 1862-63; COL 128th OH INF 1864-65; Bvt B.G. 13 Mary 1865; Bvt M.G. 13 Mar 1865; m/o 13 Jul 1865
Died: 24 Nov 1881, Toledo OH; interment in Forest Cemetery
Publications: Comments on Major-Gen McClellan's Account of his West Virginia Campaign. (1864)
(E&E, FBH, FSO)

Hill, George W. (1842-1905)

Born: 18 Dec 1842, Danville VT, son of Carleton and Amanda M. (Carr) Hill
Early Life: moved to Concord, local schools of Concord and Lunenburg, farm laborer
War Service: CPL Co. K 8th VT INF 9 Dec 1861, reen 5 Jan 1864, SGT 17 Feb 1864, 1SGT 6 Feb 1865, wdd Boutte Station 4 Sep 1862, 2LT 23 Feb 1865, m/o 28 Jun 1865
Later Life: farmer, State Rep. 1890
Affiliations: Republican, GAR
Married: 7 Nov 1865, Amanda M. Lane
Died: 29 Jun 1905; interment in Riverside Cemetery, Lunenburg VT
(JGU)

Hitchcock, Ethan Allen (1798-1870)

Born: 18 May 1798, Vergennes VT, son of Samuel and Lucy Caroline (Allen) Hitchcock (grandson of Gen. Ethan Allen)
Early Life: USMA 1817 (No standings listed), 3 LARTY Corps 17 Jul 1817, 2 LT 8th US INF 13 Feb 1818, 1 LT 8th US INF 31 Oct 1818, ADJ 8th US INF 1819-21, garrison duty, recruiting service 1821-24, CPT 1st US INF 31 Dec 1824, Commandant of Cadets and instr. of INF Tactics, USMA 1829-33, WI 1834-35, Seminole War 1836, Acting I.G., Western Dept 1836, disbursing Indian Agent 1837-39, MAJ 8th US INF 7 Jul 1838, LTCOL 3rd US INF 31 Jan 1842, Acting I.G. to Gen. Scott in Mexico 1847-48, Bvt COL 20 Aug 1847, Bvt B.G. 8 Sep 1847, COL 2nd US INF 15 Apr 1851, resgd 1855, author and student
War Service: COL 10 Feb 1862, M.G. USV 10 Feb 1862, special duty reporting to the Secretary of War 1862-66, Commissioner for Exchange of Prisoners of War 1862-67
Later Life: ret. 1 Oct 1867, moved to Sparta GA
Died: 5 Aug 1870 Sparta GA; interment in West Point Cemetery NY
Publications: Swendenborg, a Hermetic Philosopher. (1858), Christ the Spirit: Being an Attempt to State the Primitive View of Christianity. (1860), Fifty Years in Camp and Field: Diary of Major-General Ethan Allen Hitchcock.
(CCPL, CKG, FSO, GWC, HGW, LOC*)

Hitchcock, Robert E. (1839-1861)

Born: 29 Sep 1839, Shoreham VT, son of William and Emily (Hunsdon) Hitchcock
Early Life: B.S. NU 1859
War Service: 2LT, USMC, 5 Jun 1861; Marine Barracks, Washington,: kia, First Bull Run, 21 Jul 1861
Died: 21 Jul 1861, Manassas VA; interment in Lake View cemetery, Shoreham VT
Notes: first marine officer and first NU graduate killed in Civil War
(GGB, WAE*)

Hoard, Charles Brooks (1805-1886)

Born: 5 Jun 1805, Springfield VT
Early Life: public schools; moved to Antwerp NY, postmaster during Jackson and Van Buren administrations; State Rep. 1837; moved to Watertown NY 1844; clerk Jefferson Cty 1844-46; US Rep. 1857-61; manufacturer, portable engines
War Service: engaged in manufacture of arms for the Government
Later Life: moved to WV
Married: 1828, Susan Heald

Died: 20 Nov 1886, Ceredo WV; interment in Spring Hill Cemetery, Huntington WV
(CB)

Hodges, Henry Clay (1831-1917)

Born: 14 Jan 1831, Clarendon VT, son of Hannibal and Mary (Hall) Hodges
Early Life: USMA 51 (32/42), Bvt 2LT 4th US INF 1 Jul 1851, frontier duty 1851-53, 2LT 1 Aug 1852, Pacific Northwest 1853-61, 1LT 23 May 1855
War Service: AQM (CPT) 17 May 1861, Purchasing and Disbursing QM, staff of NY Gov. Morgan 1861-63, QM, AOP Jan-Feb 1863, Depot QM, Nashville, TN Apr-Aug 1863, Chief QM, AOC, Aug-Nov 1863, Chickamauga Sep 1863, Depot QM Ft Leavenworth KS Dec 1863-Feb 1865, Depot QM Moorehead City NC Mar 1865, Bvt MAJ, Bvt LTCOL 13 Mar 1865, Chief QM, Mobile, AL Apr-Jun 1865
Later Life: Chief QM New Orleans 1865, Chief QM Dept of Columbia 1865-66, MAJ 29 Jul 1866, Depot QM Ft Vancouver Dec 1866, Deputy QM Gen. (LTCOL) 29 May 1876, AQM Gen. (COL) 19 Oct 1888, ret. 14 Jan 1895
Died: 3 Nov 1917, Buffalo NY; interment in Arlington National Cemetery
(ADH1, GWC, WHP, NYTObit)

Hogan, Henry Hardy (1833-1902)

Born: 9 Sep 1833, Alburg VT
Early Life: M.D. UVM 1863
War Service: physician, NY Soldiers Home 1863, in charge of Hosp. No. 4, Quincy IL, 2LT 142nd NY INF
Later Life: MAJ NV NG 1887, editor The Plaindealer Reno NV 1881-84, 1895-99, physician
Affiliations: NV State MS
Married: 1868, Helena Elizabeth Myers
Died: 17 Mar 1902, Reno NV; interment unknown
(UVMMED)

Holabird, William Hyman (1845-1921)

Born: 29 Sep 1845, Shelburne VT, son of Oscar F. and Adelia A. (Pierson) Holabird
Early Life: local schools, Williston Acad., moved to MO, newsboy, Hannibal & St. Jo R.R., returned to VT
War Service: PVT Co. C 12th VT INF 23 Aug 1862, m/o 14 Jul 1863, 1st-class Fireman USN 1 Sep 1864, *Monadnock*, Acting Asst Paymr Dec 1864, resgd 1865
Later Life: moved to IN, then IL, gen. agent, Penn. & Grand Rapids Indiana R.R. 1876-80, special agent for Atchison, Topeka & Santa Fe R.R. 1880-93, confidential field expert, Southern Pacific R.R., special consultant, Imperial Japanese govt, reporting on Chinese and Korean R.R.s post-war with Russia; receiver CA Development Co.
Affiliations: Republican, Mason, GAR, SAR
Married: 9 Jun 1870, Phebe Jane Dorr
Died: 13 Mar 1921, Sierra Madre, Los Angeles CA; interment unknown
(FSO, JGU, JMG)

Holbrook, Frederick (1813-1909)

Born: 15 Feb 1813, East Windsor CT, son of Franklin E. and Anna E. (Nourse) Holbrook
Early Life: Berkshire (MA) Gymnasium; studied in Europe; farmer, Registrar of Probate, Marlboro 1847; pres. VT Agricultural Soc. 1850-58; State Sen. 1849-51
War Service: state's first war-time gov. 1861-63
Later Life: farmer
Married: 13 Jan 1835, Harriet Smith Goodhue
Died: 28 Apr 1909, Brattleboro VT; interment in Prospect Hill Cemetery

Notes: organized the first state-based hospitals
(GFH, HGW, JGU*, MRC)

Holbrook, William Cune (1842-1904)

Born: 14 Jul 1842, Brattleboro VT, son of Frederick and Harriet Smith (Goodhue) Holbrook
Early Life: merchant, Boston, MA
War Service: PVT 1 LT, ADJ, 4th VT INF, later MAJ, COL, 7th VT INF
Later Life: atty, New York City
Affiliations: RSVO
Married: 17 Jan 1872, Anna M. Chalmers
Died: 27 Mar 1904, New York NY; interment in Prospect Hill Cemetery, Brattleboro VT
Publications: A Narrative of the Services of the Officers and Enlisted Men of the 7th Regiment of Vermont Volunteers (Veterans) from 1862 to 1866 (1882)
(GFH, JGU, MRC*)

Holden, William Wallace (1843-1936)

Born: 28 Aug 1843, Barre VT, son of Ira and Abigail (Wales) Holden
Early Life: local schools, Barre Acad., farmer
War Service: CPL Co. I 13th VT INF 25 Aug 1862, m/o 21 Jul 1863
Later Life: farmer, teacher, alternating between Barre and IL, finally settling in Northfield, manufacturing 1867-71, returned to farming, CPT VT Militia, town lister, selectman, constable, j.p., grand juror, Deputy sheriff, school dir., auditor, trustee Northfield Public Library, trustee Brown Memorial Library, trustee Northfield Savings Bank 27 years
Affiliations: Congregational, Mason, GAR (Post Cdr, ADJ and QM 18 years; Senior vice-Commander and Chap. VT Dept)
Married: (1) 1868, Mary Elizabeth Hanson; (2) Dora L. Smith
Died: 5 May 1936, Northfield VT; interment in Mt. Hope Cemetery
(AFS*, AGO)

Holliday, Jonas P. (1832-1862)

Born: 6 Apr 1832, Alleghany Cty NY
Early Life: USMA 1850 (24/44), Bvt 2LT, Dragoons, 1 Jul 1850, frontier duty, NM 1850-51, 2LT, 2nd Dragoons, 11 Oct 1851, frontier duty TX 1851-53, sick leave 1853-54, frontier duty KS 1854-57, 1LT, 2nd Dragoons, 3 Mar 1855, QM, 2nd Dragoons, 4 Aug 1858-24 Jun 1859, frontier duty, Dakotas 1859-60, recruiting service 1860-61, CPT 2nd Dragoons, 9 May 1861, leave of absence 1861-62
War Service: COL, 1st VT CAV, 14 Feb 1862, committed suicide
Died: 5 Apr 1862, near Strasburg VA; interment Village Cemetery, Burns NY
(GGB, GWC)

Holton, Joel Huntington (1841-1912)

Born: 15 Nov 1841, Westminster VT, son of Erastus Alexander and Hannah Brainerd (May) Holton
Early Life: Westminster schools, Barre and West Brattleboro Acad., silver plater 1857-62
War Service: 5SGT Co. I 12th VT INF 18 Aug 1862, m/o 14 Jul 1863
Later Life: hardware store clerk, St. Albans, proprietor, plating and saddlery business, Derby Line, moved to Burlington 1871, wholesale and retail trade in hardware, saddlery and builders' supplies, alderman, mayoral candidate
Affiliations: Democrat, Congregational, GAR, RSVO
Married: (1) 29 Oct 1863, Emma J. Diggins; (2) 25 Jun 1883, Kate E. Wiley
Died: 11 Jan 1912; interment in Old Cemetery, Westminster VT

(JGU, familyhistory.org)

Hope, James (1818-1892)

Born: 29 Nov 1818, Drygrange, Scotland, son of Henry and Helen (Haag/Hague) Hope
Early Life: came to VT 1834, apprenticed to wagon maker, Castleton Sem. 1839-40, teacher, West Rutland 1840-41, Rutland 1843, Montreal 1844-46, returned to Castleton, art studio in NYC
War Service: CPT Co. B 2nd VT INF, 16 May 1861, due to illness, assigned as scout and mapmaker, resgd 20 Dec 1862
Later Life: studio and gallery, Glens Falls NY 1872-92
Paintings: Antietam series (Antietam National Battlefield), Winter Quarters of Vermont Brigade (VHS)
Affiliations: Presbyterian, GAR
Married: 20 Sep 1841, Julia M. Smith
Died: 20 Oct 1892, Watkins NY; interment unknown
(NPS, RJT, TVE)

Hopkins, William Cyprian (1834-aft 1911)

Born: 28 Apr 1834, Burlington VT, son of Rev. John Henry and Melusina (Muller) Hopkins
Early Life: A.B. UVM 1855, ordained 1858, St. Mary's Parish, Northfield VT 1858-61
War Service: Chap. 7th VT INF, 25 Sep 1862 - 19 Oct 1865
Later Life: Pastor, New Orleans LA 1865, Christ Church, St. Joseph MO 1865-66, Hannibal MO 1866-70, A.M. UVM 1875, Trinity Church, Aurora IL 1870-78, Emmanuel Mission, Champaign IL 1878-82, Grace Church, Toledo OH 1882-94, D.D., NU 1891, Adams Street Mission, Toledo OH 1894-97, St. Paul's Church, Toledo OH 1897-1911
Married: (1) 8 Jun 1858, Cornelia C. Stevens; (2) abt 1878, Julia Gilson
Died: aft 1911; interment unknown
(1860, 1870, 1880, 1890, 1900, HC4, UVMCat, WAE)

Horton, Edwin (1841-1926)

Born: 25 Aug 1841, Clarendon VT, son of John N. and Elsie (Potter) Horton
Early Life: local schools, Clarendon Acad., BRA, moved to Chittenden 1858, farmer, town offices, lister
War Service: 22nd NY INF, PVT Co. C 4th VT INF 22 Jul 1863, CPL 28 Dec 1864, wdd, Wilderness 5 May 1864, m/o 13 Jul 1865
Later Life: constable and collector 1870-93
Affiliations: GAR, Mason, IOOF
Married: 4 Aug 1862, Ellen L. Holbrook
Died: 12 Dec 1926, Chittenden VT; interment in Horton Cemetery
(JGU)

Hovey, Charles Edward (1827-1897)

Born: 26 Apr 1827, Thetford VT, son of Alfred and Abigail (Howard) Hovey
Early Life: DC 1852, teacher, principal, school super., founded State Teacher's University, Normal IL; pres. State Teacher's University 1857-61
War Service: COL 33rd IL INF 15 Aug 1861, B.G. USV, 5 Sep 1862, wdd, Arkansas Post Jan 1863, B.G. appointment unconfirmed by Congress, expired 4 Mar 1863, resgd due to wds May 1863, Bvt M.G. 13 Mar 1865
Later Life: pension lobbyist in Washington, D.C
Died: 17 Nov 1897, Washington, D.C; interment in Arlington National Cemetery (Section 1, Grave 33D)
(GBH, GTC, HDW, IHS)

Howard, Henry Seymour (1841-1898)

Born: 26 Feb 1841, Benson VT, son of Judson J. and Persis (Pierce) Howard
Early Life: local schools, Castleton Sem., West Rutland H.S.
War Service: CPL Co. D 14th VT INF 29 Aug 1862, m/o 30 Jul 1863
Later Life: worked for flour manufacturer 1863-68, hardware trade 1868-94, selectman, lister, town clerk and notary public, State Rep. 1884
Affiliations: Republican, Mason, GAR
Married: 13 Sep 1864, Eunice P. Balis
Died: 15 Jun 1898, Benson VT; interment in Fair View Cemetery
(AGO, JGU)

Howard, Jacob Merritt (1805-1871)

Born: 10 Jul 1805, Shaftsbury VT, son of Otis and Polley (Mittington) Howard
Early Life: Bennington Acad., Brattleboro Acad., Williams College 1830, moved to Detroit 1832, admitted to the bar 1833, City Atty 1834, State Rep. 1838, US Rep. 1841-43, MI atty Gen. 1856-61
War Service: US Sen. 1862-65, judiciary and military affairs committees
Later Life: US Sen. 1865-71 Joint Committee on Reconstruction, voted to impeach Andrew Johnson
Died: 2 Apr 1871, Detroit MI; interment unknown
(CB, HGW, TWH)

Howard, Noel Byron (1838-1871)

Born: 9 Sep 1838, Fairfax VT, son of Coridon and Harriett (Richardson) Howard
Early Life: town schools, Burlington H.S., NU 1856-58, teacher, Burlington VT, military school in NC, moved to Lyons IA early 1861
War Service: 1LT, Clinton Cty Guards, 5 May 1861, CPT 1 Apr 1861, MAJ 12 Oct 1863, judge advocate on staff of Gen. Dodge, LTCOL 10 Apr 1864, wdd, Atlanta, 22 Jul 1864, COL 8 Nov 1864, comdg 1st BGD 2d Div. XVI Corps, m/o 12 Jul 1865
Later Life: clerk of courts, Clinton Cty, IA 1867-70
Affiliations: GAR, Mason
Married: 5 Sep 1865, Elizabeth McClelland
Died: 21 Feb 1871, Palatka FL; interment unknown
Notes: N. B. Howard GAR Post, DeWitt, IA named in his honor
(WAE*)

Howe, Elwin Alva (1843-1929)

Born: 18 Sep 1843, Londonderry VT, son of Alva and Julia Ann (Miles) Howe
Early Life: public schools, farming, Chester and West River Acad., teacher
War Service: PVT Co. G 11th VT INF 30 Jul 1862, CPL 24 Jun 1864, 1LT Co. I 108th USCI 14 Jun 1864, also AACS (CPT) 11 Dec 1865, m/o 30 Mar 1866, Louisville, Ky.
Later Life: tradesman, moved to Ludlow, collar and harness business, later Ludlow Toy Manufacturing Co., 15 years, State Rep. 1878, 1880, State Sen. 1882, postmaster 1897-1914, coal business 1914-28
Affiliations: GAR, MOLLUS (#14303), Mason, Congregational
Married: 11 Nov 1865, Lydia Jane Walker
Died: 30 Aug 1929, Ludlow VT; interment in Pleasantview Cemetery
(AFS*, AGO, C&S, FSO)

Howe, Thomas Marshall (1808-1877)

Born: 20 Apr 1808, Williamstown VT, son of Thomas and Clarissa (Howard) Howe

Early Life: moved to OH 1817; Warren Acad., moved to PA 1829; dry-goods clerk; cashier and pres. Exchange National Bank, Pittsburg 1839-59; mining, steel manufacturing, banking; US Rep. 1851-55; RNC delegate 1860
War Service: Asst A.G. Penn.; chair. Allegheny Cty committee for recruiting
Later Life: one of organizers and first pres. Pittsburgh Chamber of Commerce
Married: 17 Dec 1833, Mary Anne Palmer
Died: 20 Jul 1877, Pittsburgh PA; interment in Allegheny Cemetery
(CB, FSO)

Hubbard, Lorenzo W. (1841-1911)

Born: 3 Feb 1841, Lyndon VT, son of Richard and Loraine (Weeks) Hubbard
Early Life: common schools, Lyndon Acad
War Service: CPL Co. M 11th VT INF 1 Sep 1863, SGT 29 Nov 1863, reduced 11 Sep 1864, Hosp. Steward 1 Jan 1865, m/o 25 Aug 1865
Later Life: NYMC 1867, moved to Lunenburg, physician 6 years, returned to Lyndon, State Rep. 1882, 1886, pres. St. Johnsbury Board of Pension Examining SURG 1883-85
Affiliations: Republican, Congregational, White Mountain MS, VT MS, Mason, GAR
Married: 10 Nov 1868, Mary E. Halton
Died: 25 Jun 1911, Lyndon VT; interment in Lyndon Center Cemetery
(AGO, JGU)

Hudson, Henry Norman (1814-1886)

Born: 28 Jan 1814, Cornwall VT, son of Joseph Hudson
Early Life: banker, wheelwright, MC 1840, went south to teach, KY 1840-41 and AL 1841-43, Boston 1844, A.M. Trinity College 1847, studied theology, ordained Episcopal deacon 1849, priest 1850, pastor, St. Michael's, Litchfield CT 1856-60
War Service: Chap. 1st NY ENGRS; conflict with Gen. B. F. Butler 1862-65
Later Life: lecturer Wesleyan University 1868-69, Cambridge MA, noted Shakespearean scholar and literary critic, LLD MC 1881
Married: 18 Dec 1852, Emily Sarah Bright
Died: 15 Jan 1886, Cambridge MA; interment unknown
Publications: Lectures on Shakespeare (1848), The Works of Shakespeare, with Notes, Introduction and Life (1851,1856), A Chap.'s Campaigns with General Butler (1865), Plays of Shakespeare (1870-72-74), Sermons (1874), Text Book of Poetry (1875), Text Book of Prose (1876), The Harvard Shakespeare (1880), Studies in Wordsworth and other Papers (1884)
(EAD*, MIDCat, NYTObit, RJ)

Hudson, Solomon S. (1836-1904)

Born: 22 Jul 1836, Athens VT, son of Calvin and Philomelia (Powers) Hudson
Early Life: public schools, farmer
War Service: PVT Co. A 10th VT INF 30 Jun 1862, wdd, 3 Jun 1864, m/o 22 Jun 1865
Later Life: farmer 1865-86, moved to East Haven, general trade, j.p., selectman, State Rep. 1880, postmaster 6 years
Affiliations: Republican, Mason, GAR
Married: (1) 1855, Eunecia L. Hosford; (2) Lydia Gero Partlow
Died: 30 May 1904; interment in East Burke Cemetery, Burke VT
(AGO, JGU)

Hunsdon, Charles (1830-1899)

Born: May 1830, Shoreham VT

Early Life: Pennsylvania Military Inst., Harrisburg 1846-47, NU 1847-50, farmer; postmaster 1859-61, mercantile business 1861-62; State Rep. 1861-62
War Service: CPT 13 Aug 1862, Co. B 11th VT INF 3 Sep 1862, MAJ 2 Nov 1863, LTCOL 2 Sep 1864, cmdg reg't at Opequan, Cedar Creek, Petersburg, COL 23 May 1865, m/o 24 Jun 1865
Later Life: State Rep. 1865, moved to Albany NY 1866, insurance business, school teacher, Odessa NY, Methodist clergyman 1880
Affiliations: RSVO
Died: 20 Sep 1899, South Nyack NY; interment in Ferncliff Cemetery, Springfield OH
(1850, 1880, FAG, Italo*, WAE)

Huntington, William Millet (1819-1903)

Born: 21 Oct 1819, Rochester VT, son of Daniel and Mary Huntington
Early Life: New York City Univ. 1845, physician, Rochester VT 1850-60, State Rep. 1863
War Service: Fredericksburg and Washington (May 1864), among a contingent of Vermont doctors who volunteered their services to care for Vermonters who were wounded in the battles of the Wilderness and Spotsylvania C.H.
Later Life: Physician, Rochester 1880-90, Pension Board, Randolph VT 1890-95
Affiliations: Episcopal, AMA, VT MS, White River Valley MS
Married: 13 Jun 1848, Arvilla Baker
Died: 19 Nov 1903, Rochester VT; interment unknown
(1850, 1860, 1880, 1900, HFA)

Huse, Hiram Augustus (1843-1902)

Born: 17 Jan 1843, Randolph VT, son of Hiram Sylvester and Emily Morgan (Blodgett) Huse
Early Life: moved to WI 1845, returned to VT 1858, fitted for college 1860 Orange Cty Grammar School Randolph, DC 1861
War Service: Pvt Co. F 12th VT INF 19 Aug 1862, m/o 14 Jul 1863
Later Life: DC 1865, ALS 1866-67, admitted to the bar 1867, teacher State Normal School Randolph 1871-72, moved to Montpelier 1872, ten years editorial writer Green Mountain Freeman, State Librarian 1873-1902, State Rep. 1878, State's Attorney 1882-84, atty 1883-1902
Affiliations: SAR, GAR, Mason
Married: 30 Jan 1872, Harriet Olivia Woodbury
Died: 27 Sep 1902, Williamstown VT; interment in Green Mount Cemetery, Montpelier VT
(GFH*, VHS02)

Hyde, Breed Noyes (1831-1918)

Born: 14 Aug 1831, Hyde Park VT, son of Russell B. Hyde
Early Life: USMA 1854 (non-graduate)
War Service: ADC to Gov. Fairbanks Apr 1861; LTCOL 3rd VT INF 6 Jun 1861, COL 13 Aug 1861, Peninsula Campaign 1862, Maryland Campaign 1862 Fredericksburg VA, 13 Dec 1862, resgd 15 Jan 1863
Later Life: civil engr, surveyor, Norwegian, PA 1870-1910
Died: 4 Oct 1918, Pottsville, PA; interment in Charles Baber Cemetery
Notes: accused of cowardice at Fredericksburg, resgd before court martial convened
(1870, 1880, 1900, 1910, E&E, FAG, HLA, GWC, FAG)

Hyde, Melvin John (1828-1874)

Born: 19 May 1828, Grand Isle VT, son of Jedediah and Sarah (Gilman) Hyde
Early Life: DC 1852
War Service: Asst SURG 2nd VT INF, 12 Sep 1863, SURG 1 Aug 1864, m/o 15 Jul 1865

Later Life: physician, j.p.
Affiliations: RSVO
Married: 23 Dec 1856, Phoebe Loop Hill
Died: 9 Dec 1874, Isle La Motte VT; interment unknown
Biography: In the Field, Doctor Melvin John Hyde, Surgeon, 2nd Vermont Volunteers (1999)
(DCCat, FSO, JHR69)

Hall, Horace P.

Hall, Josiah

Hanrahan, John D.

Haskins, Kittredge

Hawkins, Rush C.

Haynes, Edwin M.

Hazen, William B.

Hendee, George W.

Hitchcock, Ethan Allen

Hitchcock, Robert E.

Hoard, Charles B.

Holbrook, Frederick

Holbrook, William C.

Howard, Noel B.

Hudson, Henry N.

Hunsdon, Charles

Huse, Hiram A.

Ide, George Henry (1839-1903)

Born: 21 Jan 1839, St. Johnsbury VT, son of Joseph A. and Lucretia Ann (Fairbanks) Ide
Early Life: farmer, moved to Newport 1850, district school, Derby Acad., DC 1 yr before war
War Service: 1SGT Co. K 15th VT INF 28 Aug 1862, m/o 5 Aug 1863
Later Life: DC 1865, teacher St. Johnsbury 1865-66, ATS 1869, pastor Hopkinton MA 7 years, Central Church Lawrence MA, 4 years, Grand Ave Congregational Church Milwaukee WI 1881-1903, D.D. Ripon Coll. 1882, trustee Beloit Coll. 15 years
Married: (1) 16 Mar 1871, Mary J. Sanborn; (2) 1876, Kate Emma Bowles
Died: 23 Mar 1903, Kenosha WI; interment unknown
Publications: The Living Christ: The Vital Force in Pulpit and Pew. (1903)
(AGC, ATS, JGU)

Jackman, Henry A. (1829-1904)

Born: 18 Feb 1829, Barre VT, son of Winthrop T. and Mary (Elkins) Jackman
Early Life: farmer, district school, teamster, Boston, 9 years
War Service: PVT 2nd MA LARTY 31 Jul 1861, Baltimore, Fortress Monroe, Ship Island, New Orleans, QM SGT 16 Aug 1864, m/o Aug 1865
Later Life: moved to East Corinth, grist mill operator 4 years, moved to Topsham 1876, manufacturer of bobbins and spools, selectman, State Rep. 1876, Corinth 1900
Affiliations: Republican, GAR
Married: Oct 1869, Mrs. Nancy Rowland nee Crown
Died: before 15 Dec 1904; interment unknown
(1890, 1890, JGU, T289)

Jackson, William Henry (1843-1942)

Born: 4 Apr 1843, Keeseville NY, son of George Hallock and Harriet Maria (Allen) Jackson
Early Life: moved to Rutland VT; painter
War Service: PVT Co. K, 12th VT INF 4 Oct 1862, m/o 14 Jul 1863
Later Life: muralist, painter, photographer
Died: 30 Jun 1942, New York NY; interment in Arlington National Cemetery
Diary: New York Public Library
Publications: The Diaries of William Henry Jackson, Frontier Photographer: To California and Return, 1866-67; and with the Hayden Surveys to the Central Rockies, 1873, and to the Utes and Cliff Dwellings, 1874 (1959)
(FAG, LOC, RR)

Janes, Henry (1832-1915)

Born: 24 Jan 1832, Waterbury VT
Early Life: Woodstock College 1852; CPS NYU NYC 1855; physician NYC 1855, Chelsea MA 1856, Waterbury VT 1857-61
War Service: SURG, 3rd VT INF 24 Jun 1861; SURG USV 26 Mar 1863; Hosp. steamer *Maine* 1864; Sloan U.S. Gen. Hosp. Montpelier 1864-65; Bvt LTCOL USV 13 Mar 1865, m/o 4 Jan 1866
Later Life: physician, Waterbury VT, Surgeon-Gen. VT State Militia

Affiliations: GAR, MOLLUS (#09169), SAR, RSVO
Died: 10 Jun 1915, Waterbury VT; interment in Village Cemetery
Correspondence: Surgeon's med. records and Letters (1862-63), USAMHI
(AGO, C&S, NEB, NIH, NYTObit, RR, TGL)

Jewett, Albert Burton (1829-1887)

Born: 20 Mar 1829, St. Albans VT, son of Eleazer and Adorethy (Abells) Jewett
Early Life: merchant; 1LT State Militia
War Service: 1LT Co. A 1st VT INF 2 May 1861, m/o 15 Aug 1861; COL 10th VT INF 26 Aug 1862, resgd 25 Apr 1864
Later Life: dry goods merchant, Swanton VT 1870, Railroad Super., Swanton VT 1880
Affiliations: RSVO
Married: 20 Mar 1851, Achsa Giffin
Died: 6 Mar 1887, Jacksonville, FL; interment in Church Street Cemetery, Swanton VT
Notes: instrumental in the construction of the Lake Champlain to Portland ME railroad
(1860, 1870, 1880, AGO, EMH, FSO, Jones*, LCA1)

Jewett, Jesse E. (1837-1866)

Born: 4 May 1837, Swanton VT, son of Eleazer and Adorethy (Abells) Jewett
War Service: 2LT Co. C 5th VT INF 5 Sep 1861, 1LT 9 Jul 1862, CPT Co. K 21 Mar 1863, resgd 29 May 1863
Later Life: Swanton, died of disease contracted in service
Died: 51 May 1866, Swanton VT; interment in Church Street Cemetery
Notes: Swanton GAR Post #73 named after him
(AGO, FSO, LCA1)

Jocelyn, Stephen Perry (1843-1920)

Born: 1 Mar 1843, Browningtoη VT
Early Life: student
War Service: PVT Co. A 6th VT INF 22 Aug 1863, never joined Co. but served in office of Asst Provost Marshal General, at Brattleboro, 1863-64; dis 6 Jul 1864 to accept 1LT 115th USCI 1 Aug 1864; m/o 16 Feb 1866
Later Life: 2LT 6th US INF 23 Feb 1866, 1LT 28 Jul 1866, 21st US INF 9 Mar 1871, CPT 19 May 1874
Affiliations: MOLLUS (#03327)
Died: 8 Mar 1920; interment in Arlington National Cemetery
Publications: Mostly Alkali: A Biography. (1953)
(C&S, MOLLUS, RR)

Johnson, Estelle S. - See Read, Estelle Serena

Johnson, Martha (1822-1871)

Born: 17 Sep 1822, Peacham VT, daughter of Jeba Leonard and Betsy (Merrill) Johnson
Early Life: employee New York State Penitentiary, Blackwell's Island NYC
War Service: hired by National Freedmen's Relief Assoc of NY to teach newly freed slaves in SC Sea Islands (Port Royal Experiment) 1862-71
Affiliations: Abolitionist
Died: 24 Dec 1871; interment in Episcopal Church Cemetery, Beaufort SC
(FOH, FSO)

Johnson, Russell Thayer (1841-aft 1914)

Born: 4 Apr 1841, Newark VT, son of Ransel and Sally A. (Farmer) Johnson
Early Life: Hatley Acad. PQ, teacher, med. studies under Charles S. Cahoon (q.v.), Lyndon VT 1860
War Service: PVT Co. D 11th VT INF 9 Nov 1863, Co. C 24 Jun 1865, spent most of his service in AOP Med Dept, m/o 25 Aug 1865
Later Life: D.M., Bellevue Hosp. College 1867, physician Stanstead PQ 1865-68, Concord VT 1869-1912, super. of the insane 14 years, pension bureau examiner 1872, International Med. Congress delegate 1876, State Rep. 1884, v.p. VT MS 1886
Affiliations: AMA, Mason, IOOF, GAR
Married: 29 Mar 1869, Asenath A. Weeks
Died: aft 1914; interment unknown
(1880, GFH, JGU, PCD, WRC1)

Joyce, Charles Herbert (1830-1916)

Born: 30 Jan 1830, Wherwell, England, son of Charles and Martha E. (Grist) Joyce
Early Life: came to America in 1836, settled in Waitsfield, farming, district school, Waitsfield and Northfield Acad., Newbury Sem., page in VT House 3 sessions, Asst librarian 1 yr, librarian 1 yr, teacher, admitted to bar 1852, atty, Northfield 1855, State Rep 1856-57, State's Atty
War Service: Jun 1861, MAJ 2nd VT INF, LTCOL Jun 1862, resgd Jan 1863
Later Life: atty, Rutland, State Rep. 1869-71, US Rep. 1875-83, atty, Rutland, ret. in Pittsfield
Affiliations: Republican
Married: 21 Feb 1853, Rouene Morris Randall
Died: 22 Nov 1916, Rutland VT; interment in Greenwood Cemetery
Notes: Poultney GAR Post #49 was named after him
(CB, FAG, JGU*)

Jewett, Abner B.

Johnson, Estelle

Joyce, Charles H.

KKKKK

Kasson, John Adam (1822-1910)

Born: 11 Jan 1822, Charlotte VT, son of John Steele and Nancy (Blackman) Kasson
Early Life: UVM 1842; atty in St. Louis MO until 1857; moved to IA; RNC delegate 1860
War Service: 1st Asst. Postmaster Gen. 1861-62; US commissioner to International Postal Congress, Paris, 1863; US Rep. 1863-67
Later Life: State Rep. 1868-72; US Rep. 1873-77; Minister to Austria-Hungary 1877-81; US Rep. 1881-84; Minster to Germany 1884-85; special envoy to Congo International Conf., Berlin, 1885; special envoy to Samoan International Conf. 1889; member US/British Joint High Commission, 1898, to adjust differences with Canada
Affiliations: Republican
Married: 1 May 1850, Caroline Eliot
Died: 18 May 1910, Washington D.C; interment in Woodland Cemetery, Des Moines IA
Publications: The Evolution of the Constitution of the United States of America and History of the Monroe Doctrine. (1904)
(CB, FSO, HGW)

Kellogg, William Pitt (1831-1918)

Born: 8 Dec 1831, Orwell VT
Early Life: NU 1847 (n.g.), moved to Peoria, IL 1850, admitted to IL Bar 1853, atty, 1853-61, Chief Justice NE 27 Mar 1861
War Service: COL 7th IL CAV 8 Sep 1861, Commander, Cape Girardeau, MO, New Madrid, MO 1862, Shiloh, TN 1862, Corinth, MS 1862, resgd due to poor health, 1 Jun 1862
Later Life: Chief Justice, NE 1862-65, courier for Gen. Grant 1863, Collector, Port of New Orleans, 13 Apr 1865, US Sen., LA 1868-72, 1877-83, LA Gov. 1873-77, US Rep. 1883-85, RNC delegate 1888-96
Died: 10 Aug 1918, Washington, D.C; interment in Arlington National Cemetery
Publications: Proceedings in the Case of the United States Vs. William Pitt Kellogg: Charged with Receiving a Bribe while a United States Senator. (1884)
(CB, BDAC, JGU, PCD*)

Kelton, Dwight H. (1843-1906)

Born: 4 Oct 1843, East Montpelier VT, son of Stillman S. and Ursula (Sprague) Kelton
Early Life: common schools, Barre Acad., left to enlist
War Service: enl 13th VT INF, rejected due to youthfulness, NU 2 years, PVT Co. B 98th NY INF 29 Jan 1864, CPT 5th USCI 15 Oct 1864, m/o 10 Feb 1866
Later Life: 2LT USA 20 Jul 1866, 1LT 26 MAR 1868, 1873, studied in Leipsic, Germany, CPT 16 Feb 1885, ret. for disability 6 Mar 1888, resided Des Moines IA 1900, Bvt MAJ 23 Apr 1904
Married: 19 Jul 1889, Anna L. Donnelly
Died: 9 Aug 1906, Montpelier VT; interment in Arlington National Cemetery VA
Publications: Annals of Fort Mackinac (1882), Indian Names of Places Near the Great Lakes (1888), Indian Names and History of the Sault Ste. Marie Canal (1889), Kelton Family Items (1895)
(1900, OAR80, VHS06, WAE, WHP)

Kenfield, Frank (1838-1914)

Born: 13 Mar 1838, Sterling (Morristown) VT, son of Asaph and Eliza (Shephard) Kenfield
Early Life: local schools, People's Acad., moved to MA, teacher, travelled around the country, returned to VT 1860, lumber business

War Service: 2LT Co. E 13th VT INF, 8 Sep 1862, 1LT 4 Jun 1863, wdd, Gettysburg, 3 Jul 1863, m/o 21 Jul 18863, CPT Co. C 17th VT INF, 22 Feb 1864, wdd, Wilderness, 6 May 1864, pow, Petersburg Mine, 30 Jul 1864, at Columbia SC, prld 1 Mar 1865, m/o 15 May 1865
Later Life: mercantile pursuits, farming, stock and produce buying, town offices, State Rep. 1884, State Sen. 1894, trustee VT Soldiers' Home
Affiliations: Republican, GAR, MOLLUS (#09179), Mason
Married: (1) 5 Sep 1866, Lamott C. Wheelock; (2) 9 Feb 1874, Mrs. Mary Margaret Cruller nee Lyman
Affiliations: RSVO
Died: 11 Jun 1914, Morrisville VT; interment in Pleasant View Cemetery.
(AGO, C&S, JGU*, Morrisville Messenger)

Kennedy, Ronald Albert (1837-1902)

Born: 25 Sep 1837, Ryegate VT, son of Ronald and Isabel (Lang) Kennedy
Early Life: farm laborer, food merchant, in Concord VT 1860
War Service: SGT Co. I 3rd VT INF 16 Jul 1861, 2LT Co. D 22 Sep 1862, 1LT Co. I 13 Oct 1862, wdd Salem Heights 4 May 1863, CPT Co K 8 Jan 1864; LTCOL 5th VT INF 20 Feb 1865; COL 9 Jun 1865, m/o 29 Jun 1865 as LTCOL
Later Life: farmer, NE at least 1870-80, NE State Rep., j.p., Super. New Albany IN National Cemetery 1897-1902
Affiliations: Grange, GAR
Married: Mar 1864, Addie D. Rowell
Died: 13 Jun 1902, interment in New Albany National Cemetery IN
(1860, 1870, 1880, FAG, FSO, PSS, RR, T288, T289)

Kenny, Albert Sewall (1841-1930)

Born: 19 Jan 1841, Keosauqua, IA, son of Sewall and Mary (Strong) Kenny (parents both Vermonters)
Early Life: UVM 1861
War Service: Asst Paymr 19 Mar 1862 (credited to Burlington); steamer *South Carolina*, SABS 1862-64; steamer *Santiago de Cuba*, NABS 1864-65; Paymr 9 Mar 1865
Later Life: Paymr in charge of naval stores at Luanda, West Coast Africa 1866-67; Navy Pay Office, San Francisco 1868-71; on *Plymouth* 1872-73; ironclad *Roanoke*, North Atlantic Station, 1873-74; USNA 1875-80; Flt Paymr, North Atlantic Station, 1881-84; Pay Inspector, 31 Jul 1884; Boston Navy Yard 1885-87; Bureau of Provisions & Clothing, Washington 1887-90; General Storekeeper, Brooklyn Navy Yard 1890-93. *Chicago,* European Station 1893-95; Navy Pay Office, New York 1896; General Storekeeper, Brooklyn Navy Yard 1897-99, Pay Dir., 26 September 1897; Chief, Bureau of Supplies and Accounts, Washington 1899-1903; Paymr Gen. (RADM) 13 December 1899; Ret. 19 Jan 1903; treasurer of the Isthmian Canal or Walker Commission 1904-05
Affiliations: RSVO, MOLLUS (#08650)
Died: 17 May 1930, Washington D.C; interment in Moravian Cemetery, New Dorp, Staten Island NY
(C&S, CLL*, TJL2)

Kent, Enoch Wright (1842-aft 1903)

Born: 27 Aug 1842, Panton VT, son of Hiram and Delia Kent
Early Life: unknown
War Service: Baxter Hosp. and USA Gen. Hosp. Burlington, two years under Dr. Samuel W. Thayer
Later Life: M.D. UVM 1866, physician Fletcher 1866-67, Crown Point NY 1878-80, Moriah NY 1903
Affiliations: AMA, Essex Cty NY MS
Married: 1870, Mary J. Moore
Died: aft 1903; interment unknown
(MDNY03, NYMS78, UVMMED)

Kent, Evarts B. (1843-1924)

Born: 12 Mar 1843, Benson VT, son of Cephas Henry and Mary Abby (Clark) Kent
Early Life: Castleton Seminary, MC 1861, left to enlist
War Service: PVT Co. A 6th VT INF 6 Feb 1864, wdd, Wilderness 6 May 1864, m/o 25 Feb 1865
Later Life: MC 1865 teacher, Harvard IL 1865-66, AuTS 1866-67, ATS 1867-69, A.M. MC 1869 ordained 1871, pastor, Sterling MA 1869-70, Billerica 1870-71, Michigan City IN 1871-80, Chicago IL 1880-81, Atlanta GA 1881-89, Eldora IA 1889-98, Victor 1898-1901, Dunlap 1905, Enosburg VT 1905-09, Benson 1909-12, Sterling MA 1912-15, ret. to Grafton MA
Affiliations: Delta Upsilon Fraternity, Congregationalist, SAR
Married: 22 Aug 1872, Helen M. Beckwith
Died: 6 Nov 1924, Worcester MA; interment unknown
(FSO, LHC, MIDCat, T289)

Kenyon, Henry Lyman (1839-1909)

Born: 23 May 1839, Bennington Cty VT, adopted son of Jesse W. and Orpha (Soper) Kenyon
Early Life: district schools, marble shop employee
War Service: PVT Co. F 1st VT INF 9 May 1861, m/o 15 Aug 1861, PVT Co. C 14th VT INF 21 Oct 1862, m/o 30 Jul 1863, PVT Co. E 5th VT INF 3 Sep 1864, m/o 19 Jun 1865
Later Life: store clerk, Northfield, general merchandiser, Kenyon & Emerson, Kenyon & Newell, Kenyon & Soper, unti 1885, postmaster 1885-89, town clerk/treasurer 1892, town clerk 1900
Affiliations: Mason, GAR
Married: 20 Jan 1864, Mary E. Hill
Died: 8 Dec 1909; interment in Elmwood Cemetery, Northfield VT
(1900, AGO, GFH, HC4, RR)

Ketchum, Benjamin F. (1837-1897)

Born: 25 Dec 1837, Troy NY
Early Life: M.D. NYU 1860
War Service: SURG, 12th VT INF 19 Sep 1862, m/i 14 Jul 1863, BGD SURG 2nd VT Brig
Later Life: physician, Brattleboro until his death
Affiliations: AMA, Washington Cty MS, CT River Valley MS, Union MS of Berkshire
Married: 7 Aug 1861, Eliza Gray
Died: 9 Jan 1897, Brattleboro VT; interment unknown
(FPF, GFS, GG)

Keyser, Elizabeth (1840-1925)

Born: 1840, Page Cty VA, daughter of Alexander and Ann (Koontz) Keyser
War Service: despite having a husband and two brothers in Union prisons, when she discovered severely wounded LT Henry Bedell (q.v.) abandoned by his regiment in a nearby mill, brought him back to her home, treated him until he was well enough to travel, and returned him to Union forces a great peril to her safety
Later Life: farmer's wife Longmarsh VA 1870, commended by VT Legis. in 1915 for her services
Married: 12 Apr 1860, James S. E. Van Metre (no issue)
Died: 2 Apr 1925, Berryville VA; interment in Village Cemetery
(1850, 1870, AFW, GGB, LEC2, TJL)

Kidder, Charles Wheeler Burr (1818-1893)

Born: 13 Nov 1818, Weathersfield VT, son of Gideon and Frances (Hubbard) Kidder
Early Life: CMC 1843, physician Providence RI (5 years), Peru NY (3 years), Troy NY (4 years), Vergennes VT 1857

War Service: SURG 11th VT INF 18 Aug 1862, resgd 10 Sep 1863
Later Life: physician Vergennes 1877
Married: 18 Aug 1850, Mary A. Howe
Died: 26 Sep 1893, Pittsfield VT; interment unknown
(1880, CPT FSO, HPS, UVMMED)

Kimball, Frederick Marius (1840-1924)

Born: 14 Jun 1840, Barton VT, son of Frederick White and Mary Hinman (Chadwick) Kimball
Early Life: Orleans Liberal Inst., Glover, teacher, studying law
War Service: SGT Co. D 6th VT INF 20 Sep 1861, 1SGT, 2LT, Co. G 3 Feb 1863, wdd, Banks' Ford, 4 May 1863, wdd, Funkstown, MD, 10 Jul 1863, dis/dsb 22 Oct 1863; 2LT, later CPT VRC, Nov. 1863, served in Co. G 13th VRC, 24th Co. 2nd Btln, 246th Co. 1st Btln, Co. F 18th VRC, Co. D 3rd VRC, and Co. D 22nd VRC, St. Albans, Brattleboro, and others
Later Life: Freedmen's Bureau, Lawrenceville VA, until 1 Jan 1869; moved to Cameron MO, businessman, acting mayor and postmaster, moved to CO, real estate business, returned to MO, then Topeka, KS 1892, secretary, Aetna Building & Loan Assoc, v.p. KS Building & Loan Assoc, pres. Security Mining Co. of Idaho
Affiliations: GAR (Post commander), Mason, SAR
Married: 27 Sep 1863, Susanna S. Hoyt
Died: 7 Jul 1924, Long Beach CA; interment in Topeka KS
(FWB, JLK, KFN*, LHC, T289)

Kimball, John (1831-1897)

Born: 10 Oct 1831, Barton VT, son of John Hazen and Harriet (Chamberlain) Kimball
Early Life: St. Johnsbury Acad., DC 1856, UTS 1858; mission work NYC, moved to CA, pastor Congregational Church, Grass Valley, 2nd Congregational Church, San Francisco until Feb 1863.
War Service: US Christian Commission 1863-64, Chap., Carver Hosp., Washington DC until Jul 1865
Later Life: staff of Gen. Charles H. and Oliver O. Howard, super. schools, Freedmen's Bureau, in DC, VA, WV, MD, and DE, resgd Nov 1869, American missionary Association, San Francisco 1870, ministry in San Francisco and Oakland 10 years, preached 6 months in Chicago, Brooklyn and Europe, publisher, managing editor of The Pacific 1878
Married: 18 Jan 1864, Annie M. Eskridge
Died: 2 Jul 1897; interment unknown
(EMB, FSO, LAM, BFP)

King, Royal Daniel (1824-1904)

Born: 17 Nov 1824, Benson VT, son of Horace and Eunice (Belden) King
Early Life: local schools, Castleton Sem., UVM 1846, teacher in VT and IL, Benson town super. of schools, selectman, State Rep. 1852, 1854, recruiter
War Service: PVT Co. D 14th VT INF 10 Sep 1862, m/o 30 Jul 1863
Later Life: Benson town super. 1863-80, State Sen. 1880
Affiliations: Republican, Mason
Died: 15 Jan 1904, Benson VT; interment in Old Cemetery
Correspondence: CW correspondence at Bennington Museum
(AGO, JDM, JGU)

Kingsley, Levi Gleason (1832-1913)

Born: 21 May 1832, Shrewsbury VT, son of Harvey and Elvira (Gleason) Kinglsey
Early Life: public schools, Brandon Acad., student NU 1854-55, worked on farm until 1852, railroad 1856-59, 2LT Rutland Light Guard

War Service: MAJ 12th VT INF 26 Sep 1826, m/o 14 Jul 1863
Later Life: hardware merchant 1860-95, QMG Vt. Militia 8 yrs, B.S. NU 1882, State Sen. 1890, Mayor of Rutland 1894, dir. Baxter National Bank, Marble Savings Bank, Rutland 1909-10
Affiliations: Republican, Episcopalian, Mason, GAR, MOLLUS
Married: 4 Jun 1865, Cornelia S. Roberts
Died: 26 Jun 1913, Rutland VT; interment in Evergreen Cemetery
(1910, AGO, WAE*, WHO3)

Knapp, Lyman Enos (1837-1904)

Born: 5 Nov 1837, Somerset VT, son of Hiram and Elvira (Stearns) Knapp
Early Life: Burr Sem., MD 1862
War Service: CPT Co. I 16th VT INF, 20 Sep 1862, wdd, Gettysburg, 3 Jul 1863, m/o 10 Aug 1863, CPT Co. F 17th VT INF, 9 Apr 1864, MAJ 1 Nov 1864, Bvt LTCOL 2 Apr 1865, m/o 14 Jul 1865 as MAJ
Later Life: teaching, Burr & Burton Sem., editor Middlebury Register 13 years, clerk of VT House 1872-73, admitted to bar 1876, State Rep. 1886-87, j.p. 1869-89, register of probate 2 years, judge of probate 1879-89, school board, town clerk several years, numerous other government and private organizations, moved to Alaska 1889, Gov. of Alaska 1889-93, atty, Seattle, WA 1893-1904, LLD Whitman Coll. 1893
Affiliations: Republican, Congregational, GAR, RSVO
Married: 23 Jan 1865, Martha A. Severance
Died: 9 Oct 1904, Seattle, WA; interment unknown
Papers: Alaska State Library
(FAG, JGU, MIDCat, RJ)

Knox, James Monroe (1820-1875)

Born: 18 Mar 1820, Tunbridge VT, son of David and Silence (Cobb) Knox
Early Life: UVM 1849, CMC 1851, physician Richmond
War Service: Fredericksburg and Washington (May 1864), among a contingent of VT doctors who volunteered their services to care for Vermonters wounded at the Wilderness and Spotsylvania C.H.
Later Life: physician, Burlington, Essex Jct., committed suicide
Died: 15 Jan 1875, Essex Jct. VT; interment unknown
(FSO, HC1, LISOC)

Kellogg, William P.

Kenfield, Frank

Kenny, Albert S.

Kimball, Frederick M.

Kingsley, Levi G.

LLLLL

Lamson, Jasper H. (1837-1911)

Born: 28 Mar 1837, Randolph VT, son of Thomas and Esther (Marn) Lamson
Early Life: local schools, farming, store clerk
War Service: PVT Co. C 15th VT INF 11 Sep 1862, CPL 19 Nov 1862, m/o 5 Aug 1863
Later Life: store clerk 10 years, hardware business
Affiliations: Republican, Christian (Bethany)
Married: 1 Jan 1872, Hannah (Pratt) White
Died: 13 Aug 1911, Randolph VT; interment in South View Cemetery
(AFS*, AGO)

Langdon, Henry Huntington (1827-1881)

Born: 26 Jul 1827, Constable NY, son of Silvester and Clarissa (Huntington) Langdon
Early Life: CMC 1851
War Service: Asst SURG 7th VT INF 3 Oct 1862, resgd 27 Mar 1863
Later Life: physician, Burlington, 1880
Married: Hannah R. (Nfi)
Died: 24 Sep 1881; interment in Village cemetery, Shelburne VT
(1880, AGO, CPT FSO)

Langdon, Seth Wightman (1821-1891)

Born: 31 Jun 1821, Constable NY, son of Silvester and Clarissa (Huntington) Langdon
Early Life: AMS 1847, physician, Burlington
War Service: recruit 5th VT INF 15 Aug 1864, Asst SURG 17th VT INF 21 Nov 1864, m/o 14 Jul 1865
Later Life: physician, Sheldon VT, 1870-80
Affiliations: Franklin Cty MS
Died: 24 Mar 1891; interment in Hillside cemetery, Sheldon VT
Publications: Tubercular Phthisis (1847)
Notes: filed claim for med. services rendered, Draft Rendezvous, New Haven CT before commissioning; filed claim against Great Britain for loss of treasury notes during St. Albans Raid
(1870, 1880, AGO, AM, CPT FSO, FRUS)

Lathrop, Cyrus U. (1839-1908)

Born: 31 Oct 1839, Chelsea VT, son of Urbane and Eliza (Wiggins) Lathrop
Early Life: local schools, Chelsea and Newbury Acad
War Service: PVT Co. C 8th VT INF 19 Dec 1863, m/o 28 Jun 1865
Later Life: farmer, chair. Williamstown railroad commissioners, pioneer of Williamstown Granite Co., chair. Williamstown Construction Co., associate judge, Orange Cty Court, State Rep. 1892
Affiliations: Republican, GAR
Married: 24 Nov 1861, Frances A. Hopkins
Died: 14 Apr 1908, Williamstown VT; interment in Village Cemetery
(AGO, JGU*)

Leach, Chester K. (1830-1909)

Born: 17 Jan 1830, Fairfield VT, son of Joseph and Olive (Burton) Leach
Early Life: local schools, farmer
War Service: 2LT Co. H 2nd VT INF 23 May 1863, 1LT 14 Sep 1861, m/o 29 Jun 1864
Later Life: farmer, various town offices, State Sen. 1878
Affiliations: Republican, Mason, GAR
Married: 8 Oct 1851, Ann A. Montague
Died: 1909; interment in Binghamville Cemetery, Fletcher VT
Correspondence: UVM
Publications: "Dear Wife," the Civil War letters of Chester K. Leach (2002)
(AGO, JGU*)

Leach, Moses J. (1837-1915)

Born: 22 Dec 1837, Craftsbury VT, son of Ervin and Mary Ann (Scott) Leach
Early Life: moved to Wolcott, local schools, People's Acad., moved to MA, saw mill employee
War Service: CPL Co. E 13th VT INF, 9 Aug 1862, m/o 21 Jul 1863
Later Life: farmer 1863-69, drug store proprietor, town clerk 45 years, postmaster 1890-1914
Affiliations: Republican, GAR, Mason, RSVO
Married: 16 Mar 1864, Ellen B. Parker
Died: 25 Jan 1915, Wolcott VT; interment in Fairmont (upper) Cemetery
Correspondence: 19 Jan - 14 Jun 1863, USAMHI
(AGO, JGU*, Morrisville Messenger)

Leavenworth, Abel Edgar (1828-1901)

Born: 3 Sep 1829, Castleton VT, son of Abel and Anna (Hickok) Leavenworth
Early Life: moved to Madrid NY 1832, district school, returned to Charlotte 1844, teacher in Charlotte 1846-47; Hinesburg 1847-48; St. George 1848-50; Monkton 1850-51, Burlington 1851-52, fitted for college at Hinesburg Acad., Bolivar, MO Acad. 1852-55, principal, Hinesburg Acad. 1855, A.B. UVM 1856, A.M. UVM 1860, chair. State Teachers' Assoc 1859, established VT School Journal, principal Brattleboro Acad. 1860
War Service: 1SGT Co. K, 9th VT INF 24 May 1862, 1LT 17 Nov 1862, CPT 1 Dec 1862, Asst I.G., Wistar's BGD 2nd Div. XVIII Corps, Prov BGD Bermuda Hundreds, 2nd BGD 3rd Div. XXIV Corps, led skirmish line into Richmond 3 Apr 1865, Asst P.M., Richmond, Asst A.G. Appomattox, m/o 13 Jun 1865
Later Life: Principal, Beeman Acad., New Haven 1870-74, principal State Normal School, Randolph 1874-79, principal State Normal School, Castleton 1881-1901
Affiliations: Republican, Congregational, GAR, RSVO, Mason, IOOF, Sons of Temperance, MOLLUS (#09183)
Married: (1) 14 Sep 1853, Mary Evelina Griggs; (2) 12 Aug 1889, Lucy Elizabeth Wadsworth
Died: 3 Jun 1901, Castleton VT; interment in Hillside Cemetery
Notes: Castleton GAR Post #108 was named after him
(C&S, FHEObit, HF, JGU*)

Leavenworth, Jesse Henry (1807-1885)

Born: 29 Mar 1807, Danville VT, son of Henry and Elizabeth (Morrison) Leavenworth
Early Life: USMA 1830 (22/42), 2LT 4th US INF 30 Jul 1830, transferred 2nd US INF 18 Aug 1831, resgd 31 Oct 1836, merchant, Milwaukee WI 1850-60
War Service: COL 2nd CO INF, 17 Feb 1862, Ft Lyon CO Aug 1862, Ft Leavenworth KS Apr 1863, Commander, all troops along the Santa Fe Trail Jun 1863, dis 26 Sep 1863
Later Life: Indian Agent for the Kiowas, Commanches and Plains Apaches at Ft Larned KS 1864-68, Milwaukee WI 1870
Married: 12 Jun 1832, Elvira Caroline Cook
Died: 12 Mar 1885, Milwaukee WI; interment unknown

Notes: son of B.G. Henry Leavenworth for whom Fort Leavenworth was named
(1850-1870, DLT, FBH, GWC)

Lee, Edward Payson (1839-1922)

Born: 5 Aug 1839, Waterford VT, son of Nathaniel and Isabel Maria (Johnson) Lee
Early Life: St. Johnsbury Acad
War Service: SGT Co. A 11th VT INF 1 Sep 1862, 1LT 2 Sep 1862, CPT Co. B 2 Nov 1863, wdd Cedar Creek 19 Oct 1864, m/o 2 Jun 1865
Later Life: AC, Deputy Customs Collector, Island Pond VT 1867-78, School Super. Brighton VT 1868-69, ordained, Episcopal deacon 19 Jun 1879, ordained Episcopal priest 24 Jun 1880, Missionary VT 1879-91, rector St. James Church West Somerville MA 1892-96, missionary ME 1896-98, rector Christ Church Island Pond VT 1898-1908, ret. Waterford VT 1910
Married: (1) 1866, Permelia Ursaline Brown; (2) 1880, Sarah Bard McVicker; (3) 1891, Virginia Howard Johnson
Died: 11 Dec 1922, St. Johnsbury VT; interment in Grove Cemetery
(1910, AGO, PCD, WLM)

Leland, Oscar Hopestill (1826-1914)

Born: 21 Jul 1826, Baltimore VT, son of Joshua and Betsey (Boynton) Leland
Early Life: BRA, Wesleyan Sem., NU, withdrew for health reasons, teacher, Blakely, GA (1853-55), Waco, TX 1855-56, admitted to bar 1856, A.B. Baylor 1856, A.M. 1860, prof. of mathematics and astronomy there 1856-61, prof. of mathematics and astronomy, Waco University 1865
War Service: ADJ (CPT) 30th TX CAV 1862-65
Later Life: Internal Revenue Service 1865-70; presiding justice, McLellan Cty Court 1870-74; postmaster of Waco 1877-85 real estate 1874-77, McGregor, TX 1898
Married: 8 Jan 1863, Frances Juliett
Died: 18 May 1914; interment in Oakwood Cemetery, McLellan Cty TX
Publications: <u>Ancestors & Descendants of John Sherwin, Sr. Late of Weathersfield, VT</u>. (1922)
(1900, WAE)

Leonard, Hiram W. (1807-1883)

Born: 10 Apr 1807 VT, son of Bethuel and Zilpha (Wetherell) Leonard
Early Life: Asst Paymr USV 24 Nov 1846; MAJ & Paymr 2 Mar 1849
War Service: Deputy Paymr Gen. (LTCOL) 6 Sep 1862; Bvt COL 13 Mar 1865, Bvt B.G. 13 Mar 1865
Later Life: ret. 1 Jan 1872
Married: 23 Feb 1834, Huldah Sampson Billings
Died: 21 Dec 1883, San Francisco CA; interment in San Francisco National Cemetery
(1860, 1870, E&E, FBH, FSO, JPN, LRP, RS)

Levey, George Hugh (1841-1903)

Born: 16 Mar 1841, Cty Longford, Ireland
Early Life: moved to Canada, then Ludlow VT, 1849, farmer, employee Ludlow Woolen Mills
War Service: PVT 12 May 1861 Co. B 1st VT INF, m/o 15 Aug 1861
Later Life: boss finisher and super. at Ludlow Mills, Hoosick Falls NY, Harrisville NH, Dracut MA, returned to Ludlow 1885, mngr, then partner of Ludlow mills, moved to Gilsum NH, organized Black River Woolen Co. 1891, board of water commissioners, trustee BRA, board of dirs Ludlow Savings Bank & Trust Co., j.p. 1903
Affiliations: Mason, IOOF, GAR
Married: 3 Jul 1866, Theresa E. Nudham
Died: 10 Feb 1903, Ludlow VT; interment unknown

(AFS, AGO)

Lewis, Barbour (1818-1893)

Born: 5 Jan 1818, Alburg VT
Early Life: IL Coll. 1846; teacher Mobile AL; HLS; atty; RNC delegate 1860
War Service: CPT Co. G 1st MO INF 1 Aug 1861; civil commission court judge Memphis 1863; m/o 15 Nov 1864
Later Life: pres. Shelby Cty TN commissioner 1867-69; US Rep. 1873-75; moved to St. Louis MO 1878; US Land Office, Salt Lake City UT 1878-79; moved to WA, farmer
Died: 15 Jul 1893, Colfax WA; interment in Colfax Cemetery
Publications: Justice to the Southwest! (1874)
(CB, FAG)

Lewis, John Randolph (1834-1900)

Born: 16 Sep 1834, Edinburg PA, son of Jesse and Sara (Cambell) Lewis
Early Life: unknown
War Service: 2SGT Co. H 1st VT INF 2 May 1861, m/o 15 Aug 1861, CPT Co. I, 5th VT INF, 12 Sep 1861, MAJ 15 Jul 1861, LTCOL 6 Oct 1862, wdd (lost arm), COL VRC 4 Sep 1864, Bvt B.G. 13 Mar 1865
Later Life: cmdg post at Elmira NY Oct 1865, awaiting orders at Buffalo NY Dec 1865, I.G. on Staff of B.G. Fiske, Nashville, Mar 1866, Asst Commissioner, BRFAL, TN Jan 1867, MAJ 44th US INF 22 Jan 1867, Bvt LTCOL USA 2 Mar 1867, Bvt COL USA 2 Mar 1867, I.G., staff of Bvt B.G. Sibley, Savannah, Macon and Atlanta GA to 1869, Asst Commissioner, BRFAL to 28 Apr 1870, ret. as COL USA 28 Apr 1870; postmaster, Atlanta GA
Affiliations: GAR, RSVO
Married: 1856, Helen Mattice
Died: 8 Feb 1900, Chicago IL; interment in Arlington National Cemetery (Section WS, Site 451)
(FAG, FSO, JGU)

Lincoln, Sumner H. (1840-1928)

Born: 21 Dec 1840, Gardner MA
Early Life: Winchendon Acad., M.A. NU (n.g.)
War Service: PVT Co B 1st VT INF 2 May 1861, dis 15 Aug 1861, CPL Co B 6th VT INF 15 Oct 1861, 1LT ADJ 21 Feb 1863, wdd, Wilderness, 5 May 1864, wdd, Opequan, 19 Sep 1864, MAJ 28 Oct 1864, LTCOL 10 Mar 1864, COL 6 Feb 1865, m/o 26 Jun 1865
Later Life: 1LT 17th US INF, 23 Feb 1866, trans 26th US INF 21 Sep 1866, trans 10th US INF, 19 May 1869, CPT 24 Mar 1878, War Department, Office of Publication of Records of the Rebellion, Washington, 1893, MAJ 26 Apr 1898; wdd, San Juan Hill, Santiago, Cuba, 1 Jul 1898; LTCOL 13th US INF 12 Jul 1899; COL 10th US INF 21 Mar 1901, B.G. 26 May 1902; ret. 21 Dec 1904
Affiliations: RSVO
Died: 16 Apr 1928; interment in Arlington National Cemetery
(CFG, GGB, Jones*, WHM)

Liscum, Emerson Hamilton (1841-1900)

Born: 16 Jul 1841, Huntington VT, son of John and Phebe (Hamilton) Liscum
Early Life: student
War Service: CPL Co. H 1st VT INF 2 May 1861; m/o 15 Aug 1861; CPL, SGT, 1SGT 12th US INF 1862-63; 2LT 22 Mar 1863; 1LT 4 May 1863, wdd, Cedar Mountain, Gettysburg; Bvt CPT 11 Nov 1864, RQM 1865

Later Life: 30th US INF 1866; CPT 25th US INF 26 Mar 1867; 19th US INF 5 Jul 1870; MAJ 4 May 1892, 22nd US INF; LTCOL 24th US INF May 1896; B.G. USV 12 Jul 1898; dis USV 31 Dec 1898; COL 9th US INF 25 Apr 1899; killed in action during the Boxer Rebellion
Affiliations: MOLLUS (#08736)
Married: May Divan
Died: 13 Jul 1900, Tientsin, China; interment in Arlington National Cemetery (Section 3 DIV Site 843)
Memorial: Military Order of the Loyal Legion of the United States, Vermont Commandery. Unveiling Exercise of Memorial Tablet to Emerson Hamilton Liscum, Brigadier-General USV, Colonel 9th U.S. Infantry. Fletcher Free Library, Burlington, Vt., April 28, 1911.
Notes: His last words "Keep up the fire," became the motto of the 9th US INF; Fort Liscum, AK, named after him.
(C&S, FBH, MOLLUS, RJ*)

Little, Arthur (1837-1915)

Born: 24 May 1837, Webster NH, son of Simeon Bartlett and Harriet (Boyd) Little
Early Life: KUA, DC 1860, Teacher, Thetford Acad., BRA 1861, ATS 1861-62, Princeton Theological Sem. 1863, ordained Congregational Minister, 16 Mar 1863
War Service: Chap., 11th VT INF, 20 Mar 1863, m/o 24 Jun 1865
Later Life: Pastor, Bedford NH 1866-68, Fond du Lac WI 1868-77, Chicago, IL 1877-89, D.D., DC 1880, pres. Chicago Congregational Club 1886, Pastor, Dorchester MA 1889-1905, Boston MA 1910
Married: (1) 15 Aug 1863, Laura Elizabeth Frost; (2) 1 Feb 1898, Elizabeth Ann Wales
Died: 11 Apr 1915, Dorchester MA; interment unknown
(1910, BOS, CLL*, JLS)

Loomis, Gustavus A. (1789-1872)

Born: 23 Sep 1789, Thetford VT, son of Beriah and Mary (Benton) Loomis
Early Life: USMA 1811 (no standing listed), War of 1812, Mexican-American War, Black Hawk War, Seminole Wars in Florida; COL, 5th US INF 1851
War Service: commanding recruits on Governor's Island 1862; ret. Jun 1863, B.G. USA 13 Mar 1865, for long and meritorious services
Later Life: unknown
Married: (1) 24 Feb 1851, Mrs. A. T. Panton; (2) Mary A. L. (nfi)
Died: 5 Mar 1872, Stratford CT; interment in Grove Street Cemetery, New Haven CT
(1860, 1870, FSO, GWC, HR2500)

Lord, Nathan S. (1831-1886)

Born: 17 Jul 1831, Hanover NH, son of Nathan and Elizabeth King (Leland) Lord
Early Life: DC 1851, principal Montpelier Acad., read law with Millard Fillmore, Buffalo NY, admitted to bar Sep 1854, atty, Cincinnati OH, Foundry worker, Lawrenceburg IN 1860
War Service: CPT Co G 7th IN INF 25 Apr 1861, Philippi VA 3 Jun 1861, m/o 2 Aug 1861, LTCOL 5th VT INF 16 Sep 1861, COL 6th VT INF 16 Sep 1861, Lee's Mill VA Apr 1862, wdd Savage's Station VA 29 Jun 1862, Antietam MD 17 Sep 1862, Fredericksburg MD Dec 1862, resgd 18 Dec 1862
Later Life: Ohio State Sen. 1869-71, Railroad business, Cincinnati OH 1870, Mayor, Riverside OH 1878-82, Foundry business, Riverside OH 1880
Married: 1 Jun 1876, Julia Craik
Died: 1886, Ohio; interment unknown
Notes: Youngest son of Nathan Lord, pres. DC
(ADP, FSO, GGB, HC4, Jones*, WF)

Lovell, Frederick Solon (1813-1878)

Born: 1 Nov 1813, Bennington VT
Early Life: Hobart College; atty, moved to WI, edited revised statutes of WI 1858
War Service: LTCOL 33rd WI INF 18 Oct 1862; COL 46th WI INF 2 Mar 1865; m/o 27 Sep 1865; Bvt B.G. 11 Oct 1865
Later Life: attorney, Kenosha WI
Died: 15 May 1878, Kenosha WI; interment in Greenridge Cemetery
(E&E, FAG)

Lowry, Francis (1814-1903)

Born: 15 Jul 1814, Burlington VT, son of Heman and Margaret (Campbell) Lowry
Early Life: public schools, Midshipman 3 Aug 1831, cruised West India Squadron 1831-33, Pacific Squadron 1834-37, Brooklyn Naval School 1837, Passed Midshipman 23 Jun 1838, coast survey 1838-40, steamer *Fulton* 1841-42, LT 4 Jul 1843, New York Rendezvous 1844, Gulf of Mexico on sloop *John Adams* 1845-47, seriously injured in coal fire, "the poisonous gas produced partial paralysis of the limbs and throat, and resulted in his final retirement" on 13 Sep 1855
War Service: volunteered for service, ordered to Portland Naval Rendezvous through Jun 1862, to ill to accept additional orders, ordered to Burlington
Later Life: CAPT on ret. list 4 Apr 1867, living in Burlington 1880
Married: 4 Aug 1838, Susan Alice Nichols
Died: 2 Mar 1903, Burlington VT; interment in Lakeview Cemetery
(AFS*, FAG, GGB, TJL2)

Lowry, Horatio Barnard (1837-1901)

Born: 10 Nov 1837, Burlington VT, son of Abner Benedict and Olivia S. (Moore) Lowry
Early Life: moved to SC
War Service: 2LT USMC 16 Sep 1861; 1LT 26 Nov 1861; Marine Barracks, Washington 1861; Marine Barracks, Portsmouth NH 1861-62; Marine BTLN, Port Royal VA 1862; Marine BTLN, Morris and Folly Islands SC 1863; Marine Barracks, Boston (1864-65; receiving ship *Vermont*, Brooklyn Navy Yard 1865
Later Life: Marine Barracks Boston 1866; receiving ship *Vermont*, Brooklyn 1866; Marine Barracks Philadelphia 1867-69; frigate *Sabine* 1869-70; CPT 16 Oct 1869; Marine Barracks Philadelphia 1870-72; AQM 21 Jun 1872; HQMC 1872; Brooklyn 1873; New York, Philadelphia 1877; Acting QM HQMC 1881; MAJ and QM 1885-96; ret. 19 Jun 1897
Affiliations: MOLLUS (#02439)
Married: 15 Dec 1863, Charlotte Huntington Young
Died: 22 May 1901, Atlantic City NJ; interment unknown
(C&S, TJL2)

Lucia, Joel Howard (1842-1915)

Born: 17 Mar 1842, Bridport VT, son of Charles T. and Paulina (Macier) Luica
Early Life: Barre Acad., MC
War Service: CPL Co. D 14th VT INF 21 Oct 1862, SGT 1 May 1863, m/o 30 Jul 1863, 1SGT Co H 17th VT INF 12 Apr 1864, 1LT 2 Aug 1864, wdd Poplar Spring Church 30 Sep 1864, m/o 14 Jul 1865
Later Life: j.p. Addison Cty 1866-83, admitted to the bar 1868, atty Vergennes 1870-80, State's Atty 1872-74, mayor Vergennes 1881-83, moved to Montpelier 1883, School Board Commissioner Montpelier 1885-1901, atty Montpelier 1900-10
Affiliations: MOLLUS (#14103)
Married: 27 Jun 1871, Elizabeth Burnap Reed
Died: 22 Mar 1915, Montpelier VT; interment unknown
(1870, 1880, 1900, 1910, C&S, HC4, MOLLUS, PCD)

Lyman, Milo W. (1839-1923)

Born: 8 Apr 1839, Poultney VT, son of Isaac and Achsak (Ames) Lyman
Early Life: limited schooling, apprentice carpenter
War Service: PVT Co. K 1st VT INF 2 May 1861, m/o 15 Aug 1861, SGT, Co. K, 12th VT INF 8 Aug 1862 - 14 Jul 1863
Later Life: contracting and building, incl Old Opera House and Baxter's Bank in Rutland, St. Peter's Church, built marble factories in Florence (VT), Philadelphia PA and GA, one of the largest contractors in the state
Affiliations: GAR (Post Commander)
Married: 29 Jul 1863, Mary Turner
Died: 19 Apr 1923, Rutland VT; interment in Evergreen Cemetery
(AFS, AGO, FSO)

Lynde, Isaac (1804-1886)

Born: 23 Jul 1804, Williamstown VT, son of Cornelius and Rebecca (Davis) Lynde
Early Life: USMA 1827 (32/38), Bvt 2LT and 2LT 1 Jul 1827 5th US INF, 1LT 18 Feb 1836, CPT 5th US INF 1 Jan 1839, Ft Atkinson IA 1840, MAJ 18 Oct 1855, 7th US INF 27 Jan 1856
War Service: 26-27 Jul 1861, surrendered Ft Fillmore NM to CSA, dismissed 25 Nov 1861
Later Life: restored as MAJ 18th US INF 27 Nov 1866 to date 28 Jul 1866, ret. 27 Nov 1866 to date 28 Jul 1866
Married: 18 Sep 1827, Margaret Wight
Died: 10 Apr 1886, Picolata FL; interment unknown
(FBH, FSO, GWC)

Lyon, Emory M. (1836-1910)

Born: 27 May 1836, VT
Early Life: M.D. UVM 1861
War Service: SURG 96th NY INF, Plattsburg Barracks, 1861-62
Later Life: physician, Med. Examiner six insurance companies, Examining SURG U.S. Pensions 18 years
Affiliations: AMA, NY MS, Northern NY MS, Clinton Cty MS
Married: Mary C. Benedict
Died: 7 Sep 1910; interment in Riverside Cemetery, Plattsburg NY
(MCR, T289, UVMMED)

Lathrop, Cyruss

Leach, C. K.

Leach, M. J.

Leavenworth, A. E.

Lincoln, Sumner H.

Liscum, E. H.

Little, Arthur

Lord, Nathan S.

Lowry, Francis

MMMMM

Mack, Daniel Alva (1825-1883)

Born: 4 Jun 1825, Plainfield VT, son of John Miner and Rebecca Cordelia (Ayers) Mack
Early Life: Newbury Sem., Concord Biblical Inst, Concord NH 1847
War Service: Chap. 3rd VT INF, 11 Jan 1862-27 Jul 1864, 30 Mar 1865-11 Jul 1865
Later Life: Clergyman, Royalton VT 1870, founder and super. NH Orphans Home, Franklin NH 1871
Married: 1850, Anna Roby
Died: 1 Dec 1883, Franklin NH; interment unknown
Notes: one of the driving forces of his founding of the orphanage were the pleas of dying soldiers to "take care of my children"
(1870, DFS, EML, FSO)

Macomber, John Harrison (1836-1916)

Born: 17 Feb 1836, Chesterfield NY
Early Life: unknown
War Service: CPL Co. C 11th VT INF 12 Aug 1862, SGT 12 Apr 1863, 1LT Co. L 11 Jul 1863, wdd Cold Harbor 7 Jun 1864, pow Weldon Railroad 23 Jun 1864, prld 12 Sep 1864, Bvt CPT 2 Apr 1865, CPT Co. L 23 May 1865, Co. C 24 Jun 1865, m/o 25 Aug 1865
Later Life: Methodist-Episcopal minister, Sauk Centre, Woodbury, Anoka, MN 1866-80, Chap., USA, 16 Jun 1880, accepted 15 Sep 1880, Fort Custer, MT 20 Oct 1880-87, Fort Sherman ID 1887-93, Angel Island CA 1893-99, Presidio, San Francisco 1899-1900, ret. 17 Feb 1900
Affiliations: MOLLUS (#03558, Chap.), GAR (Post Commander, Dept mustering officer, patriotic instr.), Union Veteran League, Regular Army and Navy Union, Mason
Married: 1862, Julia Granby Pitney
Died: 3 Dec 1916, San Jose CA; interment in San Francisco National Cemetery (section OS, row 83, site 2)
Notes: MN Hist. Soc. has diaries/papers 1863-1914
(1880, C&S, CLL*, FBH, MNCensus, SJMNObit, WHP)

Mansfield, John Brainerd (1826-1886)

Born: 16 Mar 1826, Andover VT, son of Arminadab and Fanny (Prentice) Mansfield
Early Life: machinist, Nashua NH 1850, book and map seller, Boston 1860
War Service: war correspondent, New England Meridian, hosp. stew. USV, 21 Apr 1863 – 21 Dec 1864
Later Life: publisher, GPO employee, inmate, National Vets Home, Leavenworth KS Sep-Oct 1886
Married: Sarah Howard (nfi)
Died: 29 Oct 1886, Effingham, KS; interment unknown
Publications: History of the New England States (1860), The American Loyalist (1866), A Sketch of the Political History of the United States of American from the Settlement of Jamestown to the Present Time (completed, but unpublished)
(1850, 1860, HRNH, MDG)

Mansur, Zophar Mack (1843-1914)

Born: 23 Nov 1843, Morgan VT, son of Warren and Jane A. Mansur
Early Life: common schools, Derby Acad
War Service: CPL Co. K 10th VT INF 1 Sep 1862, wdd, Winchester, 19 Sep 1864; dis/wds 31 Aug 165

Later Life: atty, State Rep. 1866, postmaster Island Pond 1867, admitted to the bar 1879, State's Atty 1886-88, State Sen. 1888; LT Gov. 1894-96; customs collector 1897-1906; trustee Vermont Soldiers' Home; trustee, UVM, pres. National Bank of Derby Line
Died: 12 Mar 1914, Burlington; interment unknown
Affiliations: Republican, Methodist, Mason, GAR (Dept. Cmdr), RSVO, Vt. Soc. SAR (pres. 1894)
(FAG, LHC, PCD*, RR, WHO3)

Marsh, Carmi L. (1842-1910)

Born: 4 Aug 1842, Franklin VT, son of Lathrop and Lucy (Chadwick) Marsh
Early Life: farmer, Franklin 1860
War Service: 2LT Co K 13th VT INF 11 Sep 1862, hosp. Fairfax C.H., typhoid fever Dec 1862-Jan 1863, resgd 7 Feb 1863
Later Life: farmer Franklin 1870, State Rep. 1878-79, purchased an interest in the Kendall Spavin Cure business 1879, State JAG 1882-86, pres. Dr. B. J. Kendall Co., Enosburg Falls VT 1884-1910, State Sen. 1886
Affiliations: MOLLUS (#06106)
Married: 1865, Delia E. Pelton
Died: 29 Dec 1910; interment in Methodist Cemetery, Enosburg VT
Notes: in 1910 the State Legis. renamed Franklin Pond to Lake Carmi in honor of his valued service as a citizen; Franklin GAR Post #80 was named for him
(1860, 1870, C&S, GGK, LCA1, PCD*)

Mason, Charles W. (1837-1898)

Born: 6 Nov 1837, Potsdam NY, son of Lawrence S. and Sarah (French) Mason
Early Life: common schools, New Haven Acad., farmer
War Service: 2LT, Co. G 14th VT INF, 8 Sep 1862, m/o 30 Jul 1863
Later Life: raised and CPT Co. E 3rd VT Militia Reg't, farmer, breeder and dealer in thoroughbred Merino sheep and high-blood horses
Affiliations: Republican, Congregational, Mason
Married: 13 Oct 1864, Cornelia Ruth Rogers
Died: 28 May 1898, Los Angeles CA; interment in Evergreen Cemetery, New Haven VT
(FSO, JGU)

Mason, George M. (1831-aft 1894)

Born: 31 Dec 1831, Putney VT, son of Ephraim Hubbard and Prudence (Hills) Mason
Early Life: moved to Brookline 1832, farmer, teacher, A.B. UVM 1858
War Service: clerk, Office of US Paymr Gen., 1863-68
Later Life: LL.B. Columbian College 1868, admitted to bar of D.C. Supreme Court, specialty bankruptcy law, D.C. school board member 1869, real estate business, D.C. atty 1880
Affiliations: Republican, Mason
Married: 11 Jun 1862, Josephine Augusta Buffum
Died: aft 1894; interment unknown
(1880, JGU)

Mather, Charles D. (1847-aft 1920)

Born: 15 Dec 1847, Weathersfield VT, son of Charles and Mary (Waite) Mather
Early Life: schools in Weathersfield and Windsor; clerk Tuxbury and Stone, Windsor
War Service: PVT 3rd VT LARTY 16 Feb 1865, m/o 15 Jun 1865

Later Life: moved to Boston 1872, dry-goods business until 1920; moved to Montpelier VT, pres. Fisher Home for the Aged, pres. Heaton Hosp., RNC alternate delegate 1908
Affiliations: Unitarian, GAR, VHS
Married: (1) 29 Jun 1882, Clara Emma Fifield; (2) 1901, Mrs. Lucy Moulton nee Barrows
Died: aft 1920; interment unknown
(1920, AFS)

Maxfield, Hampton L. (1836- aft 1905)

Born: 2 Sep 1836, Fairfax VT, son of Harry and Abigail (Bishop) Maxfield
Early Life: New Hampton Inst
War Service: PVT Co. H 2nd VT INF 20 Jun 1861, wdd Marye's Heights 3 May 1863, CPL 1 Jun 1863, reen 21 Dec 1863, wdd Wilderness 5 May 1864, SGT 1 Sep 1864, m/o 15 Jul 1865
Later Life: farmer, Cambridge and Fletcher
Affiliations: GAR
Married: Oct 1866, Ermina A. McClellan
Died: aft 1905; interment unknown
Notes: "at the Wilderness he left his Springfield musket on the field, which fell into the hands of the Confederates. The name, co. and regt of the owner was carved on the gun, which 11 months later was brought back to the regt by a squad of deserters."
(WHJ*)

Maxham, Azro Job (1844-1915)

Born: 18 Nov 1844, Sherburne VT, son of Benjamin and Minerva (Shurtleff) Maxham
War Service: PVT Co F 3rd VT INF 16 Jul 1861, CPL, wdd Wilderness 5 May 1864, m/o, 27 Jul 1864
Later Life: teacher, Stockbridge VT, vocal instr., tuner, Estey Organ Co., Brattleboro VT 1890, vocalist, touring music companies and Ludlow VT 1900, campaign singer, reading clerk and messenger, US House, Asst. Door-Keeper, US Sen. 1904-12
Married: (1) before 1869, Mary Ella Baker; (2) 30 Jul 1896, Letitia Dorothea Burland
Died: 30 Aug 1915, Burlington VT; interment in Lakeview Cemetery
(1890, 1900, AGO, BS, PCD)

McFarland, Moses (1821-1911)

Born: 25 Jun 1821, Marietta OH, son of Osgood and Mary (Bartlett) McFarland
Early Life: moved to Waterville VT 1824
War Service: 1LT Co. A 8th VT INF 13 Nov 1861, CPT 24 Dec 1862, m/o 28 Jun 1865
Later Life: farmer, Waterville, j.p.
Affiliations: Democrat, Universalist, Mason, RSVO
Married: (1) 22 Oct 1849, Livonia A. Leach; (2) Julia Howard
Died: 6 Mar 1911, Waterville VT; interment in Mount View Cemetery
Publications: Some Experiences of the Eighth Vermont West of the Mississippi (1896), Some Incidents Touching the Battle of the Cotton (1896), The Eighth Vermont in the Battle of Cedar Creek (1897)
Notes: grandfather Moses served in French and Indian and Revolutionary Wars
(FSO, GFH, HC2, JVS88, WHJ*, WHO3)

McGettrick, Felix William (1847-1919)

Born: 20 Nov 1847, Fairfield VT, son of Michael and Mary (O'Connell) McGettrick
War Service: PVT Co. E 2nd USSS 1 Jan 1864, tr to Co. G 4th VT INF, 25 Feb 1865, m/o 24 Jun 1865

Later Life: New Hampton Inst., atty, town grand juror, school board member, town agent for prosecuting and defending suits, DNC delegate 1880, special customs inspector 1887, super. of construction, US Customs House and Post Office, St. Albans
Affiliations: Democrat
Married: Jan 1872, Elizabeth Morris
Died: 1919, St. Albans VT; interment in Holy Cross Cemetery
(FAG, JGU)

McKean, James Bedell (1821-1879)

Born: 5 Aug 1821, Bennington VT, son of Andrew and Catherine (Bedell) McKean
Early Life: moved to N.Y., teacher in district schools and Jonesville Acad., COL 144th NY Militia 1844; admitted to the bar 1849, atty, Ballston Spa, Saratoga Springs; Saratoga Cty Judge 1854-58; US Rep. 1859-63
War Service: COL, 77th NY INF 1861-63
Later Life: Treaty commissioner, Honduras 1865; Chief Justice, Supreme Court of UT Terr. 1870-75
Married: 20 Jun 1850, Catherine Hay
Died: 5 Jan 1879, Salt Lake City, UT; interment in Mt. Olivet Cemetery
Speeches: Democracy Vs. Slavery (6 Jun 1860, Congress), Union and Disunion (18 Feb 1861, Congress)
(CB, FAG, FSO)

McLaughen, Napoleon Bonaparte (1823-1887)

Born: 8 Dec 1823, Chelsea VT
Early Life: PVT, CPL, SGT USA 2nd Dragoons 27 May 1850; m/o 28 Apr 1859
War Service: 2LT 1st US CAV 27 Mar 1861; 1LT 3 May 1861; tr to 4th US CAV 3 Aug 1861; CPT 17 Jul 1862; COL 1st MA INF 1 Oct 1862; AIG Army of KY 1862-63; Bvt MAJ 3 May 1863; Bvt LTCOL USA, m/o 28 May 1864; COL 57th MA INF 14 Sep 1864; 3rd BGD 1st DIV IX Corps AOP 1864-65; Bvt B.G.; cmdg 1st DIV IX Corps AOP 1864-65; Bvt COL, Bvt B.G. USA 13 Mar 1865; m/o 10 Aug 1865
Later Life: MAJ 10th US CAV 17 May 1876; ret. 26 Jun 1882
Died: 27 Jan 1887, Middletown NY; interment in Maple Grove Cemetery, Worcester NY
(1870, AW, E&E, FBH, LOC*, MMB, RJ)

Mead, John Abner (1841-1920)

Born: 20 Apr 1841, Fair Haven VT, son of Roswell Rowley and Lydia Anna (Gorham) Mead
Early Life: local schools, Franklin Acad. (Malone, NY); A.B. MC 1864
War Service: PVT Co. K 12th VT INF 4 Oct 1862, m/o 14 Jul 1865
Later Life: physician; Trustee MC, UVM, NU; businessman; State Sen. 1892-93; commissioner, World Columbian Exposition, Chicago 1893; commissioner, Mexican National Exposition of Industries and Free Arts 1895; State Rep. 1906-07; LT Gov. 1908-9; VT Gov. 1910-11; RNC delegate 1912
Married: 30 Oct 1873, Mary Madelia Sherman
Affiliations: Republican, Congregational, GAR, Rutland Valley Grange, SAR, Mason
Died: 10 Jan 1920, Rutland VT; interment in Evergreen Cemetery
Biography: Barstow, John R. Sketch of the Life of John B. Mead, Colonel of the Eighth Vermont Veteran Volunteers. 1889
(JGU, MIDCat, PCD*, VHS20)

Mead, John B. (1831-1887)

Born: 15 Mar 1831, Stratham NH
Early Life: farmer, Randolph VT

War Service: 2LT Co. G 8th VT INF 7 Jan 1862, pow Bayou des Allemands LA 4 Sep 1862, prld 13 Nov 1862, 1LT 2 Apr 1863, CPT 5 May 1863, MAJ 26 Jul 1864, wdd Cedar Creek 19 Oct 1864, COL 4 Mar 1865, m/o 28 Jun 1865
Later Life: farmer, Randolph State Rep. 1867-68, Vermont State Board of Agriculture 1875, State Sen. 1878, State Super. of Agriculture 1878-80, Vermont Commissioner to the New Orleans Exposition 1884-85, New England Commissioner to the New Orleans Exposition 1886
Affiliations: RSVO
Died: 16 Dec 1887, Randolph VT; interment unknown
(GNC, JGU*)

Mead, Larkin Goldsmith (1835-1910)

Born: 3 Jan 1835, Chesterfield NH, son of Larkin Goldsmith and Mary Jane (Noyes) Mead
Early Life: grew up in Brattleboro VT, studied sculpture in Brooklyn NY pre-war works include "The Recording Angel," "Vermont," "Ethan Allen," last two in State House
War Service: six months artist for Harper's Weekly, hired by B.G. W. F. Smith to do topo. drawings of rebel positions during Peninsula Campaign, until nearly killed by a sharpshooter, moved to Florence, Italy
Later Life: Lincoln monument, Springfield, IL, "Ethan Allen" in US Capital, "America" for Soldier's monument, St. Johnsbury VT
Died: 15 Oct 1910, Toscana, Italy; interment in Cimitero Accatolico, Florence, Italy
Notes: friend of photograph George Houghton (q.v.)
(FAG, FSO, Gibson*, HTW)

Meigs, Henry Benjamin (1844-1922)

Born: 23 Nov 1844, Highgate VT, son of Luther and Phoebe (Stockwell) Meigs
Early Life: farmer
War Service: PVT Co. K 13th VT INF 11 Sep 1862, m/o 21 Jul 1863
Later Life: moved West, CPT CO CAV troop, suppression of Indian insurrection 1866-67, City Councilman, Julesburg CO 1867-69, Rancher, Hotel Proprietor, Julesburg, Prospector, Atlantic City WY Terr. 1870, merchandising and freighting 6 years, returned East, manufacturer of lime, merchandising, northern New York, and insurance agent 1871-74; life insurance business 1876-88, in New York, moved to Baltimore, MD, 1888, created largest life insurance agencies in the country, including MD, VA, WV, DE and D.C.
Affiliations: Baptist, GAR, SCW, SAR, Sons of War of 1812, NGS, GAR, Soc. of I Army Corps, 13th VT Regt Assoc, Mason
Married: (1) 18 Oct 1872, Alvira Stanley; (2) 17 Feb 1909, Nellie Merrifield
Died: 6 Mar 1922; interment in Episcopal Church Cemetery, Highgate Falls VT
Publications: Record of the Descendants of Vincent Meigs who Came from Dorsetshire, England, to America about 1635 (1901), A day in Virginia October 9, 1902, by 41 members of the 13th Vermont Regiment Association
Notes: In 1911, dedicated a bronze monument to the town of Highgate to commemorate the soldiers of all wars that served from that town
(1870, FAG, FSO, JGU, MOMM, RJM)

Meigs, John Jay (1838- aft 1920)

Born: 24 Oct 1838, Johnson VT, son of John and Laura (Waterman) Meigs
Early Life: M.D. HMS 1860
War Service: Asst SURG, 11th VT INF, 11 Aug 1862, SURG 3rd VT INF, 1 Oct 1864, m/o 8 Jul 1865
Later Life: Co. Hosp. Elko NV 1866-93, SURG Central Pacific and Southern Pacific R.R., left due to disability from septicemia, moved to Oakland, CA
Affiliations: RSVO
Married: (1) 25 Jun 1866, Diana Hyde; (2) 23 Feb 1889, Delia Wolf
Died: aft 1920, Elcho NV

(1910, 1920, Italo*, TFH)

Miles, John Fay (1820-aft 1912)

Born: 22 Jan 1820, Hinesburg VT, son of Nathaniel and Roxalana (Bishop) Miles
Early Life: Hinesburg Acad., WMS 1839, CMC 1842, physician Hinesburg 1843-90, town clerk and treasurer Hinesburg 1855-65, M.D. UVM 1856, State Rep. 1862-63
War Service: Med. Examiner VT Militia Chittenden Cty 1863, US Surgeon General's Office, Washington, 1864, sent to Fredericksburg and Port Royal to care for the wounded soldiers of VI Corps
Later Life: honorary degree, DC 1868, town clerk and treasurer Hinesburg 1880-1912
Affiliations: Republican
Married: 30 Jan 1843, Fidelia Boynton
Died: aft 1912
(FSO, PCD)

Miles, Lorenzo Dow (1838- aft 1920)

Born: 26 Sep 1838, St. Johnsbury VT, son of Orrin and Eunice (Clark) Miles
Early Life: Johnson Acad
War Service: PVT Co. E 3rd VT INF 1 Jun 1861, detached to Btry F, 5th US ARTY until winter 1863, m/o 27 Jul 1864
Later Life: farmer, Albany VT, deputy sheriff 1874, sheriff 1884-1906, since 1878, resided Craftsbury, Barton, Irasburg and Newport, 1920 in Newport
Affiliations: Republican, GAR, Mason, KOP
Married: 14 Mar 1865, Harriet E. Lord
Died: aft 1920; interment unknown
Diary: VHS
(1920, JGU*)

Miller, Crosby Park (1843-1927)

Born: 20 Oct 1843, Pomfret VT, son of Crosby and Orpha (Hewett) Miller
Early Life: unknown
War Service: CPL Co. G 16th VT INF 4 Sep 1862, dis 12 Mar 1863 to accept appointment as cadet, USMA on 1 Jul 1863
Later Life: USMA 1867 (18/67), 2LT 4th US ARTY 17 Jun 1867, QM West Point, 1LT 1 Dec 1869, duty at Fort Whipple VA, Fort McHenry, MD, Fort Riley, KS; Fort McHenry, Presidio CA, ARTY School, Ft. Monroe VA, instr. USMA, Block Point CA, Ft. Preble ME, prof. Mil. Sci and Tac. UVM, Fort Adams RI, QM 4th US ARTY, Post QM, Willet's Point, NYC, Fort Sheridan IL, War Department Washington, DC (1892), Chief QM (MAJ) Philippines 1900, Washington, 1910, US Soldiers Home Commission 1912, ret. Burlington VT, 1920
Affiliations: MOLLUS (#07005)
Married: 14 Apr 1874, Laura Haskin
Died: 30 Mar 1927, Burlington VT; interment at USMA Cemetery, West Point NY
(C&S, FBH, GWC, HC5, JAH, RR, WHP)

Montgomery, Marshall (1839-1919)

Born: 26 Mar 1839, Walden VT, son of Sereno and Hannah (Foster) Montgomery
Early Life: Peacham Acad. 1859, Walden 1860
War Service: CPL Co G 3rd VT INF 16 Jun 1861, CPT 10th USCI 18 Nov 1863, m/o, 17 May 1866
Later Life: admitted, Vermont Bar 1869, atty, St. Johnsbury VT 1870-80, State's Atty, 884-86, atty St. Johnsbury 1900
Affiliations: Congregational, GAR
Married: 1873, Flora Sibley

Died: 16 Oct 1919, St. Johnsbury VT; interment unknown
Notes: his term of service during the war was the longest of any volunteer to serve from VT
(1860, 1870, 1880, 1890, 1900, 1910, AGO, PCD)

Morrill, Justin Smith (1810-1898)

Born: 14 Apr 1810, Strafford VT, son of Nathaniel and Mary (Hunt) Morrill
Early Life: merchant's clerk 1825-31, merchant 1831-48, farmer 1848-55
War Service: US Rep. 1855-67
Later Life: US Sen. 1867-98
Affiliations: Whig, Republican
Died: 28 Dec 1898, Washington D.C.; interment in City Cemetery, Strafford VT
Notes: Author of 1861 Tariff Act and Morrill Land-Grant Bill
Publications: Self-Consciousness of Noted Persons. (1887)
(CB, HGW; LOC*)

Mott, Judd M. (1834-1863)

Born: abt 1834, Alburg VT, son of Joseph Marvin and Elizabeth A. (Mix) Mott
Early Life: moved to OH, clerk Willoughby OH 1850, moved to MI, UMI 1858
War Service: CPT 30 Sep 1861, CPT Co. B Lancers Regt MI 21 Jan 1862, CPT Co. I 16th MI INF 20 Mar 1862, GCM 18 Mar 1863 on charge of being AWOL, found guilty, sentenced "to be dismissed the service of the United States," sentence mitigated by President Lincoln to forfeiture of pay for the period of two months, mwia Middleburg 20 Jun 1863, LTCOL Jun 1863 while in hosp., d/wds Armory Square Hosp., Washington
Affiliations: Delta Phi Fraternity
Died: 28 Jun 1863, Washington D.C.; interment in Bush Cemetery, Alburg VT
Notes: Rev. David Marvin preached the sermon at his funeral in Alburg, in 1863 (St. Albans Messenger); Alburg GAR Post #88 was named after him
(1850, FSO, AGO, RCS89, TMB, TMO)

Moulton, Hosea Ballou (1843-aft 1930)

Born: 28 Jun 1843, Concord VT, son of CPT David and Harriet (Hale) Moulton
Early Life: Postal Clerk, Nelson, NH
War Service: PVT Co B 2nd NH INF 15 Aug 1862, wdd Fredericksburg Dec 1862, m/o 10 Dec 1863, foreman, US Arsenal, Washington 1863-64
Later Life: Treasury Dept, Washington 1864-74, LLB, National University 1872, LLM, Grant Memorial Univ. 1873, D.C. judge 1874-79, atty, Washington 1880-1930
Affiliations: Methodist, GAR, Mason
Married: (1) 1864, Annie Reese; (2) 1892, Elma Saunders
Died: aft 1930; interment unknown
(1880, 1900, 1910, 1920, 1930, PCD)

Mower, Joseph Anthony (1827-1870)

Born: 22 Aug 1827, Woodstock VT, son of Nathaniel and Sophia (Holmes) Mower
Early Life: carpenter, cadet, NU (1844-46), PVT Co A US ENGRS, 29 Mar 1847, m/o 25 Jul 1848, 2LT 1st US INF 18 Jun 1855, 1LT 13 Mar 1857, CPT 9 Sep 1861
War Service: COL 11th MO INF 3 May 1862, Bvt MAJ 9 May 1862, Bvt LTCOL 19 Sep 1862, wdd & cap, recaptured by Union forces when Confederate field Hosp. overrun, Corinth Oct 1862, B.G. USV, 29 Nov 1862, Bvt COL, 14 May 1863, cmdg 2nd BGD 3rd Div XV Corps, Vicksburg Campaign May-Jul 1863, Red River Campaign Mar-May 1864, cmdg 1st Div XVI Corps,

Tupelo Jul 1864, M.G. USV, 12 Aug 1864, cmdg 11th Div XVII Corps, March to the Sea Nov-Dec 1864, Bentonville Mar 1865, Bvt B.G. Bvt M.G. 13 Mar 1865, m/o 1 Feb 1866
Later Life: COL, 39th US INF 28 Jul 1866, 25th US INF 15 Mar 1869, cmdg Dept of Louisiana
Died: 6 Jan 1870, New Orleans LA; interment in Arlington National Cemetery (Section 2, Grave 1041)
(FSO, HGW, RJ)

Mudgett, Henry Edwin (1838-1918)

Born: 1 Sep 1838, Westford VT, son of John and Harriet (Starkweather) Mudgett
Early Life: Underhill Flats Acad., farm laborer Westford 1860
War Service: PVT Co E 13th VT INF 10 Oct 1862, m/o 21 Jul 1863
Later Life: farmer Hyde Park VT 1870, Johnson VT 1880-1910
Affiliations: Republican
Married: 1865, Abbie Whiting Burnham
Died: 3 May 1918; interment in Lamoille View Cemetery, Johnson VT
(1860, 1880, 1900, 1910, AGO, PCD)

Murray, John Boyce (1822-1884)

Born: 13 Aug 1822, Arlington VT, son of Edward and Phoebe (Manchester) Murray
War Service: CPT 50th NY ENGRS 30 Sep 1861; resgd 22 Jul 1862; MAJ 148th NY INF. 14 Sep 1862; LTCOL 23 Nov 1863; COL 14 Dec 1864; Bvt B.G. 13 Mar 1865; m/o 22 Jun 1865
Later Life: organized first Memorial Day, Waterloo NY, 5 May 1866
Married: 27 Jan 1847, Ageline Savage
Died: 8 Oct 1884, Seneca Falls, NY; interment in Restvale Cemetery
(E&E, FSO)

Macomber, John H.

Mansur, Zophar M.

Marsh, Carmi L.

Maxfield, Hampton L.

McLaughlen, Napoleon. B.

Mead, John A.

Mead, John B.

Meigs, Henry B.

Meigs, John J.

Miles, Lorenzo D.

Morrill, Justin S.

Mower, Joseph A.

NNNNN

Newell, Henry Clay (1835-1922)

Born: 19 Oct 1835, Burke VT, son of Selim and Emeline (Denison) Newell
Early Life: Bowdoin Coll. 1855, principal, Johnson H.S., A.B. DC 1860, M.D. DC 1864
War Service: drafted, 13 Aug 1863, Asst SURG 3rd VT INF 2 Oct 1863, resgd 20 May 1865
Later Life: physician St. Johnsbury 1866-69, 1874-1911, Barnet 1869-74, B.G., Surg. Gen. on the staff of Gov. Fairbanks, 1876
Affiliations: Delta Kappa Epsilon Fraternity
Married: 20 Mar 1866, Hannah Maria Hazen
Died: 29 Apr 1922, St. Johnsbury VT; interment in Mt. Pleasant Cemetery
(AGC, AWH, DCCat, DKECat, GTC, TEH)

Newell, Selim (1803-1871)

Born: 4 Aug 1803, Burke VT, son of Daniel and Nancy (Curtis) Newell Jr.
Early Life: D.M., Bowdoin 1830, physician, Burke 1830-41, Lyndon 1841-53, St. Johnsbury 1853-64
War Service: Fredericksburg and Washington (May 1864), among a contingent of Vermont doctors who volunteered their services to care for Vermonters who were wounded in the battles of the Wilderness and Spotsylvania C.H.
Later Life: physician St. Johnsbury 1864-71
Affiliations: AMA (1849)
Married: 1835, Emeline Denison
Died: 23 Aug 1871, interment unknown
Notes: two sons also served, Henry in the3rd VT INF, and Charles in the 10th VT INF
(1860, AMA1, B&C, BOWDcat)

Newton, Charles Marshall (1846-1911)

Born: 31 Oct 1846, Newfane VT, son of Marshall and Nancy (Tufts) Newton
Early Life: local schools
War Service: PVT Co. L 11th VT INF 6 Jul 1863, CPL 3 Jun 1865, Co. C 24 Jun 1865, SGT 1 Aug 1865, m/o 25 Aug 1865
Later Life: clothing business, Middletown CT, several terms in court of common council, US Postal Card agent 1890-93
Affiliations: Republican, GAR, SOC. AOP, Army and Navy Club, RSVO, 1st VT HARTY Soc.
Married: 26 Mar 1874, Mary Catherine Boardman
Died: 11 Feb 1911; interment unknown
Notes: brother John served in 18th US INF, brother James Holland in 9th and 17th VT INF, kia, Spotsylvania, 12 May 1864
(FSO, JGU)

Nichols, George (1827-1907)

Born: 17 Apr 1827, Northfield VT, son of James and Annis Aiken (Dole) Nichols
Early Life: WMC 1851, State librarian 1848-53
War Service: SURG 13th VT INF 24 Sep 1862, m/o 21 Jul 1863 (in charge of I Corps Hosp., Gettysburg)
Later Life: VT Sec. State 1865-84, pres. State ConCon 1870, RNC delegate 1872, member RNC 1872-84, Sec. & chair VT Republican Committee 1872-84, pres. Northfield National Bank 1875-1900, v.p. NU 1885-95, LLD NU 1881
Affiliations: Republican, Episcopal, RSVO
Married: 1852, Ellen Maria Blake
Died: 28 Apr 1907, Northfield VT; interment unknown

Publications: Vermont Legislative Directories 1866-80, Vermont, Compilation of Grand-List Laws (1875), Instructions Concerning the Registration of Births, Marriages and Deaths, in Vermont 1868
(RJ, WAE)

Nichols, William Henry (1829-1913)

Born: 23 Dec 1829, Braintree VT, son of William and Betsey (White) Nichols
Early Life: Orange Cty Grammar School, West Randolph, Acad., MC 1856, admitted to Orange Cty bar 1857, atty, moved to Cedar Falls IA 1860
War Service: PVT Co. K 3rd IA INF 21 May 1862, SGT 1 Nov 1863, Co. K 2nd IA INF 15 Aug 1864, m/o 12 Jul 1865, Louisville KY
Later Life: returned to Braintree, farmer; State Rep. 1870, judge of Cty Court 1872-74, super. of schools, clerk and treasurer, judge of probate 1879-94
Affiliations: Republican, Mason, GAR
Married: 3 Aug 1856, Ann Eliza Bates
Died: 15 Jan 1913, Braintree VT; interment in Hill Cemetery
(AGO, JGU*)

Nichols, William T. (1829-1882)

Born: 24 Mar 1829, Clarendon VT, son of James Tilson and Minerva A. (Briggs) Nichols
Early Life: Teacher, Sudbury VT 1850, Vermont State's Atty 1859-60, atty, Rutland VT 1860
War Service: PVT Co K 1st VT INF 2 May 1861, Big Bethel VA 10 Jun 1861, m/o 15 Aug 1861, State Rep. 1861-62, COL 14th VT INF 25 Sep 1862, m/o 30 Jul 1863, VT State Sen. 1863-66
Later Life: real estate agent, Proviso, IL 1870, Maywood IL 1880
Married: (1) 20 May 1856, Thyrza Stevens Cramton; (2) 23 Feb 1869, Helena Serepta Cramton (sisters)
Died: 10 Apr 1882, Maywood IL; interment in Evergreen Cemetery, Rutland VT
(1850-1880, FAG, FSO, JHG, LWR, SR, WHC)

Niles, Albert Augustus (1845-1922)

Born: 28 May 1845, Morristown VT, son of Solmon and Anna A. (Cooke) Niles
Early Life: Morristown 1860
War Service: PVT Co H 9th VT INF 9 Jul 1862, CPL 27 Jan 1863, SGT 1 Feb 1864, reduced 2 Mar 1865, m/o 22 Jun 1865
Later Life: People's Acad. 1869, Law School, Univ. of Michigan, admitted to the bar May 1870, atty, Morristown 1870-1920, State's Atty 1872-74, Secretary, Lamoille Cty Fair Assoc 1872-97, Lamoille Cty commissioner 1878-84, j.p. 1890-1912, Town Clerk and Treasurer, Morristown 1900-12
Affiliations: GAR (A.G.)
Married: 1872, Clara Minnie Bradley
Died: 1 Apr 1922, Morrisville VT; interment in Pleasant View Cemetery
(1860, 1870, 1880, 1920, AGO, HC2, PCD, WHJ*)

Noyes, Luman A. (1844-1907)

Born: 26 Jan 1844, Tunbridge VT, son of Stephen and Julia A. (Gushia) Noyes
Early Life: M.D. Univ. Penn. 1862
War Service: Asst SURG 2nd VT INF 14 Apr 1863, resgd 27 May 1863; Asst SURG 19th PA CAV 24 Sep 1863, m/o 14 May 1866
Later Life: physician, Randolph VT, 1866-80, post SURG Seal Island, Alaska
Married: 1862, Louise R. Boyle
Died: 14 Jan 1907, Randolph VT; interment unknown

(HC3, HEN, IHSR)

Nutt, William (1836-1909)

Born: 5 Aug 1836, Topsham VT, son of Isaac Brewster and Sally (Munroe) Nutt
Early Life: local schools, farmer, moved to Natick MA 1852, shoemaker Lawrence KS 1857
War Service: CPL Co. I 2nd MA INF 15 May 1861, SGT 11 Aug 1861, 2LT 54th MA 15 Mar 1863, 1LT 22 May 1863, CPT 55th MA 23 May 1863, P.M., Jacksonville FL, MAJ 23 Nov 1864, Bvt COL Mar 1865, LTCOL 25 Jun 1865, m/o 29 Aug 1865
Later Life: shoemaker, Freedman's Bureau, Halifax VA, 1868, returned to Natick, admitted to bar 1868, collector of taxes 1869-71, rep. to Gen. Court 1871-72, town meeting moderator, selectman, overseer of poor, Deputy sheriff 1877-86, trial justice 1886-92, j.p. 1867, notary public 1874-1909, State Sen. 1901
Affiliations: Republican, Mason, GAR, Officers Assoc of 55th Regt, pres. 2nd Regt Assoc
Married: 25 Apr 1863, Abigail Prentice Puffer
Died: 31 Aug 1909, Natick MA; interment unknown
(AHQ, AMB, AWS, EBC, FSO)

Niles, Albert A.

OOOOO

Olds, Edson Baldwin (1802-1869)

Born: 3 Jun 1802, Marlboro VT, son of Joseph and Sallie (Whitney) Olds
Early Life: moved to OH 1820, taught school, Univ. of Penn. Med School 1824, physician Kingston OH 1824, moved to Circleville OH 1828-37, business and mercantile pursuits, State Rep. 1842-43, 1845-46, State Sen. 1846-48, US Rep. 1849-55, moved to Lancaster OH 1857
War Service: arrested for disloyalty and imprisoned in Fort Lafayette 1862, while in prison elected to State House, released, State Rep. 1862-66
Later Life: mercantile business
Affiliations: Democrat
Married: 1 Jun 1824, Anna Maria Carolas
Died: 24 Jan 1869; interment in Forest Cemetery, Circleville, Ohio
(CB, FSO, JAM, JGU)

Olin, Abraham Baldwin (1808-1879)

Born: 21 Sep 1808, Shaftsbury VT, son of Gideon and Lydia (Myers) Olin
Early Life: Williams College 1835, atty, Troy NY 1838, city recorder 3 years, US Rep. 1857-63
War Service: associate justice, D.C. Supreme Court 1863-65
Later Life: D.C. Supreme Court 1865-79; LLD Williams College 1865
Married: Dec 1838, Martha Bushnell Danforth
Died: 7 Jul 1879, near Sligo MD; interment in Danforth Family Lot next to West Lawn Cemetery, Williamstown MA
(CB, FSO, JGU)

Ormsbee, Ebenezer Jolls (1834-1924)

Born: 8 Jun 1834, Shoreham VT, son of John Mason and Polly (Wilson) Ormsbee
Early Life: Scientific and Literary Inst. Brandon, Green Mountain Acad., Woodstock, admitted to the bar 1861
War Service: 2LT Co. G 1st VT INF 25 Apr 1861, m/o 15 Aug 1861; CPT Co. G 12th VT INF 22 Sep 1862, m/o 14 Jul 1863
Later Life: atty; IRS assessor 1868-72; State's Atty 1870-74; A.B. MC 1875, State Rep. 1872-73; State Sen. 1878-79; trustee, Vermont Reform School 1880-84; A.M. DC 1884, LT Gov. 1884-86; VT Gov. 1886-88; commissioner to Piute Indians 1891; land commissioner of Samoa 1891-93; LLD NU 1893, pres. Brandon Bank
Affiliations: GAR, RSVO, MOLLUS (#05797)
Married: (1) 1862, Jennie L. Briggs; (2) Mrs. Frances B. Davenport nee Wadhams
Died: 3 Apr 1924, Brandon VT; interment in Pine Hill Cemetery
Notes: Brandon GAR Post #18 named after him
Papers: VHS
(C&S, FSO, GFH*, JGU, MIDCat, TWH)

Otis, John Grant (1838-1916)

Born: 10 Feb 1838, Danby VT, son of Harris F. Otis and Elizabeth H. (Haviland) Otis
Early Life: Burr Sem., Williams College (n.g.), HLS, admitted to the bar 1859, moved to KS 1859
War Service: assisted in recruiting first black regt in Kansas 1862, State Paymr Gen. Gov. staff 1863-65, Kansas State Militia, activated in Sep 1864 to counter Gen. Sterling Price Raid at Kansas/Missouri border
Later Life: agricultural pursuits, dairy business, member of the Grange 18 years (State agent 1873-75, State lecturer 1889-91), US Rep. 1891-93

Affiliations: Abolitionist, Populist, National Greenback Party, National Grange
Married: 4 Sep 1865, Bina A. Numan
Died: 22 Feb 1916, Topeka KS; interment in Topeka Cemetery
(CB, JGU, WGC, politicalgraveyard.org)

Ormsbee, Ebenezer J.

PPPPP

Palmer, Cornelius Solomon (1844-1932)

Born: 2 Nov 1844, Underhill VT, son of Jonah Ferris and Chloe (Mead) Palmer
Early Life: Underhill Acad
War Service: PVT Co F 13th VT INF 10 Oct 1862, m/o 21 Jul 1863,
Later Life: admitted, Vermont Bar 1870, atty, Jericho VT 1870-82, State's Atty, Chittenden Cty 1876-77, State Rep. 1880, US Atty Dakota Terr. 1882-84, Dakota Terr. Supreme Court assoc Justice 1884-88, atty, Sioux Falls SD 1888-1901, State Sen. SD 1896-97, law firm of Palmer & Foster, Burlington VT 1904, atty Jericho 1910, moved to Plainfield NJ 1917, Plainfield 1920, Orlando FL 1930
Affiliations: Congregational, GMC, GAR (SD Commander)
Married: (1) 30 Oct 1870, Annie Rogers Fassett; (2) Jun 1905, Mrs. Mary K. Marshall nee Cropsey
Died: 13 Jun 1932, Plainfield, NJ; interment unknown
(1910, 1920, 1930, CHH, PCD, HWP)

Palmer, Edwin Franklin (1836-1914)

Born: 22 Jan 1836, Waitsfield VT, son of Aaron and Sarah (Thayer) Palmer
Early Life: DC 1862
War Service: 5SGT Co. B 13th VT INF 25 Aug 1862, 2LT Co. B 4 Nov 1862, m/o 21 Jul 1863
Later Life: atty, Waterbury VT State Rep. 1880, 1888, 1896, State Supreme Court reporter 1880-88; State Super. of Education 1880, 1890
Married: 15 Jun 1865, Addie D. Hartshorn
Died: 8 Oct 1914, Waterbury VT; interment unknown
Publications: The Second Brigade or Camp Life By a Volunteer (1864)
(LMW)

Park, Castanus Blake (1834-1891)

Born: 14 Dec 1834, Grafton VT, son of Castanus B. and Elzim (Tenney) Park
Early Life: Chester Acad., AMS 10 Jun 1856, Darlington WI 1856, St. Ausgar IA 1857, Grafton VT 1858-62
War Service: SURG 16th VT INF 18 Oct 1862, m/o 10 Aug 1863, SURG 11th VT INF 3 Oct 1863, m/o 24 Jun 1865
Later Life: Poweshiek Cty IA 1857, Grand Junction IA 1869-91, physician, farmer, banker
Affiliations: IA MS, Mason
Married: 3 Jul 1856, Nancy D. Carlton
Died: 22 Aug 1891; interment in Des Moines IA
(BHR, Charles*)

Parker, Charles Edmund (1839-1924)

Born: 21 Feb 1839, Vergennes VT, son of William Tarbell and Henrietta (Miller) Parker
Early Life: B.B. Allen's Private School, A.B. NU 1859, Dartmouth 1860
War Service: ADJ 7th VT INF 1 Jan 1862, CPT Co E 9 Dec 1862, resgd 22 Oct 1863
Later Life: manufacturer, windows and blinds, Vergennes 1863-78, clerk Vergennes 1880, mayor Vergennes 1885, State Rep. 1894, pres. Vergennes Electric Co. 1895-1910
Affiliations: Episcopal, GAR, MOLLUS (#09659), TCF, DPF
Married: 1866, Agnes Warren Ripley
Died: 31 Mar 1924, Vergennes VT; interment Prospect Cemetery

(1880, 1900, 1910, C&S, GFH, PCD)

Parker, Henry J. (1836-1897)

Born: 2 May 1836, Plainfield NH, son of Benjamin and Betsey (Fullam) Parker
Early Life: local schools, Wesleyan Sem., KUA, bookkeeper, Boston, moved to Ottawa IL, teacher and clerk, returned to Springfield VT
War Service: CPL Co. H 16th VT INF 18 Sep 1862, m/o 10 Aug 1863
Later Life: farmer, Andover, state agent for Granite State Mowing Machine Co., travelling salesman for A. P. Fuller & Co., granite and marble dealer, trustee Chester Savings Bank, dir/treasurer Andover Dairy Assoc, State Rep. 1874, State Sen. 1888
Affiliations: Republican
Married: 9 Nov 1859, Adelaide E. Putnam
Died: 19 Aug 1897, Springfield VT; interment in Oakland Cemetery
(JGU)

Parker, Myron Melville (1843-1929)

Born: 7 Nov 1843, Fairfax VT, son of Melvin Vining and Emeline R. (Story) Parker
Early Life: preparing for college, left to enlist
War Service: PVT Co. M 1st VT CAV 31 Dec 1863, Co. F 21 Jun 1865, m/o 17 Jul 1865
Later Life: moved to Washington, appointment to War Dept, Law degree Columbian Univ. 1876, postmaster of Washington 1879, member executive committee in charge of Garfield inauguration, vice chair inaugural committee for President Harrison, member of citizens' committee, second Cleveland inauguration
Affiliations: Republican, Mason
Married: 10 May 1879, Nellie S. Griswold
Died: Mar 1929, Washington, DC; interment unknown
Notes: In an 1890 passport application, he was described as age 46, 6' 4" in stature, with a high forehead, gray-blue eyes, a straight nose, mustached mouth, an oval chin, dark brown hair, fair complexion and an oval face
(FSO, JGU, PA)

Parmalee, Moses Payson (1834-1902)

Born: 4 May 1834, Westford VT, son of Rev. Simeon and Phoebe (Chapin) Parmalee
Early Life: A.M. UVM 1855, Principal, Johnson VT 1856-58, UTS 1861, ordained, 2 Jul 1861
War Service: Chap. 3rd VT INF 10 Jun 1861, resgd 18 Dec 1862
Later Life: Missionary, Erzurum, Turkey 1863-82, M.D., Long Island College Hosp. 1871, Oberlin OH when passports were issued, 19 Jul 1897, 12 Aug 1901, to return to Turkey as a missionary
Married: (1) Ellen Augusta Frost; (2) 9 Jul 1871, Julia Farr
Died: 4 Oct 1902, Beirut, Lebanon; interment in Beirut
Notes: spent his life after the war as both a religious and medical missionary in Eastern Turkey, which today is known as Armenia and Syria
Publications: <u>Life Sciences among the Mountains of Ararat.</u> (1868), <u>Home and Work by the Rivers of Eden.</u> (1888)
(GEP, JLS, NSF, PA, UTSCat, UVMCat)

Parmenter, Charles (1834-1864)

Born: 12 Feb 1834, Mt. Holly VT, son of Edward and Eliza (Frost) Parmenter
Early Life: farmer, student, MC 1861
War Service: PVT Co. C 6th VT INF 8 Sep 1864, representative recruit for Hon. Justin S. Morrill (q.v.); kia Cedar Creek

Died: 19 Oct 1864, Cedar Creek VA; interment in Winchester National Cemetery VA; cenotaph in Mechanicsville Cemetery, Mt. Holly VT
(1850, FSO, RR)

Partridge, Frederick William (1824-1899)

Born: 19 Aug 1824, Norwich VT, son of Cyrus and Mary (Loveland) Partridge
Early Life: NU 1842-44; courier for President Polk, Mexican-American War; farmer (1847-55; moved to Sandwich, IL 1857; atty
War Service: CPT 13th IL INF 24 May 1861; MAJ 25 Jun 1861; LTCOL 17 Feb 1863; wdd Chattanooga Nov 1863, m/o 18 Jun 1864, Bvt COL 13 Mar 1865
Later Life: atty, postmaster, clerk of circuit court; US Consul, Bangkok Siam 1869-76; examiner of pensions
Died: 22 Jan 1899, Sycamore IL; interment in Elmwood Cemetery
Notes: while courier for President Polk, without credentials, he was arrested as a spy by US forces
(E&E, FSO, RJ, WAE*)

Partridge, George (1829-1908)

Born: 22 Aug 1829, Randolph Centre VT, son of Oramel and Lucy (Capron) Partridge
Early Life: furniture and sleigh manufacturer, newspaper publisher, Village Acad., AC 1854, moved to Alabama, prof. Tuskegee Female Coll., principal Houston (TX) Acad., atty St. Louis MO 1859
War Service: atty for first military commission for trial of 200 rebel prisoners, atty P.M. Gen. Dept, Missouri, resgd 1863
Later Life: Springfield, Mo. correspondent 8 years, petroleum industry, Ky., Ohio, MO, sold co. to Standard Oil Co., moved to CO as silver miner, moved to San Francisco, oil and mining business
Affiliations: Pacific Coast Vermont Assoc
Married: 1860, Ann/Alice Augusta Thompson
Died: 11 Mar 1908, San Francisco CA; interment in Cypress Lawn Cemetery
(FSO, JGU)

Partridge, Henry Villiers (1839-aft 1920)

Born: 10 Dec 1839, Norwich VT, son of CPT Alden and Ann Elizabeth (Swazey) Partridge
Early Life: public schools, private instruction, Bristol Coll. PA, moved to IL 1859, studied law there and in Warren PA
War Service: 39th Regt. PA INF (10th Reserves), m/o Aug 1862 for disability; Paymr Gen. office Washington 3 years
Later Life: atty, Union Paper Collar Co., NYC, 5 years, moved to Colbrook, CT, moved to Norwich VT, State Rep. 1882
Died: aft 1920, prob. Norwich VT; interment unknown
Publications: A History of Norwich, Vermont (1905) with M.E. Goddard
(1920, JGU)

Peck, Charles William (1841-1916)

Born: 23 Feb 1841, Clarendon VT, son of Lewis and Harriet (Brown) Peck
Early Life: Fairfax Acad., Barre Acad
War Service: CPL Co F 1st USSS 13 Sep 1861, wdd Yorktown 5 Apr 1862, dis/dsb 26 Nov 1862
Later Life: D.M., Long Island College Hosp. 1866, physic., Brandon VT 1866-1910, chair. Board of Health, Brandon, State Rep. 1902,
Affiliations: Rutland Cty Med. and Surg. Soc. (pres.), VT MS (pres. 1909)
Married: (1) Oct 1869, May F. Jackson; (2) 1901, Mrs. Helen R. McLeod
Died: 21 Apr 1916, Brandon VT; interment unknown
(1870, 1880, 1900, 1910, GFH, PCD)

Peck, David Brainerd (1833-1912)

Born: 15 Mar 1833, Pompey NY, son of Nehemiah and Martha (Scoville) Peck
Early Life: unknown
War Service: CPT Co H 1st VT INF 2 May 1861, Big Bethel 10 Jun 1861, m/o 15 Aug 1861, CPT Co A 7th VT INF 14 Jan 1862, LTCOL 27 Aug 1862, COL (Not m/i) 29 Jun 1865, m/o 26 Aug 1865
Later Life: Treasury Clerk, Washington, DC 1870, Rubber Business, Cleveland OH, 1900 (resided Mentor OH)
Married: 31 May 1859, Frances A. Brainerd
Died: 28 Dec 1912, Washington, D.C; interment unknown
(1870, 1900, FSO, LAB)

Peck, George Augustus (1842-1940)

Born: 10 Jul 1842, Montpelier VT, son of William Nelson and Julia Ann (Clark) Peck
Early Life: Montpelier Acad., messenger VT Legis., farmer, tinsmith
War Service: PVT Co. I 13th VT INF 25 Aug 1861, dis/dsb 11 Jan 1863
Later Life: hardware business in partnership with his father-in-law, 45 years
Affiliations: Republican, GAR
Married: 17 Dec 1867, Laura Isabella Barrows
Died: 22 Jan 1940, Montpelier; interment in Green Mount Cemetery
(AFS, AGO, FSO)

Peck, James Stevens (1838-1884)

Born: 6 Dec 1838, Montpelier VT, son of William Nelson and Julia Ann (Clark) Peck
Early Life: UVM 1860; studied law
War Service: 2LT Co. I 13th VT INF 23 Sep 1862, ADJ 22 Jan 1863, m/o 21 Jul 1863, PVT Co. C 17th VT INF 3 Mar 1864, ADJ 12 Apr 1864, MAJ 10 Jul 1865, m/o 14 Jul 1865 as ADJ
Later Life: atty; volunteer fireman; Asst US District Atty 1869-80; Asst Secretary VT Sen. 1868-72; Asst A&IG 1868-72; A&IG 1872-81; postmaster, Montpelier 1881-84
Affiliations: RSVO, Mason
Married: 4 Mar 1869, Mary Ellen Blake
Died: 28 May 1884, Loon Lake NY; interment in Green Mount Cemetery, Montpelier VT
(FAG, FSO, HC4, RR)

Peckett, John Barron (1822-1894)

Born: 19 Dec 1822, Bradford VT, son of John Barron and Martha (Tilton) Peckett
Early Life; public schools, merchant, grist mill operator
War Service: 1LT, Co. D 1st VT INF, 1 May 1861, m/o 15 Aug 1861
Later Life: town treasurer and j.p. many years
Affiliations: Republican; GAR, temperance societies
Married: 9 Sep 1847, Caroline H. Low
Died: 12 May 1894, Bradford VT; interment unknown
(GFH, JGU*)

Perry, Carlton Holmes (1802-1880)

Born: 25 Mar 1802, Quechee VT, son of COL William and Christian (Marsh) Perry
Early Life: NU 1823, teacher Hartford and Hartland VT 1823-24, instr. in penmanship, NU 1825-27, Algebra 1827-28, Mathematics 1828-29, Corps ADJ 1828-29, teacher, St. Louis, MO, clerk, Jacksonville, IL, businessman 1830-38,

businessman, Fort Madison IA 1841-51, moved to Keokuk IA 1851, businessman, Keokuk 1860 (real estate holdings were valued at $75,000 on the 1860 census)
War Service: MAJ 3rd IA CAV 26 Aug 1861, resgd 18 Nov 1862
Later Life: businessman, Keokuk (1863-80)
Affiliations: Republican, Unitarian, pres. Keokuk Library Assoc 1874-75
Married: 28 Nov 1833, Elizabeth Ann Wolcott
Died: 26 Dec 1880, Keokuk IA; interment unknown
(1860, 1870, 1880, SW, WAE*)

Perry, Daniel (1839-1909)

Born: 8 Nov 1839, Wardsboro VT, son of James Tufts and Amy (Willis) Perry
Early Life: local schools, Westminster Acad., Powers Inst. Bernardston, MA
War Service: CPL Co. F 1st USSS 11 Sep 1861, dis/dsb 22 Dec 1862
Later Life: teacher/principal, Jacksonville, Wardsboro and North Bennington, ALS 1868, moved to Maysville MO 1872, teacher, later real estate atty, real estate dealer, Cty super. of schools, public administrator, mayor of Maysville
Married: (1) before 1880, Sarah J. (nfi); (2) 8 Oct 1885, Mrs. Ella L. Osmond nee Darden
Died: 24 Dec 1909, Maysville MO; interment unknown
(1880, 1900, JGU, T289)

Perry, Hiram Riley (1842-1915)

Born: 28 Jan 1842, Hancock VT, son of Bela Ransom and Achsah (Eaton) Perry
Early Life: Hancock 1860
War Service: PVT Co E 14th VT INF 21 Oct 1862, wdd Gettysburg 3 Jul 1863, m/o 30 Jul 1863
Later Life: farmer Hancock 1870-1910, State Rep. 1880
Married: 1876, Lucy Jane Small
Died: 26 Jan 1915, Hancock VT; interment in New Village Cemetery
(1860, 1870, 1880, 1900, 1910, AGO, PCD)

Perry, John Buckley (1825-1872)

Born: 12 Dec 1825, Richmond, MA, son of Daniel and Catharine (Aylesworth) Perry
Early Life: Burlington Acad., A.B, UVM 1847, ATS 1853, ordained, Congregational Church, Swanton VT, 12 Dec 1855, Pastor, Swanton, 1855-66
War Service: Christian Commission delegate, Chap. 10th VT INF 23 Mar 1865 - 7 Jul 1865
Later Life: lecturer Harvard Univ. 1867-71, professor Oberlin College 1871-72
Married: (1) 5 Mar 1856, Lucretia Leavenworth Willson; (2) 27 May 1867, Mrs. Sophia Harmon Wright
Died: 3 Oct 1872, Cambridge MA; interment unknown
Publications: The History of Swanton (1882)
(ACH, EWL2, OGH)

Pettengill, Samuel Barrett (1839-1909)

Born: 7 Feb 1839, Grafton VT; son of Jonathan Stickney and Sally (Barrett) Pettengill
Early Life: Burr Seminary, Manchester, MC 1857-59, Amherst College 1859-60
War Service: PVT Co. B 7th RI CAV
Later Life: ATS 1866, Home Missionary, Upper Missouri Valley 1866-67, Congregational clergyman, Royalton VT 1868-70, editor Rutland Daily Herald 1870-79, A.M. MC 1874, editor and publisher St. Albans Messenger 1879-82, ed Oregonian, Portland Daily Standard, Portland OR 1883-89, Dailey News and Ledger, Tacoma WA 1889-95, VT 1895-1909, journalist Grafton 1900

Married: 24 Dec 1880, Sue Harry Clagett
Died: 21 Oct 1909, Saxtons River VT; interment in Saxtons River cemetery, Rockingham
Publications: The College Cavaliers (1883)
(1900, MIDCat, WAE)

Pettes, William Henry (1811-1880)

Born: 25 Dec 1811, Windsor VT, son of Frederick and Harriet (Mynderse) Pettes
Early Life: NU 1824-26, USMA 1832 (23/45), Bvt 2LT, 1st US ARTY, 1 Jul 1832, garrison duty 1833, 2LT 30 Sep 1833, Creek Nation 1833-34, garrison duty 1834-36, Seminole War 1836, Defense of Volusia, FL, 14 Apr 1836, resgd, 11 Sep 1836, Asst Commissioner, for distribution of supplies to destitute Floridians 1836-37, US Civil Engr, harbor improvements at Salmon River, Genesee River, Buffalo and Dunkirk NY 1837-55, civil engr, Buffalo, NY 1855-61
War Service: LTCOL 50th NY ENGRS, 18 Sep 1861, Washington Defenses Sep-Nov 1861, Engr Depot, Washington Nov 1861-Mar 1862, Siege of Yorktown Apr-May 1862, Chickahominy & James Rivers Jun-Sep 1862, AOP, Rappahannock Campaign Mar-Jun 1863, COL 3 Jun 1863, Engr Depot, Washington (Jul-Sep 1863, Rappahannock Station Mar-Apr 1864, Wilderness, May 1864, Cold Harbor Jun 1864, Petersburg Jun 1864-Apr 1865, Engr Depot, Washington Apr-Jun 1865, m/o 14 Jun 1865
Later Life: farmer, Surrats MD 1870
Married: 3 Jan 1840, Anna Sophronia Mansfield
Died: 29 Feb 1880, Ft. Washington MD; interment unknown
(1870, FBH, GWC, LWK, WAE)

Phelps, Brigham Thomas (1841-1914)

Born: 4 May 1841, Grafton VT, son of John and Judith H. (Brigham) Phelps
Early Life: moved to Walpole NH 1849, local schools, moved to Westminster VT, 1855, Westminster Acad
War Service: CPL Co. I 12th VT INF Aug 1862, m/o 14 Jul 1863
Later Life: 1LT, Co. B 12th VT State Militia, Bryant & Stratton Commercial Coll. San Francisco, CA, wholesale commission merchant, returned to Westminster 1870, tobacco and general farming, inventor of Excelsior square system of cutting ladies' and children's garments, deputy sheriff 1871-81, first constable, auditor, tax collector, State Rep. 1888, State Sen.
Affiliations: Republican, GAR, Mason
Married: Jul 1874, Annie Olivia Holton
Died: 6 Nov 1914; interment unknown
(FSO, JGU*, TBP)

Phelps, Edward Elisha (1803-1880)

Born: 24 Apr 1803, Peacham VT, son of Elisha and Suzannah (Eastman) Phelps
Early Life: NU 1823, DCMS, Yale 1825; prof. anatomy UVM; lecturer DCMS 1841
War Service: State Board of Examining Physicians; BGD SURG 1st VT BGD 1861-62; cmdg Brattleboro Hosp.; post med. dir., Louisville KY; VT SURG-Gen.
Later Life: Stoughton museum of pathological anatomy
Affiliations: CT Valley MS, VT MS
Married: 30 Sep 1829, Phoebe Foxcroft Lyon
Died: 26 Nov 1880, Windsor VT; interment in Ascutney Cemetery
(FSO, GGB, HAK, RR, WAE*, WBA)

Phelps, George Hovey (1838-1862)

Born: 12 Feb 1838, Albany VT, son of Seth and Laura (Hovey) Phelps
Early Life: student Newbury Acad
War Service: 1LT Co. D 6th VT INF 8 Oct 1861, died of disease

Died: 2 Jan 1862, Camp Griffin VA; interment in Village Cemetery, Albany VT
Notes: Albany GAR Post #114 named after him
(1860, AGO, FSO, GGK)

Phelps, John Wolcott (1813-1885)

Born: 13 Nov 1813, Guilford VT, son of John and Lucy (Lovell) Phelps
Early Life: USMA 1836 (24/49), Bvt 2LT 4th US ARTY 1 Jul 1836, 2LT 28 Jul 1836, Seminole War 1836-39, 1LT 7 Jul 1838, Northern Frontier 1839-42, garrison duty 1842-45, recruiting 1845-46, Mexican-American War 1846-48, Bvt CPT 20 Aug 1847, garrison duty 1848-49, ARTY. Board 1849-50, CPT 31 Mar 1850, frontier duty, TX 1851-56, ARTY. Board, FT Monroe VA 1856-57, Utah Expedition 1857-59, resgd 2 Nov 1859, Brattleboro VT 1859-61
War Service: COL 1st VT INF 2 May 1861, B.G. USV 17 May 1861, Gulf of Mexico Expedition (Mississippi River and New Orleans) 1861-62, Camp Parapet LA (organized and trained negro troops) 1862, resgd 21 Aug 1862
Later Life: author of numerous articles on political, scientific and educational subjects, atty, presidential candidate 1880, gardener Brattleboro VT 1880
Affiliations: VHS VT Teachers Assoc, Anti-Mason Party
Married: (1) Judith (nfi); (2) 30 Apr 1883, Mrs. Anne B. Davis nee Mattoon
Died: 2 Feb 1885, Brattleboro VT; interment in Christ Church Cemetery, Guilford VT
Notes: deemed an outlaw by the Confederate Government for having "organized and armed negro slaves for military service against their masters, [and] citizens of the Confederacy"
Diaries and Correspondence: National Archives
Publications: The Island of Madagascar: A Sketch Descriptive and Historical (1885)
(1880, E&E, FAG, FSO, GWC, MRC)

Phillips, Edwin (1833-1911)

Born: 19 Oct 1833, Tinmouth VT, son of Seth and Miranda S. (Wilier) Phillips
Early Life: farm laborer, Oberlin Coll. 3 years, M.D. UMI 1861, returned to VT to enlist
War Service: PVT Co. G 6th VT INF 15 Sep 1861, Asst SURG 4th VT INF 4 Aug 1862, SURG 6th VT INF, 28 Oct 1863, m/o 26 Jun 1865
Later Life: CPS NYU 1866, physician, Ft. Edward, NY 3 years, moved to Minneapolis, MN 1869, founder Minneapolis CPS 1883
Affiliations: Abolitionist, Prohibition Party
Died: 31 May 1911, Minneapolis MN; interment unknown
(FSO, IA, Italo*, MDS)

Phillips, George Henry (1836-aft 1898)

Born: 3 May 1836, Athol MA, son of Aaron Jones and Susan (Walker) Phillips
Early Life: moved to Winhall VT, at an early age, local schools, farming
War Service: PVT Co. C 14th VT INF 28 Aug 1862, ORD SGT, m/o 30 Jul 1863
Later Life: farmer, Winhall, West Townshend and Putney, real estate business, town lister 3 years, town selectman 2 years, State Rep. 1882
Affiliations: Republican, GAR
Married: 25 Nov 1864, Helen Mar Barrows
Died: after 29 Jan 1898, Putney VT; interment in Mt. Pleasant Cemetery
(JGU*, T288)

Pierce, Charles Alexander (1839-1915)

Born: 22 Aug 1839, Chester VT, son of James and Dorcas Bayard Pierce

Early Life: local schools, apprenticed at *Brattleboro Phoenix*, established *Manchester (VT) Journal*
War Service: 1SGT Co. C 14th VT INF 28 Aug 1862, dis 11 May 1863
Later Life: Manchester Journal 9 years, purchased Bennington Banner, proprietor of one of the largest job printing, bookbinding and publishing establishments in the state, Cty High Bailiff 1890, postmaster 1891
Married: Abby Gibson
Died: 9 Mar 1915, Brattleboro VT; interment in Prospect Hill Cemetery
(AGO, JGU, JVS90)

Pierce, Leroy Matthew (1842-1921)

Born: 14 Jan 1842, Olney IL, son of Alvah Warren and Lydia (Atwood) Pierce, native Vermonters
Early Life: moved to Londonderry VT, 1846, Londonderry Acad., Springfield Acad., MC, 1861-61, but war interrupted
War Service: Christian Commission delegate, Washington, City Point VA, and AOP
Later Life: A.B. MC 1866, ATS 1869, moved to Glenwood, Mo., ordained, 4 Feb 1870, home missionary 2 years, returned east, pastor, Provincetown MA 1871-72, Bernardston MA 1873-83, traveled to Europe, pastor, Blackstone MA 1884-96, Medfield MA 1897-1909, Boston MA 1910
Affiliations: Congregational
Married: 24 May 1876, Catherine Billings
Died: 21 Mar 1921, Blackstone MA; interment unknown
Publications: An Appreciation of Catharine Billings Pierce. (1916)
(1910, JGU, MIDcat)

Pierson, James Smith (1840-1898)

Born: 8 Dec 1840, Shelburne VT, son of Smith F. and Lydia R. (Tabor) Pierson
Early Life: public schools, Burlington, clerk, Janesville WI 1857, several months, returned to Burlington, machinist 1858-62
War Service: PVT Co. C 12th VT INF 23 Aug 1862, dis/dsb 13 Apr 1863
Later Life: recovering from service illness 5 years, moved to NYC, invented apparatus for manufacturing water gas, gen. super. United Gas Improvement Co., Philadelphia, ret. 1886, returned to Burlington, bought father's farm, dir. Burlington and Waterbury CT Gaslight companies, dir. Burlington Electric Light Co., assoc with other gas companies
Affiliations: Republican, Protestant-Episcopal
Married: 7 Dec 1872, Lucille Blake
Died: 10 Apr 1898, Burlington VT; interment in Lakeview Cemetery
(AGO, JGU)

Pike, Paphro Ditus (1835-1917)

Born: 1 Dec 1835, Morristown VT, son of William and Nancy (Hitchcock) Pike
Early Life: farm laborer, local schools, Johnson Acad., saw mill operator until 1860, moved to Stowe, saw mill operator
War Service: PVT Co. D 11th VT INF 9 Aug 1862, CPL 11 Aug 1862, QM SGT 26 Dec 1863, 2LT 23 May 1865, m/o 24 Jun 65 at SGT
Later Life: carpenter, millwright several years, manuf. butter tubs 14 years, moved to Brooklyn NY, employee of Hatters Fur Cutting Co., returned to Stowe, saw mill and butter tub business 1890-1910, State Sen. 1900, board of dirs. and v.p., Mt. Mansfield Electric R.R.
Affiliations: Republican, Unitarian, GAR
Married: 7 Nov 1860, Abigail Towne
Died: 8 Aug 1917, Stowe VT; interment in Riverbank Cemetery
(AGO, JGU, PCD)

Pitkin, Perley Peabody (1826-1891)

Born: 9 Mar 1826, Marshfield VT, son of Truman and Rebecca P. (Davis) Pitkin
Early Life: farming, local schools, Washington Cty Grammar School, mining and trading CA 1851-54, returned to East Montpelier 1855, State Rep. 1859-60
War Service: QM 2nd VT INF 6 Jun 1861, BGD QM, AQM (CPT) USV reporting to Gen. Rufus Ingalls QM Chief AOP 19 Feb 1862, Chief QM (COL) 2 Aug 1864, resgd 7 Nov 1864
Later Life: VT QM Gen. (B.G.) 1864-70, State Rep. 1874-75, pres. Farmers' Mutual Fire Insurance Co. 1876, sawmill manufacturer, Lane Manufacturing Co. pres. 1888-91, trustee Washington Cty Grammar School, dir. First National Bank, dir. National Life Insurance Co., commissioner Green Mountain Cemetery
Affiliations: MOLLUS (#08738), RSVO (Treasurer)
Married: (1) 4 Apr 1848, Caroline M. Templeton; (2) 26 Jul 1886, Jennie A. Poland nee Dewey
Died: 28 Jul 1891, Montpelier VT: interment in Green Mount Cemetery
Papers: Western Reserve Historical Soc.
(AMH, C&S, GFH*, GGB, JGU)

Plant, Azro Melvin (1835-1900)

Born: 25 May 1835, Orwell VT, son of Lorenzo and Louisa (Hall) Plant
Early Life: HMS 1862, physician, Burlington
War Service: Asst SURG, 14th VT INF, 29 Jan 1863, joined regt. at Fairfax Station VA, BGD Hosp. Fairfax C.H., Emory Hosp., Washington, m/o 30 Jul 1863, Acting Asst SURG and Contract SURG, USA, Emory and Lincoln Hosp., Washington, dis 17 Apr 1864
Later Life: physician, Georgia, druggist, Milton
Affiliations: Congregational, VT MS
Married: 29 Nov 1864, Annie Sarah Fairchild
Died: 17 Nov 1900, Milton VT; interment in Village cemetery
(AMH, GGB, FAG, FSO, JFG, TFH)

Platt, Lemuel Bostwick (1811-1880)

Born: 1 Feb 1811, VT, son of Lemuel and Sarah Platt
Early Life: farmer, Colchester VT 1850-60, State Sen. 1847-48
War Service: COL 1st VT CAV 1 Nov 1861, resgd 27 Feb 1862
Later Life: Selectman, Burlington VT 1864, Banker, Burlington VT 1870, had business interests in the following companies, Vermont Life Insurance Co., Vermont Central R.R., Vermont & Canada R.R., and Merchants National Bank Burlington
Affiliations: RSVO
Married: Clarissa A. Munson
Died: 12 Feb 1880; interment in Greenmount Cemetery, Burlington VT
(1850, 1860, 1870, CEA, JVS47,WSR)

Plimpton, Salem Marsh (1820-1866)

Born: 21 Apr 1820, Sturbridge MA, son of Ziba and Hannah (Marsh) Plimpton
Early Life: Monson Acad., AC 1846, ATS 1849, ordained, Congregational Church, Wells River VT, 8 May 1851, Pastor, Wells River VT 1851-61
War Service: Chap. 8 Sep 1861, 4th VT INF, resgd, 1 Sep 1862
Later Life: Pastor, St. Johnsbury VT 1862-63, East Douglas 1864-65, Chelsea VT 1865-66
Married: 5 May 1851, Beulah M. Belknap
Died: 14 Sep 1866, Chelsea VT; interment unknown
(AMH, WLM)

Pollard, Henry Moses (1836-1904)

Born: 14 Jun 1836, Plymouth VT, son of Moses Pollard
Early Life: common schools, DC 1857, moved to Milwaukee WI, atty 1861
War Service: 1LT Co. I 8th VT INF 12 Jul 1863, CPT 7 Jan 1863, MAJ 6 Apr 1865, m/o 28 Jun 1865
Later Life: moved to Chillicothe, Mo. 1865, mayor 1874, Cty Atty 1876, U.S. Rep. 1877-79, atty until his death
Affiliations: Republican, MOLLUS (#04288), GAR, Legion of Honor, Mason
Married: 28 Apr 1864, Mariel Esther Adams
Died: 25 Feb 1904, St. Louis, MO, interment in Edgewood Cemetery, Chillicothe
(BPP, CB, C&S, DCN, HLC, JGU, MCC, MJP, TWH)

Porter, Edward Octavius (1836-1921)

Born: 12 Dec 1836, Cornwall VT, son of Marcus O. and Juliette Bethia (Chipman) Porter
Early Life: CMC 1859
War Service: Asst SURG, 11th VT INF, 19 Aug 1862, resgd 16 Jan 1865
Later Life: physician, Cornwall, State Rep. 1876-77
Affiliations: Congregational, RSVO
Married: 28 Aug 1867, Mary A. (nfi)
Died: 6 May 1921, Cornwall VT; interment in Central Cemetery
(1870, AGO, FSO, JHR77)

Porter, Henry Martyn (1835-1907)

Born: 25 Apr 1835, Middlebury VT, son of Cyrus and Mary Olive (Wilcox) Porter
Early Life: Peacham Acad., MC 1857, Teacher VT 1857-59), mercantile business, NY (1859-61)
War Service: 7th NY NG Jul 1860, CPT 15 Jan 1862, Co C 7th VT INF, 4 Feb 1862, Baton Rouge, La., 5 Aug 1862, MAJ, 28 Aug 1862, Provost-Marshal Dept Mar 1863, Donaldsonville, LA, 28 Jun 1863, PM, Brashear City Oct 1863, PM, New Orleans LA Oct 1863-Jul 1864, pr LTCOL, 29 Jun 1865, pr COL (Not mustered), 1 Sep 1865, m/o 14 Mar 1866
Later Life: National and American Bank-Note Co. 1867-94, solicitor, Manhattan NY 1900
Affiliations: RSVO
Married: 28 Jul 1864, Frances Ann Cornelia Fremont (Niece of GEN John C. Fremont)
Died: 6 Feb 1907, NYC; interment in West Cemetery, Middlebury VT
(1900, FAG, MIDCAT, WHP1)

Post, James E. (1840-1932)

Born: 19 Feb 1840, Rutland VT, son of Alpha and Mary (Cheney) Post
Early Life: local schools, farmer
War Service: PVT Co. K 1st VT INF 2 May 1861, m/o 15 Aug 1861, 2SGT Co. D 7th VT INF 27 Nov 1861, dis/dsb 15 Nov 1862
Later Life: farmer, travelling salesman (New England NY, PA, VA, IN), salesman, Rutland, oil burners and electric rangers, manufacturer of sewer pipes
Affiliations: GAR (QM SGT, Officer of the Day), Rutland Fair Assoc, Congregational
Married: 24 Nov 1863, Lura A. Kelley
Died: 23 May 1932, Rutland; interment in Evergreen Cemetery
(AFS, AGO, SR)

Powell, Charles Albert (1843-1931)

Born: 16 May 1843, Richford VT, son of Herman and Julia Submit (White) Powell
Early Life: public schools
War Service: PVT Co. F 10th VT INF 17 Jul 1862, m/o 16 Aug 1864, 2LT Co. C 10th USCI 15 Aug 1864, Acting RQM 31 Mar 1865, 1LT 15 May 1865, detailed to court martial duty, 27 Feb 1866 Galveston, TX, m/o 17 May 1866 Galveston

Later Life: farmer, moved to East Medway, MA, managed fancy stock farm 3 years, returned to Richford, employee I. J. Sweat & Co., partner, Powell-Comings, hardware and general merchandise, catering to retail trade, later became Sweatt-Comings, of which he was pres., funeral dir., State Rep. 1915
Affiliations: Republican, Baptist
Married: 6 Feb 1868, Mornelvia Letitia Kingsbury
Died: 1931, interment unknown
(AFS*, FSO, LCA1, M1821)

Powers, Horace (1807-1867)

Born: 28 Oct 1807, Croydon NH, son of Urias and Lucy (Wakefield) Powers
Early Life: Vermont Med. College 1832, Physician, Morristown VT 1832-56
War Service: Fredericksburg and Washington (May 1864), among a contingent of Vermont doctors who volunteered their services to care for Vermonters who were wounded in the battles of the Wilderness and Spotsylvania C.H.
Later Life: physician, Morrisville 1856-67
Married: 22 Oct 1833, Love E. Gilman
Died: 11 Dec 1867, Morrisville VT; interment unknown
(1860, AHP, HC2, ZT)

Pratt, John Edward (1835-1882)

Born: 7 Feb 1835, Bennington VT, son of Edward Stephen and Maria (Welling) Pratt
War Service: CPT Co. A 4th VT INF, 27 Aug 1861, pr MAJ 30 Apr 1864, pow, Weldon Railroad, 23 Jun 1864, prld 1 Mar 1865, pr LTCOL 14 Mar 1865, m/o 13 Jul 1865
Affiliations: RSVO
Married: 11 Jun 1856, Mary Louise Dewey
Died: 11 Oct 1882, Bennington VT; interment in Village cemetery
Notes: raised Vermont's only Zouave Co. (later Co. A 4th VT INF)
(AGO, BBObit, FSO, RR)

Pray, Rufus M. (1844-1918)

Born: 8 Apr 1844, Calais VT, son of Thomas and Polly (King) Pray
Early Life: town schools, apprentice carpenter and joiner
War Service: PVT Littleton (NH) Vols 24 Apr 1861, supposed tr to CPT Joshua Chapman's Co., m/o 12 Jun 1861, PVT Co. K, 3rd VT INF 23 Jul 1861, reen 31 Dec 1863, SGT, wdd, Wilderness, 6 May 1864, wdd, Cedar Creek, 19 Oct 1864, m/o 27 May 1865
Later Life: farmer, carpenter and joiner, postmaster, South Woodbury, 1889-92, State Rep. 1892, town treasurer 1891-92
Affiliations: Republican
Married: 8 Aug 1864, Nellie A. Whitham
Died: 7 Jul 1918, South Woodbury VT; interment South Cemetery
(AGO, JGU, T289)

Preston, Addison W. (1830-1864)

Born: 8 Dec 1830, Danville VT, son of William and Mary Preston
Early Life: Brown Univ. 1855, farmer, Danville VT 1860
War Service: CPT Co D 1st VT CAV, 15 Oct 1861, pr, LTCOL, 16 Sep 1862, Gettysburg PA Jul 1863, wdd, Hagerstown MD, 6 Jul 1863, wdd Culpepper C.H. 13 Sep 1863, pr COL 29 Apr 1864, Spotsylvania C.H. May 1864, kia Cold Harbor 3 Jun 1864
Died: 3 Jun 1864, Cold Harbor VA; interment in Danville Green Cemetery, Danville VT

Notes: Gen. George A. Custer called Preston, the best regimental cavalry officer he had ever known; Wells River GAR Post #64 was named after him
(GGB, GJU, HSB)

Preston, Simon Manley (1821-1919)

Born: 14 Apr 1821, Strafford VT, son of Warner and Esther Preston
Early Life: teacher, civil engr
War Service: 1LT 15th IL INF 24 May 1861; m/o 15 Jun 1861; AAG (CPT) 5 Aug 1861; AAG, Dept of MO 9 Nov 1861; dismissed 23 Sep 1862; COL 58th USCI 25 Mar 1864; Bvt B.G. 30 Dec 1865; m/o 30 Apr 1866
Later Life: civil engr, farmer, real estate agent
Died: 17 Oct 1919, Seattle, WA; interment in Lake View Cemetery
(E&E, FSO, TWH)

Prichard, John Brooks Wheeler (1839-aft 1920)

Born: 26 Sep 1839, Bradford VT, son of George Washington and Elizabeth (Pearson) Prichard
Early Life: town schools, Bradford Acad., clerk, Bradford Guards
War Service: PVT Co. D 1st VT INF 2 May 1861, m/o 15 Aug 1861
Later Life: merchant, moved to MA, returned to Bradford 1869, general mercantile business, town clerk 1870-94 (except 1 year), selectman, State Rep. 1882
Affiliations: Republican, GAR (Post Commander, Adj), Mason
Married: 21 Jan 1862, Orissa J. George
Died: aft 1920; interment in Village Cemetery, Bradford VT
(1920, GFH, JGU, SK)

Prindle, Cyrus Guernsey (1838-1911)

Born: 6 May 1838, East Charlotte VT, son of George and Louisa (Harris) Prindle
Early Life: student, entered UVM 1859, but dropped out during first semester due to family illness; amateur horticulturalist
War Service: drafted – PVT Co. C 4th VT INF 13 Jul 1863, dis 6 Nov 1863 by reason of being a Quaker
Later Life: horticulturalist, UVM
Married: 25 Feb 1863, Almira L. Greene (divorced 1877)
Died: 25 May 1911; interment in Morningside Cemetery, Charlotte VT
Notes: after divorce in 1877, changed his name to Pringle; Pringle only mentions one of the other two Quakers in his predicament, Lindley M. Macomber, Co. G 4th VT INF, other sources indicated the third was Peter Dakin, Co. H 4th VT INF.
Publications: The Record of a Quaker Conscience (posthumously, 1918)
(AGO, CGP, FR, FSO, HBD, LHB*)

Prindle, Franklin Cogswell (1841-1923)

Born: 8 Jul 1841, Sandgate VT, son of Hawley and Olive (Andrew) Prindle
Early Life: RPI 1859-60
War Service: 3rd Asst ENGR 3 Aug 1861, gunboat Ottawa 1861-63, 2nd Asst ENGR, 17 Apr 1863, Novelty Iron Works 1863-65, resgd
Later Life: mech. engr, Norman Wheeler, NYC 1865-67; civil engr, Brooklyn Navy Yard 1867-69; civil engr, USN, League Island 1869-76, resgd; civil and mech engr American Dredging Co. 1876-80; Brooklyn Navy Yard 1880-86, 1897-98, Mare Island Navy Yard CA 1898, CDR 1 Sep 1898; Honolulu Naval Station 1900, Civil Engr (CAPT) 5 Jan 1901; ret. 27 Feb 1901 as RADM; pres. Aztec Oil Co., 1901-23
Affiliations: NGS, MOLLUS (#02894)

Died: 6 Mar 1923, Washington, D.C; interment in Arlington National Cemetery
Publications: The Prindle Genealogy (1906)
(C&S, TJL2)

Proctor, Redfield (1831-1908)

Born: 1 Jun 1831, Proctorsville VT, son of Jabez and Betsey (Parker) Proctor
Early Life: A.B. DC 1851, A.M. 1854; atty
War Service: QM 3rd VT INF 19 Jun 1861, MAJ 5th VT INF 25 Sep 1861, resgd 11 Jul 1862; COL 15th VT INF 26 Sep 1862, m/o 5 Aug 1863
Later Life: atty; Selectman, Rutland 1866; State Rep. 1867-68, 1888; State Sen. 1874-75; LT Gov. 1876-77; VT Gov. 1878-79; RNC delegate 1884, 1888; Secretary of War 1889-92; US Sen. 1892-99
Married: 26 May 1858, Emily J. Dutton
Affiliations: RSVO, MOLLUS (#04386)
Died: 4 Mar 1908, Washington, D.C; interment in South Street Cemetery, Proctor VT
Papers: Proctor Free Library
Publications: Affairs in Cuba (1898)
(AFS, CB, C&S, JGU, RR, TWH, USA*, VHS10)

Putnam, Holden (1821-1863)

Born: 21 Feb 1821, Middlesex VT, son of Russell and Abigail (Blaisdell) Putnam
Early Life: Saddler, Montpelier VT 1850, Banker, Freeport, IL 1860
War Service: COL 93rd IL INF 13 Oct 1862, Vicksburg Campaign Apr-Jul 1863, kia, Missionary Ridge, TN, 25 Nov 1863
Married: Leonora Ormanda Robinson
Died: 25 Nov 1863, Missionary Ridge, TN; interment in Freeport, IL
Notes: bronze marker erected at the Vicksburg National Military Park in his honor, 1919
(1850, 1860, ADU, NPS)

Putney, Charles Edward (1840-1920)

Born: 26 Feb 1840, Bow NH, son of David and Mary (Brown) Putney
Early Life: public schools of Bow, fitted for college at New London NH
War Service: CPL Co. C 13th NH INF 16 Aug 1862, SGT 9 May 1865, m/o 21 Jun 1865
Later Life: DC 1870, educator, principal Boys' Boarding School, Norwich, moved to St. Johnsbury, asst and principal of St. Johnsbury Acad. 1882-95, pres. Caledonia Cty board of education, moved to MA 1895, super. schools Templeton Dist. until 1910, returned to VT, princ. Burlington H.S., state examiner, Randolph and Johnson Normal Schools
Affiliations: GAR, YMCA, Congregational
Married: 26 Jul 1876, Abbie M. Clement
Died: 3 Feb 1920, Burlington VT; interment in Lakeview Cemetery
Biography: Charles Edward Putney: An Appreciation, Charles E. Putney Memorial, 1920
Notes: future President Calvin Coolidge was a student of his
(AGO, JGU*, CSW)

Parmenter, Charles

Partridge, Frederick W.

Peckett, John B.

Perry, Carlton H.

Phelps, Brigham T.

Phelps, Edward E.

Phelps, John W.

Phillips, Edwin

Pitkin, Perley P.

Prindle, Cyrus G.

Proctor, Redfield

Putney, Charles E.

QQQQ

Quimby, George Washington (1835-1862)

Born: 18 Sep 1835, Lyndon VT, son of Thomas and Delia (Huse) Quimby
Early Life: DC 1859, teacher Mobile AL, headmaster Barton Acad., reading law
War Service: 1LT Co. D 4th VT INF 4 Sep 1861, CPT 20 Mar 1862, kia Fredericksburg
Died: 13 Dec 1862, Fredericksburg VA; interment in Free Will Baptist Cemetery, Lyndon VT
Notes: Barton GAR Post #76 was named after him
(DCCat, GTC)

RRRRR

Rand, Stephen (1844-1915)

Born: 11 May 1844, Norwich VT, son of Stephen and Rebecca Rand
Early Life: DC 1860 (n.g.)
War Service: Co. E 1st USSS 1861-63, Acting 3rd Asst ENGR USN, 1864; steamer *Merrimac* 1864-65, gunboat *Tioga* 1865
Later Life: gunboat *Tioga* 1865-66, engr corps 1864-69; Supply Corps, Asst Paymr, Portsmouth Navy Yard; PM, Tehuantepec Surveying Expedition 1870-72; iron-clad *New Orleans* 1872; Passed Asst Paymr 30 Apr 1874; steamer *Kearsarge*, Asiatic Squadron, Japan, Siberia, Transit of Venus party 1874; special duty, Washington, 1878-81; European Station 1881-83; Navy Department, Washington 1883-86, Paymr 31 Jul 84; Aspinwall, Panama 1885-87; special course in analytical chemistry 1887; sloop *Mohican* 1887-91; special duty, Navy Department 1891-93; Paymr, Washington Navy Yard 1893; Paymr Navy Pay Office 1895-99, Pay Inspector Sep 99, ret. 1911 as RADM
Affiliations: MOLLUS (#03506)
Died: 12 Jul 1915, Washington, D.C; interment in Arlington National Cemetery
(C&S, TJL2)

Randall, Francis Voltaire (1824-1885)

Born: 13 Feb 1824, Braintree VT, son of Gurdon R. and Laura Scott (Warner) Randall
Early Life: Chester Acad., Vermont Bar 1848, Law Practice, Northfield VT 1848-57, postmaster, Northfield 1853-57, State Rep. 1857-59, State's Atty 1859, atty 1860-61, Judge advocate, Vermont Militia
War Service: CPT Co F 2nd VT INF 20 May1861, resgd 9 Sep 1862, COL 13th VT INF 24 Sep 1862, m/o 21 Jul 1863, COL 17th VT INF 10 Feb 1864, m/o 14 Jul 1865
Later Life: Law Practice, Montpelier 1865-76, Law Practice and Lecturer, Brookfield VT 1876-84, v.p. and trustee NU 1883-85
Affiliations: RSVO
Married: (1) 3 Jul 1846, Caroline Elizabeth Andrus; (2) 6 Dec 1863, Fanny Gertrude Colby
Died: 1 Mar 1885, Northfield VT; interment in Elmwood Cemetery
Notes: Danville GAR Post #84 was named for him
(HC4, PGZ, WAE*)

Ransom, Dunbar Richard (1831-1897)

Born: 10 Jan 1831, Fayetteville NC, son of Truman Bishop and Margaretta Morrison (Greenfield) Ransom
Early Life: NU 1846-47, USMA 1847-50 (n.g.), BS, NU 1851, engr Peru IL 1851-53, 2LT 3rd US ARTY, 7 Jun 1855, frontier duty 1855-58, 1LT, 31 Dec 1856, garrison duty 1859-61

War Service: Defenses of Washington Apr-Oct 1861, Dept of the South Oct 1861-Jun 1862, Antietam, MD Sep 1862, CPT 1 Nov 1861, tr to AOP Jun 1862, Commander, Battery C, 5th US ARTY, Bvt MAJ 13 Dec 1862, wdd Gettysburg 2 Jul 1863, Bvt LTCOL Gettysburg 3 Jul 1863, Btry Commander, AOP 1863-64, Bvt COL 25 Aug 1864
Later Life: garrison duty 1865-72, dismissed 20 Dec 1872, reinstated by Congressional Act and placed on ret. list as CPT 1 Aug 1894
Married: Helen (nfi)
Died: 11 Jul 1897, Fort Worth, TX; interment unknown
Notes: a marker was placed near Sharpsburg, MD commemorating Battery C, 5th US ARTY, CPT Dunbar R. Ransom, Commander
(1870, GWC, NPS, WAE) Check at DAR Library

Ransom, Thomas Edward Greenfield (1834-1864)

Born: 19 Nov 1834, Norwich VT, son of Truman Bishop and Margaretta Morrison (Greenfield) Ransom
Early Life: NU, civil engr, realtor, railroad station agent at Farina, IL 1861
War Service: CPT Co. E 11th IL INF 24 Apr 1861; MAJ 4 Jun 1861; LTCOL 30 Jul 1861; wdd Charleston, MO 1861; wdd Ft. Donelson, TN 1862; COL 15 Feb 1862; wdd Shiloh, 6 Apr 1862; CoS, IG, Army of the Tennessee 1862; B.G. USV 29 Nov 1862; cmdg 2nd BGD 6th DIV XVII Corps, Vicksburg 1863; wdd, Sabine Cross Roads, LA 1864; cmdg XVI Corps, Atlanta Campaign 1864; Bvt M.G. 1 Sep 1864; cmdg XVII Corps in pursuit of Gen. Hood
Died: 29 Oct 1864, near Rome GA; interment in Rosehill National Cemetery, Chicago IL
Notes: A bronze bust of him erected at Vicksburg National Military Park in 1916
(G&P, NPS, WKA)

Rawson, Charles Hamilton (1828-1884)

Born: 16 Jul 1828, Orleans Cty VT, son of Elijah and Susan (Allen) Rawson
Early Life: WMC, physician Canada two years, CPS NYU, house SURG Bellevue Hosp., SURG SS Lewis, trips to San Francisco, surgeon Marine Hosp. San Francisco 5 years, moved to IA 1856, college student Queensbury NY 1860
War Service: SURG 5th IA INF, BGD SURG
Later Life: physician, Des Moines IA 1870-84
Married: 17 Nov 1863, Mary E. Blake
Died: 27 Jun 1884, Des Moines IA; interment unknown
(1860, 1870, 1880, STL1)

Raymond, Albert C. (1842-1895)

Born: 10 Feb 1842, Stowe VT, son of Asa and Jane (Lovejoy) Raymond
Early Life: public schools, Barre Acad., farmer Stowe 1860
War Service: PVT Co. E 13th VT INF 8 Sep 1862, m/o 21 Jul 1863, SGT Co. C 17th VT INF 5 Feb 1862, wdd, 26 Jul 1864, 1SGT 24 Dec 1864, 1LT 11 Mar 1865, CPT 26 Jun 1865, m/o 14 Jul 1865
Later Life: moved to IA, farmer; returned to VT, butcher Stowe 1880, farming, town selectman, clerk, postmaster 1889-95, State Rep. 1886
Affiliations: MOLLUS (#10070), GAR, Mason
Married: (1) 11 Jun 1865, Priscilla Moody; (2) Martha Smalley; (3) 1883, Alice Hitchcock
Died: 11 Nov 1895, Stowe VT; interment in Riverbank Cemetery
(1860, 1880, AGO, C&S, JGU)

Read, Estelle Serena (1841-1910)

Born: 2 Feb 1841, Jamaica or Windham VT, daughter of Charles Davis and Olive Charlotte (Willard) Read
Early Life: housewife, Jamaica

War Service: enl with husband as nurse with 4th VT INF, Aug 1861- Mar 1862
Later Life: housewife, Holyoke MA 1870-1900
Married: 15 Aug 1859, Judson Rufus Johnson
Died: 25 Dec 1910; interment unknown
(1850, 1860, 1870, 1880, 1900, DAR4, GWC2, JW, MAH*, WRC2)

Read, James Marsh (1833-1865)

Born: 19 Nov 1833, St. Albans VT, son of David and Emily (Marsh) Read
Early Life: moved to Burlington 1839, Burlington H.S., Phillips Acad., Andover, MA, UVM 1853, moved to Canton MS, private tutor, returned north, NY Courier and Enquirer, joined CPT Pope expedition as assist. with Barometrical and Astronomical Dept, left NYC 2 Feb 1855, stopping in Havana, New Orleans and Indianolia, Texas, marched to San Antonio, thence to upper waters of Rio Peros, camped near N.M. border, 2 1/2 years exploring central N.M., winter 1857, Washington, preparing expedition reports, returned to N.M., returned to VT late 1858, two years spent studying natural history specimens, writing for scientific journals, fall 1860, editor, Burlington Sentinel
War Service: PVT Co. H 1st VT INF 2 May 1861, m/o 15 Aug 1861, SGT, Co. D 10th VT INF 31 Aug 1861, 2LT 17 Jun 1864, 1LT Co. E 19 Dec 1864, wdd, Cedar Creek, 19 Oct 1864, ADJ 2 Jan 1865, Bvt CPT 2 Apr 1865, mwia 2 Apr 1865
Died: 6 Apr 1865, City Point VA; interment in Elmwood Avenue cemetery, Burlington VT
Biography: <u>A Young Man of Promise: The Flower of the Family, James Marsh Read 1833-1865</u> (2004)
(AGO, EMH, RR)

Read, Levant Murray (1842-1902)

Born: 26 Dec 1842, Wardsboro VT, son of Charles and Olive C. (Willard) Read
Early Life: local schools, Leland and Gray Sem.
War Service: PVT Co. H 2nd VT INF 13 Jul 1863, wdd, Wilderness, 5 May 1864, tr to VRC 21 Feb 1865, m/o 19 Jul 1865
Later Life: atty, Jamaica 1869-72, moved to Bellows Falls, probate judge 1876, State's Atty 1880-82, State Rep. 1892
Affiliations: Republican, GAR, Mason, VT Bar Assoc
Married: 13 Dec 1876, Sarah A. Perkins
Died: 17 Jun 1902, Rockingham VT; interment in Oak Hill Cemetery
(AGO, JGU)

Read, Ogden Benedict (1843-1889)

Born: 16 Sep 1843, Colchester VT, son of David and Emily (Marsh) Read
Early Life: student, Colchester VT, UVM 1861, dropped out to enlist
War Service: PVT Co. D 10th VT INF 4 Aug 1862, CPL 26 Sep 1862, dis 28 Mar 1864, CPT 39th USCI, MAJ 13 Mar 1865, m/o 4 Dec 1865
Later Life: 2LT and 1LT 11th US INF 23 Feb 1866, tr to 29th US INF 21 Sep 1866, Regt'l ADJ 18 Dec 1866 to 25 Apr 1869, tr to 11th INF 25 Apr 1869, Regt'l ADJ 23 Jan 1871 to 18 Sep 1874, CPT 28 Jun 1878
Married: 1 Jan 1872, Edith Adocia Sage
Died: 13 Apr 1889, Plattsburg Barracks, NY; interment in Elmwood Avenue Cemetery, Burlington VT
(1850, 1880, AGO, FBH, RR, TPH)

Redington, Edward Dana (1839-1931)

Born: 12 Nov 1839, Chelsea VT, son of Edward Caldwell and Caroline Dana (Stevens) Redington
Early Life: DC 1861, teacher St. Johnsbury Acad
War Service: SGM 12th VT INF 23 Aug 1862, 2LT, Co. I, m/o 14 Jul 1863, MAJ and Asst Paymr USV, 24 Feb 1864, AOP until 24 Jun 1865, Springfield IL until m/o 30 Nov 1865

Later Life: assistant cashier Passumpsic Bank 1863-64, cashier/paymaster, KS Pacific R.R. 1866-71, lumber business Lawrence KS, 1871-75, and Chicago 1875-87, insurance business 1888-
Affiliations: Republican, Congregational, MOLLUS (#07759), Western SOC. AOP, SAR, GAR, Sons of VT
Married: (1) 15 Nov 1864, Mary Ann Chamberlain; (2) 18 May 1882, Mary Julia Towne
Died: 9 Oct 1931, Evanston IL; interment unknown
Publications: Military Record of the Sons of Dartmouth in the Union Army and Navy, 1861-1865 (1907)
(C&S, DCCat2, JGU)

Reed, Marquis de Lafayette (aka Marcus L.) (1839-1912)

Born: 5 Feb 1839, Kirby VT, son of Samuel S. and Louisa (Joslin) Reed
Early Life: local schools in Kirby and Concord, moved to Burlington, business pursuits, shoe trade
War Service: 4SGT Co. G 17th VT INF 24 Feb 1864, wdd, Spotsylvania, 12 May 1864, detailed to take charge of ordnance and knapsack room, Washington, Harwood Hosp. until m/o 14 Jul 1865
Later Life: moved to Granby, farmer until 1878, moved to West Concord 1886, farmer, State Rep. 1869, 1870, 1892
Affiliations: Mason, GAR
Married: 13 Sep 1866, Emily C. Grout
Died: 7 Aug 1912, St. Johnsbury VT; interment in Grove Cemetery
(AGC, AGO, JGU*)

Reynolds, Albert (1837-1899)

Born: 18 Aug 1837, Grand Isle VT, son of Guy B. and Mary (Hyde) Reynolds
Early Life: farm laborer Rutland 1860, M.D. UVM 1864
War Service: US Army 62-64, Asst SURG 17th Regt Corps D'Afrique 63-64
Later Life: lecturer, Nervous and Mental Diseases IA State Univ. 2 years, super. Hosp. for the Insane, Washington, IA 1880, Clinton Cty MS, IA MS
Married: 1869, Sarah Rogers
Died: 23 Feb 1899, Clinton, LA; interment unknown
(1860, 1880, FSO, UVMMED)

Reynolds, William B. (1840-1864)

Born: 1840, Milton VT, son of Luther and Martha J. Reynolds
Early Life: laborer, Benson VT 1860
War Service: 1LT Co. I 6th VT INF 7 Dec 1861, CPT 18 Jan 1862, wdd/pow Golding's Farm 27 Jun 1862, prld 17 Jul 1862, MAJ 17th VT INF 12 Apr 1864, kia Petersburg Mine
Died: 30 Jul 1864, Petersburg Mine; interment unknown
Notes: Milton GAR Posts #24 and #59 named after him
(1850, 1860, GGK, RR)

Rice, John Lovell (1840-aft 1912)

Born: 1 Feb 1840, Weathersfield VT, son of Lysander Mason and Clarinda Whitmore (Upham) Rice
Early Life: KUA Meriden NH, store clerk, Cornish Flat NH 1859-61
War Service: PVT Co A 2nd NH INF 28 Apr 1861, wdd Bull Run 21 Jul 1861, pow Libby Prison, prld 2 Jan 1862, CPT Co H 16th NH INF 26 Nov 1862, LTCOL 75th USCI 31 Oct 1863
Later Life: cotton farmer, Avoyelles Parish LA 1866, provisions dealer, Springfield MA 1867-73, US Customs Inspector, Boston MA 1874-76, admitted, Suffolk Cty Bar 24 Apr 1876, atty Springfield MA 1876-1912, State Rep. Springfield 1882, chief of Police, Springfield 1882, 1892-95, postmaster Springfield 1886-90, commissioner, US Circuit Court MA District 1889-1910

Affiliations: Mason, GAR, MOLLUS (#05367)
Married: (1) 8 Jan 1867, Marion Virginia Chellis; (2) 2 Oct 1879, Clara Elizabeth Galpin
Died: aft 1912; interment unknown
Notes: received the surrender of the last organized unit of Confederates, 5 Jun 1865, at Washington LA; in 1886, contributed $235 to pay costs incurred for building Sudley Church, where he had been nursed back to health after being wdd at 1st Bull Run
(C&S, PCD, SCS, WRC1)

Richardson, Harrison A. E. (1844-aft 1912)

Born: 4 Feb 1844, Roxbury VT, son of Joel and Susannah P. (Batchelder) Richardson
Early Life: student
War Service: PVT Co H 6th VT INF 15 Oct 1861, wdd Lee's Mill 14 Apr 1862, wdd Wilderness May 1864, wdd Cold Harbor 2 Jun 1864, m/o 28 Oct 1864
Later Life: farmer, Roxbury 1870-1900, Board of Real Estate Appraisers 1898, license commissioner 1904, school dir., highway commissioner
Affiliations: Methodist, GAR, Grange
Married: (1) 23 Jan 1866, Sarah P. Packard; (2) 1888, Jennie L. Cutler
Died: aft 1912, interment in Roxbury Cemetery, Roxbury VT
(1870, 1880, 1900, AGO, FSO, PCD)

Richardson, Israel Bush (1815-1862)

Born: 26 Dec 1815, Fairfax VT, son of Israel Putnam and Susanna Richardson
Early Life: USMA 1841 (38/52), 2LT, 3rd US INF, 30 Sep 1841, Seminole War 1841-42, frontier duty 1842-45, Texas 1845-46, 1LT 21 Sep 1846, Mexican-American War 1846-47, Bvt CPT 20 Aug 1847, Bvt MAJ 13 Sep 1847, frontier duty 1848-54, CPT 3rd US INF 5 Mar 1851, resgd 30 Sep 1855, farmer, Pontiac, MI (1855-61)
War Service: COL 2nd MI INF 25 May 1861, B.G. USV, 17 May 1861, cmdg 4 Brig, 1 Div. First Bull Run Jul 1861, cmdg 1 Div II Corps, Peninsular Campaign, M.G. USV, 4 Jul 1862, cmdg II Corps, Antietam, mwia, 17 Sep 1862
Married: Mar 1851, Fannie Travor
Died: 3 Nov 1862, Sharpsburg MD; interment in Oak Hill Cemetery, Pontiac, MI
Notes: descendant of Rev. War Gen. Israel Putnam; Fairfax GAR Post #92 named after him
(HGW, GWC, LOC*, RJ)

Ricker, Isaac M. (1839-1910)

Born: 10 Apr 1839, Groton VT, son of Oronson and Lydia (Taisey) Ricker
Early Life: public schools, farmer laborer 1860
War Service: PVT Co. H 12th VT INF 15 Aug 1862, m/o 14 Jul 1863
Later Life: business and agriculture, lumber industry, sold clapboards and shingles, owned 1,000 acres of 'wild land' in Groton
Affiliations: Republican, State Rep. 1906
Married: Dec 1863, Mary Jane Taisey
Died: 15 Aug 1910, Groton VT; interment in Village Cemetery
(1860, 1910, AFS*, AGO, HC6)

Ripley, Edward Hastings (1839-1915)

Born: 11 Nov 1839, Center Rutland VT, son of William Young and Jane (Warren) Ripley
Early Life: student, UC

War Service: CPT Co. B 9th VT INF 2 Jun 1862, MAJ 20 Mar 1863, LTCOL 16 May 1863, COL 22 May 1863, wdd, Chapin's Farm, 29 Sep 1864, Bvt B.G. 1 Aug 1864, m/o 13 Jun 1865
Later Life: Ripley Brothers marble business, banker, founder and dir. of US and Brazil Steamship Line, built Raritan River Railroad in NJ
Affiliations: MOLLUS (#03013), RSVO
Married: 25 May 1878, Amelie Dyckman Van Doren
Died: 14 Sep 1915, Rutland VT; interment in Evergreen Cemetery
Publications: The Capture and Occupation of Richmond, April 3rd, 1865 (1907)
Biography: Vermont General: The Unusual War Experiences of Edward Hastings Ripley, 1862-1865 (1960)
Notes: Civil War collection given to Bennington Museum
(AMH, C&S, FTM*, HER, RR, UCA)

Roberts, Benjamin Stone (1810-1875)

Born: 18 Nov 1810, Manchester VT, son of Gen. Martin and Betsey (Stone) Roberts
Early Life: USMA 1835 (53/56), Bvt 2LT, 1st Dragoons, 1 Jul 1835, frontier duty (1835-38), 2LT, 1st Dragoons, 31 May 1836, 1LT, 1st Dragoons, 31 Jul 1837, recruiting 1838-39, resgd, 28 Jan 1839, chief engr overseeing construction of Champlain & Ogdensburg R.R. 1839-40, Assistant State Geologist, New York 1841, railroad construction in Russia 1842, atty Ft. Madison, IA 1844-46, LTC, IA Militia 1844-46, 1LT Mtd Rifles 27 May 1846, CPT Mtd Rifles 16 Feb 1847, Bvt MAJ 13 Sep 1847, Bvt LTCOL 24 Nov 1847, frontier duty 1848-49, leave of absence 1850-52, Topo. Bureau, Washington 1852-53, frontier duty 1853-61
War Service: MAJ 13 May 1861, 3rd US CAV 3 Aug 1861, New Mexico 1861-62, Bvt COL 21 Feb 1862, B.G. USV 16 Jul 1862, I.G. on Gen. Pope's staff, Second Bull Run Campaign 1862, cmdg expedition against Chippewa in MN 1862, Commander, upper defenses of Washington, cmdg Dept of IA 1863, Chief of CAV, Dept of the Gulf 1864-65, cmdg Dist. of West Tennessee 1865, Bvt B.G., Bvt M.G. USV, 13 Mar 1865, m/o 15 Jan 1866
Later Life: LTCOL 3rd US CAV 28 Jul 1866, frontier duty 1867-68, instr. Military Science, Yale 1868-70, ret. 15 Dec 1870, atty Washington, 1866-75
Married: 18 Sep 1835, Elizabeth Sperry
Died: 29 Jan 1875, Washington, D.C; interment in Dellwood Cemetery, Manchester VT
Publications: Lieut.-General U.S. Grant, his Services and Characteristics (1869)
NOTES: Invented Roberts' breech-loading rifle 1870
(BFG, FTM*, GWC, RJ)

Roberts, George Tisdale (1824-1862)

Born: 3 Oct 1824, Clarendon VT, son of Benjamin and Sophia (Hodges) Roberts
Early Life: Burr Sem., Railroad Construction, Marble Business, Manchester VT 1850), Marble Agent, Rutland VT 1860
War Service: 1LT, 1st VT INF 28 Nov 1859, Big Bethel VA Jun 1861, m/o 15 Aug 1861, COL, 7th VT INF 5 Dec 1861, capture of New Orleans LA Apr-May 1862, Vicksburg, MS Jun-Jul 1862, mwia, Baton Rouge, LA, 5 Aug 1862
Died: 7 Aug 1862, Baton Rouge, LA; interment in West Street Cemetery, Rutland VT
Notes: grandson of Revolutionary War veterans, Gen. Christopher Roberts and Continental Army SURG, Dr. Silas Hodges
(1850, 1860, ADH, WCH)

Roberts, John L. (1818-1873)

Born: 18 Mar 1818, Strafford VT, son of Jonathan and Olive Roberts
Early Life: joined M.E. Church 1845 VT Conf. 1849, ordained, 20 Jun 1849
War Service: Chaplain, 4th VT INF, 25 Sep 1862, resgd 9 May 1863, again 3 Jul 1863, m/o 13 Jul 1865
Later Life: became supernumerary Troy Conf. 1866, moved to Washington, filled several govt positions
Married: Anna H. (nfi)
Died: 24 Jun 1873, Ocean Grove, NJ; interment unknown

Notes: obituary in minutes of annual Conf. 1874, p. 70
(1870, FSO, JM)

Robie, Edward Dunham (1831-1911)

Born: 11 Sep 1831, Burlington VT, son of Jacob Carter and Louisa (Dunham) Robie
Early Life: Binghamton (NY) Acad. 1852; warrant Assistant Engr USN 1852; 3rd Asst Engr side-wheel steamer *Mississippi*, COMO Mathew Perry's flag-ship, circumnavigate globe, visited Japan 1852-55; 2nd Asst Engr 1856; side-wheel steamer *Susquehanna*, European Squadron, provided support for successful attempt to lay a trans-Atlantic cable; 1st Asst Engr 21 Jul 1858; steam frigate *Niagara* 1858-60
War Service: Chief Engr 1861; screw sloop *Mohican*, SABS; superintended building of iron-clad monitor *Dictator* 1862; steamer *Ericsson*, SABS 1863-64; ironclad *Dictator*, SABS 1864-65
Later Life: Engr Board of Examiners 1865-66; steam sloop *Ossipee* 1866; Fleet Engr, Pacific Squadron 1866-67; shore duty, Washington 1868-69; Inspector of Machinery Afloat, at the Boston Navy Yard 1870-71; frigate *Wabash*, Mediterranean; Fleet Engr European, Gulf and Pacific Squadrons 1871-74; in charge of Steam Engineering Department, Norfolk VA 1874-77; Pittsburg, PA, then Cold Spring, NY 1877-79; Fleet Engr, Pacific Station 1879-81; Chief Engr, Boston Navy Yard 1881-84; Brooklyn and Norfolk Navy Yards 1884-91; Inspection duty 1891-92; Bureau of Steam Engineering, Washington 1892-93; ret. 11 Sep 1893 as COMO; selection of auxiliary vessels during Spanish-American War; RADM 1906
Affiliations: MOLLUS (#09215)
Died: 7 Jun 1911, Washington, D.C; interment in Arlington National Cemetery
Papers: East Carolina University
Notes: In Japan, aside from taking daguerreotype pictures, he erected the first electric telegraph line in Japan, 1,200 feet long, and assisted in building the first steam railroad, one-quarter scale, all of which were designed to impress the Japanese, which they did
(C&S, TJL2)

Robinson, Calista (1839-1913)

Born: 22 Mar 1839, Chelsea VT, daughter of Cornelius and Mary A. (Pike) Robinson
Early Life: local schools, Rutgers (NY) Female Inst, teacher, Chicago 1861-64, returned to VT
War Service: assisted in collecting and distributing sanitary and hosp. supplies, IL and later VT
Later Life: charter member Women's Relief Corps, National Pres. 1901, Bradford
Married: 8 Sep 1864, Charles Jones
Died: 30 Jan 1913; interment unknown
(CRJ*, FSO, GFH, JAL, WRC3)

Robinson, Charles Henry (1831-1917)

Born: 31 Aug 1831, Bennington VT, son of Uel Merrill and Betsey (Hicks) Robinson
Early Life: businessman
War Service: QM SGT 31st NC INF (CSA)
Later Life: businessman, Wilmington NC
Died: 6 Nov 1917, Wilmington, NC; interment in Oakdale Cemetery
(JS)

Robinson, Don Alonzo (1836-aft 1880)

Born: 29 Feb 1836, West Charleston VT, son of Elijah and Eliza A. (Smith) Robinson
Early Life: M.D. UVM 1859
War Service: Asst SURG 5th NH INF 28 Feb 1865, m/o 28 Jun 1865
Later Life: Med. Examiner Equitable NY Mutual

Affiliations: VT MS, Dist. St. Francis PQ MS
Married: 28 Dec 1864, Sara Maria Noyes
Died: aft 1880; interment unknown
(1880, ADA, UVMMED)

Robinson, Frederick G. (1843-1884)

Born: 13 Jan 1843, Bennington VT, son of Uel Merrill and Betsey (Hicks) Robinson
Early Life: farmer 1860, Wilmington NC Rifle Guards
War Service: Co. I 8th NC INF (CSA), 40th NC INF (CSA); pow at Bentonville 19-21 Mar 1865; prld at end of war
Later Life: civil engr, grocery clerk 1880
Married: 13 Jun 1866, Isabel B. Costin
Died: 14 Nov 1884, Wilmington, NC; interment in Oakdale Cemetery
(1860, 1880, JS)

Rogers, Nathaniel Sewall (1840-1916)

Born: 7 Jun 1840, Moultonboro NH, son of Nathaniel and Mary (Smith) Rogers
Early Life: moved to Newport 1845, public schools, worked family farm while father served in 15th VT INF
War Service: PVT Co. M 11th VT INF 15 Sep 1863, wdd, Spotsylvania, 18 May 1864 (lost right leg), m/o 14 Sep 1865 at Montpelier Hosp.
Later Life: farmer 1865-80, j.p. 14 years, Asst Cty Judge 1892, school board member
Affiliations: Baptist, GAR (ADJ. Chap., Post commander, State Asst I.G.)
Married: 25 Sep 1866, Mary E. Whipple
Died: 20 Nov 1916, Newport VT; interment in Newport Center Cemetery
(AFS, AGO, JVS17)

Ross, Lucretius Dewey (1828-1902)

Born: 4 Jul 1828, East Poultney VT, son of Paul Mower and Charlotte Moseley (Dewey) Ross
Early Life: Troy Conf. Acad., Castleton Sem., MC 1852, CMC 1852-57
War Service: Asst SURG, 14th VT INF 8 Oct 1862, m/o 30 Jul 1863, Contract SURG, U.S. Army Hosp., Brattleboro 1864-65
Later Life: physician, Poultney 1865-1902, pres. Rutland Cty MS, Super. of Schools
Married: 4 Jul 1860, Adaline Adelia Baldwin
Died: 25 Aug 1902, Poultney VT; interment unknown
Correspondence: Letters from Home (1848-1852): Being Mostly Letters from a Mother (Charlotte Moseley Dewey Ross) to her son (Lucretius Dewey Ross) (1962)
(LHC, MIDCAT, RR, VTMS)

Royce, Homer Elihu (1819-1891)

Born: 14 Jun 1819, East Berkshire VT, son of Elihu Marvin and Sophronia (Parker) Royce
Early Life: local schools, St. Albans and Enosburg Acad., atty, State Rep. 1846-47), State's Atty (1846-47), prosecuting atty (1848), State Sen. 1849-51, 1861, 1868)
War Service: US Rep. 1857-61 VT
Later Life: VT Supreme Court justice 1870-82, LLD UVM 1882, chief justice 1882-90
Affiliations: Republican
Married: 23 Jan 1851, Mary Edmunds
Died: 24 Apr 1891, St. Albans VT; interment in Cavalry Cemetery, East Berkshire VT
(CB, JGU*, TWH)

Russell, Chandler Miller (1842-1911)

Born: 7 Dec 1842, Wilmington VT, son of Jordan Higley and Harriett (Partridge) Russell
Early Life: public schools, Wesleyan Acad
War Service: PVT Co. F 16th VT INF 3 Sep 1862, m/o 10 Aug 1863
Later Life: Wesleyan Acad. 1865, principal Wilmington H.S., mercantile business, 1867-78, teacher, National College of Elocution and Oratory at Philadelphia, 1884, public speaker, incorporator, Mount Vernon Inst. of Elocution and Languages, Philadelphia, 1885, later dir., councilor, American Inst. of Civics, NYC, 1891, j.p., school super., town lister, town constable and collector of taxes 10 years, village trustee, created 1900, Wilmington's "Old Home Week," general insurance broker 1893-1911
Affiliations: Republican, Mason, GAR
Married: Jun 1877, Gertrude E. Bowen
Died: 16 Dec 1911, Wilmington VT; interment in River View Cemetery
(AFS, AGO, JGU*)

Russell, George Kendall (1841-1926)

Born: 11 Apr 1841, Cabot VT, son of Willard and Abigail E. (Ward) Russell
Early Life: local schools and Franklin (NH) Acad., moved to Lawrence, MA, then Exeter NH, paper manufacturer
War Service: SGT Co. E 15th NH INF 1 Sep 1862, m/o 13 Aug 1863, Concord NH
Later Life: paper manufacturer, Exeter NH 1863-73, moved to Bellows Falls VT, paper manufacturer, Willard, Russell & Co., horse breeder
Affiliations: Republican, Episcopal, Free Mason (charter member, Bellows Falls Council, No. 17), GAR, RSVO
Married: 9 Nov 1863, Annie A. Colbath
Died: 1 Sep 1926, Rockingham VT; interment in Episcopal Cemetery
(ADA, HC7, JGU, LSH, RSVO2)

Russell, William Pierson (1810-1887)

Born: 6 Jan 1810, Burlington VT
Early Life: M.D. BMC 1830, physician, Middlebury 1831-61, town selectman, postmaster 1857-59, CPT Militia
War Service: SURG, 5th VT INF 15 Aug 1861, wdd/pow, Savage's Station, 29 Jun 1862, prld 17 Jul 1862, dis/dsb 11 Oct 1862
Later Life: physician, Middlebury 1862-87
Affiliations: Congregational, Mason, IOOF, GAR, RSVO, VHS, Addison Cty MS, VT MS
Married: 1835, Lydia Bass
Died: 4 Jun 1887, Middlebury VT; interment in West Cemetery
Notes: Middlebury GAR Post #89 was named after him
(AGO, FSO, GFH, HPS, RR)

Rutherford, George Valentine (1830-1876)

Born: 1830, Rutland VT
Early Life: atty, manufacturer, telegraph super.
War Service: Chief, Field Inspections & Reports Officer, QMG Dept 1861-64; AQM (CPT) 2 Apr 1863, QM (COL)1864-66
Later Life: telegrapher, lecturer
Married: (1) 14 Nov 1861, Elizabeth Worthington Hurlbut; (2) 19 Oct 1870, Lucy Emily Keyes
Died: 28 Aug 1876, St. Helena SC; interment in St. Helena Public Cemetery
Notes: Brothers Friend and Reuben, b. NY, were B.G. and Bvt B.G., respectively
(E&E, FBH, JC, JDR)

Rutherford, Joseph Chase (1818-1902)

Born: 1 Oct 1818, Schenectady NY, son of Alexander and Sally (Clifford) Rutherford

Early Life: moved to Burlington 1830, Woodstock Med. School 1849, Blackstone MA 1851-57, Derby VT 1857-60, Newport VT 1860

War Service: Asst SURG, 10th VT INF; SURG 17th VT INF; m/o Jul 1865

Later Life: physician, Newport 1865-95; U.S. Examining SURG for Pensions 1866-93

Affiliations: Congregational, GAR, IOOF, Mason, RSVO, Abolitionist

Died: 21 Oct 1902, Newport VT; interment in West Derby VT

(EMH, JGU, VTMS)

Randall, Francis V.

Ransom, Thomas E. G.

Reed, Marquis L.

Richardson, Israel B.

Ripley, Edward H.

Roberts, Benjamin S.

Royce, Homer. E.

Russell, Chandler H.

SSSSS

Safford, Mary Jane (1834-1891)

Born: 31 Dec 1834, Hyde Park VT, daughter of Joseph and Diantha (Little) Safford
Early Life: moved to Crete IL 1837, local schools, teacher, Joliet, Shawneetown, Cairo
War Service: nurse, Cairo IL, Cairo, AOT, Fort Donelson, battle of Shiloh, hosp. ships *City of* Memphis and *Hazel Dell*
Later Life: Medical college for Women, NYC, 1869, Univ. of Brewlaw, Germany, physician, Chicago, 1872, prof. Women's Diseases, Boston Univ., staff Mass. Homeopathic Hosp.
Died: 8 Dec 1891, Tarpon Springs FL; interment unknown
(B&V*, LHF)

Sanborn, Eben Kimball (1828-1862)

Born: 24 Jan 1828, New Chester NH, son of John Hilton Sanborn
Early Life: M.D. BMC 1847, lecturer VT Medical Coll. 1853, traveled to England and Germany, teacher, anatomy and chair of SURG BMC, instr. CMC, physician Rutland
War Service: SURG, 1st VT INF 26 Apr 1861, post SURG Newport News m/o 15 Aug 1861, SURG 31st MA INF 20 Feb 1862, died of typhoid fever
Married: 10 Oct 1855, Harriet Williams Avery
Died: 3 Mar 1862, Ship Island, La.; interment at sea "on account of some imperfection in embalming"
(DNP, BMJ5, JGC)

Sargeant, Francis E. (1842-1927)

Born: 1842, East Peacham VT, son of Asa and May Jane (Mealey) Sargeant
Early Life: public schools, Peacham Acad
War Service: PVT Co. G 3rd VT INF 1 Jun 1861, m/o 27 Jul 1864
Later Life: moved to Anaconda MT, banking, one of framers of constitution of State 1889, secretary, Anaconda Mining Co., Butte City MT 1887-90
Affiliations: Republican, Congregational, Mason
Married: Lou E. Harvey
Died: 6 Dec 1927, Peacham VT; interment in Peacham Corners Cemetery
(1890, AFS*, AGO, HC6)

Sargent, Joseph (1817-1863)

Born: 6 Jan 1817, Warner NH, son of Zebulon and Huldah (Collamore) Sargent
Early Life: NU 1834-36, studied under a Rev. Davis, OH, teacher, ordained, Casawago PA, 11 Jun 1840, pastor, Sutton NH 1841-45, Barnard VT 1845-48, Barre VT 1848-56, Missionary 1856-57, organized 1st Universalist Church, Essex VT 1857, pastor, Plainfield VT 1859-60, Williston VT 1860-62
War Service: Chap. 13th VT INF 4 Oct 1862, died in service
Married: 28 Dec 1840, Lucinda Skinner
Died: 20 Apr 1863, Camp Carusi near Occoquan VA; interment in Williston VT
(HC1, MNH, WAE)

Sawin, William J. (1833-1877)

Born: 8 Aug 1833, Hancock NH, son of Levi S. and Sarah (Swett) Sawin

Early Life: M.D. DC 1854, physician, Watertown WI, 1854-61, moved to Chicopee MA
War Service: Asst SURG 10th MA INF 7 Sep 1861; Hosp. Steward Co. E 3rd VT INF, Asst Surg 2nd VT INF 21 Jun 1862, wdd Savage's Station 29 Jun 1862, pow, Savage's Station, prld 22 Jul 1862, BGD SURG, m/o 29 Jun 1864
Later Life: physician, Chicopee Falls MA 1864-75
Affiliations: Mason, Hampden District MS
Married: Mary Beal Babcock
Died: 3 Dec 1877, Chicopee Falls MA; interment unknown
(BMJ5, NFC)

Sawyer, Edward Bertrand (1828-1918)

Born: 16 Apr 1828, Hyde Park VT, son of Joshua and Mary (Keeler) Sawyer
Early Life: admitted to the bar Jun 1849, Law Practice, Lamoille Cty Clerk 1849-51, 1853-61
War Service: recruited, Co. D 5th VT INF, CPT Co. I, 1st VT CAV 21 Oct 1861, MAJ 25 Apr 1862, COL 16 Sep 1862, wdd, Brandy Station, 11 Oct 1863, resgd, 28 Apr 1864
Later Life: owner/editor, Lamoille Newsdealer 1867-70, Lamoille Cty Clerk 1868-75, Owner, American Hotel 1870-77, atty, Hyde Park 1880-1910
Affiliations: RSVO
Married: (1) Jun 1849, Susan Almira (nfi); (2) Aug 1866, Helen M. Pennock
Died: 17 Mar 1918, Hyde Park VT; interment in Hyde Park Cemetery
(1880, 1900, 1910, FAG, GJU, HC2, JGU*)

Scofield, Robert Jr. (1837-1918)

Born: 22 Dec 1837, Carlton NY, son of Robert and Sallie (Curtis) Scofield
Early Life: Murray, NY 1860
War Service: 1LT, Co F 1st VT CAV 17 Oct 1861, CPT 4 Oct 1862, pow Herndon Station 17 Mar 1863, prld 5 May 1863, pow Hagerstown 12 Jul 1863, MAJ 18 Nov 1864, prld 1 Mar 1865, Bvt LTCOL, Bvt COL, 13 Mar 1865, m/o 1 Jun 1865
Later Life: farmer, Kilbourn WI 1870-1900, moved to Long Beach CA 1910
Married: 25 Nov 1867, Josephine Lophelia Holly
Died: 22 May 1918, Dell Prairie WI; interment Spring Grove Cemetery, Kilbourn WI
(1860, 1870, 1880, 1900, 1910, GGB, HNJ, RR, TSFP)

Scott, Harriet M. (?-?)

Born: VT
Early Life: Irasburg 1861
War Service: nurse, 3rd VT INF, Union Hotel Hosp., Georgetown, Armory Square Gen. Hosp., Washington, Acquia Creek, Nov 1861 - Dec 1862, Gettysburg Jul-Aug 1863
Later Life: Charlestown MA
Died: unknown
Notes: H.R. 2621 and S 1348, granting a pension to her, introduced by Mr. Grout, 55th Congress, 1st Session
(MAH)

Scott, Oscar Delieu (1843-1909)

Born: 30 Aug 1843, Townshend VT, son of Walter and Aurilla (White) Scott
Early Life: Leland and Grey Sem., MC 1858 for 1 year
War Service: CPL Co. F 17th VT INF 14 Sep 1863, wdd, Cold Harbor, 7 Jun 1864 (lost right foot), in hosp. until m/o 18 May 1865
Later Life: MC 1868, admitted to the bar 1868, atty, Magnolia AR 1870-73, Lewisville AR 1873-75, Texarkana TX 1875-1907

Affiliations: Republican, Chi Psi fraternity, Mason, IOOF (Noble Grand), Elks, GAR (Post Commander), Phi Beta Kappa
Married: 27 Jan 1875, Cornelia Frances Hulett
Died: 24 Feb 1909, Texarkana, TX; interment in Rose Hill Cemetery
(JGU, MIDCat, MIDCat3)

Scott, William (1839-1862)

Born: 9 Apr 1839, Groton VT, son of Thomas and Mary (Wormwood) Scott
Early Life: farmer
War Service: PVT Co. K 3rd VT INF 10 Jul 1861, "Sleeping Sentinel," sentenced to be executed, pardoned by Lincoln, mwia, Lee's Mill, 16 Apr 1862
Died: 17 Apr 1862; interment in Yorktown National Cemetery (marker #351)
(tbd)

Seaver, Joel Joshua (1822-1899)

Born: 17 Dec 1822, Salisbury VT, son of Joshua and Betsy (Bigelow) Seaver
Early Life: moved to Malone NY, taught school, studied law, staff, later owner and editor, Malone Palladium
War Service: CPT Co. I 16th NY INF 15 May 1861, MAJ 11 Nov 1861, LTCOL 4 Jul 1862, COL 29 Sep 1862, m/o 22 May 1863 Albany NY, Bvt B.G. 13 Mar 1865
Later Life: ConCon 1867
Married: 1849, Ann Eliza Brown
Died: 29 Nov 1899, Malone NY; interment in Morningside Cemetery
(E&E, FBH, FP, FSO, JGW)

Selden, Henry Raymond (1821-1865)

Born: 14 Mar 1821, Bennington VT, son of Martius Sinus and Minerva (Griswold) Selden
Early Life: USMA 1843 (31/39), Bvt 2LT, 1st US INF 1 Jul 1843, garrison duty 1843-46, 2LT, 5th US INF 25 Mar 1846, Mexican-American War 1846-48, 1LT, 8 Sep 1847, frontier duty 1848-51, 1854-56, garrison duty 1851-52, recruiting service 1852-54, CPT 18 Oct 1855, Seminole War 1856-57, Utah Expedition 1857-60, Navajo Expedition 1861
War Service: defense of Ft Craig NM Aug 1861-Jan 1862, Reg't Cmdr, NM operations 1862-63, MAJ 13th US INF 1 Jul 1863, Super. of Recruiting, Santa Fe NM 1863-64, COL, 1st NM INF 25 Apr 1864, ops NM 1864-65
Died: 2 Feb 1865, Ft. Union, NM; interment unknown
Notes: Ft. Selden, outside of Las Cruces NM was named in his honor
(FBH, FSO, GWC, RWF) Check at DAR Library

Seymour, Truman (1824-1891)

Born: 24 Sep 1824, Burlington VT
Early Life: NU 1840-42, USMA 1846 (19/59), Bvt 2LT, 1st US ARTY, 1 Jul 1846, 2LT, 3 Mar 1847, Bvt 1LT 18 Apr 1847, Bvt CPT 20 Aug 1847, 1LT, 26 Aug 1847, capture of Mexico City Sep 1847, Asst prof. of drawing, USMA 1850-53, Ft. Moultrie SC 1853-56, Seminole War 1856-58, CPT 22 Nov 1860, Ft. Moultrie SC 1860, Ft. Sumter SC 1860-61
War Service: bombardment of Ft. Sumter SC Apr 1861, Bvt MAJ 14 Apr 1861, 5th US ARTY 14 May 1861, recruiting duty Jul-Sep 1861, Commander, camp of instruction, Harrisburg, PA Sep-Nov 1861, Chief of ARTY, McCall's division, Defense of Washington 1862, C. of S. ARTY, Dept of the South 1862-64, B.G. USV, 28 Apr 1862, cmdg BGD Dept of Rappahannock Apr-Jun 1862, cmdg 3 BGD 3 Div V Corps, Seven Days Jun-Jul 1862, cmdg 1 BGD 3 Div III Corps, 2nd Bull Run Campaign Jun-Aug 1862, Bvt LTCOL 14 Sep 1862, Bvt COL 17 Sep 1862, cmdg Div Folly Island SC 4 Jul 1863, cmdg Ft. Wagner SC (wdd) 18 Jul 1863, Florida Expedition Feb 1864, cmdg Dist. of Florida Feb-Mar 1864, cmdg 2 Brig 3 Div. VI Corps, Wilderness May 1864, pow Wilderness, 6 May 1864, exchanged, 9 Aug 1864, cmdg Div., Shenandoah Valley Campaign Oct-Dec 1864, Petersburg Mar-Apr 1865, Bvt B.G., M.G. USV, 13 Mar 1865, m/o USV 24 Aug 1865

Later Life: A.M. Williams College 1865, cmdg Key West 1865-66, MAJ 5th US ARTY, 13 Aug 1866, Ft. Warren, MA, Ft. Preble ME 1869-75, ret. 1 Nov 1876
Married: 11 Aug 1852, Louise Weir
Died: 30 Oct 1891, Florence, Italy; interment in Cimitero Degli Allori, Florence
Papers: Smithsonian Inst. Archives of American Art
Publications: The Drawings and Watercolors by Truman Seymour (1824-1891) (1986)
(JGW, E&E, GWC, RJ, WAE*, WPG3)

Shaw, Henry Charles (1832-1862)

Born: 1832, Waitsfield VT, son of Lucius and Happylona (Steele) Shaw (brother of Lucius S. Shaw (q.v.))
Early Life: M.D. DC 1858, Hanover NH 1861
War Service: Asst SURG, 1st NH INF, 30 Apr 1861, m/o 9 Aug 1861, Asst SURG, 5th VT INF, 15 Aug 1861, d/dis 7 Sep 1862
Died: 7 Sep 1862, Alexandria VA; interment in Irasville cemetery, Waitsfield VT
(ABD, ADA, DCCat, HC4)

Shaw, Lucius Stearns (1830-1861)

Born: 24 Jul 1830, Waitsfield VT, son of Lucius and Happylona (Steele) Shaw (brother of Henry C. Shaw (q.v.))
Early Life: A.B. DC 1857, atty Lawrence KS 1861
War Service: 2LT Co. D 2nd KS INF, died by accident, Platt River bridge, Mo.
Died: 3 Sep 1861; interment in Irasville Cemetery, Waitsfield VT
(ABD, GTC)

Sheldon, Charles Henry (1840-1898)

Born: 18 Sep 1840, Johnson VT, son of Gershem and Mary Sheldon
Early Life: farmer, store clerk, abolitionist
War Service: SGT Co. E 7th VT INF 12 Feb 1862, 2LT, Co. I, 1 Mar 1863, 1LT, 21 Dec 1863, CPT 13 Jul 1865, m/o 14 Mar 1866
Later Life: farmer; lived 10 years in southern IL, three years in KY; moved to Dakota Terr. 1881; member, Territorial Council 1887; S.D. Gov. 1893-97
Married: (1) 25 Feb 1868, Mary J. Waters; (2) 29 Sep 1875, Martha Ann Frizell
Died: 20 Oct 1898, Deadwood, SD; interment in Town Cemetery, Pierpont SD
Diary: This is a True Copy of the Civil War Diaries for 1862 & 1863 (1973)
(FSO, RR, TWH)

Shepard, John Franklin (1835-1914)

Born: 4 Sep 1835, Sharon VT, son of Isaac Stevens and Lucy (Wheat) Shepard
Early Life: public schools, moved to Royalton 1848, Royalton Acad., out west 1858-59
War Service: PVT Co. E 2nd USSS 14 Oct 1861, dis/dsb 12 Oct 1862 from Judiciary Square Hosp., Washington
Later Life: farmer, miller, lumber manufacturing, town selectman 1879, State Rep. 1886, school board dir.
Affiliations: Republican, GAR (charter member, Orville Bixby Post No. 93), Patron of Husbandry, Master of White River Valley Pomona Grange 1891-92
Married: 25 Nov 1863, Mary Flynn Button
Died: 1 Oct 1914, Royalton VT; interment in Haven Cemetery
(AGO, EWL, JGU*)

Shepherd, Jonathan Avery (1816-1898)

Born: 26 Aug 1816, Brandon VT, son of Jonathan and Abigail (Avery) Shepherd
Early Life: MC 1838, Episcopal Theological Sem., NYC 1844, rector, Wilmington, NC, San Francisco Female Inst. 1856-57
War Service: Chap., Congress of the Confederacy, Montgomery, AL
Later Life: Principal, St. Clement's Hall, Ellicott City MD, rector, St. Andrew's College, MS, Church of the Incarnation, Santa Rose CA (17 years)
Married: 6 May 1854, Evelyn Turner
Died: 30 Mar 1898, Santa Rose CA; interment unknown
(MIDCAT)

Sherman, Elijah Bernis (1832-1910)

Born: 18 Jun 1832, Fairfield VT, son of Elias Huntington and Clarissa (Wilmarth) Sherman
Early Life: local schools, farmer, drug store clerk 1854, Brandon Sem., Burr Sem., A.M. LLB, MC 1860, teacher, South Woodstock and Brandon Sem.
War Service: 2LT, Co. C 9th VT INF, 24 Jun 1862, resgd 7 Jan 1863, Chicago, IL
Later Life: Univ. of Chicago Law School 1864, State Rep. 1876-79, LTCOL and Judge advocate, 1st BGD IL NG 1877-84, Master in Chancery, US Circuit Ct, Northern IL Dist. 1879-1910, atty auditor of public accounts State of IL 1877-89, chief supervisor elections, Northern Dist. IL, 1884-95; pres. IL Bar Assoc 1884, pres. ABA 1885 and 1899, LLD, MC 1885, trustee, MC from 1892
Affiliations: Republican, IOOF (Grand Master 1874), Mason, MOLLUS (#04637), GAR, IL Assoc SOV
Married: 1866, Hattie G. Lovering
Died: 1 May 1910, Chicago IL; interment in Rosehill National Cemetery
Publications: An Address in Memory of Ulysses S. Grant (1885)
(C&S, ANW, JGU, WHO1)

Sherman, Linus Elias (1835-1912)

Born: 30 Jun 1835, Fairfield VT, son of Elias H. and Clarissa (Wilmarth) Sherman
Early Life: local schools, Bakersfield Acad., Burr & Burton Sem., A.M. MC 1861
War Service: first man from Franklin Cty to enlist, 1LT, Co. A 9th VT INF, 14 Jun 1862, pow, Winchester, 3 Sep 1862, prld 28 Sep 1862, CPT 24 May 1863, m/o 13 Jun 1865
Later Life: principal, BRA, 1866, drug business 1867-76 VT ConCon 1869, moved to CO, mercantile pursuits, then Interior Department atty, mineral land and pension atty, Colorado Springs city council 1879
Affiliations: Baptist (deacon, 12 years), GAR (from 1868, Dept Council of Admin., Post Commander), RSVO
Married: 16 May 1866, Jennie C. Galer
Died: 17 Feb 1912, Colorado Springs CO; interment in Evergreen Cemetery
(DUCat, JGU, MIDCat)

Shores, Ethan Prescott (1842-1901)

Born: 7 Feb 1842, Victory VT, son of Levi P. and Sarah (Prescott) Shores
Early Life: farming, district school
War Service: PVT Co. K 8th VT INF 18 Feb 1862, CPL 26 Nov 1863, wdd Bayou Des Allemands LA 4 Sep 1862, reen 5 Jan 1864, SGT 1 Jul 1864, m/o 28 Jun 1865
Later Life: farmer, State Rep. 1876, 1878
Affiliations: International Organization of Good Templars (Worthy Chief Templar)
Married: 7 Feb 1867, Susan Maria Gleason
Died: 10 Oct 1901, Granby VT; interment in Shores Cemetery
Notes: brother Paschal, same unit, mwia at Cedar Creek, 19 Oct 1864
(AGC, JGU)

Silsby, Wendell (1846-1896)

Born: 28 Mar 1846, Lunenburg VT, son of Harvey and Celia (Bloss) Silsby
Early Life: public schools of Westmore
War Service: PVT Co. B 11th VT INF 26 Nov 1863, sick in Hosp. at Annapolis, then Montpelier until m/o 22 May 1865
Later Life: lumber manufacturer with brother 1865-72, own business 1872-90, added shingle mill in 1884, and a saw mill 2 years later, and a dressing mill in 1892, by 1883 was manufacturing 500,000 feet of lumber and 1,000,000 shingles annually, lister in Westmore and Burke, j.p. for Burke 6 years, State Rep.
Affiliations: Methodist, GAR (Post Commander), IOOF
Married: 11 Apr 1873, Ada Gaskell
Died: 7 Mar 1896, Burke VT; interment in West Burke Cemetery
(AFS, AGC, HC2)

Simons, Volney M. (1833-aft 1920)

Born: May 1833 CT, son of Clarissa Simons
Early Life: Colebrook, CT 1850, Rev., St. Albans VT 1860
War Service: Chap., 5th VT INF, 24 Aug 1861, resgd, 1 Mar 1862
Later Life: Clerk, Albany, NY 1870, pastor, M.E. Church, Woburn MA 1880-83, physician Worcester MA 1900, insurance business Worcester 1920
Affiliations: GAR (Chap.)
Married: before 1860, Sarah W.
Died: aft 1920; interment unknown
(1850-1870, 1900-1910, DH, DH1)

Simmons, Seneca Galusha (1808-1862)

Born: 27 Dec 1808, Windsor VT, son of Alfred and Deborah (Perkins) Simmons
Early Life: NU 1829, USMA 1834 (22/36), Bvt 2LT 7th US INF 1 Jul 1834, 2LT 31 Dec 1834, survey of Apalachicola Harbor, FL 1834-35, coastal survey of Maine 1835-36, 1LT 19 Jan 1837, frontier duty 1837-42, Seminole War 1842, garrison duty 1842-44, recruiting service 1844-47, Mexican-American War 1847, CPT 16 Feb 1847, garrison duty 1848-49, Seminole War 1849-50, recruiting service 1851-53, Commander, Ft Arbuckle, Indian Terr. 1853-57, garrison duty 1857-59, sick leave 1859-61
War Service: COL 5th PA INF 21 Jun 1861, defenses of Washington Jun 1861-Jun 1862, MAJ 4th US INF 9 Sep 1861, Dranesville VA, 20 Dec 1861, Peninsular Campaign, mwia Glendale VA 30 Jun 1862
Married: Aug 1834, Elmira Adelaide Simmons
Died: 1 Jul 1862, Confederate Hosp., Richmond VA; interment in Richmond VA
(GWC, WAE*)

Slack, William Henry Harrison (1844-1922)

Born: 21 Feb 1844, Springfield VT, son of John A. and Mary A. (McAllister) Slack
Early Life: local schools, Springfield Sem., machine shop employee
War Service: PVT Co. E 16th VT INF 1 Sep 1862, m/o 10 Aug 1863
Later Life: machinist 1863-71, partnered with brother John to run largest shoddy firm in the U.S., organized Springfield Electric Light Corp., State Rep. 1888, State Sen. 1890, ADC (COL) to Gov. Carroll S. Page, dir. First National Bank of Springfield, trustee Springfield Savings Bank
Affiliations: Republican, GAR (National ADC to MAJ William Warner, and Asst I.G. to COL Wheelock Veazey), Mason, Grange
Married: (1) 16 Jul 1865, Nellie L. Wyman; (2) 7 Aug 1879, Ann M. Corbett
Died: 6 Feb 1922, Springfield VT; interment in Summer Hill Cemetery

(AFS, GFH)

Sloan, William James (1813-1880)

Born: 1813, PA
Early Life: ASST SURG 12 Jul 1837; MAJ Medical Corps 20 Dec 1855, Newport Barracks 1853-56
War Service: Medical Inspector, Dept of the East; Bvt LTCOL and Bvt COL 13 Mar 1865
Later Life: Bvt B.G. 28 Sep 1866 (New York harbor, where cholera prevailed); Medical Dir., Dept of Dakota 1875-80, LTCOL USA 26 Jun 1876; COL USA 28 Sep 1877; COL Apr 1877
Died: 17 Mar 1880, St. Paul MN; interment unknown
(E&E, JBF, WC)

Smalley, Henry Adams (1834-1888)

Born: 28 Feb 1834, Jericho VT, son of David Allen and Laura (Barlow) Smalley
Early Life: NU 1850, USMA 1854 (23/46), Bvt 2LT 1st US ARTY. 1 Jul 1854, 2LT 2nd US ARTY. 2 Oct 1854
War Service: 1LT 2nd US ARTY. 25 Apr 1861; COL 5th VT INF, 30 Jul 1861; resgd from USV 10 Sep 1862; CPT 2nd US ARTY. 1 Aug 1863; resgd 8 Mar 1865; Bvt B.G. 13 Mar 1865
Later Life: asst editor, New York Star, NYC Public Works Department; receiver, several institutions and individuals, but declared bankrupt 2 Feb 1877
Died: 13 May 1888, NYC; interment in Greenmount Cemetery, Burlington VT
Notes: brothers Eugene A. and Jacob M. Smalley (q.v.) served in the Marines and Navy, respectively, during the war
(E&E, GWC, HLA, RR, WAE*)

Smalley, Jacob Maech (1837-1874)

Born: 13 Oct 1837, Jericho VT, son of David Allen and Laura (Barlow) Smalley
Early Life: NU 1856-58, merchant, Burlington
War Service: Mate, Aug 1861, Acting Ensign 1 Dec 1862, Acting master 28 Jun 1864, resgd 10 Feb 1865
Later Life: businessman, Los Angeles 1865-74
Married: 2 Dec 1864, Elizabeth S. Keyes
Died: 3 Dec 1874, Los Angeles CA; interment unknown
Notes: brother of B.G. Henry A. Smalley (q.v.)
(TJL2, WAE*)

Smart, William Stevenson (1833-1912)

Born: 10 Mar 1833, Johnstown NY, son of John and Anna Maria (Stevenson) Smart
Early Life: Washington Acad., Cambridge NY, law studies, San Francisco CA 1854, admitted to bar 1856, atty San Francisco, Clerk US Court San Francisco 1856, atty, Xenia OH 1857, attended, Xenia Theological Sem. 1857-58, D.D., UTS 1860, Pastor, Congregational Church, Benson VT, 1860-67, ordained 1861
War Service: Chap. 14th VT INF, 8 Oct 1862, m/o 30 Jul 1863
Later Life: Pastor, Congregational Church, Benson VT, 1860-67, pastor, First Church, Albany, NY 1867-89, Pastor, Brandon VT 1889-1905, Trustee, MC 1890-1912, Brandon VT 1910
Married: 8 Sep 1858, Sarah Juliet Chipman
Died: 29 Apr 1912, Burlington VT; interment unknown
Publications: Lessons from the War (1862)
(1910, EJW, SR)

Smith, Charles Carroll (1830-1906)

Born: 11 Jun 1830, Sharon CT, son of Ransom and Lydia (Burtch) Smith
Early Life: local schools, State Normal School, New Britain CT, Green Mountain Liberal Inst., A.B. MC 1862
War Service: PVT Co. E 14th VT INF 30 Aug 1862, m/o 30 Jul 1863
Later Life: A.M., M.D. UVM 1865, studied diseases at Kings Cty Hosp., Flatbush NY, physician, Gaysville, Stockbridge, State Rep. 1872, 1884, State Sen. 1890-92
Affiliations: VT MS, Republican, GAR (Post Commander), Delta Kappa Epsilon Fraternity
Married: 17 Oct 1862, Mary L. Hancock
Died: 19 Jun 1906, Stockbridge VT; interment in Mount Pleasant Cemetery
(DKECat, JGU, MIDCat)

Smith, Claudius Buchanan (1818-1904)

Born: 19 May 1818, Lanesboro MA, son of Otis and Abilene (Stearns) Smith
Early Life: A.B. MC 1845, A.M., MC 1848, Principal, BRA, Ludlow VT 1846-52, Leland and Gray Sem., Townshend VT 1852-59, ordained 1855, Pastor, Baptist Church, Brookline MA 1855-59, Principal, Brandon VT 1859-64
War Service: Chap. 2nd VT INF 6 Jun 1861 - 8 Jul 1862
Later Life: Clerk, Treasury Dept, Washington, DC 1864-85, Board of Education, Washington, Washington, DC 1900-04
Married: 24 May 1847, Melvina R. Waller
Died: 18 Aug 1904, Washington, DC; interment unknown
(1900, EJW, RUS)

Smith, Edward Worthington (1832-1883)

Born: 16 Dec 1832, St. Albans VT, son of Rev. Worthington and Mary Ann (Little) Smith
Early Life: A.M. UVM, atty Chicago, IL 1860
War Service: 1LT, 15th US INF May 1861, ADC, General Hunter Aug 1861, ADC, AAG, Army of the Missouri Sep-Dec 1861, AAG, Dept of KS Dec 1861-Mar 1862, AAG, mustering officer Dept of the South Mar 1862-Jul 1863, MAJ 30 Oct 1862, CPT 15th US INF Feb 1863, LTCOL, AAG, 10th corps AOJ Jul 1863-Sep 1864, AAG, Dept of Virginia and North Carolina, AOJ Sep 1864-Mar 1865, AAG, Dept of Virginia Apr 1865-Jul 1866), Bvt MAJ, LTCOL, COL, B.G.
Later Life: 24th US INF, 21 Sep 1866, AAG, Dept of Dakota 1866-68, St Paul, MN 1880
Married: (1) 5 Oct 1871, Kate Morgan Adams, (2) Virginia (nfi)
Died: 22 May 1883, Ft Lewis, CO; interment in Greenwood Cemetery, St. Albans VT
Publications: A Genealogical Sketch of the Families of Rev. Worthington Smith, D.D. and Mrs. Mary Ann (Little) Smith of St. Albans, Vermont (1878)
(1860, 1880, FAG, GVH, MLO, NAR, TWH)

Smith, Emery L. (1842-1928)

Born: 11 Oct 1842, Northfield VT, son of Alvin and Susan (Lewis) Smith
Early Life: farming, local schools, Orange Cty Grammar School
War Service: PVT Co. G 6th VT INF 25 Sep 1861, CPL, pow, Savage's Station, 29 Jun 1862, prld 13 Sep 1862, wdd, Wilderness, 5 May 1864, dis/wds 31 Oct 1864
Later Life: Stone cutter and granite dealer, invented capstone for derrick, introduced steam drill and electric battery to quarrying process, partnerships in Smith & Bradley, Smith & Winch, Kimball & Smith, Smith & Wells and others
Affiliations: Democratic, Mason, GAR, Knights of Honor
Married: 11 Oct 1866, Mary Wheaton Hewitt
Died: 11 Dec 1928, Barre VT; interment in Elmwood Cemetery
(AWB, GFH, JGU)

Smith, Franklin Gillette (1797-1866)

Born: 14 Dec 1797, Benson VT, son of Chauncey and Hannah (Brown) Smith
Early Life: MC 1817, A.M. Princeton 1819, teacher, Boys' School, Milledgeville, GA 1821, Female Sem., Lynchburg VA, 1823, ordained 1823, rector, St. Paul's, Lynchburg 1824-37, Columbia TN Female Inst. 1838-52, founded Columbia TN Anthenaeum 1852
War Service: too old to serve himself, he organized the Maury Rifles, Co. B, 2nd Tenn. INF CSA 1861
Married: 29 May 1836, Sarah Ann Davis
Died: 4 Aug 1866, Columbia, TN; interment unknown
Notes: two of his sons served in the unit
(APTA,MIDCAT)

Smith, Frederic Elijah (1830-1907)

Born: 11 Jun 1830, Northfield VT, son of Elijah and Anna (Robertson) Smith
Early Life: local schools, Newbury Sem., dry goods clerk, Montpelier, druggist, Montpelier, 1853-61
War Service: outfitted 6th VT INF for Gov. Fairbanks, went to the front to settle accounts with RQMs in the field, QM, 8th VT INF, 23 Nov 1861, provost judge, CS on staff of Gen. Godfrey Weitzel, m/o 30 Nov 1863
Later Life: mercantile pursuits 1865-69, New York City 1869-72, manufacturing, pres. Watchman Publishing Co., Montpelier Public Library, Colby Wringer Co., Montpelier, Maplewood Improvement Co., Tenn., trustee Diocese of VT, v.p. First National Bank VT Mutual Fire Insurance Co., Bowers Granite Co., dir. National Life Insurance Co. VT Quarry Co., Wetmore & Morse Granite Co., trustee NU, trustee Washington Cty Grammar school, Montpelier school board, military aide to Gov. Fairbanks 1876, State Sen. 1886, 1888, RNC delegate 1892
Affiliations: Republican, Episcopal, GAR, RSVO, SAR, MOLLUS (#05880)
Married: 12 Oct 1852, Abba Morrill Hale
Died: 24 Feb 1907, Montpelier VT; interment in Green Mount Cemetery
(C&S, JGU, VHS10)

Smith, John Gregory (1818-1891)

Born: 22 Jul 1818, St. Albans VT, son of John and Maria W. (Curtis) Smith
Early Life: UVM 1841; Yale Law School; railroad executive, trustee Vermont and Canada R.R. 1858
War Service: State Rep. 1860-62; VT Gov. 1863-65, "an active supporter of the union cause during the civil war"
Later Life: railroad executive, pres. Northern Pacific R.R. (1866-72), RNC delegate (1872, 1880, 1884)
Affiliations: Republican
Married: 27 Dec 1843, Ann Eliza Brainerd (q.v.)
Died: 6 Nov 1891, St. Albans VT; interment in Greenwood Cemetery
(FSO, HGW, JGU, TWH)

Smith, Rodney (1829-1915)

Born: 3 Jan 1829, Orwell VT, son of Israel Smith
Early Life: Sem. student, Castleton VT 1850, A.M. UVM 1854, Teacher, KY
War Service: Paymr (MAJ) 23 Feb 1864, Bvt LTCOL 13 Mar 1865
Later Life: San Francisco 1880, Deputy Paymr (LTCOL), 24 Jan 1881, Asst Paymr Gen. (COL) 8 Dec 1886, ret. 3 Jan 1893, B.G. 23 Apr 1904, St. Paul, MN 1900-10
Married: 1876, Julia C. (nfi)
Died: 12 Nov 1915, Brandon VT; interment unknown
(1850, 1880, 1900, 1910, FBH, GOC, IA15, OAR, UVMCat, WHO3, WHP)

Smith, William (1831- aft 1895)

Born: 26 Mar 1831, Orwell VT, son of Israel Smith

Early Life: Castleton Sem. 1850, A.M. UVM 1854, teacher, KY, MS, VT 1854-61
War Service: apptd from MN, Add'l Paymr, 29 Aug 1861, Washington, 1861-62, Louisville KY 1862-64, St Paul MN 1864-66, Bvt LTCOL 13 Mar 1865, m/o 20 Jul 1866
Later Life: MAJ & Paymr, 17 Jan 1867, LTCOL & Deputy Paymr, 6 Sep 1888, B.G. & Paymr Gen., 10 Mar 1890, ret. 26 Mar 1895
Died: aft 1895; interment unknown
(1850, NYT, UVMCat, WHP)

Smith, William Farrar (1824-1903)

Born: 17 Feb 1824, St. Albans VT
Early Life: USMA 1845 (4/41); Bvt 2LT Topo Engrs Corps 1 Jul 1845; instr. USMA 1846-48; 2LT 14 Jul 1849; 1LT 3 Mar 1853; surveys in Great Lakes, Mexico, TX, AR and FL 1845-55; instr. USMA 1855-56; Lighthouse service 1856-61; CPT 1 Jul 1859
War Service: COL 3rd VT INF 27 Apr 1861; B.G. USV and LTCOL USA 13 Aug 1861, Bvt COL USA; cmdg VI Corps at Fredericksburg; Carlisle Barracks during Gettysburg campaign; Ch. Engr, Army of the Cumberland 1863, where he opened the famous "cracker-line" at Chattanooga; M.G. Mar 1865; cmdg XVIII Corps AOJ, at Cold Harbor, Petersburg, M.G. USV 4 Jul 1862; resgd USV 1865
Later Life: resgd USA 21 Mar 1867; pres. International Telegraph Co. 1864-73; police commissioners board, NYC, 1875-81; civil engr PA 1881-1903
Died: 28 Feb 1903, Philadelphia, Pa.; interment in Arlington National Cemetery
Correspondence: UVM
Publications: Military Operations Around Chattanooga (1886), articles for Battles and Leaders of the Civil War (four volumes, 1887-1888), The Relief of the Army of the Cumberland, and the Opening of the Short Line of Communication between Chattanooga, Tennessee, and Bridgeport, Alabama, in Oct 1863 (1891), From Chattanooga to Petersburg Under Generals Grant and Butler (1893), The Re-opening of the Tennessee River Near Chattanooga, Oct 1863 (1895)
Notes: St. Albans GAR Post #20 named after him
(EJW, E&E, FAG, Gibson*, GWC)

Spafford, Henry W. (1840-1911)

Born: 2 Nov 1840, Weathersfield VT, son of William H. and Eliza (Rumrill) Spafford
Early Life: districts schools, Springfield Acad., Chester Acad., station agent, Danby and North Bennington R.R.
War Service: PVT Co. A 4th VT INF 4 Sep 1861, CMSY SGT 28 May 1862, pow 11 Oct 1863, prld 21 Mar 1864, m/o 30 Sep 1864, ADJ 25 Oct 1864, acting QM VT BGD, m/o 13 Jul 1865
Later Life: bookkeeper, New York City, returned to Bennington 1867, station agent, North Bennington, general freight agent, general passenger agent, moved to Rutland 1882, trustee VT State Soldiers' Home, 1907
Married: (1) 5 Oct 1864, Mattie E. Kingsbury; (2) 5 Dec 1878, Lydia Ella Marsh
Died: 6 Feb 1911, Rutland VT; interment in Weathersfield VT
(FSO, JGU*, RHObit)

Sparrow, Bradford Polk (1843-1920)

Born: 8 Apr 1843, Calais VT, son of Abner Doty and Almira M. (Shepard) Sparrow
Early Life: local schools, Washington Cty Grammar school, teacher, messenger at State library
War Service: PVT Co. K 4th VT INF 17 Jul 1863, pow, Weldon Railroad, 23 Jun 1864, incarcerated in Andersonville, prld 28 Apr 1865, m/o 17 Jun 1865, McDougal Hosp., NYC
Later Life: A.B. MC 1874, Columbia Law School 1876, admitted to the bar Jul 1876, Asst clerk D.C. Supreme Court until 1880, moved to Bowling Green VA, lumbering and farming, 1882-88, Stafford C.H. VA, 1888-93, Hartwood VA, 1893+, moved to Montpelier
Died: 11 Aug 1920, Calais VT; interment in Robinson Cemetery
Correspondence: UVM

Notes: UVM has letters and diary Aug 1863 - Jun 1865
(AFS, DUCat, DUCat1, DUCat2, JDM, MIDCat, T289)

Sparrow, William (1835-1923)

Born: 1 Jun 1835, Huntington PQ, Canada, son of James and Martha (Douglass) Sparrow
Early Life: local schools, harness maker, moved to Hyde Park VT
War Service: 14 Sep 1861, SDLR, Co. I, 1st VT CAV, SDLR SGT, 18 Nov 1864
Later Life: harness maker, Charlestown NH, moved to Springfield VT 1869, harness and horse equipment until 1894, ret., village trustee
Affiliations: Mason, Eastern Starr, GAR
Married: 23 Jan 1856, Jane Ford
Died: 1 Aug 1923, Springfield VT; interment in Summer Hill Cemetery
(AFS, HC5)

Sprague, Edwin Huntington (1811-1891)

Born: 24 Apr 1811, New Haven VT, son of Eseck and Sophronia (Huntington) Sprague
Early Life: MC 1842 (n.g.) physician, Middlebury 1841-43, physician, Shelburne, 1850
War Service: SURG, 14th VT INF, 8 Oct 1862, dis/incompetency 14 Nov 1862
Later Life: physician, New Haven, 1865
Married: 7 Sep 1842, Ora S. Dickinson
Died: 10 Apr 1891; interment unknown
Notes: applied for pension 14 Dec 1888, as did widow in 1891 (from MA), neither approved
(1850, FSO, MIDCat, ZT)

Stannard, George Jerrison (1820-1886)

Born: 20 Oct 1820, Georgia VT, son of Samuel and Rebecca (Pattee) Stannard
Early Life: farmer, teacher, foundry clerk, COL 4th VT Militia 1860-61
War Service: LTCOL 2nd VT INF 20 Jun 1861; COL 9th VT INF 9 Jul 1862; B.G. 11 Mar 1863; pow Harpers Ferry, 15 Sep 1862; exchanged 10 Jan 1863; 2nd BGD, Abercrombie's DIV XXII Corps 1863; 3rd BGD 3rd DIV I Corps AOP 1863; wdd, right thigh, Gettysburg, 3 Jul 1863; 2nd BGD 2nd DIV XVIII AOJ 1864; wdd left arm, Petersburg 31 Jul 1864; wdd right arm 29 Sep 1864, amputated; Bvt M.G. 28 Oct 1864
Later Life: Deputy commissioner BRFAL 1866; resgd 28 Jun 1866; Doorkeeper, USHR 1881-86
Died: 1 Jun 1886, Washington, D.C; interment in Lakeview Cemetery, Burlington VT
Notes: First Volunteer from Vermont 14 Apr 1861; Burlington GAR Post #2 named after him
(E&E, EJW, FAG, FSO, FTM*, HGW)

Start, Henry Russell (1845-1905)

Born: 28 Dec 1845, Bakersfield VT, son of Simeon Gould and Mary Sophia (Barnes) Start
Early Life: Bakersfield and Barre Acad
War Service: PVT Co. A 3rd VT INF 8 Apr 1865, m/o 11 Jul 1865
Later Life: atty, State's Atty 1876-78, State Sen. 1880, trustee VT Reform School 1880-88, State Rep. 1890, Presidential Elector 1888, Judge VT Supreme Court 1890
Married: 10 Jun 1869, Ellen S. Houghton
Affiliations: Republican, Congregational
Died: 7 Nov 1905, Bakersfield VT; interment in Maple Grove Cemetery
(DWS, HFW12, JGU)

Start, Romeo Hoyt (1837-1893)

Born: 15 Apr 1837, Bakersfield VT, son of Moses and Laura (Griswold) Start
War Service: 2LT, Co. H 3rd VT INF, 3 Jun 1861, 1LT 7 Nov 1861, ADJ, 24 Jul 1862, CPT Co. E 22 Sep 1862, resgd 19 May 1863, CPT 3rd VT LARTY, 23 Nov 1863, m/o 15 Jun 1865
Affiliations: RSVO
Married: Anna Clark
Died: 18 Jun 1893, Eau Claire, MI; interment in Maple Grove Cemetery, Bakersfield VT
(DWS, HFW12)

Stearns, John C. (1831-1914)

Born: 11 Feb 1831, Chelsea VT, son of John and Elizabeth (Chandler) Stearns
Early Life: local schools, Bradford Acad., general store clerk, later Brooks & Stearns, Worcester, MA, 6 years, joined MA Militia, returned to VT, joined Bradford Guards as 1LT
War Service: PVT Co. D 1st VT INF 2 May 1861, SGM 24 May 1861, m/o 15 Aug 1861, ADJ 9th VT INF 30 Jun 1862, resgd due to disabilities 1 May 1863
Later Life: general insurance business and farming, US Assessor of Internal Revenue 1870-73, State Sen. 1878, COL and ADC to Gov. John B. Page, 1LT and ADJ, 1st VT NG, US Collector of Internal Revenue 1881-85, State Rep. 1886, apptd commissioner by Sec. of War Redfield Proctor to map positions at battle of Antietam with Confed. Gen. Harry Heth, RNC delegate 1868, 1888, one of original trustees VT Soldier's Home, and treasurer 1890
Affiliations: Republican, GAR, Mason, MOLLUS (#09161)
Married: 12 Sep 1863, Martha F. Pecket
Died: 2 Jul 1914, Bradford VT; interment unknown
(C&S, GFH*, JGU)

Steele, Hiram Roswell (1841-1929)

Born: 10 Jul 1841, Stanstead, PQ, Canada, son of Sanford and Mary (Hinman) Steele
Early Life: local schools, Lyndon Acad., St. Johnsbury Acad., principal, Cassville H.S., Stanstead, PQ, studied law, Derby Line
War Service: CPT Co. K, 10th VT INF 12 Aug 1862, CS (CPT) USV 18 May 1864, Bvt MAJ USV 19 Dec 1865, wdd Spotsylvania 12 May 1864, m/o 14 Jan 1866
Later Life: chief CS Southern District MS, moved to LA, cotton planter, admitted to the bar 1868, Grant elector, judge parish court, district atty, atty general of La., State ConCon 1868, 1879, moved to Brooklyn NY 1890, atty, judge, dir. New York Life Insurance Co., dir. Brooklyn City Railroad, trustee, South Brooklyn Savings Inst.
Affiliations: Republican, MOLLUS (#08503), GAR, SAR VT Soc. of NY
Married: 1877, Mary E. Porter
Died: 21 Nov 1929, NYC; interment unknown
Publications: Reminiscences of a Long Life (1927)
Notes: represented, at one time, (future CSA President) Jefferson Davis
(AFS, C&S, EMH, MK*)

Stevens, Jonas T. (1842-1923)

Born: 3 Jun 1842, Eden VT, son of Amasa and Martha (Smith) Stevens
Early Life: local schools, farming, mill worker, started his own saw mill
War Service: PVT Co. I 1st VT CAV 26 Sep 1862, pow Broad Run 1 Apr 1863, prld 7 Apr 1863, CPL 1 Jun 1864, SGT 19 Nov 1864, 1SGT 23 Mar 1865, 2LT 4 Jun 1865, m/o 21 Jun 1865 as 1SGT
Later Life: saw mill operator, Eden Mills, 23 years, farming and public affairs, Deputy sheriff 1870-78, sheriff 1878-80, Deputy sheriff 1880-92, sheriff 1892, State Rep. 1872, 1874
Affiliations: Republican, Mason, GAR (Post Commander)

Married: 1867, Emma White
Died: 2 Aug 1923, Eden VT; interment in Eden Cemetery
(DFG, HC2, JGU, PCD)

Stewart, William Emmett (1843-1930)

Born: 8 Dec 1843, Castleton VT, son of Daniel and Elvira (Tuttle) Stewart
Early Life: Castleton Sem.
War Service: PVT Co H 2nd USSS 18 Feb 1862, wdd 27 Oct 1863, m/o 20 Feb 1865
Later Life: M.D., UVM 1867, physician, Dorset VT 1868-80, RI, CA, Wallingford VT 1890, 1910, Bristol VT 1900
Affiliations: Baptist
Married: (1) 1 Jan 1866, Adelia Sarah Hawkins; (2) 20 Mar 1899, Anna Saunders
Died: 8 May 1930; interment in Green Hill Cemetery, Wallingford VT
(1870-1910, AGO, HWS, PCD)

Stillson, Henry Leonard (1842-aft 1912)

Born: 19 Sep 1842, Granville NY, son of Eli Bennett and Eliza Anne (Leonard) Stillson
Early Life: Eastman Business College, Poughkeepsie NY 1862
War Service: Co. B, VT Militia 1863-65, defense of St. Albans 1864
Later Life: editor Bennington Banner 1873-98, agent, Associated Press 1877-97, Health Officer, Bennington 1893-1912
Affiliations: Episcopal, Mason, IOOF, SAR, KOP
Married: (1) 1868, Josephine Woodruff; (2) 1881, Helen Kenyon
Died: aft 1912; interment unknown
Publications: The History of Free Masonry and Concordant Orders (1891), The Official History of Odd Fellowship (1897), History of the Ancient and Honorable Fraternity of Free and Accepted Masons, and Concordant Orders (1906), The Official History of Odd Fellowship: The Three-Link Fraternity (1914)
(1900, JGU*, PCD)

Stone, Edward Payson (1830-1920)

Born: 1 Aug 1830, Quechee VT, son of John Fitch and Lydia Powers (Paddock) Stone
Early Life: student, Bakersfield Acad., A.B. MC 1853, Principal, Royalton Acad. 1853-55, teacher, NC 1855-57, Chester VT 1858, Woburn MA 1859, Newtonville MA 1860
War Service: Chap., 6th VT INF 10 Oct 1861-27 Aug 1863
Later Life: Pastor, Congregational Church, Centerville MA 1863-65, Wellesley 1865, agent, AMA, Boston 1865-69, pastor, Waterford VT 1869-71, Underhill and Essex 1871-75, Pembroke and Center Harbor NH 1875-79, missionary, Lapeer MI 1880-1905, Rutland VT 1910-20
Married: (1) 16 Aug 1855, Martha Experience Stone; (2) 7 Oct 1869, Laura Jackson Noble; (3) 27 Jan 1881, Mrs. Hannah I. Barber nee Rood
Died: 11 Sep 1920, Rutland VT; interment in Green Mount Cemetery, Montpelier VT
(1910, 1920, EWL, JGB, MIDCAT, RR, TSP)

Stone, John (1815-1868)

Born: 31 Aug 1815, Barnard VT, son of Luke and Sibyl (Adams) Stone
Early Life: NU 1835-37 (n.g.), moved to Tennill GA 1840, school teacher, moved to Linton GA, M.D. Philadelphia 1857, physician Linton 1860-68
War Service: SURG CSA
Affiliations: Baptist
Married: Martha Anna Glenn

Died: 1868, Linton GA; interment unknown
(WAE)

Stone, Levi Huntoon (1806-1892)

Born: 10 Dec 1806, Cabot VT, son of John Stone
Early Life: Pastor, Cabot VT 1836-45, Glover VT, 1845-55, honorary A.M., MC 1849, Pastor, Waitsfield VT 1855-56, Northfield VT 1856-63
War Service: Chap., 1st VT INF, 26 Apr 1861 - 15 Aug 1861
Later Life: Pastor, Pawlet VT 1866-71, Castleton VT 1872-92
Married: (1) 19 May 1829, Clarissa Osgood; (2) 1844, Lydia J. Fuller (3) 29 Jul 1847, Lydia Abigail Duncan (4) 1854, Mrs. Lucy Holbrook nee Leighton (5) Adeline French
Died: 24 Jan 1892, Castleton VT; interment unknown
(JGB)

Stone, Newton (1836-1864)

Born: 9 Dec 1836, Rowe MA, son of Rev. Ambrose and Lucy (Amidon) Stone
Early Life: law student, Bennington VT 1860, admitted to bar, Manchester VT Jun 1861
War Service: 1LT, Co A 2nd VT INF 16 May 1861, CPT Co. I 22 Jan 1862, MAJ 8 Jan 1863, staff of GEN Howe Jan 1863, LTCOL 9 Feb 1863, COL 2 Apr 1864, kia, Wilderness
Died: 5 May 1864, Wilderness VA; interment in Hill Cemetery, Bennington VT
Notes: North Bennington GAR Post #26 was named for him
(1860, GGB, BBObit)

Stoughton, Charles Bradley (1841-1898)

Born: 31 Oct 1841, Chester VT, son of Henry Evander and Laura Elmina (Clark) Stoughton
Early Life: A.B. NU 1861
War Service: ADJ 4th VT INF 1 Aug 1861, MAJ 25 Feb 1862, LTCOL 17 Jul 1862, COL 5 Nov 1862, wdd (lost right eye), Funkstown, MD, 10 Jul 1863, resgd, 2 Feb 1864, Bvt B.G. 13 Mar 1865
Later Life: admitted to the bar Sep 1864, atty, NYC 1870, A.M. NU 1872, atty, New Haven, CT 1880, LLD, NU 1884, trustee, NU 1871-87
Married: 7 Apr 1869, Ada Ripley Hooper
Died: 17 Jan 1898, Bennington VT; interment in Immanuel Cemetery, Bellows Falls VT
(1870, 1880, DWV, FAG, LSH, RR, WAE*)

Stoughton, Edwin Henry (1838-1868)

Born: 23 Jun 1838, Chester VT, son of Henry Evander and Laura Elmina (Clark) Stoughton
Early Life: USMA 1859 (17/22); Bvt 2LT 4th US INF 1 Jul 1895; 2LT 6th US INF 5 Sep 1859; resgd 4 Mar 1861
War Service: COL 4th VT INF 1 Aug 1861; B.G. USV 5 Nov 1862, 2nd VT BGD; pow Fairfax C.H. 9 Mar 1863 by John Mosby (released after 2 months); appointment expired 4 Mar 1863
Later Life: atty
Died: 25 Dec 1868, New York NY; interment in Immanuel Cemetery, Bellows Falls VT
Notes: Bellows Falls GAR Post #34 named for him
(EFP, FTM*, GGB1, GWC, RR)

Stoughton, Homer Richard (1836-1902)

Born: 13 Nov 1836, Quechee VT, son of Richard Montgomery and Polly Goddard (Fay) Stoughton

Early Life: Royalton VT 1850, Royalton Acad., Railroad Station Agent, Randolph VT 1860
War Service: CPT Co E 2nd USSS, 25 Sep 1861, pr on field at Antietam, MD, MAJ 17 Sep 1862, LTCOL 24 Jun 1863, COL 19 Jan 1864, wdd Spotsylvania 10 May 1864, pow Petersburg 21 Jun 1864, prld 1 Dec 1864, m/o 23 Jan 1865
Later Life: Central Vermont Railroad Station Agent, Randolph VT 1865-72, Railroad Station Agent, Palmer MA 1880, auditor, gen. mngr and v.p. Shelby Iron Co, Shelby, AL 1885-91, commissioner, VT committee to erect monuments at Gettysburg 1890, Central VT R.R. station agent, Barre VT 1895-1902
Affiliations: RSVO
Married: (1) 14 Feb 1860, Cleora Atwood; (2) 3 May 1869, Ellen Louise Gilchrist
Died: 17 Sep 1902, Otsego MI; interment in Elmwood Cemetery, Barre VT
Notes: named on a monument honoring Co E and Co H of the 2nd USSS, Antietam National Battlefield
(1850-1880, EML, ESS, GWF, LOC*, NPS, RR, RSVO2)

Stranahan, Farrand Stewart (1842-1904)

Born: 3 Feb 1842, New York NY, son of Farrand Stewart and Caroline M. (Curtis) Stranahan
War Service: 1SGT Co. L 1st VT CAV 29 Sep 1862; 2LT 5 Jan 1864, 1LT 28 Feb 1864, ADC to GEN George A. Custer, resgd 28 Aug 1864
Later Life: Paymr, Vermont Central Railroad 1865; businessman 1867-71; treasurer, National Car Co. 1871-1903; State Rep. 1884-85; State Sen. 1888-89; cashier then v.p. Welden National Bank 1886-92; trustee, State Reform School 1888-92; LT Gov. 1892-93; dir. Central VT R.R.; vice pres. Missisquoi R.R.; officer, National Despatch Line; v.p. Saint Albans Messenger Co.
Affiliations: GAR, MOLLUS (#03878), SAR, RSVO
Died: 13 Jul 1904, St. Albans VT; interment in Greenwood Cemetery
(C&S, FAG, HC, JGU*, LHC, TPG)

Streeter, Sebastian Russell (1818-1871)

Born: 1 Jun 1818, Springfield VT, son of Rev. Russell and Clarinda (Cook) Streeter
Early Life: A.B. NU 1837, atty Barnard VT 1841-49, Providence RI 1849-60
War Service: 1LT 61st MA INF 17 Oct 1864, CPT 9 Nov 1864, resgd 4 Jan 1865
Later Life: atty, Roxbury MA 1860-71
Died: 9 Jun 1871, Woodstock VT; interment unknown
(WAE*)

Strong, George Crockett (1832-1863)

Born: 16 Oct 1832, Stockbridge VT, son of David Ellsworth and Harriet (Fay) Strong
Early Life: NU 1853-55, USMA 1857 (5/38), Bvt 2LT Ordnance 1 Jul 1857, cmdg Mt. Vernon Arsenal, AL 1858-59, 2LT Ordnance 31 Jul 1859, 1LT 25 Jan 1861
War Service: cmdg Watervliet Arsenal Troy, NY May 1861, MAJ & Asst A.G. 1 Oct 1861, Ordnance Officer, McDowell's staff, Bull Run Jul 1861, Asst Ordnance Officer, McClellan's staff Jul-Sep 1861, cmdg expedition to Biloxi, MS Apr 1862, cmdg expedition to Ponchatoula, LA Sep 1862, CoS Gen. Benjamin Butler May 1862, B.G. USV 29 Nov 1862, sick leave Dec 1862-Jun 1863, CPT Ordnance 3 Mar 1863, cmdg 1st BGD/1st Div, Dept of the South Jun 1863, Morris Island SC Jul 1863, Ft. Wagner SC, mwia, 18 Jul 1863, M.G. 18 Jul 1863
Married: 14 Apr 1859, Margaret Elles Budd
Died: 30 Jul 1863, NYC; interment in Green-Wood Cemetery, Brooklyn, NY
Publications: Cadet Life at West Point (1862)
(FBH, FSO, GWC, JGW, LOC*, RJ)

Strong, Thomas Jefferson (1824-1885)

Born: 16 Jan 1824, Pawlet VT, son of John and Nancy (McNaughton) Strong
War Service: CPT 22nd NY INF 6 Jun 1861, MAJ 23 Mar 1863; LTCOL 7 May 1863; m/o 19 Jun 1863; MAJ 16th NY ARTY 5 Jan 1864, LTCOL 13 Sep 1864, Bvt COL 13 Mar 1865; Bvt B.G. 13 Mar 1865; dis 15 May 1865
Died: 5 Sep 1885, Sandy Hill NY; interment in Union Cemetery, Fort Edward NY
(E&E, FBH, FP, FSO, TWH)

Safford, Mary J.

Sawyer, Edward B.

Scott, Harriet M.

Seymour, Truman

Shepard, John F.

Simmons, Seneca G.

Smalley, Henry A.

Smalley, Jacob M.

Smith, Willam F.

Spafford, Henry W.

Stannard, George J.

Stearns, John C.

Steele, Hiram R.

Stillson, Henry L.

Stoughton, Charles B.

Stoughton, Edwin H.

Stoughton, Homer R.

Stranahan, Farrand S.

Streeter, Sebastian R.

Strong, George C.

TTTTT

Taylor, Herbert Edward (1837-1911)

Born: 13 Oct 1837, Guilford VT, son of Jeremiah and Mary (Edwards) Taylor
Early Life: local schools, Westminster Sem., Powers Inst., farmer
War Service: PVT Co. F 4th VT INF 31 Aug 1861, wdd, Wilderness, 5 May 1864, m/o 30 Sep 1864
Later Life: farming 1864-65, clothing and furnishing business 1865-75; Deputy collector of internal revenue 1879-85, Deputy sheriff and tax collector, Brattleboro 1886-89, VT NG 1886-90, special Customs Inspector 1889-93, insurance business Brattleboro 1893-1911
Affiliations: GAR, Mason, RSVO, SAR
Married: 7 Oct 1867, Emeline Dutton
Died: 13 Jan 1911, Brattleboro VT; interment in Prospect Hill Cemetery
(AGO, JGU*)

Temple, William Grenville (1824-1894)

Born: 23 Mar 1824, Rutland VT, son of Robert and Charlotte (Green) Temple
Early Life: Acting Midshipman 1840, USS *Constellation* 1840-44, *Potomac* 1844-45, *Norfolk* 1845, *Potomac* 1845, pr Passed Midshipman 11 Jul 1846; *Boston* 1846, Mexican-American War, siege of Vera Cruz, Naval Observatory, Washington 1848-49, Coast Survey Duty 1849-50, Tehuantepec Hydrographic Survey 1850-52, *Levant* 1852-55, Coast Survey Duty 1855-59, flag lieutenant, sloop *Lancaster* (1859-61
War Service: steamer *Flambeau* 1861-62, pr LCDR 16 Jul 1862, gunboat *Pembina* 1862-64, Defenses of Washington 1864, steamer *Pontoosuc* 1864-65, pr CDR 3 Mar 1865
Later Life: steamer *Tacony* 1866, Portsmouth Navy Yard 1866-69, pr CPT 28 Aug 1870, steamer *Tennessee* 1870-71, frigate *Wabash* 1871-73, Brooklyn Navy Yard 1875-77, COMO 5 Jun 1878, Examining and Retiring Board, Navy Advisory Board 1879-82, Jeannette Court of Inquiry 1883, RADM 22 Feb 1884, ret. 29 Feb 1884
Died: 28 Jun 1894, Washington, D.C; interment in Congressional Cemetery
Publications: Memoir of the Landing of the United States Troops at Vera Cruz in 1847 (1852)
(TJL2)

Tenney, Charles H. (1830-1874)

Born: 21 Feb 1830, Hartford VT, son of Harper and Cynthia (Marsh) Tenney
Early Life: DC Medical Coll. 1858, M.D. NYMC 61
War Service: Asst SURG, 7th VT INF, 16 May 1863, resgd due to illness 20 Jan 1864
Later Life: 1871, 2nd Asst later 1st Asst physician VT Asylum for the Insane Brattleboro 1872-74
Married: 25 Nov 1862, Fanney W. Nutt
Died: 27 Apr 1874, Brattleboro VT; interment unknown
(NYTObit, WHT)

Thayer, Charles Paine (1843-1910)

Born: 22 Jan 1843, West Randolph VT, son of Samuel White and Sarah L. (Pratt) Thayer
Early Life: student
War Service: Hosp. Stew. 13th VT INF 1 Oct 1862, reduced at own request 20 Dec 1862, tr to Co. H m/o 21 Jun 1863
Later Life: M.D. UVM 1865, SURG Northern Pacific R.R. 3 years, MN Div, Medical Dir. VT GAR, Health Officer, Burlington, prof. of Anatomy Tufts Coll. Medical and Dental Schools, UVM teacher 1899, Asst SURG 1st VT Militia 1875
Affiliations: GAR

Married: 21 Sep 1871, M. Alice Bemis
Died: 1 Feb 1910, Burlington VT; interment in Green Mount Cemetery
Publications: Medical Register of Vermont (1877)
(BT, ELH, UVMMED, WBA, WHO2)

Thayer, Samuel White (1817-1882)

Born: 21 May 1817, Braintree VT, son of Samuel and Ruth Thayer
Early Life: WMC 1838, moved to Northfield 1840, Burlington 1853, SURG prof., UVM Medical Dept
War Service: Vermont SURG General; Asst SURG USV, in charge of Baxter General Hosp.; B.G. VT Militia 22 Nov 1864; Bvt CPT USV 1865
Later Life: Prof. of Anatomy, UVM Medical School 1856-72, 1881-82
Notes: established hospitals at Brattleboro, Montpelier, and Burlington during the war
Married: 6 Jan 1841, Sarah L. Pratt
Died: 14 Nov 1882, Burlington VT; interment in Greenmount Cemetery
Publications: Family Memorial (1835)
(BT, E&E, RR, WBA)

Tinker, Charles Almerin (1838-1917)

Born: 8 Jan 1838, Chelsea VT, son of Almerin and Sophronia Burnham (Gilchrist) Tinker
Early Life: Newbury Sem., clerk, Northfield post office, telegraph operator VT & Boston Telegraph Co., mngr, Illinois & Mississippi Telegraph co., Pekin IL (became friend of A. Lincoln), Chicago & Rock Island R.R., Galena & Chicago Union R.R., Chicago Light Guard
War Service: military telegrapher, for Gen. Banks, Poolesville, MD, for Gen. Wardsworth, Upton Hill, for Gen. McClellan on steamer *Commodore*, Gen. Heintzelman's HQ, Savage Station, War Dept, Washington DC, mngr, USMTS
Later Life: mngr, Western Union, Washington, DC 1865-72, Super. VT Central, R.R., Super. Pacific Div., Atlantic & Pacific Telegraph Co. 1875; telegraph mngr, Baltimore & Ohio R.R. 1879, partner in American Union Telegraph Co. 1879-81, Gen. Super. Eastern Div., Western Union, v.p. American District Telegraph Co., Dir. and v.p. VT & Boston Telegraph Co.
Affiliations: Baptist, Brooklyn Soc. of Vermonters, IL Soc. SOV
Married: 1863, Lizzie A. Simkins
Died: Mar 1917, Winnipeg, MB, Canada; interment unknown
(DHB*, GFH, JGU, NYHObit)

Titus, Fanny H. (1840-aft 1920)

Born: 9 May 1840, Vershire VT, daughter of Simeon B. and Eliza J. (Morris) Titus
Early Life: Vershire 1860
War Service: nurse, Armory Square Hosp. and Columbian Hosp. Washington, until Jun 1865
Later Life: Lawrence MA 1870, boarding house Cambridge MA 1880-1920
Affiliations: WRC
Married: 5 Aug 1866, Charles R. Hazen
Died: aft 1920
Notes: three brothers served in VT regiments
(1860, 1870, 1880, 1900, 1910, 1920, DAR1, MAH*, WHT)

Trueworthy, Edwin Weston (1840-1912)

Born: 30 Aug 1840, Newport ME
Early Life: Bowdoin Coll. Medical School 1864, M.D. UVM 1865

War Service: 2LT Co. K 22nd ME INF Sep 1862, Medical Cadet USA Jun 1864-Jun 1865, Asst SURG 7th VT INF 17 Jun 1865, SURG 1 Oct 1865, m/o 14 Mar 1866
Later Life: physician Lowell MA
Affiliations: MA MS, National MS
Married: 1868, Emma Holmes Rackliffe
Died: 13 Sep 1912, Lowell MA; interment unknown
(BOWDCat, NAS, UVMMED, VTMS)

Trull, Daniel N. (1835-1892)

Born: 12 Jun 1835, Burke VT, son of Joel and Cynthia N. Trull
Early Life: Lyndon Acad., DC 1856, physician St. Johnsbury, physician Lyndon 1860
War Service: State Recruiting Officer
Later Life: physician Lyndon 1870, carriage business, banker, Lyndon Bank 8 years, moved to St. Johnsbury 1890, moved South due to failing health,
Died: 31 Dec 1892, St. Johnsbury VT; interment unknown
(1860, 1870, JGU*)

Trussell, Jacob (1833-1910)

Born: 20 Sep 1833, Sutton VT, son of Joshua and Electa (Curtis) Trussell
Early Life: Danville schools, Phillips and Caledonia Cty Acad., teacher, atty, Peacham
War Service: 1SGT Co. D 1st VT CAV 21 Sep 1861, 2LT 30 Oct 1862, 1LT 1 Jun 1863, wdd, Nottoway C.H., 23 Jun 1864, m/o 18 Nov 1864
Later Life: moved to Virginia City MT, Sioux City IA, railroad work for Union Pacific R.R., returned to Peacham, farmer, atty, tradesman; State Rep. 1884
Affiliations: Democrat pre-war, Republican post-war, Congregational, Mason, GAR, RSVO
Married: (1) 4 Oct 1871, Flora M. Blanchard; (2) 9 Nov 1888, Mrs. Marietta C. Walbridge
Died: 28 Nov 1910, Peacham VT; interment in Peacham Corners Cemetery
(AGO, JGU)

Tucker, Stephen S. (1807-1861)

Born: 16 Oct 1807, Randolph VT, son of Stephen and Ruth (Herrick) Tucker
Early Life: Orange Cty Grammar School, UVM 2 years, NU 1831, officer, Army of the Republic of Texas, Seminole War, CPT Mtd Riflemen, 27 May 1846, Bvt MAJ, resgd 30 Jun 1851, MAJ Red Star Guard with William Walker
War Service: COL CSA Apr 1861, comdg Ft. Morgan, near Mobile, mwia 15 Nov 1861, received commission as M.G. the night of his death
Died: 15 Nov 1861, near Mobile AL; interment unknown
(WAE*)

Tupper, Tullius Cicero (1809-1866)

Born: 9 Feb 1809, Barnard VT, son of Samuel and Mary (Green) Tupper
Early Life: UVM 1832, moved to Madison Cty MS 1835, atty, sawyer, planter, State Rep. 1840, applied to USMA 1842 unsuccessfully; owned 51 slaves in 1850, 58 in 1860
War Service: B.G. CSA MS Militia 10 Mar 1862, M.G. CSA MS Militia Jun 1862, resgd Mar 1863.
Later Life: signed loyalty oath 28 Jun 1865, filed for presidential pardon 23 Aug 1865, pardoned 28 Aug 1865, post-war wealth valued at less than $20,000
Married: 19 Mar 1842, Mary H. Drane
Died: 14 Aug 1866; interment unknown

Notes: library and many papers destroyed by fire
(1850, 1860, E&E, FLR, FSO, HFB, M688, M1003, UVMCat3)

Tuttle, Lyman M. (1837-1897)

Born: 1837, Weathersfield VT, son of Augustus and Phila (Tolles) Tuttle
Early Life: AMS 1859
War Service: Asst SURG, 6th VT INF, 7 Nov 1861, resgd 26 Sep 1862
Later Life: Springfield VT, 1878; physician Holyoke MA 1880
Died: 27 Apr 1897, Holyoke MA; interment unknown
(1880, AMT, FSO, GARM, LCA2, NAS, VTMS)

Tuttle, Oscar Stratton (1832-1881)

Born: 23 Aug 1832, Weathersfield VT, son of Augustus and Phila (Tolles) Tuttle
Early Life: merchant, Cavendish VT 1860
War Service: CPT Co E 1st VT INF 25 Dec 1860, m/o 15 Aug 1861, MAJ 6th VT INF 25 Sep 1861, LTCOL 19 Sep 1862, COL 18 Dec 1862, resgd 18 Mar 1863
Later Life: Dry Goods merchant, Holyoke MA 1870
Married: 1 Jun 1858, Ellen Maria Cook
Died: 15 Dec 1881, Holyoke MA; interment in Village Cemetery
Notes: listed on "Old Vermont Brigade" monument, Antietam National Battlefield
(1850-1870, AMT, DWV, NPS)

Twitchell, Marshall Harvey (1840-1905)

Born: 28 Feb 1840, Townshend VT, son of Harvey Daniel and Elizabeth (Scott) Twitchell
Early Life: farmer, teacher
War Service: PVT Co. I 4th VT INF 21 Sep 1861, CPL 6 Jan1862;l SGT 10 Apr 1862; 1SGT 10 Oct 1862; dis Brandy Station, for reen 15 Dec 1863; wdd, Wilderness, 5 May 1864; dis 9 Sep 1864, CPT Co. H 109th USCI 16 Jun 1864; tr to Freedman's Bureau Oct 1865; m/o New Orleans, Aug 1866
Later Life: Provost Marshall and Agent for Freedman's Bureau, LA; State Rep. 1868; parish judge 1868; State Sen. 1870-78; survived assassination attempt, but lost both arms 1876; US Consul at Kingston, Ontario (1878-1905)
Affiliations: GAR, Mason, MOLLUS (#10381)
Married: (1) 24 Apr 1866, Adele Coleman; (2) 26 Oct 1876, Henrietta Nancy Day
Died: 21 Aug 1905; interment in Oak Grove Cemetery, Townshend VT
Autobiography: <u>Carpetbagger from Vermont</u> (1989)
Papers: Louisiana Technical University
(C&S, CLL*, FAG, FSO, JGU, RR)

Tyler, John Steele (1843-1864)

Born: 29 Apr 1843, Brattleboro VT
Early Life: student
War Service: 1LT, Co. C 2nd VT INF 17 May 1861; CPT 23 Jan 1862; MAJ 9 Feb 1863; LTCOL 2 Apr 1864; mwia, Wilderness, 5 May 1864; COL 6 May 1864; d/wds 23 May 1864
Died: 23 May 1864; interment in Prospect Hill Cemetery, Brattleboro VT
(FAG, MRC*, RR)

Taylor, Herbert E.

Tinker, Charles E.

Titus-Hazen, Fanny. H.

Trull, Daniel N.

Tucker, Stephen. S.

Twitchell, Marshall M.

Tyler, John S.

UUUUU

Upham, Charles Carroll (1819-1868)

Born: 3 Apr 1819, Montpelier VT, son of William and Sarah (Keyes) Upham
Early Life: asst doorkeeper, State Rep. 1838, Purser USN 30 Jul 1852, *Cyane*, Home Squadron 1853, visited Nicaragua, steamship *Niagara* 1858, returning liberated slaves to Liberia, Boston 1860
War Service: Washington Navy Yard 1861-63, Fleet Paymr, North Atlantic Squadron, flagship *Minnesota* 1863-65, temporary duty at Beaufort NC 1863-64 to purchase naval stores, maintain accounts, and investigate discrepancies
Later Life: Paymr receiving ship *Vandalia* Portsmouth NH 1866, sick leave Montpelier VT 1 Jan 1867 until his death
Married: Abbie E. (nfi)
Died: 10 Jun 1868, Montpelier VT; interment in Greenmount Cemetery
Notes: mother's sister was grandmother of M.G. William T. H. Brooks
(TJL2)

VVVVV

Valentine, Alonzo Buckingham (1830-1904)

Born: 1 Apr 1830, Bennington VT, son of Joel and Judith (Wells) Valentine
Early Life: Bennington local schools, Union Acad. Suffield CT Acad., moved to CA, 1852-54, returned to Bennington, established grist-mill
War Service: QM, 10th VT INF, 31 Jul 1862, CS (CPT) USV 2 Mar 1864, Bvt MAJ USV 28 Jun 1864, m/o 28 Jun 1865
Later Life: managed largest knitting mill in State, established graded schools in Bennington, and Soldiers' Home, State Sen. 1886-87, State Commissioner of Agriculture and manufacturing interests, pres. board of trustees and dir. Bennington Cty Savings Bank, NU Board of Visitors
Affiliations: Republican, Agnostic (but attended Congregational Church), GAR, MOLLUS (#03017), RSVO, VI Corps Reunion Soc., SAR
Married: 1856, Alma L. Park
Died: 9 Jul 1904, Bennington VT; interment in Village Cemetery
(AFS, C&S, JGU*, LHC, WAE)

Van Deusen, George Henry (1836-1915)

Born: 24 Aug 1836, Palatine NY, son of Cornelius and Elizabeth (Cornue) Van Deusen
Early Life: teacher, 4 years, A.B. UVM 1857. M.D. UVM 1861, physician insane asylum, NYC
War Service: Asst SURG USN 14 Feb 1862, gunboat *Sachem* 1862, gunboat *Owasco* 1864, resgd 19 Mar 1864
Later Life: physician Bethel VT 4 years, Ontario Cty NY
Married: 1863, Celia A. Liscum
Affiliations: VT State MS, Steuben and Ontario Cty MS White River MS
Died: 28 Jan 1915, Strattonville PA; interment unknown
Notes: witnessed Monitor-Virginia battle in Hampton Roads
(TJL2, UVMMED)

Van Steenburg, Warner (1832-1880)

Born: 14 Jun 1832, Hinesburg VT
Early Life: Hinesburg Acad., M.D. UVM 1856

War Service: Asst SURG 1st NY INF, 3 Dec 1861, SURG 30 Nov 1861, m/o 30 Sep 1862, Asst SURG 55th NY INF 10 Oct 1862, SURG 13 Oct 1862, m/o 23 Dec 1862, SURG 120th NY INF, 11 Mar 1863, m/o 3 Jun 1865
Later Life: physician Cohoes NY 1870
Affiliations: VT MS
Married: 1858, Phoebe Houghtlin
Died: Apr 1880, Cohoes, NY; interment unknown
(1870, NYL, NYL1, UVMMED)

Van Vliet, Stewart Leonard (1815-1901)

Born: 21 Jul 1815, Ferrisburg VT, son of Christian and Rachel (Huff) Van Vliet
Early Life: USMA 1840 (9/42), 2LT 3rd US ARTY 1 Jul 1840, Seminole War 1840-42, Asst Prof. Mathematics, USMA Sep-Nov 1841, garrison duty 1842-46, 1LT 19 Nov 1843, Mexican-American War 1846-47, AQM (CPT) 4 Jun 1847, Ft. Kearney, NE 1847-49, Ft. Laramie, Dakota Terr. 1849-51, Texas 1852-54, CPT 3rd US ARTY 24 Dec 1853, Sioux expedition Apr 1855-Jul 1856
War Service: MAJ & QM 3 Aug 1861, Chief QM AOP 1861-62, B.G. USV 23 Sep 1861, expired 17 Jul 1862, Chief QM AOP, Peninsula Campaign Mar-Jul 1862, New York, furnishing supplies and transportation to armies in the field, Jul 1862-Mar 1867, Bvt LTC, Bvt COL, Bvt B.G. USA, 28 Oct 1864, B.G., Bvt M.G. USV 13 Mar 1865
Later Life: Deputy QM Gen. (LTCOL) 29 Jul 1866, m/o USV 1 Sep 1866, Depot QM Baltimore, MD 1867-69, Chief QM, Div. of the Atlantic 1869-72, AQM (COL) Gen. 6 Jun 1872, Chief QM, Dept of Missouri 1872-75, Chief QM, Philadelphia Depot 1875, Inspector of QM H.Q., Washington, 12 Nov 1875, ret. 22 Jan 1881
Affiliations: MOLLUS (#00745)
Married: 6 Mar 1851, Sarah Jane Brown
Died: 29 Mar 1901, Washington, D.C; interment in Arlington National Cemetery (Section 2)
(C&S, FSO, GWC, LOC*, RJ, WHP)

Vilas, William Freeman (1840-1908)

Born: 9 Jul 1840, Chelsea VT, son of Levi and Esther (Smilie) Vilas
Early Life: moved to WI 1851; UWI Madison 1858, ALS 1860; atty
War Service: CPT Co. A 23rd WI INF, MAJ, LTCOL
Later Life: law school professor, UWI 1868, State Rep. 1885, DNC delegate 1876, 1880, 1884; Postmaster Gen. 1885-88; Sec. of the Interior 1888-89; US Sen. 1891-97; regent, UWI 1898-1905
Married: 3 Jan 1866, Anna Matilda Fox
Died: 27 Aug 1908, Madison WI; interment in Forest Hill Cemetery
(CB, FSO, JGU)

Vincent, Walter Scott (1838-aft 1920)

Born: 4 Jun 1838, Chelsea VT, son of Stephen and Phebe Adams (Hale) Vincent
Early Life: DC, M.D. UVM 1861
War Service: Asst SURG, 9th VT INF 20 Apr 1863, SURG 15 Nov 1864, m/o 13 Jun 1865
Later Life: druggist, Burlington VT 1870-80, Manager VT Electric Co., State Rep. 1902-03
Affiliations: Republican, Episcopalian, GAR, RSVO, SAR, MOLLUS (#10075)
Married: (1) 8 Oct 1862, Harriet Frances Lawrence; (2) 28 Jun 1904, Mary Hall Ward
Died: aft 1920; interment unknown
Notes: Vincent's sister, Ann Eliza, married Dr. Story Goss (q.v.)
(1860, 1870, 1880, 1920, C&S, HFW77, UVMMED, WHO3)

Valentine, A. B.

Vanvliet, Stewart

WWWWWW

Waite, Charles (1837-1898)

Born: 1 Apr 1837, Braintree VT, son of Daniel Waite
Early Life: moved to IL 1854; Beloit College; teacher, Sycamore IL 1860; moved to MI
War Service: 1LT 27th MI INF 10 Oct 1861; CPT 1 May 1863; wdd Spotsylvania 12 May 1864; MAJ 12 May 1864; LTCOL 18 Nov 1864; COL 6 Mar 1865; Bvt B.G. 2 Apr 1865, m/o 26 Jul 1865
Later Life: banker; merchant, druggist Lena IL 1870-80
Married: Emily (nfi)
Died: 23 Jun 1898, Boulder, CO; interment in Lena Burial Ground, Lena IL
(1860, 1870, 1880, CL, E&E, FSO, JR)

Wakefield, William Wallace (1844-1919)

Born: 27 Jun 1844, Orleans Cty VT, son of Alvah and Hannah (Kimpton) Wakefield
Early Life: public schools, Johnson Acad
War Service: PVT Co. M 11th VT INF 19 Sep 1863, tr to VRC 13 Apr 1865, m/o 4 Oct 1865
Later Life: farming 1865-75, lumber business, town selectman, auditor, lister, first constable, deputy sheriff, high bailiff, State Rep. 1892
Affiliations: Republican, Baptist, Mason, GAR
Married: 11 Feb 1866, Ruth E. Newton
Died: 23 Mar 1919; interment in North Troy Cemetery, Troy VT
(AGO, JGU)

Walbridge, James Hicks (1826-1913)

Born: 29 Jul 1826, Hinsdillville VT, son of Stebbins Denio and Harriet (Hicks) Walbridge
Early Life: weaver, sailor; moved to CA 1852; miner; vigilante; returned to VT 1857; farmer, Bennington 1860
War Service: CPT Co. A 2nd VT INF 16 May 1861; MAJ 21 May 1862; LTCOL 8 Jan 1863; COL 9 Feb 1863; res. 1 Apr 1864 for medical reasons
Later Life: Internal Revenue Assessor, Bennington VT 1870-80; Agent, Fire Insurance Co, Bennington VT 1900, Panama Railroad Co. employee
Affiliations: GAR, MOLLUS (#09182), RSVO
Married: (1) abt 1851 Eliza Ann Burgess; (2) 26 Feb 1867, Delia Perry
Died: 15 Dec 1913, Bennington VT; interment in Grandview Cemetery, North Bennington
(1860, 1870, 1880, 1900, BBObit, C&S, FSO, MOLLUS, RR)

Walker, Aldace Freeman (1842-1901)

Born: 11 May 1842, West Rutland VT, son of Aldace and Mary Ann (Baker) Walker
Early Life: KUA 1858, MC 1862
War Service: 1LT Co. B 11th VT INF 13 Aug 1862, CPT 30 Nov 1862, Co. D 11 Jul 1863, MAJ 28 Jun 1864, Bvt LTCOL 10 Oct 1864, LTCOL 23 Mary 1865, m/o 24 Jun 1865
Later Life: Columbia Law School 1865-68, atty NYC 1867-73, atty Rutland VT, railroad litigation 1873-87, State Sen. 1882-83, LLD MC 1887, ICC commissioner 1887-89, chaired Interstate Commerce Railway Assoc, chaired Western Traffic Assoc, State commissioner Columbian Exposition 1893; receiver, chair. Atchinson, Topeka & Santa Fe Railroad and allied lines
Married: 6 Sep 1871, Katherine Shaw
Affiliations: Republican, GAR, MOLLUS (#05409), RSVO9

Died: 12 Apr 1901, NYC; interment in Evergreen Cemetery, Rutland VT
Correspondence: VHS, Quite Ready to be Sent Somewhere: The Civil War Letters of Aldace Freeman Walker (2002)
Publications: The Vermont Brigade in the Shenandoah Valley, 1864 (1869); James R. Langdon, Et Al., Vs. Vermont & Canada Railroad Co., Et Al. State of Vermont Supreme Court: Franklin County (1882); The Apportionment of Competitive Traffic Under the Law (1890)
(C&S, JGU, KUA, TJL, MIDCAT, Snoots)

Walker, Daniel Chase (1842-1917)

Born: 11 Dec 1842, Cambridge VT, son of Lyman and Adeline (Chase) Walker
Early Life: public schools, Bakersfield Acad
War Service: PVT Co. D 1st VT CAV 15 Aug 1862, SGT 7 Dec 1864, wdd, Weldon Railroad, 23 Jun 1864, m/o 21 Jun 1865
Later Life: carpenter and joiner, farmer, town lister, selectman, justice, school dir., postmaster, State. Rep. 1892
Affiliations: Republican, GAR
Married: 16 Apr 1867, Kate M. Converse
Died: 19 Feb 1917, Cambridge VT; interment in North Cambridge Cemetery
(AGO, JGU)

Walker, William Harris (1832-1896)

Born: 2 Feb 1832, Windham VT, son of Ephraim and Lydia (Harris) Walker
Early Life: moved to Londonderry 1838, local schools, Leland and Gray Sem., BRA, MC 1858; teacher, princ. Little Falls NY Acad., atty, Ludlow 1861-84
War Service: CPT Co. C 16th VT INF 29 Aug 1862, resgd 22 Oct 1862 due to typhoid fever
Later Life: State Rep. 1865-66, 1884, State Sen. 1867-68, Supervisor of the Insane 1878-80, probate judge 1878, Asst judge VT Sup. Court 1884-87, trustee, MC, pres. Black River Acad
Affiliations: Republican, Mason
Married: 1859, Ann Eliza Taylor
Died: 11 Aug 1896, Ludlow VT; interment unknown
(AGO, JGU)

Walton, Eliakim Persons (1812-1890)

Born: 17 Feb 1812, Montpelier VT, son of Ezekiel Parker and Prussian (Persons) Walton
Early Life: journalist, Walton's Vermont Register, State Rep. 1853,
War Service: US Rep. 1857-63, RNC delegate 1864
Later Life: State ConCon 1870, State Sen. 1875, 1877, UVM trustee 1875-87, pres. VHS 1876-90
Affiliations: Republican
Married: (1) 5 Jun 1836, Sarah S. Howes; (2) Oct 1882, Clara P. Field
Died: 19 Dec 1890, Montpelier VT; interment in Green Mount Cemetery
Publication: Records of the Governor and Council of the State of Vermont (1880), A Description of the State Houses of Vermont (1896)
(CB, FSO, HGW, JGU*)

Warner, James Meech (1836-1897)

Born: 29 Jan 1836, Middlebury VT, son of Joseph and Jane (Meech) Warner
Early Life: KUA 1854; MC 1855, USMA 1860 (40/41); Bvt 2LT 10th US INF; 2LT 28 Feb 1861; 1LT 30 May 1861, while cmdg Ft. Wise, CO
War Service: COL 11th VT INF 15 Aug 1862; wdd Spotsylvania C.H., 18 May 1864, Bvt B.G. 1 Aug 1864, B.G. USV 8 May 1865; m/o USV 15 Jan 1866; resgd USA 13 Feb 1866

Later Life: pres. Albany (NY) Card and Paper Co.; postmaster, Albany, NY 1889-92;
Affiliations: MOLUS (#01908)
Married: Matilda Allen
Died: 16 Mar 1897, NYC; interment in West Cemetery, Middlebury VT
Notes: Morrisville GAR Post #4 named after him
(GWC, Italo*, KUA, MIDCAT, RR, TJL)

Warren, Charles Carlton (1843-1928)

Born: 11 Feb 1843, Hartland VT, son of Charles Walton and Julia M. (Perry) Warren
Early Life: Hartland schools, KUA, tanner, Hartland
War Service: Musician (cornet) 2nd VT INF Band 15 Jun 1861, dis 19 Dec 1861, Musician 1st BGD Band 17 Apr 1863, m/o 29 Jun 1865
Later Life: farmer, tanner Hartland and Waterbury 1870-95, manufacturer of harness and rein leather 1900-20, State Fish Commission, dir. State fish hatchery, dir. Hartland and Waterbury bands
Affiliations: Republican, Mason, GAR
Married: 15 Dec 1873, Ella F. McElroy
Died: 2 Nov 1928, Waterbury VT; interment in Village Cemetery
Notes: had the state fish hatchery erected in Roxbury and began breeding trout for Vermont ponds and streams
(1870, 1920, AFS, JGU, PCD)

Washburn, Henry Dana (1832-1871)

Born: 28 Mar 1832, Windsor VT
Early Life: tanner, school teacher, New York State and National Law School 1853, atty, Newport IN 1853, Auditor, Vermillion Cty IN 1854
War Service: LTCOL, 18th IN INF 16 Aug 1861, Blackwater Creek MO Dec 1861, Pea Ridge MO Mar 1862, COL 15 Jul 1862, Bvt B.G., 15 Dec 1864, Bvt M.G. 26 Jul 1865, m/o 26 Aug 1865
Later Life: US Rep. IN 1866-69, Surveyor General, Montana Terr. 1869-70, headed the Washburn-Langford-Doane expedition to locate headwaters of Yellowstone River; discovered Yellowstone National Park 1870
Married: 28 Dec 1854, Serena Johnson
Died: 26 Jan 1871, Clinton IN; interment in Riverside Cemetery
Notes: Mt. Washburn in Yellowstone Park is named in his honor
(AR, FBH, FSO, VCHS, WHB)

Washburn, Peter Thacher (1814-1870)

Born: 7 Sep 1814, Lynn MA, son of Reuben and Hannah Blaney (Thacher) Washburn
Early Life: moved to VT 1817; DC 1834; atty 1838; VT Supreme Court reporter (1844-52; State Rep. 1853-54; militia officer; RNC 1860
War Service: LTCOL 1st VT INF 26 Apr 1861; m/o 15 Aug 1861
Later Life: VT Asst & I.G. 1862-66; atty; VT Gov. 1869-70
Affiliations: RSVO
Married: 1839, Almira E. Ferris
Died: 7 Feb 1870, Woodstock VT; interment in River Street Cemetery
Papers: UVM
Publications: Practical Forms (1836), A Digest of all Cases Decided in the Supreme Court of the State of Vermont (1845), The American Bookseller's Complete Reference Trade List (1847)
Speeches: An Oration Before the Re-Union Society of Vermont Officers in the Representatives' Hall, Montpelier, Vt., October 22d, 1868
(FSO, OFW, PCD, RR)

Waterman, Arba Nelson (1836-1917)

Born: 5 Feb 1836, Greensboro VT, son of Loring Franklin and Mary (Stevens) Waterman
Early Life: Montpelier, Johnson and Peacham Acad., NU 1852-53, teacher, Georgia Acad. 1853-54; moved to Illinois 1854, teacher, Goodings Grove, IL 1854-55, Aurora, IL 1856-57, studied law in IL, ALS 1862, admitted to NY bar, returned to IL late 1861, atty Joliet 1862
War Service: LTCOL 100th IL INF 30 Aug 1862, dis/dsb Jul 1864
Later Life: atty, Chicago, judge Circuit Ct, Cook Cty, 1887, judge appellate court 16 years, private practice 1903, Waterman, Thurman and Ross, trustee, Chicago Public Library
Affiliations: GAR, MOLLUS (#02174), Grand Army Hall and Memorial Assoc (pres. 1901-02)
Married: 16 Dec 1862, Eloise Hall
Died: 16 Mar 1917, Chicago IL; interment unknown
Publications: Washington at the Time of the First Bull Run (1887)
(ANW, C&S, JGU, WAE*)

Watson, Austin H. R. (1842-aft 1902)

Born: 24 Apr 1842, Wilmington VT, son of Patrick J. and Caroline (Lathrop) Watson
Early Life: mill laborer
War Service: PVT Co. F 16th VT INF 3 Sep 1862, pr QM SGT 4 Jul 1863 (Gettysburg), m/o 10 Aug 1863
Later Life: junior clerk, Western Union Telegraph Co., Rochester NY 1864-65, storekeeper for same, NY (1866-79), James E. Vail, Jr., & Co., dry goods wholesaler 1879-85, moved to Stamford CT 1886, Watson, Bull & Co., wholesalers, pres. CT Witch Hazel Co.
Married: 28 Oct 1879, Julia Brainerd Vail
Died: aft 1902; interment unknown
(JGU*)

Webster, Alonzo (1818-1887)

Born: 27 Jan 1818, Weston VT, son of Jonathan and Lucy (Sterling) Webster
Early Life: Newbury Sem., Pastor, Brattleboro VT, Greenfield NH, Northfield NH, Chesterfield NH, Chaplin VT State Sen. 1848, M.E. Clergyman, Danville 1850, Pastor Grace Methodist Church St. Johnsbury 1856, honorary A.M. MC 1859, D.D., Allegany College, PA, M.E. Clergyman, Hartford VT 1860
War Service: Chap., 16th VT INF, 16 Oct 1862 - 10 Aug 1863, Chap. 6th VT INF, 3 Oct 1863 - 28 Oct 1864, Chap. Sloane Hosp., Montpelier 1865
Later Life: M.E. Church, Charleston SC 1866-68, founder, Claflin Univ., Orangeburg SC 1869, pres. 1869-73, trustee 1869-83, Clergyman, Orangeburg SC 1880
Married: (1) 26 May 1840, Martha Jane (nfi); (2) 16 Jun 1844, Laura Ann Peaslee
Died: 15 Aug 1887, Brattleboro VT; interment unknown
Notes: Claflin University chartered to assist freed slaves with higher education
(1850, 1860, 1880, CF, ETF, GFH, MOC, MRC)

Webster, Harvey A. (1826-1899)

Born: 6 Jun 1826, Weston VT, son of Jonathan and Lucy (Sterling) Webster
Early Life: Newbury Sem., Concord Biblical Inst., Pastor, Methodist Church, Putney VT (1848), Reading VT (1852-53), Waitsfield VT 1860, Royalton VT 1862
War Service: Chap., 6th VT INF, 13 Nov 1864, m/o 26 Jun 1865
Later Life: Methodist Pastor, Essex VT 1870, Barre VT 1880, Moretown VT 1890, Free Methodist Church, Burlington VT (1893)
Married: Lucy (nfi)

Died: 6 Jan 1899, Swanton VT; interment unknown
Notes: brother of Alonzo Webster (q.v.)
(1860, 1870, 1880, 1890, AF, B1893, EWL, GAD, GFH)

Welch, Alvin Colby (1817-1888)

Born: 28 Apr 1817, Canaan NH, son of Bailey and Priscilla (Barbour) Welch
Early Life: A.M. DC 1843, M.D., CMC, physician, Williston VT 1850-80
War Service: Fredericksburg and Washington May 1864, among a contingent of Vermont doctors who volunteered their services to care for Vermonters who were wounded in the battles of the Wilderness and Spotsylvania C.H.
Later Life: M.D., Dartmouth 1868, Commissioner of the Insane, Vermont; committed suicide
Affiliations: VT Med Soc
Married: 27 Apr 1845, Abigail Chittenden
Died: 21 Oct 1888, Williston VT; interment unknown
(1850, 1860, 1880, AMT1860, AMW, BMJ1)

Wells, Charles James Stewart (1836-1881)

Born: 24 Aug 1836, Palatine NY
Early Life: A.B. UVM 1857. M.D. UVM 1861, physician insane asylum, NYC
War Service: Asst SURG USN 24 Jan 1862, *Brooklyn* 1863, Mississippi Squad. 1864, Naval Asylum, Philadelphia 1865, Passed Asst SURG 30 Oct 1865, *Shamrock* 1866-69, screw frigate *Colorado* 1870-71, expedition to Korea, SURG 6 Jul 1872
Died: 1 Jan 1881; interment unknown
(TJL2, UVMCat3, UVMMED)

Wells, Edward (1835-1907)

Born: 30 Oct 1835, Waterbury VT, son of William Wellington and Eliza (Carpenter) Wells
Early Life: dry goods clerk
War Service: Musician 5th VT INF Band 6 Sep 1861, unit disbanded 20 Feb 1862, further service as transportation clerk, AOP, under P. P. Pitkin three years
Later Life: clerk for VT QM Gen. 1864-66, clerk for State Treasurer 1866-68, partner Henry & Co., wholesale druggists 1868-72, pres., Wells & Richardson Co., Burlington Trust Co., dir. Burlington Cotton Mills, State Rep. 1890
Married: (1) 26 Apr 1858, Mary Frances Parmalee; (2) 14 Oct 1879, Effie E. Parmalee (sisters)
Died: 19 Feb 1907, Miami FL; interment in Lakeview Cemetery, Burlington VT
(AGO, JGU*, LHC, VHS10)

Weston, Edmund Jr. (1830-1901)

Born: 6 Feb 1830, Randolph VT, son of Edmund and Sarah (Edson) Weston
Early Life: NU 1848, dentist, Boston 1852-57, M.D. UVM 1859, physician 1859-61
War Service: CPT Co. F 1st USSS 15 Aug 1861, resgd due to illness 2 Aug 1862
Later Life: dentist in Randolph 1862-81, Board of Health Washington DC 1881-85, clerk, War Dept, Washington DC 1885-93
Affiliations: Episcopal, Mason
Died: 3 Jul 1901, Washington, DC, interment in family plot in West Randolph
(HHW*, UVMMED, WAE)

Weston, Eugene Sydney (1847-1922)

Born: 14 Aug 1847, Cavendish VT, son of Freeman F. and Sarah J. (Evans) Weston
Early Life: Chester Acad

War Service: PVT Co. C 7th VT INF 27 Aug 1864, m/o 14 Jul 1865
Later Life: DC, UVM 1871, physician, Heath, Coleraine and Pittsfield MA 1871-79, physician, Newfane 1879-1922, State Rep. 1892-94
Affiliations: Republican, Congregational, Mason, GAR, VT MS, MA MS
Married: 6 Jun 1871, Eva S. Hall
Died: 29 Nov 1922, New Haven VT; interment unknown
(GFH, JGU, T289)

Wheeler, Charles Willard (1839-1909)

Born: 13 Apr 1839, Enosburg VT, son of Willard and Maria (Page) Wheeler
Early Life: Enosburg Acad., mercantile pursuits, St. Albans, Burlington
War Service: PVT Co. I 10th VT INF 5 Aug 1862, CPL 30 Jan 1863, SGT 1 Jul 1864, 1SGT 4 Jul 1864, 2LT 9 Aug 1864, 1LT Co. K 9 Feb 1865, wdd, Cedar Creek, 19 Oct 1864, QM 22 Mar 1865, m/o 28 Jun 1865
Later Life: State Rep. 1886, State Sen. 1890, introduced secret ballot act, prop. gen. store, real estate
Affiliations: Republican, Congregational, GAR
Married: 7 Jun 1871, Louise E. Nichols
Died: 14 Sep 1909; interment unknown
(EMH, JGU*)

Wheeler, Henry Orson (1841-1918)

Born: 7 Oct 1841, Williston VT, son of Orville Gould and Aurelia Maria (Sanford) Wheeler
Early Life: South Hero Acad
War Service: CPL 1st VT CAV 19 Nov 1861, SGT 1 Dec 1862, 1LT 24 Sep 1863, wdd Wilderness 5 May 1864, wdd/pow Columbia Furnace 7 Oct 1864, Libby Prison, prld 22 Feb 1865, m/o 8 Mar 1865, BVT CPT 13 Mar 1865
Later Life: A.B. UVM 1867, Law Studies, Univ. of Michigan 1867-69, atty Fort Dodge IA 1869-71, atty Burlington VT 1871-86, admitted to the bar Apr 1872, School Super., Burlington 1880-1912, treasurer, UVM 1882-92
Affiliations: Republican, Congregationalist, GAR, MOLLUS (#09162), SAR
Married: 19 Jul 1871, Elizabeth Lavina Martin
Died: 27 Jul 1918, San Dimas, CA; interment unknown
(AGW, C&S, MA, PCD, WSR)

White, Azro 'Hank' (1833-1899)

Born: 2 Oct 1833, Reading VT, son of George and Electa (Cushman) White
Early Life: local schools, apprenticed at offices of Vermont Journal, printer, engraver, moved to NYC, studied theatre and Negro minstrel performances, partnered with George M. Clark, 'Broadway Minstrels'
War Service: Musician Co. E 16th VT INF 1 Sep 1862, m/o 10 Aug 1863
Later Life: Whitmore and Clark's Minstrels 25 years, New England, Canada, State Rep. 1886
Affiliations: Republican
Married: 19 Nov 1867, Catherine Felch
Died: 14 Feb 1899, Felchville, Reading VT; interment in Bailey Cemetery
Notes: "It's the greatest State in the Union and has only one thing I don't like. For about six weeks in midsummer when the snow melts off, we have to drag around on wheels" – Azro White
(AFS)

Whiting, Henry (1818-1887)

Born: 7 Feb 1818, Bath NY, son of John and Nancy (Carter) Whiting

Early Life: USMA 1840 (17/42); 2LT 5th US INF 1 Jul 1840; Ft. Snelling 1840-41; Jefferson Barracks 1841; Fort Mackinac 1841-45; TX 1845-56; resgd 25 Mar 1846; teacher St. Clair, MI 1846, Bath NY 1846-47; merchant, St. Clair 1847-61; regent, MI U. 1858-63
War Service: COL, 2nd VT INF 6 Jun 1861; resgd 9 Feb 1863
Later Life: merchant, St. Clair, MI
Married: Oct 1859, Mary T. Rice
Died: 23 Jun 1887, Ypsilanti, MI; interment in Hillside Cemetery
(CCPL, COM, GWC, Italo*, RR)

Whitney, Abel D. (1847-1864)

Born: 9 Jul 1847, Tunbridge VT, son of Joseph and Caroline (Pierce) Whitney
War Service: PVT Co. D 9th VT INF 2 Jan 1864, pow Newport Barracks 2 Feb 1864, died in prison
Died: 8 Aug 1864; interment in Andersonville National Cemetery GA
Notes: Tunbridge GAR Posts #21 and #29 were named after him
(DA, FSO, GGK)

Wilcox, Henry Clay (1842-aft 1894)

Born: 20 Aug 1842, Cambridge VT, son of Edmund W. and Matilda (Farnsworth) Wilcox
Early Life: Cambridge and Johnson Public Schools
War Service: US Armory, Springfield MA, duration of war
Later Life: farm laborer, manufacturer (butter tubs), hotel clerk, foreman in lumber trade, Gen. Super. Buck & Wilcox Lumber Co. 1882-85, C. H. Stevens & Co., Northern Lumber Co., deputy sheriff Johnson, justice, selectman Granby, State Rep. 1886-90
Affiliations: Republican, Mason
Died: aft 1894; interment unknown
(JGU*)

Wiley, Daniel Day (1837-1893)

Born: 10 Aug 1837, Readsboro VT
Early Life: merchant, Templeton MA 1860
War Service: SGT, Co A 21st MA INF 19 Jul 1861, m/o 20 Nov 1861, CPT Cmsry of Subsist., USV, 28 Aug 1862, Bvt MAJ USV 1 Aug 1864, Bvt LTCOL, COL and B.G. USV, 13 Mar 1865, m/o 26 Oct 1866
Later Life: Templeton MA 1870, Customs Appraiser Boston MA 1880
Died: 25 Jan 1893, Sudbury Centre MA; interment in Greenlawn Cemetery, Baldwinville MA
(1860, 1870, 1880, E&E, TWH)

Willard, Henry Augustus (1822-1909)

Born: 14 May 1822, Westminster VT, son of Joseph Willard and Susan Dorr (Clapp) Willard
Early Life: Walpole Acad., store clerk, hotel clerk, moved to Troy NY, steward, steamer *Niagara*, moved to Washington 1847, leased and later bought Benjamin Tayloe's 'City Hotel,' renaming it Willard's Hotel, 1853 took his brother as full partner
War Service: co-owner of Willard's Hotel, Washington, with his elder brothers Edwin Dorr and Joseph Clapp Willard; many luminaries stayed there, including President-elect Lincoln
Later Life: hotel keeper, Board of Health, Washington 1869-71, Board of Public Works 1873-74, pres. Columbia R.R. 1873-89, pres. National Savings Bank 1867-1909
Married: 6 Nov 1855, Sarah Bradley Kellogg
Died: 4 Dec 1909, Walpole NH; interment in Old Cemetery, Westminster VT

(FAG, FSO, HKW*, VHS10)

Williams, Carlos Dutton (1843-1921)

Born: 29 Sep 1843, Royalton VT, son of Erastus and Charlotte (Safford) Williams
Early Life: public schools, Northfield Acad
War Service: 1SGT Co. F 12th VT INF 19 Aug 1862, 2LT 4 Dec 1862, 1LT 10 Mar 1862, m/o 14 Jul 1863
Later Life: drug business 1863-86, moved to Burlington, employee Burlington Drug Co. 1886-1921, trustee VT Soldiers' Home 1917
Affiliations: MOLLUS (#12172), GAR (Post ADJ, Dept Asst ADJ, and QM Gen., registrar, recorder), Mason
Married: (1) 8 Dec 1869, Mary Elizabeth Woodbury; (2) 15 Jan 1879, Ellen M. Thayer
Died: 16 Dec 1921, Burlington VT; interment in Elmwood Cemetery, Northfield VT
(AFS, AGO, C&S)

Williams, Francis Charles (1824-1910)

Born: 2 Nov 1824, Brighton MA
Early Life: A.B. Harvard 1843, ordained, Unitarian Church, Andover, MA, 27 Feb 1850, Pastor, Andover 1850-56, Brattleboro VT 1856-64
War Service: Chaplin 8th VT INF 20 Dec 1861, m/o 22 Jun 1864
Later Life: Pastor, East Bridgewater MA 1865-70, Hyde Park MA 1870-79, Clergyman Boston 1880-90, Wayland MA 1893-94
Married: 20 Oct 1857, Mary Hancock Gardner
Died: 27 Nov 1910, Brookline MA; interment unknown
(1880, 1890, DH2, GNC, HDCAT, SLB)

Williams, John C. (1843-1908)

Born: 25 Jun 1843, Danby VT, son of Olney and Susan (Roberts) Williams
Early Life: farm laborer, store clerk
War Service: CPL Co. B 14th VT INF 21 Oct 1862, reduced by request, tr to Co. K 1 Mar 1863, m/o 30 Jul 1863
Later Life: school teacher, Super. of common schools 1865-67, constable and collector 1866, assistant marshal for 1870 census, town historian, publisher <u>Otter Creek Valley News</u>
Affiliations: Rutland Cty Hist. Soc.
Married: 5 Feb 1868, Nora Colvin
Died: 18 Oct 1908, Denver CO; interment unknown
Publications: <u>Life in Camp: A History of the Nine Months' Service of the Fourteenth Vermont Regiment, From October 21, 1862, When It was Mustered into the U.S. Service, to July 21, 1863, Including the Battle of Gettysburg</u> (1864), <u>The History and Map of Danby, Vermont</u> (1869), <u>Sheriffs of Rutland County</u> (1881)
(1860, 1870, 1880, JCW, LWR, MDG, RR)

Williamson, Charles H. (1841-1922)

Born: 14 Aug 1841, Middlebury VT, son of Isaac and Catherine M. (White) Williamson
Early Life: livery business, Middlebury 1860
War Service: PVT Co B 5th VT INF 16 Sep1861, SGT, 1SGT, 2LT Co K 21 Mar 1863, Co. B 25 Mar 1863, 1LT 7 Nov 1863, wdd Spotsylvania C.H. 10 May 1864, m/o 15 Sep 1864
Later Life: livery business, Middlebury 1864-1907, chair. Middlebury Village, Super. of Parks, Middlebury 1911, Middlebury 1920, never married
Affiliations: Republican, GAR
Died: 25 Mar 1922, Middlebury VT; interment in West Cemetery

(1860, 1880, 1900, 1920, AGO, PCD)

Willson, Melvin A. (1847-1909)

Born: 31 Jul 1847, Lowell, MA, son of Sydney and Lucy (Boutwell) Willson
Early Life: moved to Victory VT 1855, farm laborer
War Service: PVT Co. K 8th VT INF 13 Sep 1864, m/o 13 May 1865
Later Life: general farming, raising, buying and selling stock, trades in feed, flour and grain, State Rep. 1884
Married: 6 Mar 1872, Jean Wells
Affiliations: Republican
Died: 19 Dec 1909, Granby VT; interment in Church Cemetery
(AGO, JGU)

Winslow, John Flack (1810-1892)

Born: 5 Nov 1810, Bennington VT, son of Richard and Mary (Corning) Winslow
Early Life: Iron manufacturer, Troy NY 1860
War Service: government contracted with his firm for the construction of ironclad *Monitor*, which was begun in 1861 at Greenpoint, Long Island, and launched in 1862
Later Life: pres. Poughkeepsie and Eastern R.R., bridge builder
Married: 12 Sep 1832, Nancy Beach Jackson
Died: 10 Mar 1892, Poughkeepsie, NY; interment unknown
Publications: The Pneumatic or Bessemer Process of Making Steel (1865)
(1860, FSO, VHS13)

Wisewell, Moses N. (1827-1888)

Born: 15 May 1827, Brandon VT
Early Life: civil engineer, merchant, princ. Yonkers (NY) Collegiate and Military Inst, princ. Eagleswood Military and Collegiate Inst. Perth Amboy NJ
War Service: COL 28th NJ INF 22 Sep 1862; wdd Fredericksburg 13 Dec 1862; COL VRC 25 Sep 1863; Mil. Gov. Washington 1864; Bvt B.G. 13 Mar 1865 for Fredericksburg VA; resgd 1 Oct 1865
Later Life: Railroad contractor Brooklyn NY 1870
Died: 11 Apr 1888, NYC; interment in First Reformed Church Cemetery, Pompton Plains NJ
(1870, E&E, FAG, FBH, JAH2)

Wood, Lydia A. (see Johnson, Estelle S.)

Woodbridge, Frederick Enoch (1818-1888)

Born: 29 Aug 1818, Vergennes VT, son of Enoch Day and Clarissa (Strong) Woodbridge
Early Life: UVM 1840, atty 1843-49, State Rep. 1849, 1857-58, Mayor of Vergennes, State auditor 1850-52, Prosecuting atty 1854-58
War Service: State Sen. 1860-61, US Rep. 1863-69
Affiliations: Republican
Married: 1846, Mary P. Halsey
Died: 25 Apr 1888, Vergennes VT; interment in Prospect Cemetery
(CB, FSO, HGW, JGU, LOC*)

Woodbury, Urban Andrain (1838-1915)

Born: 11 Jul 1838, Acworth NH, son of Albert Merriam and Lucy Lestina (Wadleigh) Woodbury
Early Life: M.D. UVM 1859, physician
War Service: 1SGT Co. H 2nd VT INF 20 Jun 1861, wdd/pow Bull Run 21 Jul 1861, prld 5 Oct 1861; disch/wds 18 Oct 1861; CPT Co. D 11th VT INF 17 Nov 1862; tr to VRC 17 Jun 1863; resgd 27 Mar 1865
Later Life: lumberman; entrepreneur; mayor of Burlington 1885-86, LT Gov. 1888 VT Gov. 1894-96, member War Investigation Committee 1898
Affiliations: Republican, Mason, IOOF, GAR (Dept. Cmdr), MOLLUS (#05799), SAR, KOP, RSVO
Married: 1860, Paulina Livonia Darling
Died: 15 Apr 1915, Burlington VT; interment in Lakeview Cemetery
Notes: lost his right arm at First Bull Run, becoming Vermont's first "empty sleeve"
(BBObit, C&S, CCC*, GGB, JGU, LHC, PCD, TWH, WHO3)

Woodruff, Charles Albert (1845-1920)

Born: 26 Apr 1845, Burke VT, son of Erastus Woodruff
Early Life: Lyndon Acad., St. Johnsbury Acad., Bryant & Stratton's Business Coll., Burlington
War Service: PVT Co. A 10th VT INF 5 Jun 1862, CPL 19 Mar 1864, wdd, Cold Harbor, 3 Jun 1864, dis/dsb 18 Aug 1865
Later Life: recovered, surrendered invalid pension, USMA 1871 (11/41), 2LT, 7th U.S. INF, 12 Jun 1871, Frontier Duty, Mont. 1872-75, Indian Camp. ID, Yellowstone, Nez Perces, 1876-77, rescue of survivors of Custer's Command; 1LT 9 Aug 1877, Ft. Leavenworth 1878-79, CS (CPT) 28 Mar 1878, ACS, AAGC Dept of MO 1879, CS Dept of NM 1879-84, Dept of Columbia 1884-89, Bvt CPT 27 Feb 1890, CS (MAJ) 27 Dec 1892, ACG Washington DC, 1894-98, ACGS (LTCOL) 4 Feb 1898, ACGS (COL) 11 May 1898, super. CS Branch, A.T.S., New York 1898-1900, CS Philippines 1900-02, C. S., Dept of CA 1902-03, B.G. 27 Jul 1903, ret. 28 Jul 1903
Affiliations: MOLLUS (#05448), Military Order of the Carabao
Died: 13 Aug 1920; interment in National Cemetery, San Francisco CA
Publications: American Patriotism (1891)
(C&S, FBH, GWC, GWC1, JGU)

Woodward, Adrian Theodore (1827-1908)

Born: 17 Jul 1827, Castleton VT, son of Theodore and Mary (Armington) Woodward
Early Life: Castleton Sem., CMC 1847, physician in Whitehall NY, Castleton and Brandon VT, honorary A.M. UVM 1857, prof. obstetrics and gynecology CMS and prof. surgical disease of women, UVM
War Service: SURG, 14th VT INF 9 Feb 1863, m/o 30 Jul 1863
Later Life: physician, Brandon 1870-1900
Affiliations: Mason, IOOF, MOLLUS (#09187), GAR, RSVO, VT MS
Married: (1) 1850, Martha Chapin; (2) 1855, Lois Cornelia June
Died: 9 Jan 1908, Brandon VT; interment in Pine Hill Cemetery
(1870, 1880, 1890, C&S, FSO, RR, WBA, WRS)

Woodward, Edwin T. (1843-1894)

Born: 8 Mar 1843, Castleton VT, son of Edwin Carlos and Charlotte (Barney) Woodward
Early Life: entered USNA 21 Nov 1859, in 3rd year, ordered to Boston
War Service: side-wheel steamer *Mississippi*, garrison ship *Island*, and gunboat *Sciota* 1861-62, prize-crew of steamer *Henry Lewis*, captured rebel battery, sloop *Cyane*, Pacific Squadron 1863, LT Feb 1864, steam frigate *Minnesota*, commanded landing party during assault on Fort Fisher 14 Jan 1865, screw sloop *Kearsarge* 1865-66
Later Life: LCDR 25 Jul 1865, screw sloop *Guerriere* 1867, gunboat *Quinnebaug*, gunboat *Kansas* 1869, Brooklyn Navy Yard 1869-71, Philadelphia Navy Yard, commanded pre-com crews for monitors *Canonicus* and *Saugus*, screw sloop *Brooklyn* 1874-76, screw sloop *Vandalia* 1876-77, torpedo duty 1877, CMDR Feb 1878, Philadelphia Navy Yard 1879-80, commanded gunboat *Yantic* 1881, commanded squadron including coastal monitors *Passaic*, and *Nantucket*, torpedo boat

Alarm, commanded screw sloop *Swatara* 1885-86, commanded monitor *Terror* 1888, command screw steamer *Adams* 1889-90 during Hawaiian revolution, lighthouse inspector, St. Lawrence River, Lakes Ontario and Eire and Niagara River, 1892-93, ret. 3 Jul 1893
Affiliations: MOLLUS (#01825)
Married: 9 Aug 1866, Mary Elizabeth Hawley
Died: 22 Feb 1894, Saratoga Springs NY; interment in Greenridge Cemetery
(C&S, CLL*, EWC, GGB, LRH, ORN)

Woodward, John H. (1809-1886)

Born: 1809, Charlotte VT
Early Life: UC 1833, minister 1826-61, State Sen. 1856-57, 1860-61, pastor, Westford VT 1860
War Service: Chap. 1st VT CAV 16 Nov 1861, resgd 17 Jul 1863
Later Life: pastor, Irasburg 1864, Milton 1870-85, school super. Milton
Affiliations: Congregational
Married: Emily D. Morehouse
Died: 1886; interment unknown
Notes: known as "The Fighting Chaplin" for being in front with the men during engagements; monument in Westford is topped with statue of Woodward; Westford GAR Post #20 was named after him
(1860, 1870, 1880, HC1, WHC)

Woodward, Rollin Carlos Mallory (1820-1873)

Born: 10 Feb 1820, Castleton VT, son of Theodore and Mary (Armington) Woodward
Early Life: CMC 1842, physician Bakersfield VT 1850, St. Albans 1860
War Service: SURG, 6th VT INF, 10 Oct 61, dis/dsb 29 Oct 1861
Later Life: physician, St. Albans 1870
Affiliations: Franklin Cty MS
Married: Elizabeth (nfi)
Died: 21 Nov 1873, St. Albans VT; interment in Greenwood Cemetery
(1850, 1860, 1870, AGO, BMJ4, FSO, LCA1, RR)

Wright, George (1803-1865)

Born: 21 Oct 1803, Norwich VT, son of Roswell and Jemima (Rose) Wright
Early Life: NU 1818, USMA 1822 (24/40), 2LT 3rd US INF, 1 Jul 1822, frontier duty 1822-28, 1LT 23 Sep 1827, CPT 30 Oct 1836, 8th US INF 7 Jul 1838, Seminole War 1840-42, Bvt MAJ 15 Mar 1842, Bvt LTCOL 20 Aug 1847, Bvt COL 8 Sep 1847, Pacific Northwest 1848-55, MAJ 4th US INF 1 Jan 1848, LTCOL 3 Feb 1855, COL 9th US INF 3 Mar 1855, cmdg Northern Dist. Dept of the Pacific 1855-57, cmdg Dept of Oregon 1858-61
War Service: B.G. USV, 28 Sep 1861, cmdg Dept of the Pacific 1861-64, Bvt B.G. USA, 19 Dec 1964, shipwrecked on *Brother Jonathan* off the CA coast while on his way to assume command of the Dept of the Columbia
Died: 30 Jul 1865, at sea; interment in City Cemetery, Sacramento CA
Notes: remembered as general who had almost nothing to do with the Civil War
(FBH, FSO, FTM*, GWC, JGW)

Wright, James Edward (1839-1914)

Born: 9 Jul 1839, Montpelier VT, son of Jonathan Edwards and Fanny Wyman (Houghton) Wright
Early Life: Boston Public Latin School 1852-57, A.B. Harvard 1861, ATS
War Service: PVT Co F 44th MA INF 12 Sep 1862, SGT 16 May 1863, m/o 18 Jun 1863, Christian Commission delegate 1864

Later Life: ATS 1865, ordained Henry IL 1866, pastor Jacksonville IL 1866-69, Unitarian Pastor, Church of the Messiah, Montpelier 1869-1909, Unitarian Fellowship 1881, D.D., Harvard 1902, Dir, American Unitarian Association 1903-09, Montpelier 1910
Affiliations: Republican, Unitarian
Married: 4 Oct 1876, Julia Ann Whitney
Died: 5 Sep 1914, Montpelier VT; interment unknown
(1910, HAR, PCD, VHS16, WRC1)

Wright, Riley Erastus (1839-1930)

Born: 24 Jul 39, Westminster VT, son of Erastus and Mary A. (Fairbrother) Wright.
Early Life: Derby Acad., Green Mountain Inst, Powers' Inst., Bernardson MA, DC, MC, but left to enlist
War Service: CPT Co. H 15th VT INF 18 Sep 1862, resgd 16 Jun 1863; led militia Co. at Derby Line after St. Albans Raid.
Later Life: atty, counsel for several large corporations, judge, chief judge of Orphans Court 1897-99, numismatist
Affiliations: Republican, Mason, GAR, SPCA
Married: 11 Sep1866, Mary E. Collier
Died: Apr 1930, Baltimore MD; interment unknown
Publications: An Account of the Erection and Exercises at the Dedication of the Monument Erected and Presented to the Town of Coventry, VT. (1912)
Notes: proposed and funded CW memorial in Coventry VT, dedicated 14 Aug 1912
(DHC*, JGU)

Wright, Thomas Foster (1830-1873)

Born: 1830, Jefferson Barracks MO, son of George Wright (q.v.)
Early Life: moved to Norwich VT 1846; NU 1848, USMA 1849 (19/43); Walker filibustering expedition, Nicaragua and Honduras, 1851
War Service: 1LT and RQM 2nd CA INF 2 Oct 1861; resgd 31 Jan 1863; MAJ 6th CA INF 1 Feb 1863, 2nd CA INF 3 Oct 1864, LTCOL 23 Nov 1864, COL 6 Jan 1865, Bvt B.G. 13 Mar 1865; m/o 16 Apr 1866
Later Life: 1LT 32nd US INF 28 Jul 1866, RQM 1867-69, 12th US INF 31 Jan 1870, killed during expedition against Modoc Indians
Died: 26 Apr 1873, Lava Beds OR; interment in City Cemetery, Sacramento CA
(FAG, GWC, WAE)

Wait, Horatio L.

Walker, Aldace F.

Walton, Eliakim P.

Warner, James M.

Washburn, Peter T.

Waterman, Arba N.

Watson, Austin. H.

Wells, Edward

Weston, Edmund

Wheeler, Charles W.

Hite, Azro

Whiting, Henry

Wilcox, Henry C.

Willard, Henry A.

Woodbridge, Frederick E.

Woodbury, Urban A.

Woodward, Edwin T.

Wright, George

Wright, Riley E.

Sources Cited

1850 - Seventh Census of the United States, 1850. Washington, D.C.: NARA, 1850. M432, 1,009 Rolls.

1860 - Eighth Census of the United States, 1860. Washington, D.C.: NARA, 1860. M653, 1,438 Rolls.

1870 - Ninth Census of the United States, 1870. Washington, D.C.: NARA, 1870. M593, 1,761 Rolls.

1880 - Tenth Census of the United States, 1880. Washington, D.C.: NARA, 1880. T9, 1,454 Rolls.

1890 - Special Schedules of the Eleventh Census (1890) Enumerating Union Veterans and Widows of Union Veterans of the Civil War. Washington D.C.: NARA, 1890. M123, 118 Rolls.

1900 - Twelfth Census of the United States, 1900. Washington, D.C.: NARA, 1900. T623, 1,854 Rolls.

1910 - Thirteenth Census of the United States, 1910. Washington, D.C.: NARA, 1910. T624, 1,178 Rolls.

1920 - Fourteenth Census of the United States, 1920. Washington: NARA, 1920. T625, 2,076 Rolls.

1930 - Fifteenth Census of the United States, 1930. Washington: NARA, 1930. T626, 2,667 Rolls.

55IL - The Story of the Fifty-Fifth Regiment Illinois Volunteer Infantry in the Civil War 1861-1865. Clinton, MA: W.J. Coulter, 1887.

AAH - Humphreys, Andrew A. The Virginia Campaign of '64 and '65: The Army of the Potomac and the Army of the James. New York: Charles Scribner's Sons, 1883.

AB - Buono, Anthony. Vermont, Her Men, and the Civil War. Colchester, VT: Saint Michael's College, 1991.

ABD - Dascomb, Alfred Brooks. The Memorial Record of Waitsfield, Vermont. Montpelier, VT: Freeman Steam Printing Establishment, 1867.

ACBR - Amherst College Biographical Record, Centennial Edition, 1927, sighted at www3.amherst.edu/~rjyanco94/genealogy/acbiorecord/; Internet.

ACD - Dennis, Ann Carter, San Antonio, Texas. Family material on Henry Gray Carter, her great-grandfather.

ACH - Harmon, Artemas C. The Harmon Genealogy Comprising all Branches in New England. Washington, DC: Gibson Bros., 1920.

ADA - Ayling, Augustus D. Revised Register of the Soldiers and Sailors of New Hampshire in the War of the Rebellion 1861-1866. Concord, NH: Ira C. Evans, 1895.

ADG - Gaff, Alan D. On Many a Bloody Field: Four Years in the Iron Brigade. Bloomington, IL: University Press, 1999.

ADH - Hodges, Almon D. Genealogical Record of the Hodges Family of New England, Ending December 31, 1894. 3rd Edition. Boston: Frank H. Hodges, 1896.

ADH1 - Hodges, Almon D. Genealogical Record of the Hodges Family in New England. Boston: Dutton and Wentworth, 1853.

ADP - Catalogue of the Alpha Delta Phi. New York: Executive Council Alpha Delta Phi Fraternity, 1899.

ADU - Dunbar, Aaron. History of the Ninety-Third Regiment Illinois Volunteer Infantry from Organization to Muster Out. Chicago: Blakely Printing Co., 1898.

AF - Foster, Amos. The History of the Town of Putney. Ludlow, VT: A.M. Hemenway, 1884.

AFS - Stone, Arthur Fairbanks. The Vermont of Today With Its Historical Background, Attractions and People. New York: Lewis Historical Publishing Co., 1929.

AFW - Walker, Aldace F. The Vermont Brigade in the Shenandoah Valley, 1864. Burlington, VT: The Free Press Association, 1869.

AGC - Albert G. Chadwick. Soldiers' Record of the Town of St. Johnsbury, Vermont, in the War of the Rebellion, 1861-5. St. Johnsbury: C. M. Stone & Co., 1883

AGO - Adjutant General's Office Burial Records, transcribed by Vermont Commandery, SUVCW.

AGW - Wheeler, Albert Gallatin. The Genealogical and Encyclopedic History of the Wheeler Family in America. American College of Genealogy, 1914.

AHP - Powers, Amos H. The Powers Family: A Genealogical and Historical Record of Walter Power and Some his Descendants. Chicago: Fergus, 1884.

AHQ - Quint, Alonzo H. The Record of the Second Massachusetts Infantry, 1861-1865. Boston: James P. Walker, 1867

AM - MacFarlane, Andrew. Albany Medical Annals. Journal of the Alumni Association of the Albany Medical College. Albany: Weed-Parsons, 1897.

AMA1 - Transactions of the American Medical Association, Instituted 1847. Volume XVI. Philadelphia: Collins 1866.

AMB - Bridgman, A. M. A Souvenir of Massachusetts Legislators, 1901. Stoughton, MA: A. M. Bridgman, 1901.

AMH - Hemenway, Abby Maria. The Vermont Historical Gazetteer, Burlington: A. M. Hemenway, 1867 (vol. 1), 1871 (vol. 2), 1877 (vol. 3), 1882 (vol. 4)

AMM - One Thousand American Men of Mark of To-Day. Chicago: American Men of Mark, 1916.

AMT - Tuttle, Alva M. Tuttle-Tuthill Lines in America. Columbus (OH): Estel Printing, 1968.

AMT1860 - Smith, Stephen. The American Medical Times. Vol. I. July to December 1860. New York: Bailliere Brothers, 1860.

AMW - Welch, Alexander McMillan. Philip Welch of Ipswich Massachusetts 1654 and His Descendants. Richmond: William Byrd Press, 1947.

ANW - Waterman, A. N. Historical Review of Chicago and Cook County and Selected Biography. Chicago: The Lewis Publishing Co., 1908.

APM - Sanjek, Russel. American Popular Music and Its Business. New York: Oxford University Press, 1988.

APTA - Maury County APTA. Anthenaeum History. Association for the Preservation of Tennessee Antiquities, 2005; sighted at www.athenaeumrectory.com/index.php; Internet.

AR - Runte, Alfred. National Parks: The American Experience. 3rd Edition. Lincoln (NE): University Press, 1997.

AS - Shaw, Albert. The American Review of Reviews: January-June 1915. New York: Review of reviews Co., 1915.

ASR - Roe, Alfred S. The Tenth Regiment Massachusetts Volunteer Infantry 1861-1864. Springfield, MA: Tenth Regiment Veteran Associations, 1909.

ATA - Andreas, A. T. History of Chicago from the Earliest Period to the Present Time. Chicago: A. A. Andreas, 1886.

ATS - Andover Theological Seminary. Necrology, 1902-1903. Boston: The Everett Press Co., 1903.

AW - Woodbury, Augustus. Major General Ambrose E. Burnside and the Ninth Army Corps: A Narrative of Campaigns. Providence: Sidney S. Rider, 1867.

AWB - Brayley, Arthur W. History of the Granite Industry of New England. Boston: E.L. Grimes Co., 1913.

AWE - Welles, Albert. History of the Buell Family in England ... and in America, from Town, Parish, Church, and Family Records. New York: Society Library, 1881.

AWH - Hafner, Arthur Wayne. Directory of Deceased American Physicians, 1804-1929. Chicago: American Medical Association, 1993.

AWS - Spencer, Arthur W. The Green Bag; An Entertaining Magazine for Lawyers. Boston: The Riverdale Press, 1909.

B&C - Baldwin, John Denison and William Clift. A Record of the Descendants of Capt. George Denison of Stonington, Conn. Worcester: Tyler & Seagrave, 1881.

B&K - Beyer and Keydel. Deeds of Valor: How American's Civil War Heroes Won the Congressional Medal of Honor. Stamford CT: Longmeadow Press, 1992.

B&V - Brockett, L. P. and Mary C. Vaughan. Woman's work in the Civil War: A Record. Philadelphia: Zeigler, McCurdy Co., 1867.

B1893 - Burlington City Directory for 1893. Burlington: L.P. Waite & Co., 1893.

BAAM – Bulletin of the American Academy of Medicine, Vol. 1, January 1891, to April 1895, Easton, PA: Chemical Publishing Co., 1895.

BBObit - Obituary extracted from the Bennington Banner.

BDAC - Biographical Directory of the American Congress, 1774-1949. Washington: GPO, 1950.

BEO - The Biographical Encyclopedia of Ohio of the Nineteenth Century. Columbus: Galaxy Publishing, 1876.

BFB - Butler, Benjamin F. Autobiography and Personal Reminiscences of Major General Benjamin F. Butler: Butler's Book. Boston: A.M. Thayer & Co., 1892.

BFG - Gue, Benjamin F. History of Iowa: From the Earliest Times to the Beginning of the Twentieth Century. New York: The Century History Co., 1903.

BFP - Prescott, Benjamin F. History of the Classes, 1856, Dartmouth College. Concord, NH: Republican Press Association, 1888.

BHR - Biographical and Historical Record of Greene and Carroll Counties, Iowa. Chicago: Lewis Publishing Co., 1887

BIA - Ballou, Adin. An Elaborate History and Genealogy of the Ballous in America. Providence, RI: E.L. Freeman & Son, 1888.

BMJ1 - Smith, J.V.C. The Boston Medical and Surgical Journal. Vol. XXVII. Boston: D. Clapp, 1843.

BMJ2 - Moreland, W.W. The Boston Medical and Surgical Journal. Volume LVII. Boston: David Clapp, 1858.

BMJ3 - The Boston Medical and Surgical Journal. Volume CIII, July-December 1880. Boston: Houghton, Mifflin & Co., 1880.

BMJ4 - Smith, J.V.C. The Boston Medical and Surgical Journal. XXV. Boston: D. Clapp Jr., 1842.

BMJ5 - Collins, Warren, J. and Thomas Dwight. The Boston Medical and Surgical Journal. XCVII. July-December 1887. Boston: H. O. Houghton & Co., 1877.

BML - Baxter Memorial Library, Rutland VT

BOS - One Hundred and Fiftieth Anniversary of the Settlement of Boscawen and Webster, Merrimack Co., NH, August 16, 1883. Concord NH: Republican Press, 1884.

BOWDCat - General Catalogue of Bowdoin College and the Medical School of Maine 1794-1912. Brunswick, ME: published by the college, 1912.

BPP - Poore, Ben. Perley. The Political Register and Congressional Directory. Boston: Houghton, Osgood and Co., 1878.

BrownCat - Historical Catalogue of Brown University, Providence, R.I., 1764-1894. Providence: P. S. Remington, 1895.

BS - Shurtleff, Benjamin. Descendants of William Shurtleff of Plymouth and Marshfield, Massachusetts. Revere, MA: unknown, 1912.

BSObit – Obituary extracted from the Baltimore (MD) Sun

BT - Thayer, Bezaleel. Memorial of the Thayer Name, from the Massachusetts Colony of Weymouth and Braintree. Oswego, NY: R. J. Oliphant, 1874.

BWD - Dwight, Benjamin W. The history of the Descendants of Elder John Strong of Northampton, Mass. Albany, NY: Joel Munsell, 1871.

BYU - Bulletin of Yale University, First Series, No. 5, July, 1905. New Haven, CT: Yale University, 1905.

C&S – Carroon, Robert G. and Dana B. Shoaf. Union Blue: The History of the Military Order of the Loyal Legion of the United States. Shippensburg, PA: White Mane, 2001.

CAB - The National Cyclopaedia of American Biography. New York: James T. White, 1896.

CAW - Walworth, Clarence A. The Walworths of America. Albany, NY: Weed-Parsons Printing Co., 1897.

CB - Biographical Directory of the United States Congress 1774-Present; sighted at bioguide.congress.gov/biosearch/biosearch.asp; Internet.

CCC - Coffin, Charles Carleton. Stories of our Soldiers: War Reminiscences, by "Carleton," and by Soldiers of New England. Boston: The Journal Newspaper Co., 1893.

CCI - The Biographical Record of Clinton County, Iowa. Chicago: S. J. Clarke Publishing Co., 1901.

CCM - Biographical Review: Leading Citizens of Cumberland County Maine.Boston: Biographical Review Publishing Co., 1896.

CCPL - U.S. Mexican War, The Zachary Taylor Encampment in Corpus Christi, 1845-1846. Corpus Christi Public Libraries, 2004; sited at www.library.ci.corpus-christi.tx.us/MexicanWar/alvordb.htm; Internet.

CDC - Cowles, Calvin Duvall. The War of Rebellion: A Compilation of the Official Records of the Union and Confederate Armies. Washington: GPO, 1894.

CE – The Catholic Encyclopedia and Its Makers. New York: The Encyclopedia Press, Inc., 1917.

CEA - Allen, Charles E. Burlington, Vermont Statistics: 1763-1893. Burlington: Free Press Association, 1992.

CEF - Fonvielle, Chris Eugene. The Wilmington Campaign: Last Rays of Departing Hope. Mechanicsburg, PA: Stackpole Books, 2001.

CF - Fitch, Charles Elliot. Encyclopedia of New York. Boston: American Historical Society, 1916.

CFG - Goss, Charles Frederic. The Queen City, 1788-1912. Chicago: S. J. Clarke Publishing Co., 1912.

CGP - Pringle, Cyrus Guernsey. The Record of a Quaker Conscience, Cyrus Pringle's Diary. New York: The McMillan Co., 1918.

CHH - Hayden, Chauncey H. et al. The History of Jericho Vermont. Burlington, VT: Free Press Printing Co., 1916.

CKG - Gardner, Charles K. A Dictionary of all Officers, Who Have Been Commissioned, or Have Been Appointed and Served, in the Army of the United States, Since the Inauguration of their First President in 1789, to the First January, 1853. New York: G.P. Putnam and Co., 1853.

CL - Lanman, Charles. The Red Book of Michigan; A Civil, Military and Biographical History. Detroit: E.B. Smith Co., 1871.

CLK - Kenner, Charles L. Buffalo Soldiers and Officers of the Ninth Cavalry, 1867-1898, Black and White Together. Norman: University of Oklahoma Press, 1999.

CLL - Companions of the Military Order of the Loyal Legion of the United States. New York: L. R. Hamersly Co., 1901.

CLS - Skinner, Mrs. C. L. F. The Universalist Register... for 1880. Boston: Universalist Publishing House, 1880.

CMS - Transactions of the Medical Society of the State of California, during the years 1874 and 1875. Sacramento: H. S. Crocker & Co., 1875.

COM - Cyclopedia of Michigan, Historical and Biographical: Compromising a Synopsis of General History of the State and Biographical Sketches of Men Who Have, in Their various Spheres, Contributed Toward its Development. New York: Western Publishing & Engraving Co., 1890.

CPT - Thayer, Charles P. The Vermont Medical Register for the year 1877. Burlington: Free Press Printing House, 1877.

CSW - Woodruff, Caroline S. Charles Edward Putney: An Appreciation. Charles E. Putney Memorial Pub., 1920.

CWB - Bowen, Clarence Winthrop. The History of Woodstock, Connecticut. Norwood, MA: Plimpton Press, 1930.

CZ - Ziller, Carl. History of Sheboygan County Wisconsin Past and Present. Chicago: S.J. Clarke Publishing Co., 1912.

DA - Atwater, Dorence. A List of the Union Soldiers Buried at Andersonville. Copied from the Official Record in the Surgeon's Office at Andersonville. New York: Tribune Association, 1866.

DAB - Johnson, Allen and Dumas Malone. Dictionary of American Biography; New York: Charles Scribner's Sons, 1958.

DAR1 - Lineage Book (vol. 35). Washington, DC: Daughters of the American Revolution, 1912.

DAR2 - Lineage Book (vol. 59). Washington, DC: Daughters of the American Revolution, 1922.

DAR3 - Lineage Book (vol. 88). Washington, DC: Daughters of the American Revolution, 1926.

DAR4 - Lineage Book (vol. 87). Washington, DC: Daughters of the American Revolution, 1926.

DBEK - Kent, Dorman B. E. One Thousand Men. Montpelier, VT: Vermont Historical Society, 1915.

DBK - Kent, Dorman B. E. and Michael R. Doyle. Events of This Day: Facts of Interest to Montpelier Folks Briefly Told. iUniverse, 2005.

DC63 - Scales, John, A Series of Biographical Sketches of the Class of 1863, in Dartmouth College, privately published, 1883.

DCCat - General Catalogue of Dartmouth College and The Associated Institutions. Hanover, NH: Dartmouth College, 1890.

DCCat2 - Dartmouth College, General Catalogue, 1769-1940. Dartmouth College Publications. 1940.

DCI - The History of Dubuque County Iowa, Containing a History of the County, its Cities, Towns Etc. Chicago: Western Historical Co., 1880.

DCN - Dartmouth College Necrology, Hanover, NH: Dartmouth Press, various years, 1899 through 1913.

DFG - Twenty-Fourth Biennial Report of the Department of Fisheries and Game State of Vermont from June 30, 1916 to Jun 30, 1918. Rutland: Tuttle Co., 1918

DFS - Secomb, Daniel F. History of the Town of Amherst, Hillsborough County, New Hampshire. Concord, NH: Evans, Sleeper and Woodbury, 1883.

DH - Hurd, D. Hamilton. History of Essex, County, Massachusetts. Philadelphia: J.W. Lewis, 1888.

DH1 - Hurd, D. Hamilton. History of Middlesex County, Massachusetts. Philadelphia: J.W. Lewis, 1890.

DH2 - Hurd, D. Hamilton. History of Plymouth, County, Massachusetts. Philadelphia: J.W. Lewis, 1884.

DHB - Bates, David Homer. "Lincoln in the Telegraph Office." The Century: Illustrated Monthly Magazine, vol. vxxiv, May to October 1907. New York: The Century Co., 1907.

DHB2 - "Daniel Harmon Brush," History of the First Presbyterian Church of Carbondale, Illinois, sighted at www.firstprescdale.org/html/history/history14.html; Internet.

DHC - Carroll, David H. and Thomas G. Boggs. Men of Mark in Maryland. Baltimore: B.F. Johnson, Inc., 1911.

DKECat - Catalogue of the Delta Kappa Epsilon Fraternity. New York: Council Publishing Co., 1900.

DLT - Thrapp, Dan L. Encyclopedia of Frontier Biography. Lincoln, NE: University Press, 1991.

DNP - Patterson, David Nelson. A Necrology of the Physicians of Lowell and Vicinity, 1826-1898. Lowell, MA: Courier-Citizen Co., 1992.

DPF - Catalogue of the Delta Psi Fraternity of the University of Vermont, 1850-1896. Glens Falls, N.Y.: C. H. Possons. 1896.

DUCat - The Delta Upsilon Decennial Catalogue. Publ. by the Fraternity 1902.

DUCat1 - Bevan, Lynne J. and W. H. Dannat Pell. Catalogue of Delta Upsilon 1917. Delta Upsilon Fraternity, Inc., 1917.

DUCat2 - Chase, William Shaefe. The Delta Upsilon Qiunquennial Catalogue. Boston: Rockwell Churchill Press, 1884.

DWS – Duprey, William R. Descendants of William Start. FamilyTreeMaker Online, sighted at familytreemaker.genealogy.com/users/d/u/p/William-R-Duprey-CT/ODT1-0005.html; Internet.

DWV - Card Records of Headstones Provided for Deceased Union Civil War Veterans, 1879-1903. Quartermaster General Records, NARA, Record Group 92, Washington, D.C.

E&E - Eicher, John H. and David J. Eicher, Civil War High Commands. Stanford, CA: University Press, 2001.

EA - The Encyclopedia Americana. New York: Encyclopedia Americana Corporation, 1918.

EBC - Crane, Ellery Bicknell. Historic Homes and Institutions and Genealogical and Personal Memoirs of Worcester County Massachusetts. New York: Lewis Publishing, 1907.

EBQ - Quiner, E. B. The Military History of Wisconsin. Chicago: Clarke & Co., 1866.

EC - Child, Elias. Genealogy of the Child, Childs and Childe Families, Of the Past and Present in the United States and the Canadas, from 1630 to 1881. Utica, NY: Curtiss & Childs, 1881.

EED - Dana, Elizabeth Ellery. The Dana Family in America. Boston: Wright & Potter, 1956.

EFP - Palmer, Edwin Franklin. The Second Brigade: or, Camp Life. Montpelier, VT: E. P. Walton, 1864.

EH - Holcomb, Edward. Recollections and Sketches of Notable Lawyers and Public Men of Early Iowa. Des Moines: Homestead Publishing, 1916.

EHC - Hoffman, Elliot. History of the First Vermont Cavalry Volunteers in the War of the Great Rebellion. Baltimore: Butternut and Blue, 2000.

EHN - Newton, Ephraim H. The History of the Town of Marlborough Windham Count Vermont. Montpelier, VT: Vermont Historical Society, 1930.

EHR - In memory of Edward Hastings Ripley, November 11, 1839-September 14, 1915. Military Order of the Loyal Legion of the United States. New York, 1915.

EJW - Warner, Ezra J. Generals in Blue. Baton Rouge: Louisiana State University Press, 1992.

ELH - Heintz, Edward Louis. Catalogue of Alpha Kappa Kappa Fraternity. Chicago, 1909.

EMB - Bliss, Edwin Munsell. The Encyclopaedia of Missions. New York: Funk & Wagnalls, 1891.

EMH - Haynes, Edwin Mortimer. A History of the Tenth Regiment, Vermont Volunteers. Rutland: Tuttle Co., 1894.

EML - Lovejoy, Evelyn M. Wood. History of Royalton, Vermont with Family Genealogies 1769-1911. Burlington: Free Press Printing, 1911.

ERH - Harlan, Edgar R. The Annals of Iowa, A Historical Quarterly. Des Moines: Historical Department of Iowa, 1912.

ESS - Stearns, Ezra S. Genealogical and Family History of the State of New Hampshire. New York: The Lewis Publishing Co., 1908.

ETF - Fairbanks, Edward T. The Town of St. Johnsbury, VT: A Review of One-Hundred Twenty-Five Years, to the Anniversary Pageant, 1912. St. Johnsbury, VT: Cowles Press, 1992.

EWC - Callahan, Edward W. List of Officers of the Navy of the United States and of the Marine Corps from 1775 to 1900. New York, L. R. Hamersly & Co., 1901.

EWL - Lovejoy, Evelyn M. Wood. History of Royalton, Vermont with Family Genealogies 1769-1911. Burlington: Free Press Printing Co., 1911.

EWL2 - Leavenworth, Elias Warner. A Genealogy of the Leavenworth Family in the United States with Historical Introduction. Syracuse: S. G. Hitchcock & Co., 1873.

EWR - Rolfe, Eugene William, Diaries and correspondence (1864-1865); family collection; sighted at vermontcivilwar.org/units/ar/rolfe.php; Internet.

FAG – "Find A Grave," sighted at www.findagrate.com; Internet.

FBH - Heitman, Francis B. Historical Register and Dictionary of the United States Army. Washington: GPO, 1903.

FCB - The Hundredth Anniversary of the Founding of the First Church of Burlington, VT: February Twenty-Third to Twenty-Sixth, 1905. Burlington: The Church, 1905.

FEB - Blake, Francis E. Increase Blake of Boston: his Ancestors and Descendants: with a Full Account of William Blake of Dorchester and his Five Children. Boston: D. Clapp, 1898

FGF - Fleetwood, Frederick G. Vermont Legislative Directory, Biennial Session, 1902.

FGW – Wickware, Francis G. The American Yearbook, a Record of Events and Progress 1912. New York: D. Appleton and Co., 1913.

FHB - Brown, Francis H. Harvard University in the War of 1861-1865. Boston: Cupples, Upham and Co., 1886.

FHC - Churchill, Franklin Hunter. Sketch of the Life of Bvt. Brig. Gen. Sylvester Churchill, Inspector General U.S. Army, with Notes and Appendices. New York: Willis McDonald, 1888.

FHD - Dyer, Frederick H. A Compendium of the War of the Rebellion, 1861-1865. Dayton, OH: Morningside, 1979.

FHEObit – Obituary extracted from the Fair Haven Era

FLB - Byrne, Frank L. and Andrew T. Weaver. Haskell of Gettysburg. Kent State University Press, 1989.

FLR – Riley, Franklin L. Publications of the Mississippi Historical Society. Oxford, MS: Mississippi Historical Society, 1902.

FOH - Berolzheimer, Alan "Finding Martha," The Flow of History, Spring 2006, sighted at www.flowofhistory.org/pdf/fohspring06.pdf; Internet.

FP - Phisterer, Frederick. New York in the War of the Rebellion 1861 to 1865. Albany: Weed, Parsons and Co., 1890.

FPF - Foster, Frank P. The New York Medical Journal. LXV, January to June, 1897. New York: D. Appleton and Co., 1897.

FPW - Wells, Frederic P. History of Barnet, Vermont: from the Outbreak of the French and Indian War to Present Time. Burlington: Free Press Printing, 1923.

FR – Rhoads, Samuel (ed.). Friends Review: A Religious, Literary and Miscellaneous Journal. Philadelphia: Merrihew & Son, 1864.

FRUS - Papers Relating to the foreign relations of the United States, transmitted to Congress with the annual Message of the President, December 1, 1873. Part II, Volume III. Washington: GPO, 1874.

FSO – Family Search, An official Web site of The Church of Jesus Christ of Latter-day Saints, sighted at www.familysearch.org; Internet.

FTM - Miller, Francis Trevelyan. The Photographic History of the Civil War. New York: The Reviews of Reviews, Co., 1911.

FWB - Blackmar, Frank W. Kansas: A Cyclopedia of State History. Chicago: Standard Publishing Co., 1912.

FWJ - Johnson, Frank W. A History of Texas and Texans. Chicago: American Historical Society, 1914.

FWS – Scott, Franklin William. Newspapers and Periodicals of Illinois 1814-1879. Chicago: R. R. Donnelley, 1910.

G&P - Goddard, M. E. and Henry V. Partridge. A History of Norwich Vermont. Hanover, NH: The Dartmouth Press, 1905.

GAD - Davis, Gilbert A. Centennial Celebration, Together with an Historical Sketch of Reading, Windsor County, Vermont. Bellows Falls, VT: A.N. Swain, 1874.

GAR54 - Journal of the Fifty-Fourth National Encampment Grand Army of the Republic Indianapolis, IND. September 19 to 25, 1920. Washington: GPO, 1921.

GARM - Journal of the Thirty-Second Annual Encampment Department of Massachusetts, Grand Army of the Republic, Tremont Temple, Boston, Mass., February 8 and 9, 1898. Boston: E. B. Stillings & Co., 1898.

GARM2 - Journal of the Thirtieth Annual Encampment, Department of Massachusetts, Grand Army of the Republic. Boston: B. Stillings & Co., 1896.

GBA - Anderson, George Baker. Our County and its People: a Descriptive and Biographical Record of Saratoga County, New York. Boston: Boston History Co., 1899.

GBH - Harrington, George B. Past and Present of Bureau County, Illinois. Chicago: Pioneer Publishing, 1906.

GC - Chandler, George. The Chandler Family, the Descendants of William and Annis Chandler, who Settled in Roxbury, Mass.. Worcester, MA: Charles Hamilton, 1883.

GEP - Parks, G. Elton. Sexennial Record of the Class of 1904 Yale College. New Haven: University Press, 1911.

GFH - Hiram Carleton. Genealogical and Family History of the State of Vermont. New York: Lewis Publishing Co., 1903.

GFS - Shrady, George F. Medical Record: A Weekly Journal of Medicine and Surgery (vol. 60). New York: William Wood, 1901.

GG - Grow, Gerald. Milo Grow: Letters from the Civil War. Longleaf Publications, sighted at www.longleaf.net/milo/index.html; Internet.

GGB - Benedict, George Grenville. Vermont in the Civil War. Burlington: The Free Press, 1888.

GGK - Kane, George G. Grand Army of the Republic Collection, Vermont Commandery.

GJU - Urwin, Gregory J.W. Custer Victorious: The Civil War Battles of George Armstrong Custer. Lincoln, NE: University Press, 1990.

GNC - Carpenter, George N. History of the Eighth Regiment Vermont Volunteers, 1861-1865. Boston: Deland & Barta, 1886.

GNK - Kreider, George N. Illinois Medical Journal. July to December, 1906, Springfield, Ill.

GOC - General Orders and Circulars, Adjutant General's Office 1893. Washington: GPO, 1894.

GRB - Brush, George Robert. St. James Episcopal Church Arlington, Vermont: Privately Printed, 1941.

GSM - "Necrology." The Granite Monthly. A New Hampshire Magazine. XXVI, January-June 1899. Concord, NH: Granite Monthly Co., 1899.

GTC - Chapman, George Thomas. Sketches of the Alumni of Dartmouth College: From the First Graduation in 1771 to the Present Time, with a Brief History of the Institution. Cambridge: Riverside, 1867.

GVH - Henry, Guy V. Military Record of Civilian Appointments in the United States Army. New York: D. Van Nostrand, 1873.

GWC - Cullum, George W. Biographical Register of the Officers and Graduates of the U.S. Military Academy at West Point, NY. from its Establishment, in 1802 to 1890. Boston: Houghton, Mifflin and Co., 1891.

GWC1 - Cullum, George W.. Biographical Register of the Officers and Graduates of the U.S. Military Academy at West Point, N.Y. From Its Establishment, in 1802. (Supplement, Volume V, 1900-1910), Saginaw, Mich.: Sermann and Peters, Printers, 1910.

GWC2 - Chapin, Gilbert Warren. The Chapin Book of Genealogical Data: Eighth to Twelfth Generations. 1924.

GWF - Fuller, George W. Descendants of Thomas Stoughton (1600-1661): of Dorchester Mass. Potsdam (NY): Herald-Recorder Press, 1998.

GWH - Hilton, George Woodman. American Narrow Gauge Railroads. Stanford: Stanford University Press, 1990.

H&D - Hubbard, C. Horace and Justus Dartt. History of the Town of Springfield, Vermont: with a Genealogical Record 1752-1895. Boston: Geo. H. Walker & Co., 1895.

HAK - Kelly, Howard Atwood. A Cyclopedia of American Medical Biography. Philadelphia: W. B. Saunders Co., 1912.

HAR - 1861-1892, Fifth Report: Harvard College Class of 1861. New York: 1892.

HBD - Davis, Helen Burns. Life of Cyrus Guernsey Pringle. UVM, 1936; sighted at www.uvm.edu/~plantbio/pringle/pringlebio.html; Internet.

HC - Copee, Henry. Grant and His Campaigns: A Military Biography. New York: Charles B. Richardson, 1866.

HC1 - Child, Hamilton. Gazetteer and Business Directory of Chittenden County, Vermont for 1882-83. Syracuse: H. Child, 1882.

HC2 - Child, Hamilton. Gazetteer and Business Directory of Lamoille and Orleans County, VT for 1883-84. Syracuse: Journal Office, 1883.

HC3 - Child, Hamilton. Gazetteer of Orange County, VT 1762-1888. Syracuse: H. Child, 1888.

HC4 - Child, Hamilton. Gazetteer of Washington County, Vt. 1783-1899. Syracuse: Journal Co., 1889.

HC5 - Child, Hamilton. Gazetteer and Business Directory of Windsor County, VT for 1883-84. Syracuse: H. Child, 1884.

HC6 - Child, Hamilton. Gazetteer and Business Directory of Caledonia and Essex Counties, 1764-1887. Syracuse: H. Child, 1887.

HC7 - Child, Hamilton. Gazetteer and Business Directory of Windham County, 1724-1884. Syracuse: Journal Office, 1884.

HCAS - Casson, Henry. The Blue Book of the State of Wisconsin. Milwaukee: Henry Gugler Co., 1895.

HCC - Campbell, Henry Colin. Wisconsin in Three Centuries, 1634-1905. New York: The Century History Co., 1906.

HDCAT - General Catalogue of the Divinity School of Harvard University, 1915. Cambridge: University Press, 1915.

HDW - History of De Witt County, Illinois with Illustrations, Description of the Scenery, and Biographical Sketches ..., Philadelphia: W.R. Bring, 1882.

HEN - Noyes, Henry E. and Harriette E. Noyes. Genealogical Record of Some of The Noyes Descendants of James, Nicholas and Peter Noyes. Vol. 1. Boston, 1904.

HF - Farnsworth, Harold and Robert Howard Rodgers. New Haven in Vermont, 1761-1983. Published by Town of New Haven, 1984.

HFA - The Huntington Family in America: A Genealogical Memoir of the Known Descendants of Simon Huntington from 1633 to 1915. Hartford: Huntington Family Assoc., 1915.

HFB - Hunting For Bears, comp. *Mississippi Marriages, 1776-1935* [database on-line]. Provo, UT, USA: The Generations Network, Inc., 2004.

HFK – Kett, Henry F. The Voters and Tax-payers of DeKalb County, Illinois. Evansville, IN: Unigraphic, 1977.

HFS - Stevens, Hiram F. History of the Bench and Bar of Minnesota. Minneapolis: Legal Publishing and Engraving Co., 1904.

HFW12 - Waters, Henry Fitz-Gilbert. The New England Historical and Genealogical Register. (Vols. 37-52, 1883-98), Boston: NEHGS, 1912.

HFW77 - Waters, Henry Fitz-Gilbert. The New England Historical and Genealogical Register for the Year 1877. Volume. XXXI. Boston: NEHGS, 1877.

HGW - Hubbell, John T., James W. Geary and Jon L. Wakelyn. Biographical Dictionary of the Union: Northern Leaders of the Civil War. Westport, CT: Greenwood Press, 1995.

HHB - Bancroft, Hubert Howe. The Builders of the Commonwealth. San Francisco: The History Co., 1892.

HHM - Metcalf, Henry Harrison. The Granite State Monthly, vol. L (XIII), Concord, NH: Granite Monthly Co., 1918

HHW - Wells, Harriett Hyde and Harry Weston Van Dyke. Several Ancestral Lies of Josiah Edson and His Wife, Sarah Pinney. Albany, NY: Joel Munsell's sons, 1901.

HKW - Willard, Henry Kellogg. "Henry Augustus Willard: His Life and Times." Records of the Columbia Historical Society Washington D.C. Volume 20. Washington, 1917.

HLA - Abbot, Henry L. Half century record of the Class at West Point 1850 to 1854. Boston, MA: T. Todd, Printer, 1900.

HLC - Conrad, Howard L. (ed.) Encyclopedia of the History of Missouri. Vol. V. New York: The Southern History Co., 1901.

HNJ - Jackson, Horatio Nelson. Dedication of the statue to Brevet Major General William Wells and the officers and men of the First regiment Vermont Cavalry, on the battlefield of Gettysburg. Privately printed, 1914.

HNW - History of Northern Wisconsin Containing an Account of its Settlement, Growth, Development, and Resources ..., Chicago: Western Historical Co., 1881.

HPS - Smith, H. P. History of Addison County Vermont. New York: D. Mason & Co., 1886.

HR2500 - Library of Congress, A Century of lawmaking for a New Nation: U.S. Congressional Documents and Debates, 1774-1875, Bills and Resolutions, House of Representatives, 42nd Congress, 2nd Session, H.R. 2500.

HRNH - Historical Register of National Homes for Disabled Volunteer Soldiers, 1866-1938; (National Archives Microfilm Publication M1749, 282 rolls); Records of the Department of Veterans Affairs, Record Group 15; National Archives, Washington, D.C.

HSB - Burrage, Henry S. Civil War Record of Brown University. Providence: 1920.

HSD - Dana, Henry Swan. History of Woodstock, Vermont. Boston: Houghton, Mifflin, 1889.

HTW - Wade, Herbert Treadwell. The New International Encyclopaedia. New York: Dodd, Mead and Co., 1930.

HWH - Hill, Henry Wayland. Municipality of Buffalo New York: A History 1720-1923. New York: Lewis Historical Publishing Co., 1923.

HWP - Palmer, Horace Wilbur. Palmer Families in America. Neshanic (NJ): Neshanic Printing Co., 1966.

HWR - Rugg, H. W. The Universalist Register: Giving Statistics of the Universalist Church, and other Denominational Information 1884. Boston: Universalist Publishing, 1884.

HWS - Stevens, Harriet Weeks. Wadhams genealogy, Preceded by a Sketch of the Wadham Family in England. New York: Frank Allaben Genealogical Co., 1913.

IA - Atwater, Isaac. History of the city of Minneapolis, Minnesota. New York: Munsell & Co., 1893.

IA15 - Information Annual 1915: A Continuous Cyclopedia and Digest of Current Events. New York: R.R. Bowker Co., 1916.

IHS - Journal of the Illinois State Historical Society. Vol. 2 No. 1, Apr 1909. Springfield: Phillips Bros., 1909.

IHSR - "Illustrated Historical Souvenier of Randolph, Vermont"; Randolph, Vt.: Nickenson & Cox, 1895.

JAB - Boutelle, John Alonzo. The Burke and Alvord Memorial: A Genealogical Account of the Descendants of Richard Burke of Sudbury, Mass. Boston: Dutton and Son, 1864.

JAH - Haskin, Joseph A., A Haskin History. Little Rock, AR: James A. Hatcher, 1981.

JAH2 - Holmes, J. Albert. "Frederick Norton Freeman, Alpha '57, Originator and One of the Founders of Theta Chi." Paper read at Troy, NY, April 10, 1915, on the fifty-ninth anniversary of the founding of the Fraternity, www.thetachi.org

JAL - Logan, Mrs. John A. The Part Taken by Women in American History. Wilmington, DE: The Parry-Nalle Publishing Co., 1912.

JAM - Marshall, John A. American Bastille. A history of the illegal Arrests and Imprisonment of American Citizens During the Late Civil War. Philadelphia: Thomas W. Hartley, 1869.

JBF - Fry, James B. The History and Legal Effect of Brevets in the Armies of Great Britain and the United States from their origin in 1692 to the Present Time. New York: D. Van Norstrand, 1877.

JC - Chapman, Jacob. Lane Genealogies... Exeter, NH: The News-letter Press, 1891.

JCR - Ridpath, John Clark. The Ridpath Library of Universal Literature. New York: The Globe Publishing Co., 1898.

JCW – Williams, J. C. The History and Map of Danby, Vermont. Rutland: McLean & Robbins, 1869.

JDM - Marshall, Jeffrey D. A War of the People: Vermont Civil War Letters. Lebanon, NH: University Press of New England, 1999

JDR - Reid, James D. The telegraph in America and Morse Memorial. New York: J. Polhemus, 1886

JEP - Journal of the Executive Proceedings of the Senate of the United States of America from March 13, 1867 to November 29, 1867, Inclusive. Vol. XV, Part II. Washington: GPO, 1887.

JF - Fitch, John. Annals of the Army of the Cumberland. Philadelphia: J. B. Lippincott & Co., 1864.

JFG - Gilmore, Jean Fairchild. Early Fairchilds in America and Their Descendants. Baltimore, MD: Gateway Press, 1991.

JG - Gray, John. Gray Genealogy. Terrytown, NY: M. D. Raymond, 1887.

JGB - Bartlett, J. Gardner. Simon Stone Genealogy: Ancestry and Descendants of Deacon Simon Stone of Watertown, Mass., 1320-1926. Boston: Pinkham Press, 1926.

JGC - Carter, Jane G. and Susie P. Holmes. Genealogical Record of the Dedham Branch of the Avery Family in America. Plymouth, MA: Press of Avery & Doten, 1893.

JGU - Ullery, Jacob G. Men of Vermont: An Illustrated Biographical History of Vermonters and Sons of Vermont. Brattleboro: Transcript Publishing Co., 1894.

JGW - Wilson, James Grant. Appletons' Cyclopaedia of American Biography. New York: D. Appleton and Company, 1901.

JHA - Aubin, J. Harris. Register of the Military Order of the Loyal Legion of the United States. Boston: Commandery of the State of Massachusetts. 1906.

JHB - Brown, John Howard. Lamb's Biographical Dictionary of the United States. Boston: James H. Lamb Co., 1900.

JHG - Goulding, J.H. Official Military and Naval Records of Rutland, Vermont, in the War of Rebellion 1861-1866. Rutland: Tuttle Co., 1891.

JHG1 - Goulding, Joseph Hiram. Memorial day address Wheelock G. Veazey as a soldier and comrade. Brattleboro: 1898., Source: UVM

JHR69 - Journal of the House of Representatives of the State of Vermont. Annual Session, 1869. Montpelier, VT: Poland's Steam Printing Establishment, 1870.

JHR77 - Journal of the House of Representatives of the State of Vermont. Biennial Session, 1876. Rutland: Tuttle & Co., 1877.

JHR80 - Journal of the House of Representatives of the State of Vermont. Biennial Session, 1880. Montpelier, VT: Freeman Steam Printing House, 1881.

JHR90 - Journal of the House of Representatives of the State of Vermont. Biennial Session, 1890. Burlington: Free Press Association, 1890.

JLK - King, James L. History of Shawnee County, Kansas and Representative Citizens. Chicago: Richmond & Arnold, 1905.

JLS - Seward, Josiah Lafayette. A History of the Town of Sullivan New Hampshire 1777-1917. Keene, NH: J.L. Seward, 1921.

JM - McClintock, Rev. John and James Strong. Cyclopaedia of Biblical, Theological, and Ecclesiastical Literature. New York: Harper & Brothers, 1889.

JMA - Aubery, James Madison. The Thirty-Sixth Wisconsin Volunteer Infantry: 1stBrigade, 2d Division, 2d Army Corp, Army of the Potomac. 1900.

JMC - Currier, John M. Memorial Exercises held in Castleton, Vermont, in the year 1885. Albany: Joel Munsell's Sons, 1885.

JMG - Guinn, James Miller. A History of California and an extended history of Los Angeles and Environs. Los Angeles, CA: Historic Record Company, 1915.

JMP - Palmer, John M. The Bench and Bar of Illinois: Historical and Reminiscent. Chicago: Lewis Publishing Co., 1899.

JOW - Williams, John Oliver. A Genealogy of the Williams Families. Brookline, MA: privately printed, 1938.

JPN - Nicholson, John Paige. Register of the Commandery of the State of Pennsylvania, April 15, 1865 - September 1, 1902. Philadelphia: John T. Palmer, 1902.

JR - Robertson, Jonathan. Michigan in the Civil War. Lansing: W. S. George & Co., 1882.

JS - James Sprunt. Chronicles of the Cape Fear River, 1660-1916. Raleigh, NC: Edwards & Broughton Printing Co., 1916.

JVS02 - Journal of the Senate of the State of Vermont. Biennial Session, 1902. Albany, NY: J. B. Lyon Company, 190e.

JVS17 - Journal of the Senate of the State of Vermont. Biennial Session, 1917 and Special Session 1916. Montpelier, VT: Capital City Press, 1917.

JVS47 – Journal of the Senate of the State of Vermont. October Session, 1847. Montpelier, VT: E. P. Walton & Sons, 1848.

JVS88 - Journal of the Senate of the State of Vermont. Biennial Session, 1888. Montpelier, VT: Argus and Patriot, 1889.

JVS90 - Journal of the Senate of the State of Vermont. Biennial Session, 1890. Burlington: Free Press Association, 1891.

JVS98 - Journal of the Senate of the State of Vermont. Biennial Session, 1898. St. Albans, VT: St. Albans Messenger Co., 1899.

JW - Willard, Joseph, Charles Wilkes Walker and Charles Henry Pope. Willard Genealogy, Sequel to Willard Memorial. Boston, MA: 1915.

JWS – Siddall, John William. Men of Hawaii. Honolulu Star-Bulletin, Ltd., Territory of Hawaii, 1917..

KC - Cuccinello, Karen. Independent Ministerial Register. New York: Independent Press, 1892, 1893, 1895 editions.

KFN - The Kimball Family News, Being Supplementary to the History of the Kimball Family in America. Topeka, KS: Gustavus F. Kimball, 1902.

KUA - Kimball Union Academy, Meriden, NH, General Catalogue 1813-1930. Hanover: Dartmouth Press, 1930.

LAA - Abbott, Lemuel Abijah. Personal Recollections and Civil War Diary, 1864. Burlington: Free Press Printing Co., 1908

LAB - Brainard, Lucy Abigail. The Genealogy of the Brainerd-Brainard Family in America 1649-1908. Vol. 1. Hartford: Hartford Press, 1908.

LAM - Morrison, Leonard Allison and Stephen Paschall Sharples. History of the Kimball Family in America, From 1634 to 1897, and of its Ancestors The Kemballs or Kemboldes of England. Boston: Damrell & Upham, 1897.

LB - Brown, Leonard. History of Whitingham: From its Organization to the Present Time. Brattleboro: F.E. Housh, 1886.

LCA1 - Aldrich, Lewis Cass. History of Franklin and Grand Isle Counties Vermont. Syracuse, NY: D. Mason & Co., 1891.

LCA2 - Aldrich, Lewis Cass and George S. Conover. History of Ontario County New York. Syracuse, NY: D. Mason & Co., 1893.

LCB - Butler, L. C. The Memorial Record of Essex, Vermont. Burlington: R. S. Styles, 1866.

LDI - Ingersoll, Lurton Dunham. Iowa and the Rebellion. Philadelphia: J. B. Lippincott & Co., 1866.

LEC1 - Chittenden, L. E. Recollections of President Lincoln and His Administration. New York: Harper & Brothers, 1904.

LEC2 - Chittenden, L. E. An Unknown Heroine: An Historical Episode of the War Between the States. New York: George H. Richmond & Co., 1894.

LFP - Parker, L. Fletcher. History of Poweshiek County Iowa. Chicago: S. J. Clarke, 1911.

LHB - Bailey, L. H. The Standard Cyclopedia of Horticulture. New York: The MacMillan Company, 1917.

LHC - Cornish, Louis H. A National Register Sons of the American Revolution. New York: Andrew H. Kellogg, 1902.

LHF - Fischer, Leroy H., "Cairo's Civil War Angel, Mary Jane Stafford." Journal of the Illinois State Historical Society, No. 54, 1961.

LHI - Irvine, Leigh H. History of the New California Its Resources and People. Vol. II. New York: The Lewis Publishing Co., 1905.

LISOC - Lambda Iota Society, University of Vermont

LMG – Gross, Lewis M. Past and Present of DeKalb County, Illinois. Chicago: Pioneer Publication Co., 1907.

LMW – Welch, Linda M. F. Unpublished biographical sketches of Dartmouth College students from school archives.

LMW3 - Welch, Linda M. F. Families of Cavendish and the black River Valley of Windsor County, Vermont, vol. 3, Cavendish Historical Society, 1998

LMW4 - Welch, Linda M. History of the Families of the Black River Valley in Southern Windsor County, Vermont, draft manuscript, 2005.

LOC – Historic American Sheet Music, 1850-1920, Duke University Collection, Library of Congress.

LOC1 – Civil War Treasures from the New York Historical Society, Library of Congress

LPB - Brockett, L. P. Men of Our Day; or Biographical Sketches of Patriots, Orators, Statesmen, Generals, Reformers, Financiers and Merchants. Philadelphia: Ziegler and McCurdy, 1872.

LRP – Paige, Lucius Robinson. History of Hardwick, Massachusetts. Boston: Houghton, Mifflin & Co., 1883.

LSH - Hayes, Lyman Simpson. History of the Town of Rockingham Vermont, including the Villages of Bellows Falls, Saxtons River, Rockingham, Cambridgeport and Bartonsville 1753-1907. Bellows Falls, Vt.: 1907.

LWK - Kingman, Leroy W. Our Country and its People: A Memorial History of Tioga County, New York. Elmira, NY: W.A. Fergusson, 1897.

LWR - Redington, Lyman Williams. Centennial Celebration of the Organization of Rutland County Vermont, Held Under the Auspices of the Rutland County Historical Society, ...Rutland Vt., March 4, 1881. Montpelier, VT: Argus & Patriot, 1882.

M1821 - National Archives. Compiled Service Records of Volunteer Union Soldiers Who Served with the United States Colored Troops: Infantry Organizations, 8th through 13th, including the 11th (new). Publication Number: M1821. (www.footnote.com)

M688 - U.S. Military Academy Cadet Application Papers, 1805-1866; (National Archives Microfilm Publication M688, 1 roll); Records of the Adjutant General's Office, 1780's-1917, Record Group 94; National Archives, Washington, D.C.

MA - The Michigan Alumnus, Vol. XXVI. October, 1919-August, 1920. Ann Arbor: Alumni Association, 1920.

MAG - Massachusetts. Adjutant General. Massachusetts Soldiers, Sailors, and Marines in the Civil War. 9 vols. Norwood: Norwood, 1931.

MAH - Holland, Mary A. Our Army Nurses: Interesting Sketches, Addresses, and Photographs of Nearly One Hundred of the Noble Women who Served in Hospitals and on Battlefields During Our Civil War. B. Wilkins & Co., 1895.

MAR - Ruiz de Burton, Maria Amparo. Conflicts of Interest: The Letters of Maria Amparo Ruiz de Burton. Houston, TX: Arte Publico Press, 2001.

MCC - Wilson, Mehitable Calef Coppenhagen. John Gibson of Cambridge, Massachusetts and His Descendants 1634-1899. Washington: McGill & Wallace, 1900.

MCR - McLellan Cemetery Records (Clinton Cty, N.Y.), Plattsburg, N.Y. Public Library.

MCW - Board of Commissioners. Minnesota in the Civil and Indian Wars, 1861-1865. St. Paul: Pioneer Press Company, 1899.

MDB - Bisbee, Marvin Davis. Dartmouth College: Necrology 1910-11. Hanover: Dartmouth Press, 1911.

MDE - Edwards, Maurice Dwight. Richard Edwards and his wife Catherine Pond May: Their Ancestors Lives and Descendants. St. Paul: Webb Publishing Co., 1931.

MDG - Gilman, Marcus Davis. The Bibliography of Vermont, or A List of Books and Pamphlets Relating in Any Way to the State. Burlington: Free Press Association, 1897.

MDNYC03 - Medical Directory of the City of New York. 1903. Medical Society of the County of New York, 1905.

MDR - Raymond, M.D. Gray Genealogy: Being a Genealogical Record and History of the Descendants of John Gray, of Beverly, Mass. Tarrytown NY, 1887.

MDS - Shutter, Marion Daniel. History of Minneapolis: Gateway to the Northwest. Minneapolis: S. J. Clarke Publishing Co., 1932.

ME72 - Minutes of the Annual Conferences of the Methodist Episcopal Church for the year 1872. New York: Nelson & Phillips, 1872.

MG - Grossman, Mark. Political Corruption in America: An Encyclopedia of Scandals, Power, and Greed. Santa Barbara, CA: ABC-CLIO, 2003.

MHS - Minnesota Historical Society: Eighteenth Biennial Report for the Years 1913 and 1914. Saint Paul (MN): Minnesota Historical Society, 1915.

MIDCat - Wiley, Edgar J. Catalogue of the Officers and Students of Middlebury College in Middlebury, Vermont ... 1800-1915. Middlebury College, 1917.

MIDCat2 - Robinson, Duane L. General Catalogue of Middlebury College, Middlebury: Publications Department of Middlebury College. 1950.

MIDCat3 - Boyce, Thomas E. Catalogue of the Officers and Alumni of Middlebury College in Middlebury, Vermont, 1800 to 1889. Middlebury: Register Company, 1890.

MJP – Pollard, Maurice J. The History of the Pollard family of America. Dover, NH: M. J. Pollard, 1961.

MK - King, Moses. Notable New Yorkers 1896-1899. New York: The Orr Press, 1899.

MLO – Olcott, Mary Louise Beatrice. The Olcotts and Their Kindred: from Anglo-Saxon times through Roncesvalles to Gettysburg and After. New York: National Americana Publications, 1956

MMB - Boatner, Mark Mayo. The Civil War Dictionary. New York: Vintage, 1991.

MMS - Medical Communications of the Massachusetts Medical Society. vol. viii. Boston, for the society, 1854.

MNCensus - Minnesota Historical Society. Minnesota State Population Census Schedules, 1865-1905. St. Paul, MN, USA: Minnesota Historical Society, 1977. Microfilm.

MNH - Carter, N. F. The Native Ministry of New Hampshire: The Harvesting of more than Thirty Years. Concord, NH: Rumford Printing, 1906.

MOC - Cyclopedia of Eminent and Representative Men of the Carolinas of the Nineteenth Century. Vol. 1. Madison (WI): Brant & Fuller, 1892.

MOHR - Medal of Honor Recipients, 1863-1978. 96th Congress, 1st Session, Senate Committee Print No. 3. Prepared by the Committee on Veterans' Affairs, United States Senate. Washington: GPO, 1979.

MOLLUS - Military Order of the Loyal Legion of the United States, Headquarters Commandery of the State of Vermont. Circular No. 3, Series of 1913. Burlington, Vt., May 1, 1913.

MOMM - Men of Mark in Maryland. Johnson's Makers of America Series; Biographies of Leading Men of the State. Volume IV. Baltimore: B. F. Johnson, Inc., 1912.

MRC - Cabot, Mary Rogers. Annals of Brattleboro, 1681-1895. Brattleboro: E. L. Hildreth & Co., 1922.

MTC - Minutes of the Tory Annual Conference of the Methodist Episcopal Church held in Gloversville, NY Apr 14-19, 1909. New York: Eaton & Maines, 1909.

NAR - The National Almanac and Annual Record for the Year 1864. Philadelphia: George W. Childs, 1864.

NAS - Strait, N. A. Roster of all Regimental Surgeons and Assistant Surgeons in the late war. Washington, DC: United States Pension Office, 1882.

NEB - Boone, Nancy E. and Michael Sherman. "Designed to Cure: Civil War Hospitals in Vermont" Vermont History, Vol. 69, Winter/Spring 2001, pp. 173-200.

NFC - Gregory, John. Northfield's First Century: Centennial Proceedings and Historical Incidents Of the Early Settlers of Northfield, VT. Montpelier, VT: Argus and Patriot, 1878.

NIH - National Institutes of Health, National Library of Medicine. "Finding Aid to the Sloan U.S. Army Hospital Records, 1857-1866." sighted at www.nlm.nih.gov/hmd/manuscripts/ead/sloan.html; Internet.

NPS - National Park Service, www.nps.gov/; Internet.

NSF - Frost, Norman Seaver. Frost Genealogy in Five Families. West Newton, MA: Frost Family Association, 1926.

NSR - Richardson, N.S. The American Quarterly Church Review, and Ecclesiastical Register. New York: N.S. Richardson, 1867.

NYAG - Annual Report of the Adjutant-General of the State of New York For the Year 1903. Serial No. 35. Albany: Oliver A. Quayle, 1904.

NYHObit – New York Herald obituary

NYL - New York Legislature. Report of the Adjutant-General. 32 vols. Albany: Argus, 1895-1906.

NYL1 - New York Legislature. New York in the War of the Rebellion. 6 vols. 3rd ed. Albany: Lyon, 1912.

NYMS78 - Transactions of the Medical Society of the State of New York for the Year 1878. Syracuse: Truair, Smith & Bruce, 1878.

NYTObit – Obituary extracted from the New York Times Online

OAR - Official Army Register for 1868. Washington: Adjutant General's Office, 1868.

OAR80 – Official Army Register for 1880. Washington: Adjutant General's Office, 1880.

OFW - Waite, Otis Frederick Reed. Vermont in the Great Rebellion. Claremont, NH: Tracy, Chase, 1869.

OGH - Quinquennial Catalogue of the Officers and Graduates of Harvard University 1636-1915. Cambridge: University Press, 1915.

OLC - Oread Literary Club. History of the Town of Johnson, Vt. 1784-1907. Burlington: Free Press Printing Co., 1907.

ORN - Naval War Records Office. Official Records of the Union and Confederate Navies in the War of the Rebellion. Washington, D.C.: GPO, 1894-1922. 1987 reprint.

PA - Passport Applications: 1795-1905. Washington, D.C.: National Archives, General Records of the Department of State, Record Group 59.

PAH - Hazelton, Philip A. Descendants of Stephen Hazelton. Littleton, NH: Courier Printing, 1977.

PCD - Dodge, Prentiss C. Encyclopedia Vermont Biography. Burlington: Ullery Publishing Co., 1912.

PDW - Watson, Peter D. et al. A History of Greensboro The First Two Hundred Years. Greensboro VT: Greensboro Historical Society, 1990.

PEC - Journal of the Proceedings of the One Hundred and Fifth Annual Convention of the Protestant Episcopal Church in the Diocese of New Hampshire. Concord, NH: Rumford, 1906.

PGZ - Zeller, Paul G. The Second Vermont Volunteer Infantry Regiment 1861-1865. Jefferson (NC): McFarland & Co., 2002.

PK - Kelley, Phyllis. Sycamore. Arcadia Publishing, 2007.

PL - Loatman, Paul. "Seeing the Light." History of the City of Mechanicville. Sighted at www.mechanicville.com/; Internet.

PSS - Presidents, Soldiers, Statesmen. New York: H. H. Hardesty, 1895.

PTW - Washburn, Peter T. Report of the Adjutant & Inspector General of the State of Vermont from Oct. 1, 1864, to Oct. 1, 18655. Montpelier, VT: Walton's Steam Printing, 1865.

RCS89 - Reports of Committees of the Senate of the United States for the Second Session of the Fiftieth Congress. 1888-'89. Washington: GPO, 1889.

RHObit – Obituary extracted from the Rutland Herald.

RJ - Johnson, Rossiter and John Howard Brown. The Twentieth Century Biographical Dictionary of Notable Americans. Boston: The Biographical Society, 1904.

RJM - Meigs, Return Jonathan. Record of the Descendants of Vincent Meigs who Came from Dorsetshire, England, to America about 1635...Who Came from Dorsetshire, England, to America about 1635. 2nd Edition (1st Ed. by Henry Benjamin Meigs). Baltimore: John S. Bridges & Co., 1935.

RJT - Titterton, Robert J. Julian Scott Artist of the Civil War and Native America. Jefferson, NC: McFarland & Co., 1997.

RLO - Records of Living Officers of the United States Army. Philadelphia: L.R. Hamersly & Co., 1884.

RMB - Bashford, R.M. Legislative Manual of the State of Wisconsin, Sixteenth Annual Edition. Madison: R. R. Bolens, 1877.

RMS - Seeds, Russell M. (Ed) History of the Republican Party of Indiana: Biographical Sketches of the Party Leaders. Vol. 1. Indianapolis: Indiana History Co., 1899.

ROS - Sturtevant, Ralph Orson and Carmi Lathrop Marsh. Pictorial History: Thirteenth Regiment Vermont Volunteers War of 1861-1865. Published by the regiment, c1910. Modern reprint.

RR - Vermont. Adjutant and Inspector General's Office. Revised Roster of Vermont volunteers and lists of Vermonters Who Served in the Army and Navy of the United Sates During the War of the Rebellion, 1861-66. Montpelier, Press of the Watchman Pub. Co., 1892.

RSVO - Proceedings of the Reunion Society of Vermont Officers, 1864-1884, Burlington: Free Press Association, 1885.

RSVO2 - Proceedings of the Reunion Society of Vermont Officers, Vol. II 1886-1905, Burlington, Free Press Printing Company, 1906.

RUS - Official Register of the United States: Containing a List of Officers and Employees in the Civil, Military, and Naval Service on the First of July 1885. Washington: GPO, 1885.

RWF - Frazer, Robert W. Forts of the West: Military Forts and Presidios and Posts Commonly Called Forts West of the Mississippi River to 1898. Norman, OK: University Press, 1980.

SAH - The Story of American Heroism: Thrilling Narratives of Personal Adventures During the Great Civil War as told by The Medal Winners and Roll of Honor Men. Springfield, OH: J. W. Jones, 1897.

SAT - Report of the Proceedings of the Society of the Army of the Tennessee at the Twenty-Third Meeting Held at Detroit, Mich., November 14-15, 1900. Cincinnati: F. W. Freeman, 1901.

SAW - Vermont, Adjutant and Inspector General's Office. Vermont in the Spanish-American War. Montpelier, VT: Capital City Press, 1929.

SCS - Schatzki, Stefan C. "Sudley church, Used as a Hospital During the Battle of Bull Run." American Journal of Roentgenology. 2007; sighted at www.ajronline.org/cgi/content/full/188/6/1723; Internet.

SCW - Portrait and Biographical Record of Sheboygan County, Wis. Chicago, Excelsior Publishing Co., 1894.

SJA - The Saint Johnsbury Academy. Listing of Trustees, Teachers, and Students Academical year Ending 1846. Janice Boyko, 2004, sighted at freepages.genealogy.rootsweb.ancestry.com/ ~nekg3/ schools/school_st-johnsbury-academy-1846.htm, Internet.

SJC - Churchill, Samuel Joseph. Genealogy and biography of the Connecticut branch of the Churchill family in America. Lawrence, KS: Journal Publishing Co., 1901.

SJMNObit – Obituary extracted from the San Jose (CA) Mercury News

SK - McKeen, Silas. A History of Bradford, Vermont. Montpelier, VT: J. D. Clark & son, 1875.

SLA - Abbott, Samuel L. and James C. White. The Boston Medical and Surgical Journal, vol. LXXII. Boston: David Clapp & Son, 1865.

SLB - Bailey, Sarah Loring. Historical Sketches of Andover, Massachusetts. Boston: Houghton, Mifflin & Co., 1880.

SOVI - Annual Reports. Sons of Vermont, Illinois, 1882-1886.

SP - Catalogue of the Sigma Phi By Sigma Phi, Sigma Phi, undated (aft 1876)

SR - Smith, H.P. and W.S. Rann. History of Rutland County Vermont. Syracuse: D. Mason & Co., 1886.

SS – Sifakis, Stewart. Who Was Who in the Union. New York: Facts On File, 1988.

STL1 - Lewis, S. Thompson. A Memorial and Biographical Record of Iowa. New York: Lewis Publishing Co., 1896.

SW - Wolcott, Samuel. Memorial of Henry Wolcott, one of the First Settlers of Winsor, Connecticut. New York: A.D.F. Randolph & Co., 1881.

T288 - National Archives. General index to Pension Files, 1861-1934 (NARA Record Group T288, alphabetical sort)

T289 - National Archives. Pension applications for service in the US Army between 1861 and 1917 (NARA Record Group T289, unit sort)

TBC - Shook, John. "Significant American Professors of Philosophy, Natural Philosophy, and Theology from 1637 to 1920." The Pragmatism Cybrary, sighted at
www.pragmatism.org/american/american_professors.htm; Internet.

TBP - Peck, Thomas Bellows. William Slade of Windsor, Conn. and his Descendants. Keene, NH: Sentinel Printing Co., 1910.

TBP1 - Peck, Thomas Bellows. Richard Clarke of Rowley, Massachusetts, and his Descendants in the Line of Thomas Clark of Rockingham, VT. 1638-1904. Boston: David Clapp, 1905.

TCE - The Columbia Encyclopedia, Sixth Edition, Columbia University Press, 2008.

TDC - The Shield: Official Publication of the Theta Delta Chi Fraternity, April 1890.

TEH - Hazen, Tracy Elliot. The Hazen Family in America: A Genealogy. Thomaston, CT: R. Hazen, 1947.

TFH - Harrington, Thomas Francis. The Harvard Medical School, A History, Narrative and Documentary, 1782-1905. New York: Lewis Publishing Co., 1905.

TGL - Lewis, Theodore Graham. History of Waterbury Vermont 1763-1915. Waterbury: The Record Print, 1915.

THC - The Texas Historical Commission; sighted at www.thc.state.tx.us/index.html; Internet.

THS - Streets, Thomas Hale. Samuel Giffin of New Castle County on Delaware, Planter; and his Descendants to the Seventh Generation. Philadelphia: Thomas Hale Streets, 1905.

TJL - Ledoux, Thomas J. Quite Ready to be Sent Somewhere: The Civil War Letters of Aldace Freeman Walker. Victoria, BC: Trafford Publishers, 2002.

TJL2 - Ledoux, Thomas J. Green Mountain Mariners in the Civil War. Victoria, BC: Trafford Publishers, 2010.

TJM - McCrory, Thomas J. Grand Army of the Republic, Department of Wisconsin. Black Earth, WI: Big Earth Publishing, 2005.

TLB - Bolton, Thaddeus Lincoln. Genealogy of the Dart Family in America. Philadelphia: Cooper Printing, 1927.

TMB - The Michigan Book. Ann Arbor: 1898.

TMO - O'Brien, Thomas M. & Oliver Diefendorf. General Orders of the War Department, Embracing the Years 1861, 1862 & 1863. New York: Erby & Miller, 1864.

TPG - The Political Graveyard, politicalgraveyard.com

TPH - Hughes, Thomas Patrick and Frank Munsell. American Ancestry: Giving Name and Descent, in the Male Line, of Americans Whose Ancestors Settled in the United States Previous to the Declaration of Independence, A. D. 1776. New York: Munsell, 1894.

TPL - Lowry, Thomas P. and Jack D. Welsh. Tarnished Scalpels: The Court-Martials of Fifty Union Surgeons. Mechanicsburg, PA: Stackpole Books, 2000.

TSFP - "Our Family History," The Scofield Family Project, www.tsfp.org; Internet.

TSP - Pearson, Thomas Scott. Catalogue of the Graduates of Middlebury College. Windsor, VT: Vermont Chronicle Press, 1853.

TVE - Duffy, John J., Samuel B. Hand and Ralph H. Orth, The Vermont Encyclopedia. Lebanon, NH: University Press of New England, 2003.

TWD - Draper, Thomas Waln-Morgan. The Drapers in America, being a History and Genealogy. New York: John Polhemus Printing Co., 1892.

TWH - Herringshaw, Thomas William. Herringshaw's National Library of American Biography. Chicago: American Publishers' Association, 1914.

UCA - Fearey, Thomas H. Union College Alumni in the Civil War, 1861-1865. Schenectady NY: Union College Graduate Council,1915..

UJH - Hoffman, U.J. History of LaSalle County, Illinois. Chicago: S.J. Clarke Publishing Co., 1906.

UTSCat - General Catalogue of Union Theological Seminary in the City of New York, 1836-1876. New York: S.W. Green, 1876.

UVMCat - General Catalogue of the University of Vermont and State Agricultural College, Burlington, Vermont, 1791-1900. Burlington: Free Press Association, 1901.

UVMCat2 - General Catalogue of the University of Vermont and State Agricultural College, Burlington, Vermont, 1891-1892. Burlington: Free Press Association, 1892.

UVMCat3 - Catalogue of the Officers of Government and Instruction, the Alumni and Other Graduates of the University of Vermont and State Agricultural College, Burlington, Vt., 1791-1875. Burlington: Free Press Steam book and Job Printing House, 1875.

UVMMED - Catalogue of the University of Vermont Medical Department, Burlington, Vermont 1823-36 and 1854-1903. Burlington: Free Press Association, 1904.

UY11 - Unitarian Yearbook July 1, 1911. Boston: American Unitarian Association, 1911.

VBA - Vermont Bar Association: Officers, Proceedings, Papers and Address. 1904. Vol. VII, No. 1. Montpelier, VT: Argus and Patriot Press, 1907.

VCHS - Vermillion County Historical Society. Vermillion County, Indiana, History and Family. Turner Publishing Co., 1989.

VHS02 - Proceedings of the Vermont Historical Society 1901-1902 With Lists of Members, Necrology and Reports, Burlington: Free Press Association, 1903.

VHS06 – Proceedings of the Vermont Historical Society 1905-1906. Vermont Historical Society, 1906.

VHS13 - Proceedings of the Vermont Historical Society 1912-1913. Vermont Historical Society, 1913.

VHS16 - Proceedings of the Vermont Historical Society 1915-1916. Vermont Historical Society, 1918.

VHS20 - Proceedings of the Vermont Historical society 1919-1920. Vermont Historical Society, 1921.

VM - Vermont Marriages. Volume 1: Montpelier, Burlington, Berlin. Burlington, VT: Research Publication Co., 1903.

VMS64 - Transactions of the Vermont Medical Society at the Annual Session. Held at Montpelier, October ...1864. Woodstock, VT: Vermont Standard, 1864.

VSR - The Thirty-First Vermont School Report, October, 1890. Montpelier, VT: Watchman Publishing, 1890.

VTMS - Vermont State Medical Society. Transactions of the Vermont Medical Society, published by The Society, 1864, 1886, 1902, 1903.

WAE - Ellis, William Arba. Norwich University 1819-1911: Her History, Her Graduates, Her Honor Roll. Montpelier, VT: The Capitol City Press, 1911.

WBA - Atkinson, William Biddle. The Physicians and Surgeons of the United States. Philadelphia: Charles Robson, 1878.

WC - Carpenter, Walter. "During the Bloody Civil War, Sloan Army Hospital a Place of Healing & Recovery." The Montpelier Bridge, September 2000, sighted at www.nlm.nih.gov/hmd/manuscripts/ead/sloan.html; Internet.

WCH - Holbrook, William C. A Narrative of the Services of the Officers and Enlisted Men of the 7th Regiment of Vermont Volunteers (Veterans) from 1862 to 1866. New York: American Bank Note Co, 1882.

WCW - Wile, William C. New England Medical monthly. Medicine and Surgery. Volume 10, Oct 1890-Oct 1891, Danbury, VT: Danbury Medical Printing Co., 1891.

WD - Duff, William. History of North Central Ohio: Embracing Richland, Ashland, Wayne, Medina, Lorain, Huron and Knox Counties. Topeka: Historical Publishing Co., 1931.

WFD - Doolittle, William Frederick. The Doolittle Family in America. Cleveland: Sayers & Waite, 1904.

WFF - Fox, William F. Regimental Losses In The American Civil War 1861-1865. Albany: Albany Publishing Co.. 1889.

WFS - Scott, William Forse. The Story of a Cavalry Regiment: the Career of the fourth Iowa Veteran Volunteers from Kansas to Georgia 1861-1865. New York: G. P. Putnam's Sons, 1893.

WGC - Cutler, William G. History of the State of Kansas. Chicago: A. T. Andreas, 1883.

WGP4 - Twenty-Sixth Annual Reunion of the Association of Graduates of the United States Military Academy, at West Point, New York, June 10th, 1895. Saginaw, MI: Seemann & Peters, 1895.

WHB - Barnes William H. History of the Thirty-Ninth Congress of the United States. New York: Harper & Brothers, 1868.

WHC - Crockett, Walter Hill. Vermont, The Green Mountain State. New York: The Century History Company, Inc., 1921.

WHJ - Jeffrey, William H. Successful Vermonters: A Modern Gazetteer of Lamoille, Franklin and Grand Isle Counties. East Burke, VT: Historical Publishing Co., 1907.

WHM - Michael, W. H. Fifty-Second Congress (Second Session): Official Congressional Directory. 2nd Edition. Washington: GPO, 1893.

WHO1 - Leonard, John W. Who's Who in America 1903-1905. Chicago: A. N. Marquis & Company, 1903.

WHO2 - Leonard, John W. Who's Who in America 1908-1909. Chicago: A. N. Marquis & Company, 1908.

WHO3 - Marquis, Albert Nelson. Who's Who in New England. Chicago: A. N. Marquis & Company, 1916.

WHP - Powell, William H. Powell's Records of Living Officers of the United States Army. Philadelphia: L.R. Hamersly & Co., 1890.

WHP1 - Powell, William H. Officers of the Army and Navy (Volunteer) Who Served in the Civil War. Philadelphia: L.R. Hamersly & Co., 1893.

WHT - Tucker, William Howard. History of Hartford, Vermont Jul 4, 1761-April 4, 1889. Burlington: Free Press Association, 1889.

WKA - Ackerman, Wm. K. Early Illinois Railroads. Chicago: Fergus Printing Co., 1884.

WLM - Montague, W. Lewis. Biographical Record of the Alumni of Amherst College, During Its First Half Century. Amherst Mass., 1883.

WNE - Marquis, Albert Nelson. Who's Who in New England. Chicago: A. N. Marquis & Co., 1916

WPG1 - Twenty-Second Annual Reunion of the Association of Graduates of the United States Military Academy, at West Point, New York, June 12th, 1890. Saginaw, MI: Evening News Printing and Binding House, 1890.

WPG2 - Twenty-Second Annual Reunion of the Association of Graduates of the United States Military Academy, at West Point, New York, June 12th, 1891. Saginaw, MI: Seemann & Peters, 1891.

WPG3 - Twenty-Third Annual Reunion of the Association of Graduates of the United States Military Academy, at West Point, New York, June 9th, 1892. Saginaw, MI: Seemann & Peters, 1892.

WR - Reid, Whitelaw. Ohio in the War; Her Statesmen, Her Generals and Soldiers. Cincinnati: Moore, Wilstach & Baldwin, 1868

WRC1 - Cutter, William Richard. New England Families Genealogical and Memorial. New York, 1915.

WRC2 - Journal of the Thirtieth Annual convention of the Department of Massachusetts Woman's Relief Corps. Boston: Griffith-Stillings Press, 1909.

WRS - Steiner, Walter R. Proceedings of the Connecticut State Medical Society 1908, 116th Annual Convention. New Haven, CT: Tuttle, Morehouse & Taylor, 1908.

WSR - Rann, W. S. History of Chittenden County, Vermont. Syracuse: D. Mason & Co., 1886.

WT - Thorpe, Walter. History of Wallingford, Vermont. Rutland: The Tuttle Co., 1911.

WU - Upham, Warren. Collections of the Minnesota Historical Society, vol. XIV, Minnesota biographies 1655-1912. St. Paul, MN: June, 1912.

WVR - Walton's Vermont Register, Farmers' Almanac, and Business Directory, for 1879. Claremont, NH: Claremont Manufacturing Company, 1879.

WWD - Davis, William W. History of Whiteside County, Illinois. Chicago: The Pioneer Publishing Co., 1903.

ZT - Thompson, Zadock. History of Vermont, Natural, Civil, and Statistical, in Three Parts. Burlington: Chauncey Goodrich, 1842

Appendix A – Place of Birth Index

Williams, Francis C.
Brimfield, MA
Fairbanks, Erastus
Bristol, VT
Dunton, Walter C.
Brookfield, VT
Peck, Cassius
Brownington, VT
Baxter, Portus
Jocelyn, Stephen P.
Burke, VT
Newell, Henry C.
Newell, Selim
Trull, Daniel N.
Woodruff, Charles A.
Burlington, VT
Aubery, James M.
Benedict, George G.
Blinn, Charles H.
Doolittle, Charles C.
Hopkins, William C.
Lowry, Francis
Lowry, Horatio B.
Peck, Theodore S.
Robie, Edward D.
Russell, William P.
Seymour, Truman
Sherman, Marshal
Cabot, VT
Russell, George K.
Stone, Levi H.
Cadwell, NY
Hack, Lester G.
Calais, VT
Dwinell, Melvin
Pray, Rufus M.
Sparrow, Bradford P.
Cambridge, VT
Brush, Edwin R.
Walker, Daniel C.
Wilcox, Henry C.
Canaan, NH
Welch, Alvin C.
Canada
Cargill, John D.
Carr, Anthony
Coffey, Robert J.
Damon, George B.
Greene, Theodore P.
Grout, Josiah
Grout, William W.
Hall, Elmore John
Hanscom, Willis G.
Rich, Carlos H.
Scott, Alexander Jr.
Sparrow, William
Steele, Hiram R.
Canojoharie, NY
Burnap, Wilder L.
Canton, NY
Gray, Edmund B.
Carlton, NY
Scofield, Robert
Castleton, VT
Higley, Edwin H.
Leavenworth, Abel E.
Stewart, William E.
Woodward, Adrian T.
Woodward, Edwin T.
Woodward, Rollin C. M.
Cavendish, VT
Fletcher, Henry A.
Seaver, Thomas O.
Sperry, William J.
Weston, Eugene S.
Wheeler, Daniel D.
Charleston, VT
Robinson, Don A.
Charlotte, VT
Kasson, John A.
Pringle, Cyrus G.
Woodward, John H.
Chelsea, VT
Bixby, Orville
Lathrop, Cyrus U.
McLaughen, Napoleon B.
Redington, Edward D.
Robinson, Calista
Stearns, John C.
Tinker, Charles A.
Vilas, William F.
Vincent, Walter S.
Chester, VT
Atwood, Henry C.
Baldwin, Melvin R.
Beaman, Fernando C.
Boutin, Charles W.
Edson, Ptolemy O.
Henry, Hugh
Pierce, Charles A.
Stoughton, Charles B.
Stoughton, Edwin H.
Chesterfield, NH
Harris, Broughton D.
Mead, Larkin G.
Chesterfield, NY
Macomber, John H.
Chios, Greece
Colvocoresses, Geo. M.
Clarendon, VT
Dyer, Jay
Emmons, George F.
Hodges, Henry C.
Horton, Edwin
Nichols, William T.
Peck, Charles W.
Roberts, George T.
Colchester, VT
Read, Odgen B.
Concord, MA
Haynes, Edwin M.
Concord, VT

Perrysburgh, OH
  Thompson, Charles A.
Petersham, MA
  Gale, George F.
Piermont, NH
  Evans, Ira H.
Pittsford, VT
  Child, Willard A.
Plainfield, NH
  Bullard, Gates B.
  Parker, Henry J.
Plainfield, VT
  Mack, Daniel A.
Plymouth, VT
  Pollard, Henry M.
Pomfret, VT
  Crooker, Lucien B.
  Hawkins, Gardner C.
  Hawkins, Rush C.
  Miller, Crosby P.
Pompey, NY
  Peck, David B.
Potsdam, NY
  Mason, Charles W.
Poughkeepsie, NY
  Dayton, Durrell W.
Poultney, VT
  Lyman, Milo W.
  Ross, Lucretius D.
Pownal, VT
  Barber, Merritt L.
Proctorsville, VT
  French, Winsor B.
  Proctor, Redfield
Putney, VT
  Mason, George M.
Quechee, VT
  Perry, Carlton H.
  Stone, Edward P.
  Stoughton, Homer R.
Randolph, VT
  Bradford, Philander D.
  Carpenter, Benjamin W.
  Chandler, Albert B.
  Hebard, Salmon B.
  Herrick, Lucius C.
  Huse, Hiram A.
  Lamson, Jasper H.
  Partridge, George
  Thayer, Charles P.
  Tucker, Stephen S.
  Weston, Edmund
Reading, VT
  White, Azro
Readsboro, VT
  Gillette, Henry O.
  Wiley, Daniel D.
Richford, VT
  Blaisdell, Edson G.
  Powell, Charles A.
Richmond, MA
  Perry, John B.
Richmond, VT
  Hall, George B.
Rochester, MA
  Heyer, Charles A.
Rochester, VT
  Blodgett, Gardner S.
  Huntington, William M.
Rockingham, VT
  Butterfield, Franklin G.
  Butterfield, Frederick D.
Rowe, MA
  Stone, Newton
Roxbury, VT
  Clark, Francis G.
  Richardson, Harrison A.
Royalton, VT
  Williams, Carlos D.
Rutland, VT
  Alvord, Benjamin
  Beaman, George W.
  Conline, John
  Post, James E.
  Ripley, Edward H.
  Rutherford, George V.
  Temple, William G.
  Walker, Aldace F.
Ryegate, VT
  Beattie, Alexander M.
  Kennedy, Ronald A.
Salem, NY
  Hooker, George W.
Salisbury, NH
  Pingree, Samuel E.
Salisbury, VT
  Seaver, Joel J.
Sandgate, VT
  Prindle, Franklin C.
Saxtons River, VT
  Baxter, Horace H.
  Gilchrist, Charles A.
Schenectady, NY
  Rutherford, Joseph C.
Scotland
  Bayne, Thomas
  Hope, James
Shaftsbury, VT
  Howard, Jacob M.
  Olin, Abraham B.
Sharon, CT
  Smith, Charles C.
Sharon, VT
  Shepard, John F.
Sheffield, VT
  Gray, Jacob G.
Shelburne, VT
  Barstow, John L.
  Holabird, William H.
  Pierson, James S.
Sheldon, VT
  Ballou, Newton H.

Sherburne, VT
- Maxham, Azro J.

Shoreham, VT
- Brookins, Harvey S.
- Hitchcock, Robert E.
- Hunsdon, Charles
- Ormsbee, Ebenezer J.

Shrewsbury, VT
- Kingsley, Levi G.

Somerset, VT
- Knapp, Lyman E.

South Hero, VT
- Corbin, Job

Springfield, VT
- Davis, George F.
- Ferris, Eugene W.
- Hoard, Charles B.
- Slack, William H. H.
- Streeter, Sebastian R.

St. Albans, VT
- Alford, Albert G.
- Brainerd, Anna Eliza
- Hall, Horace P.
- Jewett, Albert B.
- Jewett, Erastus W.
- Read, James M
- Smith, Edward W.
- Smith, John G.
- Smith, William F.
- Tilton, William

St. Johnsbury, VT
- Ide, George H.
- Miles, Lorenzo D.

Stafford, VT
- Baxter, Jedediah H

Starksboro, VT
- Hill, Charles W.

Sterling, VT
- Kenfield, Frank

Stockbridge, VT
- Strong, George C.

Stockholm, NY
- Webster, Henry S.

Stonington, CT
- Austine, William

Stowe, VT
- Boynton, Joseph J.
- Butts, Lemuel P.
- Dutton, Ira B.
- Hendee, George W.
- Raymond, Albert C.
- Sargent, Jackson G.

Strafford, VT
- Morrill, Justin S.
- Preston, Simon M.
- Roberts, John L.

Stratham, NH
- Mead, John B.

Stratton, VT
- Glazier, Nelson N.

Sturbridge, MA
- Plimpton, Salem M.

Sullivan, NH
- Frost, Carlton P.
- Frost, Henry M.

Sutton, VT
- Beckwith, Amos S.
- Brown, Andrew C.
- Trussell, Jacob

Swanton, VT
- Barney, Elisha L.
- Brown, Stephen F.
- Jewett, Jesse E.

Thetford, VT
- Allen, Cyrus H.
- Gillett, Herman H.
- Hovey, Charles E.
- Loomis, Gustavus A.

Tinmouth, VT
- Ballard, Henry
- Phillips, Edwin

Topsham, VT
- Dustin, Daniel
- Nutt, William

Townshend, VT
- Scott, Oscar D.
- Twitchell, Marshall H.

Troy, NY
- Collamer, Jacob
- Ketchum, Benjamin F.

Troy, VT
- Bedell, Henry E.
- Currier, John W.
- Dix, Samuel N.

Tunbridge, VT
- Chandler, Charles M.
- Chandler, George C.
- Goodwin, David M.
- Haskell, Franklin A.
- Knox, James M.
- Noyes, Luman A.
- Whitney, Abel D.

Underhill, VT
- Burdick, Arthur F.
- Dixon, Lucius J.
- Dunton, Charles H.
- Palmer, Cornelius S.

Vergennes, VT
- Brush, Daniel H.
- Hitchcock, Ethan A.
- Parker, Charles E.
- Woodbridge, Frederick E.

Vermont
- Coburn, Joseph L.
- Fremont, Sewell L.
- Hazelton, John H.
- Leonard, Hiram W.
- Lyon, Emory M.
- Platt, Lemuel B.
- Scott, Harriet M.

Vershire, VT
- Titus, Fanny H.

Victory, VT
Shores, Ethan P.
Waitsfield, VT
Fisk, Perrin B.
Palmer, Edwin F.
Shaw, Henry C.
Shaw, Lucius S.
Walden, VT
Bell, Charles J.
Foster, George P.
Livingston, Josiah O.
Montgomery, Marshall
Wardsboro, VT
Gleason, Newell
Perry, Daniel
Read, Levant M.
Warner, NH
Sargent, Joseph
Warren, VT
Chesmore, Alwyn H.
Curtis, Edward M.
Dana, Samuel J.
Waterbury, VT
Dillingham, Edwin
Henry, William W.
Janes, Henry
Wells, Edward
Wells, William
Waterford, ME
Harrington, Ephraim W.
Waterford, VT
Benton, Jacob
Benton, Reuben C.
Goss, Story N.
Lee, Edward Payson
Waterville, VT
Bailey, Myron W.
Weathersfield, VT
Dartt, Justus N.
Dickinson, Lucius C.
Dudley, William W.
Kidder, Charles W. B.
Mather, Charles D.
Rice, John L.
Spafford, Henry W.
Tuttle, Lyman M.
Tuttle, Oscar S.
Webster, NH
Little, Arthur
Westford, VT
Allen, Heman W.
Mudgett, Henry E.
Parmelee, Moses P.
Westminster, VT
Hall, Josiah
Holton, Edward A.
Holton, Joel H.
Willard, Henry A.
Wright, Riley E.
Weston, VT
Carter, Henry G.
Gilmore, Joseph A.
Webster, Alonzo
Webster, Harvey A.
Whitingham, VT
Closson, Henry W.
Eddy, Samuel E.
Williamsburg, MA
Lyon, Frederick A.
Williamstown, VT
Coughlin, John
Howe, Thomas M.
Lynde, Isaac
Williston, VT
Chapin, Cornelius A.
Chittenden, Lucius E.
Wheeler, Henry O.
Wilmington, VT
Russell, Charles M.
Watson, Austin H. R.
Windham, VT
Gould, Charles G.
Walker, William H.
Windsor, VT
Pettes, William H.
Simmons, Seneca G.
Washburn, Henry D.
Winhall, VT
Grant, Lewis A.
Woodstock, VT
Allen, Benjamin
Churchill, Sylvester
English, Charles H.
Mower, Joseph A.

Appendix B – Place of Burial Index

The following lists the final burial place or place of death (which may not be where they are buried).

Platt, Lemuel B.
Putney, Charles E.
Read, James M.
Read, Ogden B.
Smalley, Henry A.
Smart, William S.
Stannard, George J.
Thayer, Charles P.
Thayer, Samuel W.
Wells, Edward
Wells, William
Woodbury, Urban A.
Burns, NY
Holliday, Jonas P.
Calais, VT
Livingston, Josiah O.
Sparrow, Bradford P.
California
Browne, Francis F.
Cambridge, MA
Beaman, George W.
Cowdin, Robert J.
Hudson, Henry N.
Perry, John B.
Cambridge, VT
Brush, Edwin R.
Walker, Daniel C.
Canon City, CO
Colburn, Amanda M.
Carbondale, IL
Brush, Daniel H.
Castleton, VT
Atwood, Henry C.
Higley, Edwin H.
Leavenworth, Abel E.
Stone, Levi H.
Cavendish, VT
Davis, George F.
Fletcher, Henry A.
Sperry, William J.
Cedar Rapids, IA
Clark, Francis G.
Champaign, IL
Harmon, James C.
Charlotte, VT
Prindle, Cyrus G.
Chaska, MN
Baxter, Luther L.
Cheboygan, MI
Davis, Henry G.
Chelsea, VT
Goss, Story N.
Hebard, Salmon B.
Plimpton, Salem M.
Cheshire, CT
Woodbury, Eri D.
Chester, VT
Henry, Hugh
Chesterfield, MA
Eddy, Samuel E.
Chicago, IL
Coburn, Joseph L.
Drury, Lucius H.
Ransom, Thomas E.
Sherman, Elijah B.
Waterman, Arba N.
Chicopee Falls, MA
Sawin, William J.
Chillicothe, MO
Adams, Charles A.
Chittenden, VT
Horton, Edwin
Circleville, OH
Olds, Edson B.
Clinton, IN
Washburn, Henry D.
Clinton, LA
Reynolds, Albert
Cohoes, NY
Van Steenburg, Warner
Cold Harbor, VA
Ford, Arba A.
Colfax, WA
Lewis, Barbour
Colorado Springs, CO
Sherman, Linus E.
Columbia, TN
Smith, Franklin G.
Columbus, OH
Herrick, Lucius C.
Concord, MA
Farmer, Edward
Concord, NH
Gilmore, Joseph A.
Concord, VT
Cutting, Oliver B.
Cook Cty, IL
Gray, Edmund B.
Corinth, VT
Darling, Joseph K.
Cornwall, VT
Porter, Edward O.
Coventry, VT
Nichols, Henry C.
Dandridge, TN
Dewey, Joel A.
Danville, VT
Brainerd, Charles D.
Preston, Addison W.
Dayton, OH
Downs, Henry W.
Denver, CO
Dorsey, Stephen W.
Williams, John C.
Derby Line, VT
Butterfield, Frederick D.
Grout, Josiah
Des Moines, IA
Boutin, Charles W.
Damon, George B.
Kasson, John A.
Park, Castanus B.
Rawson, Charles H.
Detroit, MI
Howard, Jacob M.
Dorchester, MA
Little, Arthur
Dorset, VT
Dunton, Warren R.
Dubuque, IA
Cram, Dewitt C.
Duluth, MN
Baldwin, Melvin R.
East Berkshire, VT
Royce, Homer E.
East Calais, VT
Dwinell, Melvin
East Montpelier, VT
Arms, Austin D.
Noyes, Wallace W.
Eden, VT
Stevens, Jonas T.
Effingham, KS
Mansfield, John B.
Elcho, NV
Meigs, John J.
Enfield, NH
Tilton, William
Enid, OK
Blair, Robert M.
Enosburg, VT
Marsh, Carmi L.
Essex Jct., VT
Ferrin, Chester M.
Knox, James M.
Evanston, IL
Redington, Edward D.
Fairfield, VT
Burleson, George W.
Fairhaven, VT
Webster, Henry S.
Fayston, VT
Dana, Samuel J.
Fletcher, VT
Leach, Chester K.
Florence, Italy
Mead, Larkin G.
Seymour, Truman
Fort Edward, NY
Strong, Thomas J.
Fort Worth, TX
Ransom, Dunbar R.
France, Paris, France
Bissell, Simon B.
Franklin, NH
Mack, Daniel A.
Fredericksburg, VA
Wheeler, Daniel D.
Freeport, IL
Putnam, Holden
Fremont, CA
Allen, Cyrus H.
Fresno, CA

Hall, Josiah
Ft. Union, NM
Selden, Henry R.
Ft. Washington, MD
Pettes, William H.
Galena, OH
Dyer, Jay
Glade Mills, PA
Allen, Charles L.
Glendale, CA
Bates, Norman F.
Glens Falls, NY
Johndro, Franklin
Granby, VT
Shores, Ethan P.
Willson, Melvin A.
Greensboro, VT
Cook, John B.
Grinnell, IA
Grinnell, Josiah B.
Groton, VT
Ricker, Isaac M.
Guilford, VT
Flagg, Joel
Hancock, VT
Perry, Hiram R.
Hanover, NH
Frost, Carlton P.
Hartford, VT
Allen, Samuel J.
Highgate Falls, VT
Meigs, Henry B.
Hinesburg, VT
Allen, John H.
Holland, VT
Blake, Isaac
Holyoke, MA
Tuttle, Lyman M.
Tuttle, Oscar S.
Honolulu, HI
Hemenway, Lewis H.
Huntington Park, CA
Aubery, James M.
Huntington, VT
Chesmore, Alwyn H.
Huntington, VW
Hoard, Charles B.
Huntsville, AL
Brooks, William T.
Hyde Park, VT
Sawyer, Edward B.
Irasburg, VT
Ingalls, Lewis J.
Isle La Motte, VT
Hyde, Melvin J.
Jackson, MI
Lyon, Frederick A.
Jaffrey, NH
Greene, Theodore P.
Johnson, VT
Andrews, Sumner A.
Mudgett, Henry E.
Kalaupapa, HI
Dutton, Ira B.
Kansas City, MO
Cummings, William G.
Kenosha, WI
Ide, George H.
Lovell, Frederick S.
Keokuk, IA
Perry, Carlton H.
Kilbourn, WI
Scofield, Robert
Lakewood, NJ
Robbins, Augustus J.
Lancaster, NH
Beattie, Alexander M.
Benton, Jacob
LaPorte, In
Gleason, Newell
Lawrence, KS
Churchill, Samuel J.
Lebanon, Beirut, Lebanon
Parmalee, Moses P.
Lena, IL
Waite, Charles
Leominster, MA
Day, Hannibal
Linton, GA
Stone, John
Litchfield, CT
Colvocoresses, George M.
Colvocoresses, George P.
Londonderry, VT
Buxton, Albert
Los Angeles, CA
Goodwin, David M.
Holabird, William H.
Smalley, Jacob M.
Sweeney, James
Lovilia, IA
Drury, James J.
Lowell, MA
Trueworthy, Edwin W.
Ludlow, VT
Hathorn, Ransom E.
Howe, Elwin A.
Levey, George H.
Walker, William H.
Lunenburg, VT
Hill, George W.
Lyndon, VT
Chase, Charles M.
Copeland, John W.
Farnsworth, Orrin
Gleason, Joseph T.
Hanscom, Willis G.
Hubbard, Lorenzo W.
Quimby, George W.
Lynn, MA
Draper, Alonzo G.
Madison, WI
Vilas, William F.
Malone, NY
Seaver, Joel J.
Manchester, NH
Blunt, Asa P.
Manchester, VT
Roberts, Benjamin S.
Marlin, TX
Carter, Henry G.
Maysville, MO
Perry, Daniel
McLean Cty, IL
Blanchard, Enoch
McLellan Cty, TX
Leland, Oscar H.
Mechanicville, NY
Ballou, Newton H.
Medina, OH
Blake, Harrison G.
Mendota, IL
Crooker, Lucien B.
Middlebury, VT
Porter, Henry M.
Russell, William P.
Tracy, Amasa S.
Warner, James M.
Williamson, Charles H.
Milton, VT
Dixon, Lucius J.
Fairchild, Benjamin
Plant, Azro M.
Milwaukee, WI
Leavenworth, Jesse
Minneapolis, MN
Benton, Reuben C.
Gilfillan, John B.
Grant, Lewis A.
Phillips, Edwin
Mobile, AL
Tucker, Stephen S.
Montana
Batchelder, James E.
Montgomery
Dix, Samuel N.
Montpelier
Brown, Andrew C.
Chandler, Charles M.
Clark, John W.
Clarke, Dayton P.
Coffey, Robert J.
Cross, Lewis B.
Foster, Elihu S.
Huse, Hiram A.
Lucia, Joel H.
Peck, George A.
Peck, James S.
Pitkin, Perley P.
Smith, Frederic E.
Stone, Edward P.
Thomas, Stephen
Upham, Charles C.

Walton, Eliakim P.
Wright, James E.
Moretown, VT
Foster, Ebenezer J.
Morristown, VT
Hendee, George W.
Morrisville, VT
Camp, Lyman L.
Doty, George W.
Gates, Amasa O.
Hall, Elmore J.
Kenfield, Frank
Niles, Albert A.
Powers, Horace
Natick, MA
Nutt, William
New Albany, IN
Kennedy, Ronald A.
New Dorp, NY
Kenny, Albert S.
New Haven, CT
Loomis, Gustavus A.
New Haven, VT
Mason, Charles W.
Weston, Eugene S.
New Orleans, LA
Blackmar, Armand E.
New York, NY
Steele, Hiram R.
Newburg, NY
Boynton, Edward C.
Newport, VT
Bedell, Henry E.
Rogers, Nathaniel S.
Newton, NJ
Dodge, George S.
North Walden, VT
Bell, Charles J.
Northfield, VT
Bradford, Philander .
Browne, William F.
Holden, William W.
Kenyon, Henry L.
Nichols, George
Randall, Francis V.
Williams, Carlos D.
Norwich, VT
Currier, Samuel H.
Oberlin, OH
Steele, John W.
Ocean Grove, NJ
Roberts, John L.
Ohio
Lord, Nathan S.
Orwell, VT
Abell, Charles E.
Owtonna, MN
Harrington, Joseph L.
Palatka, FL
Howard, Noel B.
Peacham, VT
Sargeant, Francis E.
Trussell, Jacob
Pepin, WI
Allen, Benjamin
Picolata, FL
Lynde, Isaac
Pierpont, SD
Sheldon, Charles H.
Pittsburgh, Pa
Howe, Thomas M.
Pittsfield, VT
Kidder, Charles W.
Pittsford, VT
Child, Willard A.
Plainfield, NJ
Palmer, Cornelius S.
Plattsburg, NY
Lyon, Emory M.
Pompton Plains, NJ
Wisewell, Moses N.
Pontiac, MI
Richardson, Israel B.
Portage, WI
Haskell, Franklin A.
Portland, ME
Adams, Cephas G.
Mattocks, Charles P.
Portsmouth, NH
Dimick, Justin
Pottsville, pa
Hyde, Breed N.
Poughkeepsie, NY
Winslow, John F.
Poultney, VT
Bixby, Armentus B.
Dunton, Charles H.
Ross, Lucretius D.
Prague, NE
Glazier, Nelson N.
Proctor, VT
Proctor, Redfield
Providence, RI
Hawkins, Rush C.
Putney, VT
Phillips, George H.
Randolph, VT
Babbitt, Robert A.
Chandler, Albert B.
Cleveland, James P.
Lamson, Jasper H.
Mead, John B.
Noyes, Luman A.
Weston, Edmund
Reading, VT
White, Azro H.
Reno, NV
Hogan, Henry H.
Richmond, VA
Simmons, Seneca G.
Rochester, VT
Eaton, Henry A.
Huntington, William
Rockingham, VT
Buxton, Charles
Read, Levant M.
Russell, George K.
Rockville, IN
Ferris, Eugene W.
Roxbury, VT
Hall, George B.
Rich, Carlos H.
Richardson, Harrison
Royalton, VT
Shepard, John F.
Rutland, VT
Baker, Joel C.
Baxter, Horace H.
Dayton, Durell W.
Dunton, Walter C.
Foot, Solomon
Haynes, Edwin M.
Hazelton, John H.
Joyce, Charles H.
Kingsley, Levi G.
Lyman, Milo W.
Mead, John A.
Nichols, William T.
Post, James E.
Ripley, Edward H.
Ripley, William Y.
Roberts, George T.
Thompson, Charles
Walker, Aldace F.
Sacramento, CA
Wright, George
Wright, Thomas F.
Salt Lake City, UT
McKean, James B.
San Dimas, CA
Wheeler, Henry O.
San Francisco, CA
Blinn, Charles H.
Leonard, Hiram W.
Macomber, John H.
Partridge, George
Woodruff, Charles A.
Santa Rosa, CA
Shepherd, Jonathan A.
Saratoga Springs, NY
French, Winsor B.
Woodward, Edwin T.
Saxtons River, VT
Butterfield, Franklin
Pettengill, Samuel B.
Scotch Plains, NJ
Scott, Julian A.
Scottsburg, IL
Gilchrist, Charles A.
Seattle, WA
Knapp, Lyman E.
Preston, Simon M.
Seneca Falls, NY

Appendix C – Wartime Ranks/Positions

The following is the highest rank or position held by the individuals during the war.

Acting Assistant Commissary of Subsistence
- Howe, Elwin A.

Acting Assistant Paymaster (Navy)
- Beaman, George W.

Acting Master (Navy)
- Smalley, Jacob M.

Adjutant
- Dwinell, Melvin
- Spafford, Henry W.
- Stearns, John C.

Adjutant & Inspector General
- Babbitt, Elbridge H.

Arms Manufacturer
- Hoard, Charles B.

Artificer
- Alford, Albert G.

Artist
- Mead, Larkin G.

Assistant Adjutant General
- Howe, Thomas M.
- Leavenworth, Abel E.

Assistant Engineer (Navy)
- Farmer, Edward
- Prindle, Franklin C.
- Rand, Stephen

Assistant Paymaster
- Holabird, William H.
- Kenny, Albert S.
- Redington, Edward D.

Assistant Postmaster General
- Kasson, John A.

Assistant Quartermaster
- Peck, Theodore S.

Boatswains Mate (Navy)
- Blair, Robert M.

Brigadier General
- Benton, Jacob
- Connor, Seldon
- Dewey, Joel A.
- Hill, Charles W.
- Loomis, Gustavus A.
- Phelps, John W.
- Roberts, Benjamin S.
- Smith, Edward W.
- Stannard, George J.
- Stoughton, Edwin H.
- Thomas, Stephen
- Tupper, Tullius C.
- Warner, James M.
- Wells, William
- Wright, George

Brigadier General (Bvt)
- Alvord, Benjamin
- Avery, Matthew H.
- Babcock, Orville E.
- Blunt, Asa P.
- Brush, Daniel H.
- Burton, Henry S.
- Churchill, Sylvester
- Coughlin, John
- Davis, Henry G.
- Day, Hannibal
- Dimick, Justin
- Draper, Alonzo G.
- Dudley, William W.
- Dustin, Daniel
- Foster, George P.
- French, Winsor B.
- Gilchrist, Charles A.
- Gleason, Newell
- Hawkins, Rush C.
- Henry, William W.
- Leonard, Hiram W.
- Lewis, John R.
- Lovell, Frederick S.
- Mattocks, Charles P.
- McLaughen, Napoleon B.
- Murray, John B.
- Preston, Simon M.
- Ripley, Edward H.
- Seaver, Joel J.
- Smalley, Henry A.
- Strong, Thomas J.
- Tompkins, Charles H.
- Waite, Charles
- Wiley, Daniel D.
- Wisewell, Moses N.
- Wright, Thomas F.

Captain (Army)
- Abell, Charles E.
- Baldwin, Melvin R.
- Barto, Alphonso
- Beattie, Alexander M.
- Bixby, Orville
- Brainerd, Charles D
- Branch, Charles F.
- Brookins, Harvey S.
- Brown, Stephen F.
- Burleson, George W.
- Butterfield, Frederick D.
- Buxton, Albert
- Carter, Henry G.
- Chamberlin, Preston S.
- Clark, John W.
- Clarke, Dayton P.
- Crooker, Lucien B.
- Davis, George E.
- Dickinson, John Q.
- Dorsey, Stephen W.
- Dunton, Walter C.
- Dyer, Jay
- Ferris, Eugene W.
- Hebard, Salmon B.
- Holton, Edward A.
- Hope, James
- Horton, Edwin
- Howard, Squire E.
- Jewett, Jesse E.
- Kelton, Dwight H.
- Kenfield, Frank
- Kimball, Frederick M.
- Lee, Edward P.
- Leland, Oscar H.
- Lewis, Barbour
- Livingston, Josiah O.
- Lynde, Isaac
- Macomber, John H.
- McFarland, Moses
- Montgomery, Marshall
- Nichols, Henry C.
- Ormsbee, Ebenezer J.
- Parker, Charles E.
- Quimby, George W.
- Raymond, Albert C.
- Sheldon, Charles H.
- Sherman, Linus E.
- Start, Romeo H.
- Streeter, Sebastian R.
- Twitchell, Marshall H.
- Walker, William H.
- Weston, Edmund
- Woodbury, Urban A.
- Wright, Riley E.

Captain (Army) (Bvt)
- Liscum, Emerson H.
- Read, James M.
- Wheeler, Henry O.
- Woodbury, Eri D.

Captain (Navy)
- Emmons, George F.
- Greene, Theodore P.
- Lowry, Francis

Chaplain
- Bayne, Thomas
- Bradford, James H.

Brastow, Lewis O.
Cummings, Ephraim C.
Dayton, Durell W.
Dickinson, Lucius C.
Frost, Henry M.
Goodrich, John E.
Hale, Charles S.
Haynes, Edwin M.
Hopkins, William C.
Hudson, Henry N.
Kimball, John
Little, Arthur
Mack, Daniel A.
Parmalee, Moses P.
Perry, John B.
Plimpton, Salem M.
Roberts, John L.
Sargent, Joseph
Shepherd, Jonathan A.
Simons, Volney M.
Smart, William S.
Smith, Claudius B.
Stone, Edward P.
Stone, Levi H.
Webster, Alonzo
Webster, Harvey A.
Williams, Francis C.
Woodward, John H.
Chief Engineer (Navy)
Robie, Edward D
Chief Quartermaster
Dodge, George S.
Hodges, Henry C.
Pitkin, Perley P.
Christian Commission Delegate
Fisk, Perrin B.
Pierce, Leroy M.
Civilian
Smith, Franklin G.
Civilian Contractor
Winslow, John F.
Civilian Pay Clerk
Mason, George M.
Civilian Quartermaster
Arms, Austin D.
Colonel
Allen, Benjamin
Andross, Dudley K.
Barney, Elisha L.
Baxter, Luther L.
Blake, Harrison G.
Cowdin, Robert J.
Cummings, William G.
Floyd, Horace W.
Fremont, Sewell L.
Hall, Josiah
Haskell, Franklin A.
Herrick, Lucius C.
Holbrook, William C.
Holliday, Jonas P.
Howard, Noel B.
Hunsdon, Charles
Hyde, Breed N.
Jewett, Albert B.
Kellogg, William P.
Kennedy, Ronald A.
Leavenworth, Jesse H.
Lincoln, Sumner H.
Lord, Nathan S.
McKean, James B.
Mead, John B.
Nichols, William T.
Peck, David B.
Pettes, William H.
Phelps, Charles E.
Platt, Lemuel B.
Porter, Henry M.
Preston, Addison W.
Proctor, Redfield
Putnam, Holden
Randall, Francis V.
Ripley, William Y. W.
Roberts, George T.
Rutherford, George V.
Sawyer, Edward B.
Seaver, Thomas O.
Selden, Henry R.
Simmons, Seneca G.
Stoughton, Charles B.
Stoughton, Homer R.
Tuttle, Oscar S.
Tyler, John S.
Veazey, Wheelock G.
Walbridge, James H.
Whiting, Henry
Colonel (Bvt)
Adams, Charles A.
Cram, Dewitt C.
Damon, George B.
Hazelton, John H.
Nutt, William
Partridge, Frederick W.
Ransom, Dunbar R.
Scofield, Robert
Sloan, William J.
Smith, William
Tracy, Amasa S.
Wheeler, Daniel D.
Williston, Edward B.
Commander (Navy)
Bissell, Simon B.
Colvocoresses, George M.
Temple, William G.
Commissary of Subsistence
Smith, Frederic E.
Contract Photographer
Browne, William F.
Contract Surgeon
Plant, Azro M.
Ross, Lucretius D
Corporal
Bell, Charles J.
Copeland, John W.
Doty, George W.
Farnsworth, Orrin
Flagg, Joel
Gray, Jacob G.
Hall, George B.
Holden, William W.
Howard, Henry S.
Lamson, Jasper H.
Leach, Moses J.
Mansur, Zophar M.
Maxham, Azro J.
Miller, Crosby P.
Parker, Henry J.
Peck, Charles W.
Perry, Daniel
Phelps, Brigham T.
Scott, Alexander
Scott, Oscar D
Smith, Emery L.
Williams, John C.
Woodruff, Charles A.
Deputy Provost Marshall
Hendee, George W.
Ensign (Navy)
Clark, Charles E.
Fleet Paymaster (Navy)
Upham, Charles C.
Governor
Fairbanks, Erastus
Gilmore, Joseph A.
Holbrook, Frederick
Smith, John G.
Hospital Steward
Ferrin, Chester M.
Thayer, Charles P.
Hostler
Willard, Henry A.
Judge
Olin, Abraham B.
Landsman (Navy)
Webster, Henry S.
Lieutenant (Army/Marine)
Abbott, Lemuel A.
Allen, John H.
Aubery, James M.
Baker, Joel C.
Ballard, Henry
Bedell, Henry E.
Benedict, George G.
Blackmer, John C.
Bliss, Charles M.
Clark, Francis G.
Clarke, Albert
Cleveland, James P.
Dartt, Justus N.
Downs, Henry W.
Drury, James J.
Gilfillan, John B.
Gillette, Henry O.
Glazier, Nelson N.

Greenleaf, William L.
Haskins, Kittredge
Hawkins, Gardner C.
Henry, Hugh
Hill, George W.
Hitchocock, Robert E.
Jewett, Erastus W.
Jocelyn, Stephen P.
Leach, Chester K.
Lowry, Horatio B.
Lucia, Joel H.
Marsh, Carmi L.
Mason, Charles W.
Palmer, Edwin F.
Peckett, John B.
Phelps, George H.
Pike, Paphro D
Robbins, Augustus J.
Sargent, Jackson G.
Shaw, Lucius S.
Sherman, Elijah B.
Stevens, Jonas T.
Stranahan, Farrand S.
Thompson, Charles A.
Trussell, Jacob
Valentine, Alonzo B.
Williams, Carlos D
Williamson, Charles H.

Lieutenant (Navy)
Woodward, Edwin T.

Lieutenant Colonel
Benton, Reuben C.
Brown, Andrew C.
Butterfield, Franklin G.
Gray, Edmund B.
Grout, William W.
Joyce, Charles H.
Mott, Judd M.
Pingree, Samuel E.
Pratt, John E.
Rice, John L.
Sperry, William J.
Vilas, William F.
Walker, Aldace F.
Washburn, Peter T.
Waterman, Arba N.

Lieutenant Colonel (Bvt)
Closson, Henry W.
Hooker, George W.
Knapp, Lyman E.
Smith, Rodney
Steele, John W.

Lieutenant Colonel (Honorary)
Brainerd, Anna E.

Lieutenant Commander (Navy)
Converse, George A.
Dewey, George

Major
Austine, William
Barstow, John L.
Boutin, Charles W.
Boynton, Joseph J.
Buxton, Charles
Crandall, Richard B.
Dillingham, Edwin
Drury, Lucius H.
Eaton, Henry A.
Farnham, Roswell
Grout, Josiah
Kingsley, Levi G.
Peck, James S.
Perry, Carlton H.
Pollard, Henry M.
Read, Ogden B.
Reynolds, William B.
Stone, Newton

Major (Bvt)
Barber, Merritt L.
Baxter, Henry C.
Blodgett, Gardner S.
Boynton, Edward C.
Coburn, Joseph L.
Dunton, Warren R.
Evans, Ira H.
Gould, Charles G.
Harrington, Ephraim W.
Hathaway, Forrest H.
Higley, Edwin H.
Steele, Hiram R.

Major General
Brooks, William T.
Hazen, William B.
Hitchcock, Ethan A.
Howard, Oliver O.
Richardson, Israel B.
Smith, William F.
Strong, George C.
Tucker, Stephen S.

Major General (Bvt)
Beckwith, Amos S.
Caldwell, John C.
Doolittle, Charles C.
Grant, Lewis A.
Hovey, Charles E.
Mower, Joseph A.
Ransom, Thomas E.
Seymour, Truman
Van Vliet, S.
Washburn, Henry D.

Military Attorney
Partridge, George

Military Telegrapher
Tinker, Charles A.

Musician
Blackmar, Armand E.
Blake, Isaac
Chase, Charles M.
Foster, Ebenezer J.
Johnston, Willie
Scott, Julian A.
Warren, Charles C.
Wells, Edward
White, Azro H.

Nurse
Colburn, Amanda M.
Keyser, Elizabeth
Read, Estelle S.
Robinson, Calista
Safford, Mary J.
Scott, Harriet M.
Titus, Fanny H.

Ordnance Sergeant
Phillips, George H.

Paymaster General
Partridge, Henry V.

Peace Conference Delegate
Baxter, Horace H.
Harris, Broughton D.

Private
Allen, Heman W.
Andrews, Sumner A.
Babcock, Volney C.
Bailey, Myron W.
Baker, Edward
Batchelder, James E.
Blinn, Charles H.
Bond, George H.
Browne, Francis F.
Butts, Lemuel P.
Camp, Lyman L.
Conline, John
Cook, John B.
Cutting, Oliver B.
Dana, Samuel J.
Darling, Joseph K.
Dix, Samuel N.
Dunton, Charles H.
Eddy, Samuel E.
English, Charles H.
Evans, Goin B.
Ford, Arba A.
Gleason, Joseph T.
Grow, Milo W.
Hanscom, Willis G.
Hatch, Isaac W.
Hathorn, Ransom E.
Hemenway, Lewis H.
Heyer, Charles A.
Hudson, Solomon S.
Huse, Hiram A.
Ingalls, Lewis J.
Jackson, William H.
Johndro, Franklin
Johnson, Russell T.
Kent, Evarts B.
Kenyon, Henry L.
King, Royal D.
Lathrop, Cyrus U.
Levey, George H.
Mather, Charles D.
McGettrick, Felix W.
Mead, John A.
Meigs, Henry B.

Miles, Lorenzo D
Moulton, Hosea B.
Mudgett, Henry E.
Noyes, Wallace W.
Palmer, Cornelius S.
Parker, Myron M.
Parmenter, Charles
Peck, George A.
Perry, Hiram R.
Pettengill, Samuel B.
Pierson, James S.
Prichard, John B.
Prindle, Cyrus G.
Read, Levant M.
Richardson, Harrison A.
Ricker, Isaac M.
Rogers, Nathaniel S.
Russell, Chandler M.
Sargeant, Francis E.
Scott, William
Shepard, John F.
Sherman, Marshal
Silsby, Wendell
Slack, William H.
Smith, Charles C.
Sparrow, Bradford P.
Start, Henry R.
Stewart, William E.
Sweeney, James
Taylor, Herbert E.
Wakefield, William W.
Weston, Eugene S.
Whitney, Abel D.
Willson, Melvin A.

Quartermaster
Cushman, Henry T.
Derby, Buel J.
Dutton, Ira B.
Wheeler, Charles W.

Quartermaster Clerk
Blaisdell, Edson G.

Quartermaster Sergeant
Churchill, Samuel J.
Gilmore, William H.
Jackman, Henry A.
Robinson, Charles H.
Watson, Austin H.

Railroad Manager
Canfield, Thomas H.

Regimental Quartermaster
Powell, Charles A.

Registrar of Treasury
Chittenden, Lucius E.

Saddler Sergeant
Sparrow, William

Sergeant
Bates, Norman F.
Cargill, John D.
Carr, Anthony
Coffey, Robert J.
Dolloff, Charles W.
Flagg, George W.
Gates, Amasa O.
Godfrey, Frederick
Hack, Lester G.
Hannon, Thomas
Harmon, James C.
Holton, Joel H.
Hubbard, Lorenzo W.
Ide, George H.
Lonergan, John
Lyman, Milo W.
Lyon, Frederick A.
Maxfield, Hampton L.
Newton, Charles M.
Nichols, William H.
Niles, Albert A.
Peck, Cassius
Pierce, Charles A.
Post, James E.
Pray, Rufus M.
Putney, Charles E.
Reed, Marquis de L.
Rich, Carlos H.
Russell, George K.
Shores, Ethan P.
Tilton, William
Walker, Daniel C.
Wright, James E.

Sergeant Major
Fletcher, Henry A.

Ship's Clerk
Colvocoresses, George P.

Soldier
Burnap, Wilder L.
Robinson, Frederick G.
Stillson, Henry L.

Springfield Arsenal employee
Currier, John W.
Wilcox, Henry C.

State Paymaster General
Otis, John G.

State Quartermaster General
Arthur, Chester A.
Davis, George F.

State Recruiting Officer
Trull, Daniel N.

State Representative
Olds, Edson B.

State Surgeon General
Phelps, Edward E.
Thayer, Samuel W.

Surgeon
Allen, Charles L.
Allen, Cyrus H.
Allen, Samuel J.
Babbitt, Robert A.
Ballou, Newton H.
Baxter, Jedediah H.
Blanchard, Enoch
Bradford, Philander D
Bullard, Gates B.
Carpenter, Benjamin W.
Chandler, Charles M.
Chesmore, Alwyn H.
Child, Willard A.
Clarke, Almon
Corbin, Job
Curtis, Edward M.
Dixon, Lucius J.
Edson, Ptolemy O.
Frost, Carlton P.
Gale, George F.
Gillett, Herman H.
Goodwin, David M.
Hogan, Henry H.
Janes, Henry
Kent, Enoch W.
Ketchum, Benjamin F.
Kidder, Charles W.
Lyon, Emory M.
Meigs, John J.
Nichols, George
Park, Castanus B.
Phillips, Edwin
Rawson, Charles H.
Russell, William P.
Rutherford, Joseph C.
Sanborn, Eben K.
Sprague, Edwin H.
Stone, John
Van Steenburg, W.
Vincent, Walter S.
Woodward, Adrian T.
Woodward, Rollin C.

Surgeon (Assistant)
Atwood, Augustus A.
Atwood, Henry C.
Bixby, Armentus B.
Brooks, Nathaniel G.
Brush, Edwin R.
Burdick, Arthur F.
Chapin, Cornelius A.
Colburn, Daniel L.
Conn, Granville P.
Crandall, John B.
Currier, Samuel H.
Fairman, Erastus P.
Foster, Elihu S.
Goss, Story N.
Hall, Elmore J.
Hall, Horace P.
Hanrahan, John D.
Harrington, Joseph L.
Hyde, Melvin J.
Langdon, Henry H.
Langdon, Seth W.
Newell, Henry C.
Noyes, Luman A.
Porter, Edward O.
Reynolds, Albert
Robinson, Don A.
Shaw, Henry C.

- Tenney, Charles H.
- Trueworthy, Edwin W.
- Tuttle, Lyman M.
- Van Deusen, G.
- Wells, Charles J.

Surgeon (Brigade)
- Sawin, William J.

Surgeon (Civilian)
- Adams, Cephas G.
- Cahoon, Charles S.
- Fairchild, Benjamin
- Hazelton, Daniel W.
- Huntington, William M.
- Knox, James M.
- Miles, John F.
- Newell, Selim
- Powers, Horace
- Welch, Alvin C.

Sutler
- Chandler, George C.
- Cross, Lewis B.

Teacher
- Johnson, Martha

Telegraph Operator
- Chandler, Albert B.

US Representative
- Baxter, Portus
- Beaman, Fernando C.
- Davis, Thomas T.
- Grinnell, Josiah B.
- Morrill, Justin S.
- Royce, Homer E.
- Walton, Eliakim P.
- Woodbridge, Frederick E.

US Senator
- Collamer, Jacob
- Foot, Solomon
- Howard, Jacob M.

War Correspondent
- Mansfield, John B.